WATFIV-S FUNDAMENTALS AND STYLE

Walter S. Brainerd
University of New Mexico
Charles H. Goldberg
Trenton State College
Jonathan L. Gross
Columbia University

BOYD & FRASER PUBLISHING COMPANY
BOSTON

Cover photo: "Special Effects," © Erik Andersen, Stock, Boston

Editor: Tom Walker
Production coordinator: Traute Marshall
Development editor: Sharon Cogdill
Artwork: Len Shalansky/Dixie Clark
Production editor: Dixie Clark
Ancillaries editor: Donna Villanucci
Typesetting: UNICOMP Technical Type
Printer: Crest Litho

Manufactured in the United States

10 9 8 7 6 5 4 3 2 1

Library of Congress Cataloging-in-Publication Data

Brainerd, Walter S.
WATFIV-S fundamentals and style.

(Boyd & Fraser programming language series)
Includes index.
1. FORTRAN (Computer program language)
I. Goldberg, Charles. II. Gross, Jonathan L.
III. Title. IV. Series.
QA76.73.F25B74 1986 005.13'3 86-2243
ISBN 0-87835-174-4

WATFIV-S FUNDAMENTALS AND STYLE

The Boyd & Fraser Programming Language Series includes these fine titles:

BASIC Fundamentals and Style
Beginning Structured COBOL
Advanced Structured COBOL: Batch and Interactive
Comprehensive Structured COBOL
Fortran 77 Fundamentals and Style
Pascal

Other outstanding programming language texts from Boyd & Fraser include:

BASIC Programming with Structure and Style
Complete BASIC: For the Short Course
Standard BASIC Programming: For Business and Management Applications
Structured Fortran 77 Programming
Structured Fortran 77 Programming: For Hewlett-Packard Computers
Pascal Programming: A Spiral Approach

Also available from Boyd & Fraser are these quality texts:

Data Communications Software Design
The Business Computing Primer: Using Microcomputer Software
Computers and Man

CONTENTS

PREFACE

Fortran

Fortran was the first major higher level programming language and is the most widely used programming language for scientific and engineering purposes. Fortran structures and constructs permeate almost all major programming languages. It is perhaps the most stable and portable programming language available, and Fortran programs can be run on almost any computer. Fortran evolved according to the needs of its users, with major revisions of the Fortran standard in 1966 and 1977. The current standard Fortran includes the features deemed both desirable and practical by a large committee of users and computer manufacturers, working under the aegis of the American National Standards Institute and the International Standards Organization. One of the authors of *WATFIV-S Fundamentals and Style*, Walter S. Brainerd, currently is on the ANSI Fortran Standards Committee. The name "Fortran" comes from *For*mula *tran*slation; it was originally written using all uppercase letters, but we have adopted the currently preferred way of writing it for this book.

WATFIV

WATFIV-S is the latest in a series of Fortran implementations provided by the University of Waterloo, the first of which was WATFOR (Waterloo Fortran). It is written to provide an excellent environment for students learning to use the Fortran programming language.

Need for Another Book

The 1977 revision of the Fortran standard, widely known as Fortran 77, introduced new and powerful features into the language. Many of these new features, as well as some features not found in the standard, have been added to WATFIV to produce WATFIV-S, or structured WATFIV. We have taken advantage of these features to teach a highly structured and modern programming style. When necessary, we use structures from other programming languages in the planning stages of our top-down design process, and refine them to the best Fortran approximation in the finished program. Modern programming structure and good programming practice are as much a part of this book as Fortran.

Who Should Use This Book

Our book was designed to be used in a one-semester course in Fortran programming or in an introductory course in computer science. No previous experience with a computer is assumed, and no mathematics beyond high-school level is required. We agree with the recommendations of the ACM Curriculum Committee and have prepared this text with the objectives of Curriculum 78 (course number CS 1, Computer Programming) in mind. Recognizing that many of the students who learn Fortran in this course will be science and engineering majors, we have included examples that illustrate the use of Fortran to solve problems in these areas.

We feel that the primary objectives of a course using our book are two-fold: students should develop skills in analyzing and solving problems in their original context; and students also should become proficient in designing, coding, debugging, and documenting programs to solve these problems, using good programming style in a high-level programming language. Analyzing a problem is pretty much the same, no matter what computer language is used to write the program, but writing instructions the computer will follow can be made easier by a suitable programming language. Fortran is an excellent language for introducing the major concepts of computer programming.

Complete Tested Programs

As experienced instructors of introductory programming courses, we recognize the value and importance of accuracy in the presentation as well as the implementation of a programming language. Nothing is more unsettling for students or instructors than example programs that contain errors (except for those programs designed to teach debugging). In addition to the over 125 complete, tested programs and their executions, the entire text of this book was typeset by one of the authors, Walt Brainerd, at UNICOMP Technical Type, using a DEC PDP* 11/73 with the Unix** operating system.

Problem Solving and Structured Programming

Great care and attention to detail went into the writing of this text. We feel that our emphasis on problem-solving techniques and structured programming concepts encourages students to develop good programming practices from the beginning of their programming experience. Discussions of subprograms and modularity start in Chapter 1 and continue throughout the book. All large programs are planned by top-down design and successive refinement. Full-scale examples appear in Chapters 1, 3, 4, 5, 6, 7, and 8.

Pace

A typical chapter contains about the amount of material that a student can master in one or two weeks. Each chapter has four to six sections plus special features.

Section Previews

Each section begins with a Section Preview. Consistent with our own philosophy of top-down design, the Section Preview describes in condensed form the major syntactic structures and concepts introduced in a section. Not only does it provide a concise preview of the section, it provides students with an excellent format for reference after the section is completed. This review is made easy, since the Section Preview are printed in blue. Students familiar with some Fortran or with the concepts presented in a particular section can skim the Section Preview, pick up the general forms of the Fortran statements and constructs, and decide if the section requires closer reading. Instructors can use the Section Previews for preparing lesson plans.

---

* PDP is a registered trademark of Digital Equipment Corporation.

** Unix is a trademark of Bell Laboratories.

Complete Sample Programs

It is one thing to see the general form of a Fortran statement; it is another to see the statement used in a complete, correct program, including echoes of input data and actual sample output. Every Fortran programming feature taught in this book is used in a complete program. Therefore, students can see not only the general form but the specific details necessary to make programs work.

Case Studies

The purpose of writing computer programs is to solve real problems. Each chapter has at least one section devoted to the complete treatment of a real problem through the use of a Case Study. Many other sections also include Case Studies. There is a wide range of applications treated in these Case Studies, including sorting, searching, simulations, text editing, word processing, digital image acquisition, image enhancement, graphics, histograms, and function plotting. Case Studies also deal with such problems as escape velocity, quadratic equations, telephone directories, ecology, grade reports, payroll, and credit card checking.

Formatting

Fortran has capabilites for very complex and versatile formatting of input and output data. We have introduced only those formatting features that are necessary to produce readable output in the most common cases, letting the student rely on default formatting most of the time. However, many of the more sophisticated formatting features are discussed in Appendix B.

Testing and Debugging

Over the years of teaching Fortran, we have collected typical bugs that are likely to show up in student programs. Each bug presented arises from an honest attempt to get the program right. We discuss the design of test cases which will detect the presence of a bug. Ultimately, the sample execution of a test case will indicate that the program contains an error. Techniques of debugging appropriate to locating that particular kind of bug are discussed, and the bug is systematically located and corrected. Every attempt is made to present the testing and debugging process and the bug itself in a realistic setting. Students will find these Testing and Debugging studies extremely useful.

Every chapter introducing major new syntactic features of Fortran has a Testing and Debugging section illustrating the typical problems that can arise in programs using these features. The Case Studies include additional material on this important topic.

Concise Treatment of Roundoff

Since science and engineering students are more apt to be using real quantities in their programming assignments, they are more apt to see slight traces of roundoff in their output. Because this can be quite disconcerting for the unprepared student, we have included a concise treatment of the elementary causes of roundoff, its suppression by the use of output formatting, and in Appendix B some effective elementary means of roundoff reduction or elimination.

Use of Second Color

A second color, blue, is used to highlight important features and to draw the student's attention to regularly occurring elements like the Section Previews, Warnings, and Style, Programming, and Debugging Notes. These elements are printed in blue to make it easier to find them for purposes of preview and review. Selected lines of the Fortran programs are highlighted in blue, drawing attention to the new or important features of the program.

Style Notes, Debugging Notes, Programming Notes, and Warnings

Style Notes, Debugging Notes, Programming Notes, and Warnings appear frequently in the text to identify ideas and hints that will help students deal with problems as they arise. They come from years of experience both teaching and programming in Fortran. We believe these notes are an invaluable pedagogical tool, reinforcing major ideas of top-down design, structured programming, thorough testing of designs and programs, and programming style.

Self-Test Questions

Self-Test Questions allow students to assess individually their understanding of the material. Self-Test Questions are short answer or true/false questions covering the major concepts and finer details presented in each section. Self-Test Questions are grouped by section at the end of each chapter, and answers to all Self-Test Questions appear in the Answer section at the end of the book.

What You Should Know

Each chapter contains a concise, list-formatted chapter review entitled "What You Should Know", reinforcing key concepts, good programming practices, and important vocabulary of Fortran and computer programming.

Fully Expanded Programming Exercises

There are over 125 fully expanded programming exercises, some with several parts, covering every aspect of the material taught in the book. Each exercise has a purpose, a clear and complete statement of the problem, a discussion of background information and proposed method of solution, sample input data, and sample execution output. Programming exercises range in difficulty from routine applications of the techniques in the chapter to challenging extended projects.

Glossary

All major programming concepts and terminology are marked in boldface in the text at the place where they are first defined. They are also collected, with complete definitions, at the end of the book in the Glossary.

Summary of the Fortran Language

Appendix C summarizes the syntax and general forms of all the Fortran statements described in the book. It can serve as a convenient reference guide.

Instructors Manual

The *Instructor's Manual and Answer Book*, available from our publisher, Boyd & Fraser, includes the following:

- chapter-by-chapter objectives
- discussions of teaching strategy
- chapter-by-chapter vocabulary lists
- transparency masters from each chapter
- Test bank, including true/false, short answer, fill-in, and multiple choice questions for quizzes and tests
- additional programming assignments

Thoroughly Tested

WATIFV-S Fundamentals and Style has been written for the student. We have tested this material with great success and trust that others will find it equally successful. We would appreciate hearing from both students and instructors who might have any comments or suggestions regarding this book. Write us in care of our publisher, Boyd and Fraser, 20 Park Plaza, Boston, Massachusetts 02116.

Walter S. Brainerd
Charles H. Goldberg
Jonathan L. Gross

NOTES

1. The Section Previews describe in condensed form the major syntactic structures and concepts introduced in the section.

2. Fortran and programming terms are printed in **boldface** when they are first explained. These terms are defined in "The Glossary" section at the end of the book.

3. Answers to all Self-Test Questions are provided in a section at the end of the book.

4. The Appendices are valuable reference tools. They provide a summary of the Fortran built-in functions, a succinct review of formatting, and a description of the Fortran syntax.

WATFIV-S FUNDAMENTALS AND STYLE

1 COMPUTERS AND PROGRAMMING

A **computer** is a device for processing information in a wide variety of ways, both simple and complex. It can perform arithmetic and read, remember, transcribe, modify, and print information with speed and accuracy. In fact, some computers can do more arithmetic in one second than a person can do in a lifetime, even if the person were to work 12 hours a day, every day, from birth to the age of 100. Moreover, the computer is unlikely to make even a single mistake in the process.

Computers are versatile, general-purpose machines. The same computer that prepares a payroll one minute can also perform a scientific calculation or alphabetize a list of names the next minute. Computers are versatile because they combine relatively simple basic operations like reading, writing, and arithmetic into meaningful sequences, called **programs**. The more programs there are for a computer, the more different things it can do.

This book is an introduction to **computer programming**, the writing of computer programs, and to the computer programming language Fortran, which is the most widely used programming language for scientific and engineering programming applications. Most of the features of the popular Fortran dialect WATFIV-S implemented at the University of Waterloo, Ontario, are introduced in this book, with typical applications showing what a computer can do. Complete programs and sample executions are given throughout. Comparisons are also made between the WATFIV-S version of Fortran and the American and international standard, Fortran 77.

Learning a computer language is like learning a natural language in the sense that it is not necessary to know the entire unabridged dictionary before anything meaningful can be said. In fact, using only a few dozen different words, it is possible to communicate quite well with a computer in Fortran.

We believe you should start reading and writing programs as soon as possible. After a brief discussion of the history and nature of computers and computer programming in this chapter, Chapter 2 shows that it is possible to read, write, and run meaningful programs with a minimum of fuss and bother.

This book assumes no prior knowledge of computers or of computer programming. However, some readers already may know another programming language or may know some Fortran constructions.

Each section begins with a Section Preview, which condenses the major syntactic structures and concepts presented in the section. If you are already

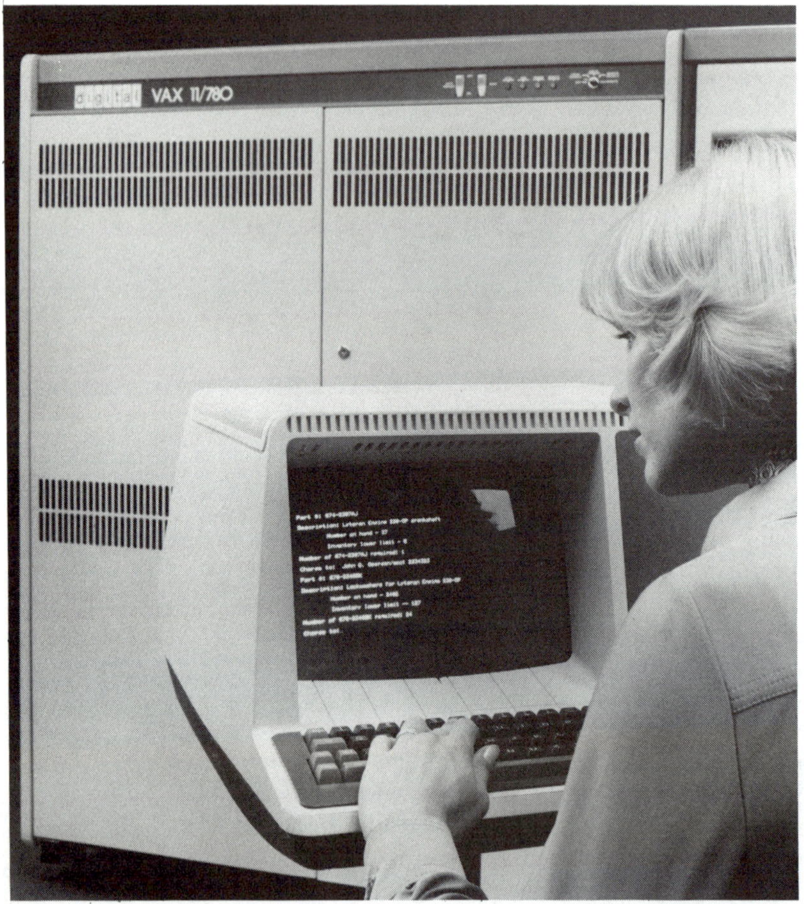

Figure 1.1 DEC VAX 11/780, a medium-scale computer system with interactive processing capability. *Courtesy Digital Equipment Corporation.*

familiar with a programming construct and know how to program it in another computer language, then the Section Preview will give you the WATFIV-S Fortran syntax for the construct in condensed form and you probably will be able to skip the section. The same holds true if you already know some Fortran. The Section Preview provides a quick review of the topics covered.

1.1 What is a Computer?

This section describes some computers and discusses the characteristic attributes and capabilities they share.

Section Preview

The first computer was Charles Babbage's Analytical Engine, which was designed in 1834 but never built. Howard Aiken's Mark I, built in 1939-44, is often considered the second computer.

A computer is a device with the following capabilities. Some computers have additional capabilities, but all computers have the ones listed below. A computer can

1. Operate automatically without step-by-step human control
2. Perform arithmetic calculations
3. Accept input data
4. Send output data to the user
5. Save data in its memory and later retrieve the data
6. Move data from place to place in its memory
7. Be programmed to execute any meaningful sequence of its built-in operations
8. Choose between programmed alternatives while operating automatically
9. Access its memory in a flexible manner
10. Store its program in the same memory cells that can at other times store data

Ancient History

At one time, a computer was a person who performed arithmetic computations. In the eighteenth and nineteenth centuries, when knowledge of the basic arithmetic operations was far from universal, and proficiency in the more difficult operations of multiplication and division was quite rare, these human computers were in some demand, especially for computing the astronomical tables essential to navigation and the tables used in trade and insurance.

Unfortunately, it is not humanly possible to manipulate great volumes of numbers without error, and consequently mathematical, astronomical, and navigational tables until relatively recently contained a profusion of errors. Even the most carefully prepared and edited tables might average one error per page, while less carefully prepared tables might have many more. Some of the errors were due to the human computers, but others entered later in the process, for instance in recopying the table for the printer, in typesetting, and even in the printing process itself.

One remarkable error originated in Vlacq's table of logarithms, printed in Gouda in 1628. Two digits, one above the other on successive lines of the table, were interchanged. It seems probable that this error occurred when two adjacent pieces of type came loose from the printing matrix at the same time during the printing of the table and were replaced by the pressman in the wrong positions. All subsequent copies of this table, which was reprinted for over 300 years, contained this error.

The First Modern Computer

The first modern computer was Charles Babbage's Analytical Engine, designed in 1834 to eliminate these sources of error and to produce perfectly accurate tables. Even though Babbage's machine was never built in its entirety, its design is remarkable because it was so innovative. Before Babbage, there were only calculators. In 1645 Blaise Pascal built a mechanical calculator that could add and subtract. In 1671 Gottfried Wilhelm von Leibniz designed a calculating machine that could add, subtract, and multiply automatically (once the numbers

Figure 1.2 IBM Personal Computer. *Courtesy International Business Machines Corporation.*

were entered), and divide with only a small amount of human assistance. One original model of Leibniz's machine may be found in the Lower Saxony Public Library in Hannover, Germany.

Babbage's Analytical Engine could not only perform all four arithmetic operations automatically, but it incorporated almost all of the features of the modern computer described below. Babbage was unable to construct his "engine" because of the state of the art of machining in his day. He was trying to construct a machine with thousands of gears at a time when even the gears of most clocks had to be hand-fitted to mesh properly.

The first operational computer, the Mark I, was designed by Howard Aiken at Harvard from 1939 to 1944, over 100 years after Babbage designed his Analytical Engine. In design, the Mark I is fundamentally the same as Babbage's machine, with improved flexibility in accessing its memory. The difference is in the hardware, which consists of electrical circuits instead of gears. A number of other computers were also built at about the same time.

Figure 1.3 CRAY X-MP computer system, a supercomputer. *Courtesy Cray Research, Inc.*

Characteristics of a Computer

Computers, from Babbage's Analytical Engine to the most modern computer, have a great deal in common. Improvements in technology have continually changed their size, speed, and physical appearance, but the fundamental principles on which they are based have changed little. The remainder of this section describes ten attributes of computers that enable them to perform the applications of this book.

Computer Attribute 1: Automatic Operation

The most fundamental principle in computer design from Babbage's time to the present is **automatic operation**, that is, the ability of a computer to operate as much as possible without human direction or assistance. According to Babbage's own account, the idea of performing repetitive computations by machine first came to him in the following way. On one occasion, his longtime friend, the scientist John Hershel, brought in some calculations done for the Astronomical Society by a (human) computer. In the course of their tedious checking, Hershel and Babbage found a number of errors, and at one point Babbage said, "I wish to God these calculations were executed by steam", by which he meant "automatically". If Babbage's metaphor seems strange to modern ears, it is because now, more than a century and a half later, steam power is no longer the new and innovative source of energy for industry and commerce it was in the 19th century. Had he lived to see the invention of the vacuum tube, the transistor, and the integrated circuit, Babbage might well have wished the calculations were executed by electronics, as indeed they are today.

The principle of requiring as little human assistance and direction as possible can be found in every aspect of computer design. In most instances, not only does accuracy improve with the elimination of unnecessary human intervention, but speed increases as well.

Computer Attribute 2: Arithmetic Calculations

The heart of Babbage's Analytical Engine, an apparatus called the "mill", is capable of performing the four basic arithmetic operations without human intervention once the numbers have been entered. Other automatic devices had been built earlier, notably a device built by Blaise Pascal, after whom a programming language was named, and another by Wilhelm Leibniz, one of the inventors of calculus. Also, before building the Analytical Engine, Babbage had built a Difference Engine, which was used to calculate mathematical tables. However, only Leibniz's machine could perform multiplication without human assistance, and none previously had been invented to perform division automatically. Modern computers still rely on the four arithmetic operations as the basis for numeric computing.

A working model of Babbage's mill was constructed from his drawings by his son, Henry P. Babbage. It worked as well as Babbage had anticipated. With the main axis turning approximately once per second, the addition or subtraction of two 29-digit numbers takes approximately 1 second. Multiplication or division of 29-digit numbers requires up to 3 minutes, depending on the sum of the digits in the multiplier or quotient. The original mill, which still works, is in the Science Museum, London.

Today, a battery-powered electronic hand calculator that performs these four basic arithmetic operations in fractions of a second can be purchased for less than the price of a book, but until recently a mechanical desk calculator with the same capabilities was at least as large as a typewriter, weighed twice as much, and cost several hundred dollars.

Computer Attribute 3: Input

A computer or calculator must have some means of receiving information, the data of the problem, from its human operators. All operations supplying a computer with information are **input**. Babbage's Analytical Engine had "number cards" for receiving information, an adaptation of the pattern cards used by Jacquard in his automatic loom for weaving brocaded silk cloth. As shown in Figure 1.4 each column of a pasteboard number card had nine positions; no holes were punched for the digit 0, one hole for the digit 1, two holes for the digit 2, and so on. Thus each digit required a full column of the card for its representation in holes, and the number of digits encoded on a number card corresponded exactly to the number of columns on the card.

The modern computer **punchcard** is very much the same as Babbage's number cards (see Figure 1.5). In the most commonly used punchcard code, named for its inventor, Herman Hollerith, each column still represents 1 digit of input information. In the Hollerith code, each digit from 0 to 9 is encoded as a single punch in an appropriate position in the column. Alphabetic characters, requiring two holes per column, and other special characters like punctuation marks, dollar signs, and arithmetic symbols, requiring up to three holes per column, are added to augment the simple numeric code. A standard 80-column Hollerith card is capable of encoding up to 80 digits, letters, or other characters of input information. Punchcards are still used at some computer installations to supply information to a computer. A typical punchcard reader can read 500 Hollerith punchcards per minute.

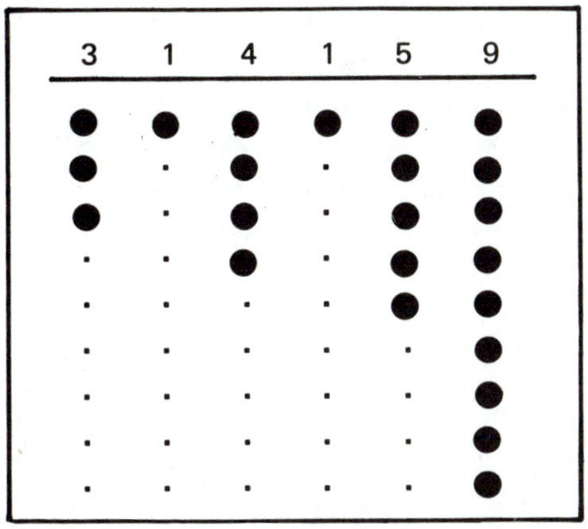

3 1 4 1 5 9

Figure 1.4 A number card for Babbage's Analytical Engine.

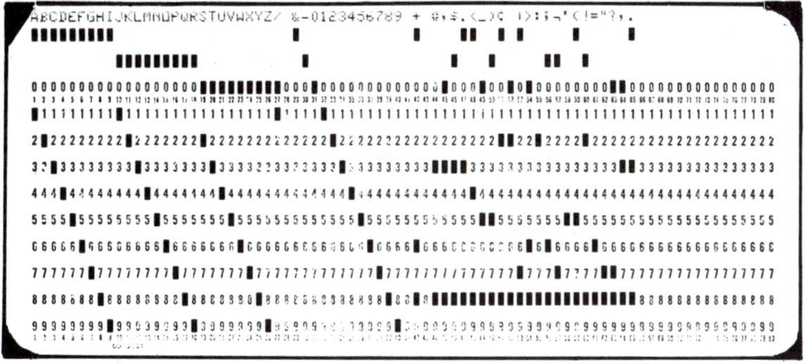

Figure 1.5 A computer punchcard, punched with the complete Hollerith code.

In contrast, input to most hand or desk calculators is accomplished by means of the entry keys. If two numbers are to be multiplied, each is entered into the machine by way of the entry keys before multiplication can begin.

Today, the primary means of supplying input information to a computer is a typewriterlike **computer terminal** keyboard. Basically, this is an electric typewriter keyboard equipped to encode electronically the letters and numbers that are typed and to transmit the encoded information directly to a computer. Like calculator keyboards, a computer terminal can supply input information only as fast as a person can press the keys.

Much greater input speeds are possible using **magnetic tapes** and **magnetic disks**. Many efficient operating systems accept input information entered from cards or terminals at whatever speeds these devices can manage and then recopy the input information onto magnetic disk or tape files for faster availability when the information is needed. Many computer systems now support creation and editing of disk files from a terminal. Similarly, calculated results that are to be reread at a later time as input data are written on magnetic disks and tapes, because of the higher reading and writing speeds of these devices.

A wide variety of other computer input devices are used at the present time, though they are much less common than punchcards and computer terminals. For example, optical scanners can read carefully printed block letters and numerals; magnetic ink scanners are used to read account numbers on bank checks. Television cameras are used as input devices to computer-controlled robots; pictures transmitted from Mars and Jupiter are analyzed and enhanced by computer. Instruments that measure temperature and size are used as input devices when a computer directly controls industrial processes. In fact, nearly any device capable of producing numeric or alphabetic information can be connected to a computer if there is good reason to do so.

Figure 1.6 DEC Rainbow personal computer. *Courtesy Digital Equipment Corporation.*

Computer Attribute 4: Output

A computer must be able to communicate its answers back to the proposer of the problem. Omitting a statement instructing the computer to print the answer is a mistake often made by beginners in their first programs. Since a computer does exactly what it is told, the computer may compute the answer when such a program is run, but it will never tell anyone what the answer is.

Any means of transcribing information held within a computer into a form external to the computer is **output**. Programmers usually speak of **writing** output, regardless of whether the result is printed, typed, displayed on a television screen, plotted, or encoded as magnetic spots on a tape or disk.

Figure 1.7 IBM 3084, a large-scale computer system. *Courtesy International Business Machines Corporation.*

Babbage was especially careful in designing the output for his Analytical Engine, because so many of the errors in the tables of his day were introduced after the computation. He provided for three types of output, a printing device capable of printing one or two copies of the results, a means for producing a stereotype mold from which printing plates for the tables could be made directly, and a mechanism for punching the numerical results of its computations into blank pasteboard cards for error-free rereading by the Analytical Engine. Great pains were taken in the design of these output features to ensure that no human error could intervene between the correct computation of the results and the final printing of the table.

At a modern computer installation, a principal form of output for human consumption is still the printed page. Direct computer typesetting has made a comeback in recent years with the complete computerization of the printing of several major newspapers. However, using modern photographic reproduction and printing processes, a computer text-editing system that produces clean high-quality printed copy also eliminates errors in printing. The text of this book was produced this way.

Another form of computer output that dates back to Babbage is the punchcard. Babbage wanted his computer to be able to punch cards so that results calculated by the machine could later be reentered into the machine without the consequent opportunities for error. This technique is still in use for bills sent through the mails. Customers are requested to return their prepunched billing card with their payment to minimize errors in crediting the payment. Most of the programs in this book were put in disk files, run, and then the program and output files were edited directly into the text to eliminate copying errors.

Most desk calculators, especially those of the hand-held electronic variety, have only one form of output, visual display. A numerical answer is displayed in lights or other readable form, and the user must copy it onto paper if a more permanent record is desired. Persons who have had occasion to copy quantities of numbers, or even to copy notes from the blackboard in a technical course, know that this process introduces many opportunities for error. Because there is a practical limit to how many figures can be copied without making a mistake, desk calculators become progressively less suitable as the volume of output information increases. Most adding machines and a few desk calculators provide a printed record of their calculations.

Many modern computers also have a provision for visual display. A television-type screen can be used to display several dozen lines of printing at the same time, or it can be used to produce other shapes for viewing. Used as an alternative to printing, this type of output can reduce substantially the amount of **hard copy** needed at a computer installation. Graphic display is also important when computers are used to teach languages like Japanese, Hebrew, Russian, and graphic arts like architectural drawing, all of which require shapes and characters not found in the usual English alphabet and consequently not available on standard printers. Graphic displays, including diagrams, line drawings, and computer-generated cartoons, can be produced in this way, and the result photographed for a more permanent record. Dot-matrix printers also can produce printed copies of graphic displays.

Other specialized output devices include plotters and electronic sound synthesizers for producing computer-generated or computer-processed music. For direct control of other machinery, output can be in the form of control impulses to that machinery, as is the case in airplane guidance systems, numerically controlled milling machines, and forms of industrial process control.

Computer Attribute 5: Memory

In a computer or calculator, **memory** is the capacity to retain information and to recall that information later. Many simple hand calculators have no memory capacity beyond what is required to retain the two numbers being added, subtracted, multiplied, or divided, and to produce the answer. Unless they are used in the very next step, intermediate results must be copied on paper and reentered later in the calculation on simple calculators. Thus, the calculation

$$(2 \times 3) / 4 = 6 / 4 = 1.5$$

can be performed without recording the intermediate result 6, but calculation of the expression

$$(2 + 3) / (4 + 5)$$

requires the recording of at least one intermediate result. Writing intermediate results on paper is jokingly called using the calculator's "paper memory", because this memory is a feature of the user and not of the calculator.

The most straightforward way to perform the intended calculation is to compute

$2 + 3 = 5$	which is recorded on paper or stored in the calculator
$4 + 5 = 9$	which is recorded on paper or stored in the calculator

and finally

5 / 9 = 0.5555555556   which is the answer

A standard trick, known to experienced users of desk calculators, is to compute and record the denominator first. Then the numerator does not have to be recorded, because it is used in the very next step when it is divided by the already calculated denominator to produce the answer. This trick also is used in efficient machine language programming of a computer.

In principle, the calculation

(2.345678 + 3.456789) / (4.567890 + 5.678901)

is similar to the previous example, because it involves the same sequence of arithmetic operations, but the penalty for having to copy and reenter a number and the probability of making a mistake are both increased by the larger number of digits in the intermediate results for the numerator and denominator. A large number of desk calculations can be made significantly easier by the addition of a small number of **memory cells**. For example, Table 1.1 shows the steps a person might follow to perform the harder calculations using a hand calculator that has an additional memory cell. The error-prone process of copying and reentering a number is replaced by use of the relatively error-free features called **store** and **recall** on some programmable calculators.

Table 1.1 A hand calculation that uses memory.

STEP	USER ACTION	DISPLAYED NUMBER
1	Enter 4.567890	4.56789
2	Add	
3	Enter 5.678901	5.678901
4	Equals	10.246791
5	Store displayed number	
6	Enter 2.345678	2.345678
7	Add	
8	Enter 3.456789	3.456789
9	Equals	5.802467
10	Divided by	
11	Recall stored number	10.246791
12	Equals	0.5662716259

Among typical desk calculators can be found simple machines with no additional memory, more powerful calculators with 1 to 3 memory cells, calculators designed for statistical or financial use with 6 to 10 memory cells, and even calculators with several dozen memory cells, each capable of storing one piece of data with the same number of digits as handled by the rest of the calculator. For his Analytical Engine, Babbage wanted 1000 memory locations in what he called the "store", but this part of his computer was never built. Modern computers have thousands, and sometimes millions, of memory locations. With recent technological advances, the cost of manufacturing and operating large memories is dropping rapidly, and they are becoming more common.

The ease and speed with which a piece of information can be stored and recalled from a memory location may be different for different parts of a computer's memory. Many computers have a variety of different types and speeds of memory. At the slow end of the scale, the distinction between a computer storing a piece of information in a memory location and a computer preserving the same piece of information by writing it on an output device like a magnetic disk for eventual recall as input data is almost imperceptible.

In a Fortran program, each memory location is given a name that reminds the programmer what the values stored in that location represent. These names for memory locations, called **variable names**, usually are taken from the original problem statement and are easier to remember than the numeric **addresses** used in hand calculators and machine languages.

Computer Attribute 6: Data Transfers

Many data processing tasks require rearranging the input data during the processing. **Sorting**, the arranging of data in alphabetic or numeric order, is such a task commonly performed by computers.

In most computer systems, all input data, regardless of their ultimate destination in the computer's memory, are read first into a set of fixed locations called the **input buffer**. Then, they are transferred from the input buffer to other parts of the memory. Output data usually follow a similar path, but in reverse. All output data are transferred first to an **output buffer**, from which they are written onto an output device.

On a hand calculator with more than one memory cell, the following sequence of operations might copy a value from memory cell 7 to memory cell 10.

Recall from memory cell 7
Store in memory cell 10

The **data transfer** takes place in two stages. First, the value in memory cell 7 is copied to the display register by the recall operation. Then the value in the display register is copied to memory cell 10 by the store operation. As a result, the old value from memory cell 7 now appears in both cells as well as the display register.

All computers have similar sequences of operations for moving a single piece of data. Many computer also have more powerful operations for moving whole blocks of data at one time.

In Fortran, the transfer of information from a memory cell named OLDX to a memory cell named NEWX is done by an **assignment statement**

```
NEWX = OLDX
```

which is read "NEWX is assigned the value of OLDX".

Computer Attribute 7: Programmability

Every hand or desk calculator has a set of basic operations which may be used individually or in meaningful combination to accomplish a desired computation. Typical basic operations include the four arithmetic operations—addition, subtraction, multiplication, and division—and the input operation of keying in a number. If a calculator has memory, the store and recall operations also are included. Many hand calculators also have more complex basic operations, like reciprocal ($1/x$), square root, logarithms, and trigonometric functions. With simpler hand calculators, human direction is required to initiate all basic operations, although they are completed automatically.

A calculator is **programmable** if meaningful sequences of basic operations can be selected in advance and an entire preselected sequence of operations executed automatically. Usually, the entire preselected sequence of operations is stored in a special **program memory** so that the sequence can be rerun easily, perhaps using different input data. Of course, input operations cannot be completely automatic if the only available form of input is a person using the entry keys.

Table 1.2 Raising 1.06 to the fifth power on a hand calculator.

STEP	USER ACTION	DISPLAYED NUMBER
1	Enter 1.06	1.06
2	Store displayed number	
3	Multiply by	
4	Recall store number	1.06
5	Equals	1.1236
6	Multiply by	
7	Recall stored number	1.06
8	Equals	1.191016
9	Multiply by	
10	Recall stored number	1.06
11	Equals	1.26247696
12	Multiply by	
13	Recall stored number	1.06
14	Equals	1.3382255776

For example, the operation of raising a number to the fifth power is useful in finding compound interest over a 5-year period, but it is not a basic operation on many hand calculators. On these hand calculators, a number may be raised to the fifth power by multiplying it by itself five times. To raise 1.06 to the fifth power, the user might perform the sequence of basic operations shown in Table 1.2.

If it is also desired to raise 1.0625 to the fifth power on a nonprogrammable calculator, the same 14 steps shown in Table 1.2 must be repeated by the user, this time with the number 1.0625 entered in step 1. However, if the calculator is programmable, this sequence of basic operations can be made into a program by replacing the specific first step, "Enter 1.06", with a more general input request to enter any number. A program like that in Table 1.3 can be stored in the program memory of a programmable hand calculator and easily run to raise any desired number to the fifth power.

Once this program has been entered and stored in the calculator's program memory, both of the desired calculations, raising 1.06 and 1.0625 to the fifth power, can be obtained as shown in Table 1.4.

Computers are programmable. The set of basic operations available on a computer is that computer's **machine language**. A large number of the machine language instructions for most computers are variants of the basic arithmetic operations, the input and output operations, and the store and recall operations.

If the computer is powerful enough to support a **compiler**, the programs do not have to be written in machine language, because the compiler automatically translates from Fortran to machine language. The following program steps written in Fortran are equivalent to the machine language program for raising an input number to the fifth power.

```
READ, VALUE
ANSWER = VALUE ** 5
PRINT, ANSWER
STOP
END
```

The commas following the words READ and PRINT mean that reading of the input value and printing of the answer are to be done in the usual way. The

Table 1.3 A program for raising any number to the fifth power.

PROGRAM STEP	BASIC OPERATION
1	Halt for input (user must enter a number and resume program execution to complete this step)
2	Store displayed number
3	Multiply by
4	Recall stored number
5	Equals
6	Multiply by
7	Recall stored number
8	Equals
9	Multiply by
10	Recall stored number
11	Equals
12	Multiply by
13	Recall stored number
14	Equals
15	Halt so user can read the result

two consecutive asterisks (**) on the second line are the symbol for exponentiation (raising to a power) in Fortran. Everything else is more or less self-explanatory.

Both the modern computer and Babbage's Analytical Engine are designed to allow the user to specify nearly any sequence of basic operations. Of course, this transfers the responsibility for ensuring that the sequence of computational steps produces a meaningful result from the designer of the machine to the designer of the program, the programmer. This is what computer programming is all about: how to design sequences of computational steps to produce meaningful and useful results.

Probably the first computer programmer, aside from Babbage himself, was his longtime supporter, Augusta Ada, Countess of Lovelace, a knowledgeable mathematician in her own right. Her mother, Annabella Milbanke, also was interested in mathematics and her father was Lord Byron, the poet. The programming language Ada, developed by the Department of Defense, was named after her.* She translated into English the first published description of the Analytical Engine, adding a set of translator's notes more than twice the length of the original article, in which she gave several computer programs for the Analytical Engine. These programs are equivalent to machine language programs for a modern computer.

Programming Note: Computer programming is the art of designing sequences of computational steps to produce meaningful and useful results.

* Ada is a trademark of the United States Department of Defense (Ada Joint Program Office).

Table 1.4 Using a program twice on a programmable hand calculator.

STEP	USER ACTION	DISPLAYED NUMBER
1	Start program	
2	Enter 1.06 and resume execution	1.06
		1.06
		1.1236
		1.06
		1.191016
		1.06
		1.26247696
		1.06
		1.3382255776
3	Start program	
4	Enter 1.0625 and resume execution	1.0625
		1.0625
		1.12890625
		1.0625
		1.199462891
		1.0625
		1.274429321
		1.0625
		1.354081154

Computer Attribute 8: Decisions

While operating automatically, that is, not under direct step-by-step human control, a computer can "choose" what to do next based on computed values or input data. The **decision** is made automatically, but the programmer must first indicate in the program exactly when the decision is to be made, what test is to be applied, and what step is to be executed next for every possible result of the test.

Two important programming techniques, loops and alternative computations, rely on the ability of a computer to decide. It is a rare and straightforward computer program that does not use one or the other of these techniques.

A **loop** is a sequence of program steps that may be repeated more than once during a single running of a program. For example, if the same computations are to be performed on the data for each student in a class or each worker in a factory, it is a dreadfully inefficient use of both the programmer's time and the computer's memory to write the computational steps out in full as many times as they are needed. A loop is written instead.

The decision step in a loop can almost always be based on the answer to the questions, "Are we done?" or "Have the computational steps in the loop been executed a sufficient number of times?" or a more specific inquiry of the same sort. If the computational steps in the loop have not been executed a sufficient number of times, the next thing the computer should do is to repeat them. If they have been executed the correct number of times, the computer should not repeat but go on to the next instruction after the loop, perhaps to compute an average or to print summary totals, or even to stop if nothing else needs to be done by the program.

Alternative computational procedures use the same decision capability of a computer, but for a different purpose. Here the choice is not whether to repeat, but which computational procedure is to be performed next. This technique allows overtime pay to be calculated by a different formula than nonovertime pay and deposits to be handled differently from withdrawals.

Both Babbage's Analytical Engine and the modern computer or programmable desk calculator can make these kinds of decisions. Some relatively simple devices also can make decisions. For example, a digital alarm clock "decides" each minute whether to start its alarm or not and "decides" again several minutes later whether to turn the alarm off, in case no one has done so in the meanwhile.

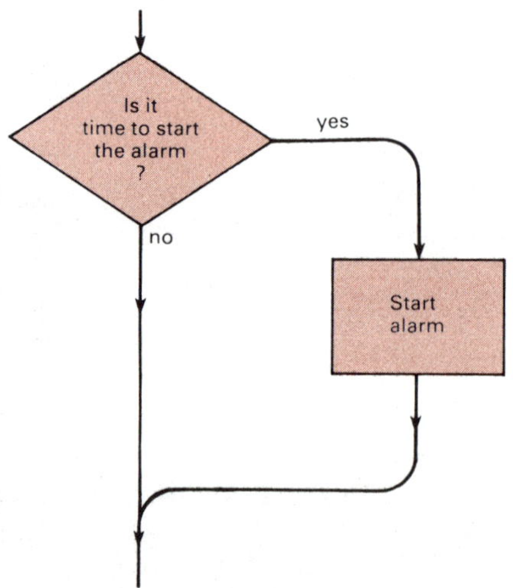

Figure 1.8 Flowchart for an alarm program on a digital watch.

Computer Attribute 9: Flexible Memory Access

In a modern computer, individual operations like store and recall operations need not be tied permanently to a specific memory cell at the time the program is written. The computer can calculate during automatic operation which memory cell will supply data for the operation or receive the results of the operations.

To be more specific, the hand calculator operations

Recall the contents of memory cell 7
Store in memory cell 10

are tied to specific memory cells. The former can only retrieve a value from memory cell 7, and the latter can only store a value in memory cell 10. Some programmable hand calculators and many computers have an operation similar to the following operation.

Look in memory cell 10.
The value you find there will tell you which memory cell
to store the answer in.

For example, if memory cell 10 contains the value 3, this operation has the same effect as the operation

Store in memory cell 3

However, if memory cell 10 contains the value 5, this operation has a different effect, namely the same as the operation

Store in memory cell 5

This two-step specification of which memory cell is intended is **indirect addressing**. Since the contents of memory cell 10 may be the result of a previous calculation, the access this operation provides to memory is very flexible. The computer's ability to process lists of data depends on such flexible memory access.

Computer Attribute 10: Stored Program

In most computers, the program is stored in the computer's memory in exactly the same memory cells that at other times could store data. In order to run its programs rapidly and efficiently, a programmable calculator or computer must be able to locate and read its next instruction about as fast as a typical instruction is executed. Usually this means that a program, or as much of one as will fit, is stored in memory cells of the same general accessibility and speed as those used to store data.

In most programmable calculators, the program memory is distinct from the data memory. Many computers allow the same memory cells to be used for either data or program steps, however, and there are advantages to this. First, the computer's design is simplified because certain parts of the circuitry do not have to be duplicated for separate program and data memories. Second, short programs with a great deal of data and long programs with comparatively little data both can be run on the same computer without wasting valuable memory capacity.

These ideas, called the stored program concept, are attributed to John von Neumann, one of the greatest mathematicians of the century and a pioneer in the early development of computers. They first appeared in print in a 1946 paper written by Arthur Burks, Herman Goldstine, and von Neumann. A side effect of program and data sharing the same memory is that a program can act on its own instructions as data, changing itself as it runs. This idea has spurred much research in artificial intelligence, but it is not ordinarily used outside that field. Babbage imagined this process as a computer eating its tail.

1.2 Top-Down Design

Solutions to computer problems do not grow on trees. This section introduces a methodology known as **top-down design** that enables you to analyze hard problems. The discussion is by necessity general since details of the Fortran language are not introduced until Chapter 2.

Section Preview

Top-Down Design:

A method of analyzing problems in which the solution is attempted first at the highest possible conceptual level, in terms closest to the problem statement. Then, details are added to each step of the proposed solution until a fully implemented solution results.

Successive Refinement:

The process of adding detail to a step of a problem solution to make it more specific is refinement. If a refined step is still not perfectly clear and unambiguous, each of its substeps is refined again. Successive stages of refinement continue until each step of the solution is clear and unambiguous. If the solution is to be expressed as a computer program, refinement continues until each step is an executable Fortran statement.

Modules:

A module is a coherent set of instructions that serve a specific and well-defined purpose in the solution of a problem. Each step in a high-level breakdown of the solution to a problem is often a module.

Subprograms:

When the solution to a problem is expressed as a computer program, each module becomes a programmer-defined subprogram: either a subroutine or a function subprogram.

Order of Refining Modules:

In general, this order depends on the individual nature of the problem. However, when the modules are relatively independent, refinement may proceed in any order. Modules may even be refined in parallel by different programmers at the same time.

Initialization Steps:

The first module executed is rarely the first module refined. Usually, decisions relating to the refinement of the main computation modules must be made before it is possible to refine the initialization modules that prepare for them.

Documentation:

Documentation is material that explains, describes, annotates, clarifies, or elucidates the nature of the problem, the plan for its solution, the organization of the modules, the details of the solution, or which describes how to use the program, when to use the program, when not to use the program, etc.

Top-Down Design and Documentation:

The hierarchical organization of a program designed top-down provides a natural and effective framework for documenting a program.

Bugs and Debugging:

A mistake in a computer program is called a bug. Removing bugs from a program is called debugging. It is much easier to debug a well-organized and well-documented program than to debug a program which falls short on either account.

Top-Down Testing

A program designed top-down may be tested top-down. First the main program is tested with fake versions of its subprograms that produce the correct answers without necessarily doing all the calculations. Then successively lower-level subprograms are tested in the same fashion.

Bottom-Up Testing:

A program designed top-down may also be debugged bottom-up. This means that the lowest-level subprograms are tested first. When they are known to be error-free, they are put together to form the next higher level subprograms, which are tested, and so on up the tree until the highest-level program unit, the main program that solves the problem, is debugged.

Top-Down Design

Top-down design is fundamentally a common-sense way to construct a solution to any difficult problem. It means you begin with strategic planning and gradually become more specific.

If the problem is so difficult that your first attempt does not reveal completely how the available tools and methods can solve it, you **refine** the steps of the proposed solution into simpler steps. You **divide and conquer**, continuing with this **stepwise refinement** until all the steps to the solution become clear.

In computer programming, the final step in the top-down design process is to write the solution as an executable Fortran program. However, an executable program by itself is not enough. For a number of reasons, it is also desirable to retain a record of the stepwise analysis of the problem.

In structured Fortran programming, the reasoning that leads to an executable program is retained by organizing the instructions in that program into groups called **subprograms**. Each subprogram performs a well-defined subtask that contributes to the solution of the original problem. The organization of a program into subprograms is what preserves sense amid the details of the Fortran code.

A Case Study in Stepwise Refinement

Let's suppose you have a goal to become a millionaire by 1990. It's all very well to say you will work hard every day until it happens, but most people who work hard don't make a million. Here is the question: what will you work hard at doing? Will you carry grains of sand one at a time from the beach to the top of the mountain? That can be very hard work.

An Initial Version of the Solution

Perhaps you finally have an inspiration that a way to make money is to sell people what they want. As obvious as this sounds, it is great progress, because it transforms the vague problem of making a million into a more concrete problem of selling people what they want. This inspiration is rendered as a flow chart in Figure 1.9.

Wanting to put a person on the moon is another general goal. Using a rocket, rather than jumping, is an inspired idea for a method. It narrows down what you have to do next. In this case, it lets you work on rocket engineering rather than on improved nutrition and athletic training.

Once you have the main inspiration of how you will achieve your goal, the analytic process becomes more systematic. Think of your fundamental

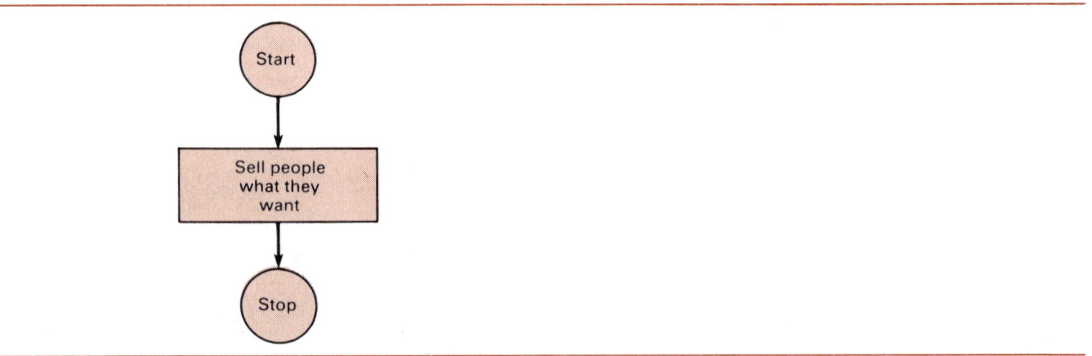

Figure 1.9 How to make a million: the initial inspiration.

inspiration as a first refinement or a restatement of the problem into a statement of the solution. If the fundamental inspiration is not itself a detailed solution, you will break it down into smaller steps. You will do this over and over again, until the resulting steps are small enough for the purposes of implementation.

Often there is more than one way to do the breakdown at each stage. After all, there are many ways to solve a problem and this certainly applies to the problem of making a million.

A First Refinement

One possible refinement of the basic strategy of selling people what they want assumes that you will have a product to sell. This refinement is shown in Figure 1.10.

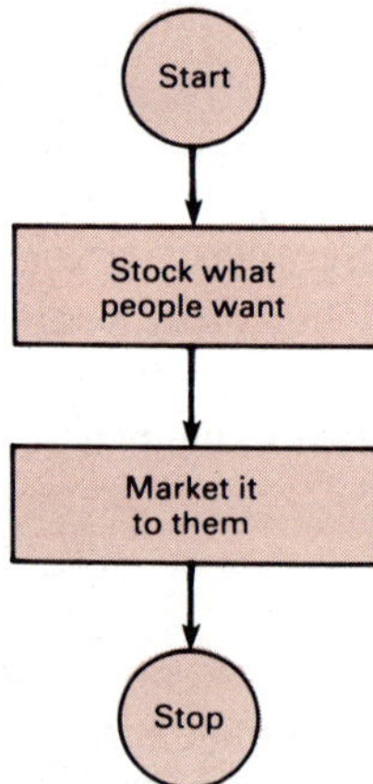

Figure 1.10 This refinement of the initial inspiration to sell something assumes that you will sell a product.

A different refinement might suppose that you will sell a professional service. Other alternatives might be in entertainment or athletics.

If you can think of more than one way to refine a problem into steps, pick one and pursue it. You can always return to one of the others if the first way doesn't work out. The one you pursue first should be the one that seems the best to you.

One refinement might be the fastest to construct. Another might be more expensive to construct, but cheaper to use after it is built. A third might be the most resistant to error. It is an unusual problem if a single approach exists that is the best in all regards. Good judgement is needed in the choice of an approach.

In order to continue the example, we shall exercise our good judgement and proceed with the plan to sell a product. Further refinements of our program will be in that direction. If we happened to encounter an insurmountable obstacle, we could backtrack and pursue one of the other directions.

A Second Refinement

There is still a long way to go from the flow chart in Figure 1.10 to an executable plan to get rich. To stock what people want, you have to find out what they want and then acquire a supply. To market what people want, you have to find the people who want whatever it is you are stocking, let them know you have it, take orders for it, deliver it, and collect the money. Figure 1.11 incorporates this level of detail.

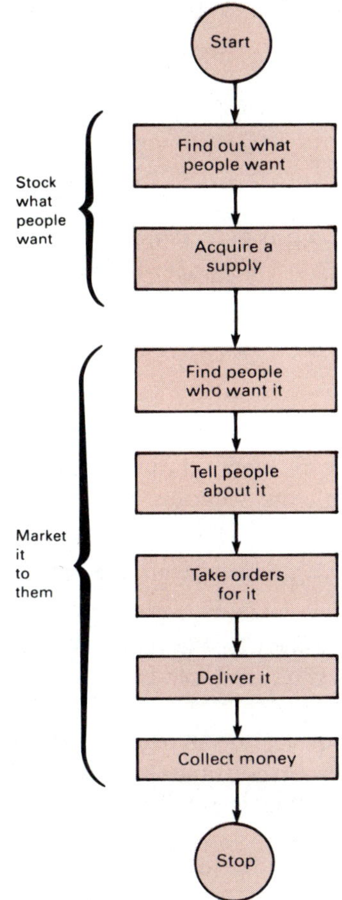

Figure 1.11 A deeper level of refinement.

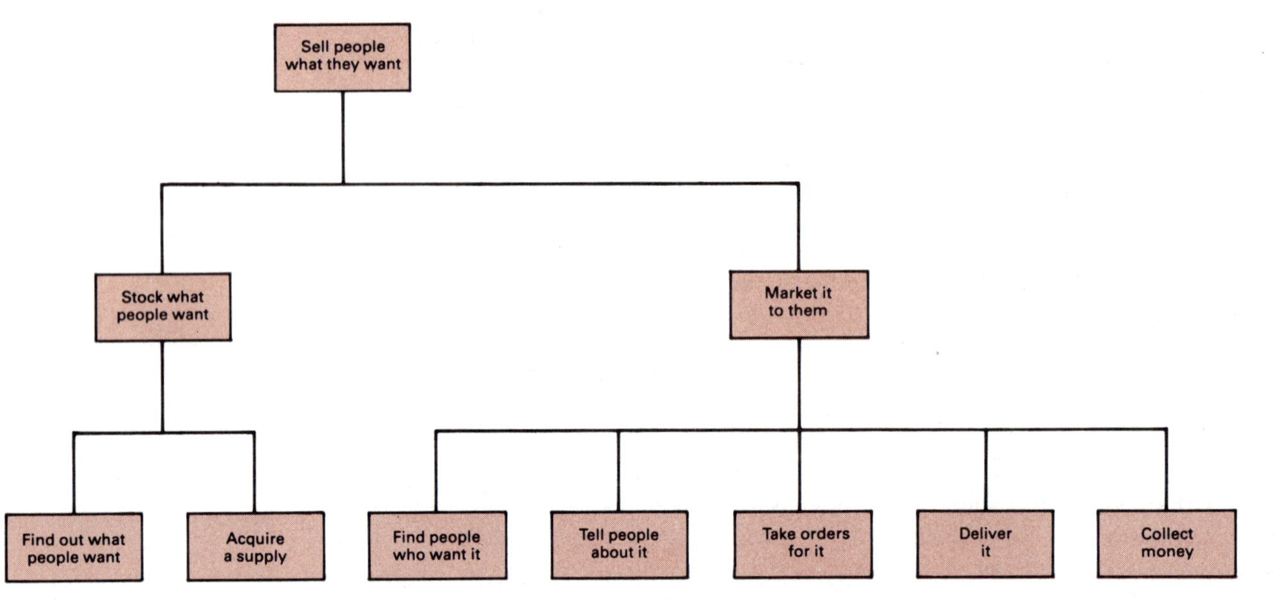

Figure 1.12 Hierarchical organization of subproblems in the task of becoming a millionaire.

Overview of the Refinement Process

Figures 1.9, 1.10, and 1.11 show how a large problem, when viewed in increasing detail, breaks up into a sequence of smaller problems. Figure 1.12 shows the refinement process from a different point of view. It shows the dependence of each subproblem on the larger problem it helps solve.

Continuing the Refinement Process

The refinement process must continue until you have written the steps precisely and unambiguously, so that they may be executed by whoever or whatever will carry them out. Ultimately, you will need to break the solution down, at least to a level with steps like this:

> Send Jodi to Chicago in mid-November with a list of all the retail outlets there.

More likely, you will need even more minute detail, such as the name of the airline, the hotel where your sales representative will stay, and her exact agenda in Chicago.

By the time you have refined the program down to an executable level, there might be hundreds, thousands, or even tens of thousands of steps. This section explains how to modularize your program so that a reader won't get lost in the details.

Two sequences of steps have been bracketed according to the higher level of design illustrated in Figure 1.10. Using subprograms, Fortran and other structured programming languages provide a natural way to represent this bracketing.

In this example of getting rich, the first two steps of Figure 1.11 are the body of the first subprogram, whose name is "Stock what people want". The last five steps of Figure 1.11 are the body of the second subprogram, whose name is "Market it to them". The program for getting rich would look like this when it is organized into subprograms.

```
Program:  Make a Million
  Stock What People Want
  Market It To Them
  end
Subprogram:  Stock What People Want
  Find out what people want
  Acquire a supply
  end
Subprogram:  Market It To Them
  Find people who want it
  Tell people about it
  Take orders for it
  Deliver it
  Collect money
  end
```

There is a **main program** that contains two major steps. Each step is regarded as a **module** that can be called upon to do its job. Below the main program, both of the subprogram modules are broken down into steps. The last step of each subprogram is to return to the **calling program** so that it may continue with the steps that come after the **subprogram call**.

One benefit of decomposing the problem into modules is that it often enables us to analyze and refine each module independently of the others. We might even want to parcel out separate modules to a group of programmers who work as a team.

If we were to continue the refinement process, we might represent each of the steps of the subprogram as a subprogram, so that high-level subprograms would call lower-level subprograms. There would be a hierarchy, rather like a large business. The president delegates work to the vice presidents. The vice presidents delegate work to the department heads. The department heads parcel out work to the supervisors. Finally, the supervisors assign well-defined tasks to the persons who carry them out.

Order of Refining Modules: A Second Case Study

Sometimes the order in which you refine the modules depends on the problem itself. As a second example, let's consider the pleasant problem of taking a vacation. What follows is a top-level breakdown of the solution of the vacation problem:

```
Program:  Vacation
   Collect information
   Make reservations
   Pack luggage
   Travel to vacation spot
   Do vacation things
   Travel home
```

The crucial factor in deciding everything else is likely to be step 5: which things do you want to do on your vacation. If you wish to lie in the sun and swim, you will pick a time and a place where these activities are possible. If you wish to ski or to hike, you will pick different times and places. Thus, the first module to be refined is likely to be

```
Do vacation things
```

Once you have that straight, you can choose where to do them, which will enable you to refine the statements

```
Travel to vacation spot
```

and

```
Travel home
```

The last statements you will refine are the initialization statements

```
Make reservations
```

and

```
Pack luggage
```

What often happens in life, as well as computer programming, is that the part of your program that is to be executed first is the very last that can be planned in detail.

Planning a vacation is an example of a program in which the top-level steps could not be delegated to separate analysts at the outset. In fact, considerable refinement might be necessary before independent analysis would be possible. For instance, the choice of a hotel might depend on what you want to do.

Top-Down Testing

A natural way to test a program written top-down is to test the modules in the order in which they are refined, proceeding from the main program down to the lowest-level subprogram. It is not necessary to have subprograms written before you test the main program, because they can be replaced during testing by fake versions that return the correct answers. For example, in the vacation program, you can verify that if you follow the six steps of the main program in the stated order your vacation will be successful. This can be verified without first having determined the procedure by which the six steps would be carried out. Then, each of the six steps would be refined and tested similarly.

Bottom-Up Testing

You can also test a program from the bottom level up.

The principle is that once you establish that the individual components of a system work correctly, all that remains to be tested is whether they are assembled correctly into the higher-level units.

Of course, when you test a subprogram, you have to make sure that it operates correctly under every possible combination of conditions. After all, you wouldn't want a distributor in your car that doesn't work on rainy days.

Why Document A Program?

If you design your program from the top down, your program becomes self-documenting. That is, it explains itself to people reading the program. The level-by-level breakdown into subprograms is organized to coincide with human experience, so that human readers can interpret higher-level modules of the program from their own context, instead of having to simulate a computer to understand the lower-level details.

Beginners often ask why it is necessary to worry about stylistic matters like **documentation**, when the program is to be read only by a computer. Here are some reasons.

Even when you write a program strictly for your own purposes, you might come back to it months later. For instance, you might need to run it on some different input. Suppose there was apparently an error the second time around and you could not remember what you had in mind when you wrote the program the messy way. How would you debug it? You might have to start over.

Well, what if you knew that the program would be run exactly once, and then never again? Would there be any point in designing it top-down? Would it pay to modularize it and divide it into subprograms? The answer is still yes, but most programmers have to learn this by experience. What often happens is that the first attempt at a complete program simply does not run correctly. It is much harder to locate and correct the flaws in a program that is not segmented into modules.

Flaws in computer programs are **bugs** and correcting them is **debugging**. Searching for problems subprogram by subprogram is much easier than line by line.

The temptation to plunge right in and get the job done is so great that nearly every programmer succumbs to it from time to time. Writing lines of Fortran code may seem like progress, but doing so before you plan your program carefully may not be progress at all.

Would you want to live in a house that was built without plans or to drive a car that was manufactured without a design? Do you think houses or cars could be built faster without plans? Even if the house stands or the car runs, remember that it is the plan that enables someone to fix it when something goes wrong.

1.3 Case Study: A Payroll Program

It is nice to think about how to become a millionaire, but in this section, we will apply some of the ideas discussed in the previous section to a more mundane problem: computing the company payroll. The program developed is not complex enough to warrant using subprograms, but we will use a stepwise refinement process and end up with a complete Fortran program, which we will run using the WATFIV compiler. You should be able to read and understand the program, but the details of how to write such a program must be covered in succeeding chapters.

Section Preview

Statement of the Problem:

Before a correct computer program can be written to solve a problem, the problem must be described accurately.

The Input:

The form of the input must be described for the programmer.

The Output:

The manner in which the results are to be printed also must be described.

Bugs:

In spite of the best intentions and the most careful programming, bugs, or errors, will be present. They must be found and corrected.

The Problem

Suppose there is a small company with 3 employees. Each employee is paid an hourly wage, with provision for extra pay for working overtime. We would like to have a program that computes the weekly wage for each employee, given their hourly wage and the number of hours worked during the week.

The Input

Before the program is run, a computer data file is prepared containing all the relevant information. This consists of a name, hourly wage rate, and number of hours worked this week for each employee. This information must be supplied to the WATFIV compiler along with the Fortran program to run it. A typical input file might look like this.

```
'WALT BRAINERD', 9.83, 55
'CHARLIE GOLDBERG', 6.29, 38
'JONATHAN GROSS', 5.89, 17.25
```

Three characteristics of the form of this input file may stand out as being slightly different than if this input file were prepared for a person to read. First, each name is surrounded by apostrophes (single quotes). Second, no dollar sign precedes each wage rate: 9.83, not $9.83. Third, fractions of an hour are written as decimals: 17.25 instead of 17¼ hours or 17:15.

The Output

The output should consist of a neatly printed echo, which is a summary of all the input data, plus the calculated gross pay for the week for each employee. For the input data shown above, the output might be the following.

```
INPUT DATA  NAME:   WALT BRAINERD
            RATE:          9.8299990
            HOURS:         55.0000000
            GROSS PAY = $614.38

INPUT DATA  NAME:   CHARLIE GOLDBERG
            RATE:                6.2899990
            HOURS:               38.0000000
            GROSS PAY = $239.02

INPUT DATA  NAME:   JONATHAN GROSS
            RATE:                5.8900000
            HOURS:               17.2500000
            GROSS PAY = $101.60
```

Problem Analysis: A First Step

The first and most important thing to realize about the solution to this problem is that the exact same process of calculating gross pay must be repeated several times, once for each employee. Thus the program has the following structure.

```
Compute the pay for each employee
```

The displayed statement above is **pseudocode**. Although it is intended to be an instruction to a computer, it is not written in any language a computer can understand. Pseudocode expresses the solution to a programming problem in a pidgin dialect combining elements of the target programming language Fortran, other programming languages, English, mathematics, and phrases and notations specific to the domain of the problem being solved. A pseudocode solution is easier to write because it deals in terms closer to the problem statement. The only requirement is that the pseudocode directions be unambiguous. Of course, since pseudocode solutions must ultimately be transformed into Fortran programs, the more closely the pseudocode resembles Fortran constructions, the easier it is to complete the task. To this end, we rewrite the pseudocode in a style that resembles programming languages.

```
For each employee
   Compute the employee's pay
```

It is almost second nature for experienced programmers to realize that it doesn't do any good to do computations unless the results are made available. This requires us to decide whether the wage of each employee should be printed immediately after it is computed or should be saved and all wages printed together after all have been computed. In this problem, it really doesn't make much difference to the user, so we may as well print the information as soon as it is computed. The resulting pseudocode below is indented in outline form to indicate that the repetition described in the first line applied to each of the other two lines.

```
For each employee
   Compute the employee's pay
   Print the pay for the employee
```

This program doesn't look like much, but we have accomplished quite a bit in realizing that the overall structure of the program consists of a series of actions to be repeated for each employee. We may now concentrate on the steps necessary to compute the pay for one employee.

The Second Refinement

There are two possible situations that may arise when computing the wage of any one employee. One possibility is that the employee worked overtime and the other is that the employee did not. The program must make provisions to handle each of the two cases. This leads to the conclusion that the structure of the part of the program that refines the statement

```
Compute the employee's pay
```

consists of making a test and doing one of two possible alternative computations based on the result of the test. We express this insight in pseudocode as follows.

```
If the employee worked overtime then
   Compute pay by the overtime formula
else
   Compute pay by the regular formula
```

Thus, computing an employee's pay reduces to three simpler tasks: (a) determining whether the employee worked overtime, (b) computing the pay by the overtime formula, and (c) computing the pay by the regular formula. These tasks are quite easy to program, once you become familiar with a programming language.

Background Information About Pay Calculations

The remaining tasks involve fairly routine computational steps. However, before they can be expressed in detail, some additional information about pay computation is needed. We need to know how many hours make up the normal work week and what formula is used for calculating overtime pay. We will assume that regular pay is computed by multiplying the number of hours worked by the hourly wage. We further assume that overtime work is all work that exceeds 40 hours per week, and that an employee is paid 1½ times the regular hourly wage for overtime work. This means that a formula for computing overtime pay is

$$1.5 \times (\text{hours worked} - 40) \times \text{hourly wage}$$

and a formula for computing regular pay is

$$\text{hours worked} \times \text{hourly wage}$$

A Bug

A **bug** is a mistake in the program. About this time we may realize you can't compute the employee's pay unless you first read into the computer the data on which the calculations are based. According to our analysis, the computer needs the number of hours worked and the hourly wage. The programmer doesn't know this information when the program is written, so the program must contain instructions to obtain this information when the program is run. The numbers are different for each employee, but the instructions for the computer are the same: Get the hourly wage and number of hours worked. It is also probably a good idea to get the employee's name to identify whose pay is computed. This necessitates a revised first refinement. Our first bug has been found and corrected before a single line of Fortran is written. Following a good programming practice, we echo the input data to the printer.

```
For each employee
   Obtain employee's name, hourly wage, and hours worked
   Echo the name, hourly wage, and hours worked
   Compute the employee's pay
   Print the pay for the employee
```

Third Refinement

None of the work on the second refinement has been wasted. We simply now have more steps to refine. Inserting the refined steps to compute the employee's pay, we obtain the most complete pseudocode version of the solution.

```
For each employee
   Obtain employee's name, hourly wage, and hours worked
   Echo the name, hourly wage, and hours worked
   If the employee worked overtime then
      Compute pay by the overtime formula
   else
      Compute pay by the regular formula
   Print the pay for the employee
```

We are about at the point where further refinements of these steps should be expressed in Fortran. Since we begin the study of Fortran proper in Chapter 2, you cannot expect to be able to write the final Fortran version of the payroll program at this point. However, to a large extent, it may be possible to read selected parts of the Fortran program and to relate them to the corresponding statements in the pseudocode version.

The major divisions of this Fortran program are

1. Comments documenting the purpose of the program and the names of the variables used. Comments are recognized by a C in column 1 and are intended only for human readers of the program. They have absolutely no effect on the computer execution of the program. Variable

names in Fortran are limited to six or fewer characters, so they are rarely completely self-explanatory.

2. Declarations of variables. These details should probably be ignored until they are explained in Section 2.2.
3. The executable statements which embody the **algorithm** are the precise unambiguous steps the computer will follow during the course of computation. This is the part of the Fortran program that corresponds directly to the pseudocode. You can see some of the pseudocode statements appearing as comments in the Fortran program; they have a C in column 1. Since it will take the next three chapters to fully explain the features of the Fortran language used in this program, we suggest comparing the executable Fortran statements with the pseudocode refinement. Some of the Fortran statements will make sense without further explanation. The remainder of the program should be reviewed after reading Chapter 4.

```
C     PROGRAM PAYROL
C     COMPUTES THE PAYROLL FOR A COMPANY WITH 3 EMPLOYEES.
C     OVERTIME IS PAID AT TIME-AND-A-HALF.
C
C     VARIABLES
C        NREMPS = NUMBER OF EMPLOYEES
C        EMPLOY = LOOP COUNTER FOR EACH EMPLOYEE
C        RATE   = HOURLY PAY RATE
C        HOURS  = HOURS WORKED THIS WEEK
C        PAY    = GROSS PAY FOR THE WEEK
C        REGPAY = PAY FOR THE FIRST 40 HOURS
C        OTPAY  = PAY FOR OVERTIME HOURS
C        REGHRS = 40 = HOURS IN NORMAL WORK WEEK
C        OTHRS  = OVERTIME HOURS
C        OTFACT = FACTOR FOR OVERTIME
C        NAME   = EMPLOYEE'S NAME
C
      INTEGER NREMPS, EMPLOY
      REAL RATE, HOURS, PAY
      REAL REGPAY, OTHRS, OTPAY
      REAL REGHRS, OTFACT
      CHARACTER NAME *20
      NREMPS = 3
      REGHRS = 40
      OTFACT = 1.5
C
C     FOR EACH EMPLOYEE
      DO 18 EMPLOY = 1, NREMPS
         PRINT, ' '
         READ, NAME, RATE, HOURS
         PRINT, 'INPUT DATA  NAME:', NAME
         PRINT, '            RATE:', RATE
         PRINT, '            HOURS:', HOURS
C
```

```
C         COMPUTE THE EMPLOYEE'S PAY
          IF (HOURS .GT. REGHRS) THEN DO
C            COMPUTE PAY BY THE OVERTIME FORMULA
             REGPAY = RATE * REGHRS
             OTHRS = HOURS - REGHRS
             OTPAY = OTFACT * RATE * OTHRS
             PAY = REGPAY + OTPAY
          ELSE DO
C            COMPUTE PAY BY THE OVERTIME FORMULA
             PAY = RATE * HOURS
          END IF
          PRINT 15, PAY
   15     FORMAT (T14, 'GROSS PAY = $', F6.2)',
   18  CONTINUE
       STOP
       END
```

```
INPUT DATA   NAME:  WALT BRAINERD
             RATE:        9.8299990
             HOURS:       55.0000000
             GROSS PAY = $614.38

INPUT DATA   NAME:  CHARLIE GOLDBERG
             RATE:              6.2899990
             HOURS:             38.0000000
             GROSS PAY = $239.02

INPUT DATA   NAME:  JONATHAN GROSS
             RATE:              5.8900000
             HOURS:             17.2500000
             GROSS PAY = $101.60
```

1.4 History of Fortran

In the mid 1950s, a group was formed at International Business Machines to develop a programming system that would permit the programmer to express computations in a language that a computer would not understand directly, but which would more directly express the computations using the languages of the programmer, namely English and mathematics. This group was led by John Backus. The programming language was called Fortran (Formula translation) and the first system was delivered in 1957 for the IBM 704 computer.

It is a little difficult to realize what a radical concept it was in those days to consider using a system in which the programmer did not write instructions directly understood by the computer. (Assembly language had eased the burden of writing machine code somewhat by allowing mnemonic abbreviations for operation codes and symbolic names for addresses, but assembler programs still corresponded instruction-for-instruction to the machine language code they specified.) Most programmers believed that they could write much more efficient assembler programs than any that could be produced by a compiler. Thus it was important that Backus' group produce a system that generated efficient programs. They succeeded remarkably well. Efficient programs have been a hallmark of Fortran compilers from the very first one to those generated now. Since computers are becoming less expensive and programmers are becoming more expensive, the gain in overall efficiency obtained by using a language like Fortran becomes ever more important. Even though a clever assembler programmer may produce a faster program than a compiler, given enough time, the cost of doing so is usually much greater than the cost of some additional computer time.

The introduction in the 1958 Fortran II Reference Manual* describes the intent and purpose of Fortran as it was then conceived.

> The original Fortran language was designed as a concise, convenient means of stating the steps to be carried out by the IBM 704 Data Processing System in the solution of many types of problems, particularly in scientific and technical fields. As the language is simple and the 704, with the Fortran Translator program, performs most of the clerical work, Fortran has afforded a significant reduction in the time required to write programs.
>
> The original Fortran language contained 32 types of statements. Virtually any numerical procedure may be expressed by combinations of these statements. Arithmetic formulas are expressed in a language close to that of mathematics. Iterative processes can be easily governed by control statements and arithmetic statements. Input and output data are flexibly handled in a variety of formats.

In 1958, Fortran II introduced six new statements, all concerned with subroutines and the modularizing of programs. Large Fortran programs which had required several hours of error-free computer time to compile could be split into independently compilable subroutines, each requiring just a few minutes of computer time. If a change was made in one part of a program, only that subroutine had to be recompiled.

In the late 1950s and 1960s, most major computer companies produced a Fortran compiler to run on their computing systems. Many added new features to the language, but not always the same features and not always with the same syntax, so a committee was formed to produce a standard version of the language. The goal was to allow Fortran programs written for one computer to be run on all computers with a modest amount of change. In 1966, Fortran became the first programming language to be standardized. The 1966 standard version of Fortran was based on a version of Fortran called Fortran IV. Major improvements were in the area of the logical IF statement, logical variables, explicit type declarations, and more uniform treatment of all input and output.

The Fortran language continued to grow in power and popularity. The University of Waterloo, Ontario, produced a set of student compilers: WATFOR (Waterloo Fortran), WATFIV (Waterloo Fortran IV), and WATFIV-S (WATFIV-structured) that provided fast turnaround and excellent error messages, as well as significant extensions of 1966 standard Fortran. Major extensions include default formatted input and output, an IF-THEN-ELSE block, character data type, and a DO-WHILE loop.

In 1977, the language standard was revised; this version is known as Fortran 77. The International Standards Organization (ISO) also has adopted this same document as an international standard for Fortran. Many of the features of WATFIV were adopted in the Fortran 77 standard, although in some cases there are minor differences in syntax, which we describe.

Fortran is still the most widely used programming language for scientific and engineering computing. Its development continues and a new standard version of the language probably will be completed by 1988.

---

* *Reference Manual, Fortran II for the IBM 704 Data Processing System*, International Business Machines Corporation, 1958.

1.5 What You Should Know

1. A computer is a device for processing information in a wide variety of ways, both simple and complex.
2. The first computer was the Analytical Engine, designed by Charles Babbage in the 1830s.
3. One of the first operational computers, the Mark I, was built in the 1940s.
4. The most fundamental principle in computer design from Babbage's time to the present is automatic operation, that is, the ability of a computer to operate as much as possible without human direction or assistance.
5. Modern computers rely on the four arithmetic operations as the basis for numeric computing.
6. Computers can receive input data from many sources, including terminals, magnetic disks, punchcards, and other computers.
7. Computers write output in many forms, including printed output, video display, plotted graphic output, and disks, tapes, and punchcards.
8. Regardless of what the actual medium is, computer scientists speak of reading all input and writing all output.
9. In its memory, a computer can save information and retrieve it later.
10. In a Fortran program, each memory location is referenced by a variable name that reminds the programmer what the values stored in that location represent.
11. A computer can move data around in its memory.
12. A computer is a general-purpose machine that can perform a specific task only if it has been programmed.
13. The instructions to a computer are not always executed in sequence. The computer's instruction set includes instructions to change the sequence on the basis of computed results.
14. A loop is a sequence of program steps that may be repeated more than once during a single execution of a program.
15. The computer can choose between computational alternatives on the basis of a calculated selector variable or expression.
16. In most computers, the program is stored in the computer's memory in exactly the same memory cells that at other times could store data.
17. Top-down design means beginning with strategic planning and gradually becoming more specific.
18. A step in the solution of a problem is refined when it is rewritten in greater detail.
19. The refinement process continues until the steps are precise and unambiguous. For our purposes, this means an executable Fortran program.
20. A module is a more or less self-contained part of the program. Modules are often refined as subroutines.
21. One benefit of decomposing the problem into modules is that it often enables us to analyze and refine each module independently of the others.
22. The organization of a program that has been designed from the top down is hierarchical. The main program calls subprograms to perform its subtasks. The subprograms in turn call lower-level subprograms to perform their subtasks.
23. Modules rarely are refined in the order in which they are executed.
24. Documentation helps readers of the program understand what it does.
25. A program that has been well-organized from the top down is self-documenting.
26. Bugs are flaws in computer programs; debugging is finding and removing bugs.

27. It is unwise to rush into writing executable code until the structure of the solution has been thoroughly planned and verified.

1.6 Self-Test Questions

Section 1.1

1. Which of the ten characteristic attributes of a computer are possessed by the following devices? You may need to refer to sources outside this book for sufficient information to help you make your decisions.
    1. A clock radio
    2. A digital clock radio
    3. A desk calculator or hand calculator. Use the one you are most familiar with.
    4. A programmable hand calculator
    5. Babbage's Analytical Engine
    6. A computer you have seen, or are using in conjunction with this book
    7. A player piano or music box
    8. A multichanger record player, that is, one that accepts more than one record at a time
    9. The automatic speed control mechanism in an automobile (cruise control)
    10. A Jacquard loom for weaving brocades

Section 1.2

1. True/false:
    a. You should discipline yourself so that when you want to solve a problem, you begin writing Fortran code immediately.
    b. Stepwise refinement means deepening the level of detail of a proposed solution.
    c. What distinguishes outstanding programmers from others is that the outstanding ones invariably can find the best all-around way to solve a problem.
2. Why don't you have to refine a program all the way down to machine language? (See if you know this one, even though the text does not tell you the answer explicitly.)
3. True/false:
    a. The body of a main program might consist of nothing but calls to programmer-defined subprograms.
    b. The systematic way to refine a program is to refine the individual steps in the sequential order in which they appear in the program.
4. True/false:
    a. When you test a program, you should test all cases equally, with no special stress on the cases most likely to occur.
    b. Good documentation means frequent comments throughout a program.
    c. The purpose of organizing a program into subprograms is so that someone else can read it.

PROGRAM SOLVING AND PROGRAMMING IN FORTRAN

A computer solves problems by executing a planned sequence of instructions. The computer's considerable success in solving problems is built on advances in two areas of computer science. First, in an area not treated in this book, major achievements have been made in designing electronic circuits that perform with speed, reliability, and at increasingly low cost. Second, much is now known about how to analyze problems for computer solution and how to write reliable computer programs to solve the problems. This book is about analyzing problems and writing Fortran computer programs to implement their solution.

Analyzing a problem is pretty much the same no matter what computer language is used to write the program. However, writing the instructions the computer will follow can be made much easier by a suitable choice of programming language. Fortran is a powerful language, particularly for writing programs involving numerical calculations, but it is also a good language to introduce the major concepts in computer programming. Surprisingly for a language reputed for its calculational power and ease, Fortran has also always had powerful and convenient features for producing beautifully formatted output.

You can begin writing meaningful programs to solve real problems as soon as you know just a few words of Fortran. Section 2.1 shows how to write Fortran programs to perform standard arithmetic calculations, and the rest of Chapter 2 shows how to write programs to do more complex calculations and how to run these programs on a computer.

We believe you should start reading and writing programs immediately. If a computer is available, write and *run* programs modelled on our sample programs for a start. A short set of directions from the instructor or computer center or, better yet, a brief demonstration using the computer will show you how to enter and run a program at your local installation.

2.1 Programs That Calculate and Print

Since computers are very good at arithmetic, one reasonable thing to learn first about computer programming is how to tell a computer to do the sort of arithmetic that otherwise might be done by hand or with the aid of a hand calculator. This section describes how to write programs to calculate and to print the answer.

Section Preview

General form of a Fortran program:

Fortran statements

. . .

END

Example:

```
C       PROGRAM CALC1
        PRINT, 84 + 13
        STOP
        END
```

COMMENT statement

General form:

C *any text whatsoever*

Example:

```
C       THIS IS A COMMENT
```

PRINT statement

General form:

PRINT *format* , *list of expressions to be printed*

Example:

```
        PRINT, 'THE ANSWER IS ', +(92 + 12) / 2
```

STOP statement

General form:

STOP

Simple Calculations

The first example is a program that prints the result of an addition

```
C       PROGRAM CALC1
        PRINT, 84 + 13
        STOP
        END
```

The program CALC1 tells the computer to add the numbers 84 and 13 and then to print the sum, 97. When the WATFIV compiler runs the program CALC1, it does precisely that: it adds the two numbers and prints their sum. The execution printout will look something like this.

```
97
```

Comment Lines

The first line of the program CALC1 is a **comment line**, identified by a C in column 1. It helps to identify the program to people who read it, but it has no effect on the program execution. Nevertheless, we always include such a statement as a matter of good programming style. We believe that a good program should be readable as well as able to calculate the correct answers.

Default Print Format

The comma immediately following the keyword PRINT tells the computer that the programmer will not be specifying the exact **format** or layout for the printed answer. The WATFIV compiler will therefore use a **default format**, designed to be satisfactory in most cases. The Fortran standards allow some freedom in the design of default formats, so your output may differ slightly from the sample execution shown above if you use a different Fortran compiler.

> *Fortran 77 Note:* WATFIV-S and Fortran 77 differ slightly on how to denote the default format in a PRINT statement. WATFIV places nothing before the comma; Fortran 77 requires an asterisk (*) before the comma.
>
> ```
> PRINT *, 84 + 13
> ```
>
> In WATFIV, one must be careful not to omit the comma
>
> ```
> PRINT, 84 + 13
> ```

STOP Statement

A WATFIV-S program execution ends when a STOP statement is executed. If the STOP statement is omitted, WATFIV-S prints an annoying error message and then stops because of the error, ironically exactly what was intended. We prefer the STOP statement.

END Statement

The END statement is a kind of "closing parenthesis" for a program. It is not an executable statement in WATFIV, but it must not be omitted. The END statement consists of the keyword END and nothing else. Every Fortran program must have an END statement as its last statement.

Program Listing

A printed copy of a program is a **program listing**. The previous display of the program CALC1 is a program listing. The complete printed output of a WATFIV job consists of a program listing, an execution output, and a few lines of identification and echoes of control cards. The program listing and the execution output are the only parts of immediate concern.

Six questions of immediate relevance are brought up by the program CALC1. Their answers will occupy the rest of this chapter.

1. How does the computer know that it is supposed to write the sum 97, and not the statement of the problem "84 + 13" instead?
2. What kinds of expressions may be written after the comma in the PRINT statement?
3. Just how much English is incorporated into the Fortran programming language? For example, are there any acceptable synonyms for PRINT, STOP, and END?
4. What is the meaning of the program name CALC1?
5. How is a computer told what the program is and when to run it?
6. Does every Fortran statement have to start in column 7?

Printing Messages

If you want the computer to print the exact typographic characters that you specify, you enclose them in apostrophes (or single quotes), as illustrated by the program QUOTES. The apostrophes are not printed in the output.

```
C       PROGRAM QUOTES
        PRINT, '84 + 13'
        STOP
        END
```

```
84 + 13
```

In a Fortran program, a sequence of typographic characters enclosed in apostrophes is a **character string**. A character string may contain alphabetic characters as well as numeric characters and may contain other special characters such as punctuation marks and arithmetic symbols. For example, the program HELLO prints a largely alphabetic character string.

```
C       PROGRAM HELLO
        PRINT, 'HELLO, I AM A COMPUTER.'
        STOP
        END
```

```
HELLO, I AM A COMPUTER.
```

Printing both exact literal characters and a computed value produces the following easy-to-read output.

```
C       PROGRAM CLC1V2
        PRINT, '84 + 13 =', 84 + 13
        STOP
        END
```

```
84 + 13 =              97
```

In the program CLC1V2 (calculation 1 version 2), there are two items in the PRINT list, a **character constant** '84 + 13 =' to be printed exactly as written, and an arithmetic expression whose value is first calculated and then printed. Although the two items may look identical, they are not. Enclosing the character string in apostrophes means that it is to be transcribed *character for character*, including the three blank characters (spaces, in ordinary typing), while the same expression written without apostrophes is to be evaluated so that the sum can be printed. Commas are used to separate the items in a PRINT list.

Constants: Character, Real, and Integer

All of the numbers and character strings in the programs in this section are examples of constants. There are several **types** of constants. A **character constant** is a character string enclosed in apostrophes. A **real constant** is a number with a decimal point. All the following are real constants in Fortran.

```
13.5  0.1234567  123.45678  3.0  00.30
.1234567  3.  12345.  .0
```

A real constant may have no digits to the left of the decimal point or it may have no digits to the right of the decimal point, but a decimal point by itself is not a legal real constant.

An **integer constant** is a string containing only the digits 0 to 9. The following are examples of integer constants.

```
23  0  1234567
```

In Fortran, the distinction between **integer type** and **real type constants** is a matter of the appearance of a decimal point, not whether the number is whole or has a non-zero fractional part. Thus 23.0 is a real constant, not an integer constant.

Integer Division

Sometimes this distinction mades a difference in a Fortran program. For example, the arithmetic expression

```
23 / 2
```

is the quotient of two integer constants and produces the integer answer 11, while the expression

```
23.0 / 2
```

is the quotient of a real constant and an integer constant and produces the real answer 11.5.

Signed Numbers

A **number** is a real constant or an integer constant. A **signed number** is a number optionally preceded by a plus sign (+) or a minus sign (−). The following are examples of signed numbers.

```
-23.7955   -6   +7.42   +3453   0.7    1
```

Exponential Notation Versus Positional Notation

The usual way of writing real numbers, like 32.17, 0.0021, or 384.41, is called **positional notation** because the place value of each digit is determined by its position relative to the decimal point. Since computers ordinarily store only a limited number of significant digits, there is another common representation of numbers to allow for very large or very small numbers.

A real or integer constant may be followed by the letter "E" and an integer to form a real constant written in **exponential notation**. The letter "E" is read as "times ten to the power" and the integer following the "E" is a power of ten to be multiplied by the number preceding the "E". Exponential notation is useful for writing very large or very small numbers. For example, 2.3E5 is 2.3 times ten to the power 5, 2.3×10^5, or $2.3 \times 100000 = 230000$. The integer power may have a minus or plus sign preceding it, as in the real constant 2.3E−5, which is 2.3×10^{-5} or $2.3 \times 0.00001 = 0.000023$. Two more examples are 1E9, which is one billion, and 1E−3, which is one one-thousandth.

Default Print Formats for Reals

The comma immediately following the word PRINT in a PRINT statement instructs the computer to print each item in the PRINT list according to a default print format chosen by the designers of the WATFIV-S system. Unfortunately, many WATFIV-S systems choose to print reals in exponential notation, as the next several sample executions show. We find WATFIV's exponential notation more difficult to read for ordinary sized numbers than positional notation, and therefore we will feel compelled to introduce explicit PRINT formatting earlier than we would when using dialects with better default formats.

Arithmetic Expressions

Just about any arithmetic expression may appear in the list of a PRINT statement, and the computer will evaluate it and print the result. The Fortran notation for arithmetic operations conforms generally to ordinary notation, except in cases where the ordinary notation is difficult or impossible to type on standard computer input devices. For example, asterisk (*) is used to denote multiplication, and slash (/) is used to denote division. Even when the notation is modified, as in CALC2, the evaluation is the usual one:

```
C       PROGRAM CALC2
        PRINT, 3.375 * (12 * 3 - 143 / 11)
        STOP
        END
```

```
          77.6250000
```

To calculate the answer, the number 3.375 is multiplied by the value of the expression in parentheses. Within the parentheses, the number 12 is multiplied by 3 to give 36. The term 143 / 11 is written all on one line because Fortran does not allow typing the numerator over the denominator. 143 / 11 has the value 13. Therefore the value of the expression in parentheses is the difference 36 − 13, which is 23. The product of 3.375 and 23 is 77.625, the answer. Some WATFIV systems print the answer as 0.7762500E+02. Either way, the answer is printed as a real number because in Fortran the result of multiplying a real number by an integer is a real number.

Integer Division: A Caution

Experienced Fortran programmers become very nervous when they see division of integer constants. Even if the final answer is type real, calculation of the quotient of two integers in a subexpression results in an integer quotient with the remainder lost. This characteristic of Fortran did not matter in CALC2 because 143 is exactly divisible by 11. However, in the program INTDIV, it does matter.

```
C       PROGRAM INTDIV
        PRINT, 10.0 * (5 / 2), 10.0 * (5.0 / 2.0)
        STOP
        END
```

```
          20.0000000            25.0000000
```

The WATFIV answers are 20.0000000 = 20 and 25.0000000 = 25, because the first expression uses integer division 5 / 2 = 2 and the second uses real division 5.0 / 2.0 = 2.5.

As further illustration of the evaluation of expressions, the program CALC3 uses the notation double asterisk (**) to denote exponentiation, that is, raising a number to a power. This compromise notation is necessary because the ordinary notation using a superscript, usually in smaller type, cannot be produced easily on computer input devices.

```
C       PROGRAM CALC3
        PRINT, -9.7E6 * (4 ** 3 - 128 / 16)
        STOP
        END
```

```
 -543199900.0000000
```

This expression is evaluated as follows. The number 9.7E6 (which is 9,700,000) is multiplied by the value of the expression in parentheses and the sign of the result is reversed. The term 4 ** 3 means 4^3 or 4 cubed, which is 64. The term 128 / 16 has the value 8, so the expression in parentheses has the value 64 − 8, which is 56. The product of 9.7×10^6 and 56 is 5.432×10^8. Hence the answer is -5.432×10^8. With a little thought, you can see that this is equivalent to the WATFIV-S answer after rounding. See section 2.3.

As in ordinary algebra, the evaluation of a complicated expression with many parentheses begins with evaluation of a subexpression enclosed by an innermost pair of parentheses. In Fortran, as in algebra, exponentiation takes precedence over multiplication and division. Multiplication and division are performed before addition or subtraction. Nevertheless, it is always permissible, and often advisable, to insert parentheses to clarify the meaning of an arithmetic expression. The precedence rules as they apply in the absence of overriding parentheses are illustrated in the following example.

```
4 + 12 / 2 - 1 + 5 * 3 ** 2
= 4 + 12 / 2 - 1 + 5 * 9      first exponentiation
= 4 + 6 - 1 + 5 * 9           then multiplications and divisions,
= 4 + 6 - 1 + 45                going from left to right
= 10 - 1 + 45                 then additions and subtractions,
= 9 + 45                        going from left to right
= 54
```

Expressions involving repeated divisions are evaluated from left to right, as shown below:

```
432 / 12 / 6 / 3
= 36 / 6 / 3      leftmost division first
= 6 / 3           leftmost remaining division next
= 2
```

As in algebra, it is a good practice to insert parentheses to distinguish this meaning more clearly from such other possible interpretations as

(432 / 12) / (6 / 3)   and   432 / (12 / (6 / 3))

which have different values. Similarly, expressions involving a mixture of multiplications and divisions are evaluated from left to right. Thus

```
12 / 6 * 2
= 2 * 2     leftmost operation first
= 4
```

When the calculated expression 12 / (6 * 2) is desired, the parentheses must not be omitted.

Does A Computer Understand English?

A computer understands only as much English as it is programmed to understand. The similarity between English and a programming language represents a compromise between what is convenient for English-speaking programmers and what is convenient for the computer, which "speaks" machine language. In general, the more a programming language resembles English, the more computational time and power are required to translate a program into machine language for execution, so the more it costs to operate. Fortran is really not much like English, but instead borrows much of its notation from mathematics. However, every bit of similarity with familiar English words and common mathematical expressions makes it that much easier to write readable and correct Fortran programs.

Keywords

The instructions given to a computer must be precise, unambiguous, and complete. When English words are used in Fortran, they acquire a precise, unambiguous, technical meaning. For example, STOP means: "Terminate the execution of a program" and END means: "This is the physical end of a Fortran program. There are no more Fortran statements to follow."

An English word like PRINT, STOP, or END used in a program for its precise, technical meaning is a **keyword**. Program steps that use a keyword make sense on two different levels. First, using the technical meaning, they are precise and unambiguous directions to a computer. Second, using the ordinary meaning of the English word, they are understandable by people who speak English. This is a great convenience to programmers and an incalculable aid to clear thinking. Almost every Fortran statement begins with a keyword.

The PROGRAM Statement of Fortran 77

Fortran 77 permits each Fortran program to begin with a PROGRAM statement, a sort of "opening parenthesis" to match the "closing parenthesis" of the END statement. Since WATFIV does not have a PROGRAM statement, we identify each program with a comment statement. Under the assumption that WATFIV-S programmers someday may have to program in a standard version of Fortran, we choose the form of the comment to exactly match the form of a standard PROGRAM statement. It consists of the keyword PROGRAM followed by a **program name** of the programmer's choosing. The name must start with a letter and consist of at most six letters and digits. The program name CALC1 does not mean anything to the computer. Any other name following the rules would work just as well. However, the first calculation program in this book is named CALC1 for the benefit of its human readers.

> *Warning:* Fortran systems, including WATFIV-S, written before the 1977 revision of the standard do not support the PROGRAM statement. On such older systems, we suggest putting the program name in a comment statement.

Running a Program

How to tell a computer to run a program depends very much on the computer being used. It also may depend on the type of device that is used to enter the program into the computer. You should get instructions specific to the computer you will be using from your instructor or computer center. It is rarely very complicated for WATFIV systems.

A complete WATFIV-S run file contains four kinds of information

1. The Fortran program
2. The data, if any.
3. WATFIV-S control cards
4. Other system-specific control cards.

We have seen several examples of Fortran programs, and will see examples of data in Section 2.2. WATFIV control cards all start with a dollar sign ($) in column 1. The $JOB card introduces the Fortran program. The $ENTRY separates the Fortran program from the data, and the $END control card ends the WATFIV-S job. The other control cards are for the local operating system and are likely to be different at different computer centers.

```
$JOB                NOEXT
C      PROGRAM ADD2
       INTEGER X, Y
       READ, X
       PRINT, 'INPUT DATA  X:', X
       READ, Y
       PRINT, 'INPUT DATA  Y:', Y
       PRINT, 'X + Y =', X + Y
       STOP
       END
$ENTRY
84
13
$END
```

In order to run a Fortran program, you must present it to the computer in a form the computer can accept. The two most common media for transmitting a program to a computer are terminals and, to a steadily decreasing extent, punched cards. Originally, WATFIV programs were entered mainly on punched cards; hence the term "control card" for the WATFIV $-separator lines. Now, the same information that used to be punched in cards is usually entered as lines of a disk file. At this point, we suggest you learn how to submit a program to your computer system, and run at least one demonstration program to verify the procedures. Detailed instructions are available from your instructor, computer manuals, or computer center memoranda.

Fields in a Fortran Source Line

Fortran statements are written in columns 7 through 72. Blank columns are ignored, so judicious use of spacing may be used to improve readability. Columns 73 to the end of the line are ignored. Columns 1 to 5 are used for statement labels, which will be discussed later. Column 1 is also used to designate **comment lines**, which have no effect on the execution of a program, but can be used to explain features of the program to human readers. A C in column 1 indicates that a line is a comment line, and is subject to no further rules of Fortran grammar. For example,

```
C      PROGRAM COMMNT
C      THIS LINE IS A COMMENT.
C      HUMAN READERS OF THE PROGRAM WILL SEE IT,
C      BUT IT WILL HAVE NO EFFECT ON THE PROGRAM EXECUTION.
C
       PRINT, 'THIS LINE IS EXECUTED.'
       STOP
       END
```

```
THIS LINE IS EXECUTED.
```

Each line of a comment must have a C or asterisk in column 1.

Continuing a Statement onto the Next Line

In Fortran, any line that contains a character other than a blank or zero in column 6 is assumed to be a continuation of the statement on the previous line. The contents of columns 7 to 72 are treated just as if they were appended immediately after column 72 of the previous line. Although it is not required, we recommend that the break between two lines be made so that the result is as readable as possible. For example, in the program CONTIN, the PRINT statement is continued to a second line by typing the character "+" in column 6 of the continuation line. This character is not considered part of the PRINT statement. It merely indicates a continuation. An asterisk or any character other than 0 would serve as well.

```
C     PROGRAM CONTIN
      PRINT, 'THE SUM OF THE NUMBERS FROM 1 TO 5 IS',
     +           1 + 2 + 3 + 4 + 5
      STOP
      END
```

```
THE SUM OF THE NUMBERS FROM 1 TO 5 IS             15
```

Calculating an Average of Four Numbers

To further demonstrate the convenience of doing routine calculations on a computer using Fortran, this section closes with the program AVG4 for computing the average of four numbers.

```
C     PROGRAM AVG4
      PRINT, +(92.1 + 71.9 + 83.3 + 89.0) / 4
      STOP
      END
```

```
       84.0749500
```

A second version of this program is named AVG4V2. It identifies the answer by specifying a character string to be printed along with the computed answer.

```
C     PROGRAM AVG4V2
      PRINT, 'THE AVERAGE IS', +(92.1 + 71.9 + 83.3 + 89.0) / 4
      STOP
      END
```

```
THE AVERAGE IS            84.0749500
```

2.2 Variables, Input, and Output

One benefit of writing a computer program for doing a calculation rather than obtaining the answer using pencil and paper or a hand calculator is that when the same sort of problem arises again, the program already written can be applied to it. The use of **variables** gives the programs in this section the flexibility needed for such reuse.

Section Preview

Variables:

Variables hold values during execution.

Variable names start with a letter and consist of any mixture of from one to six letters and digits.

Three intrinsic variable types are introduced: INTEGER, and REAL, and CHARACTER.

Declarations:

Following good programming practice, the type of every variable should be declared.

Example:

```
C       PROGRAM EXMPL1
        INTEGER FIRST, LAST, NEXT
        REAL X, Y, PI, D2YDX2
        CHARACTER NAME *4, INITAL *1
C
        LAST = 99
        PI = 3.14159
        NAME = 'JOAN'
        ...
        END
```

Assignment statement:

General form:

variable = *expression*

Example:

```
        AVERAG = (A + B) / 2
```

READ statement:

General form:

READ *format* , *list of variables*

Example:

```
        READ, THIS, THAT, OTHER
```

Variables

The programs in Section 2.1 direct the computer to perform the indicated arithmetic operations on numeric constants appearing in the PRINT statements. The first program in this section, ADD2, will find the sum of any two integers supplied as input. The numbers to be added do not appear in the program listing. Instead, two integer **variables**, X and Y, are reserved to hold the two values supplied as input. Since Fortran statements can operate on variables as well as constants, their sum can be calculated and printed. The first sample run shows how this new program could be used to find the sum of the numbers 84 and 13, previously calculated by the program CALC2 in the previous section.

```
C       PROGRAM ADD2
        INTEGER X, Y
        READ, X
        PRINT, 'INPUT DATA  X:', X
```

```
          READ, Y
          PRINT, 'INPUT DATA  Y:', Y
          PRINT, 'X + Y =', X + Y
          STOP
          END
```

```
INPUT DATA  X:              84
INPUT DATA  Y:              13
X + Y =            97
```

After declaring that the variables X and Y will hold integer values, the program ADD2 tells the computer to read a number from an input device and call it X, then to read another number and call it Y, and finally to print the value of X + Y, identified as such. Two additional PRINT statements that echo the values of the input data complete the program ADD2. The two numbers which are the values of X and Y must be supplied to the computer by placing them between the $ENTRY and $END control cards, or the computer cannot complete the run.

Declaration of Variables

Type declarations appear before the first executable statement of the program. Each declaration consists of a keyword specifying a Fortran intrinsic type, followed by a list of variable names separated by commas. For example, the program ADD2 uses the type declaration

```
INTEGER X,Y
```

Corresponding to the INTEGER, REAL, and CHARACTER constants introduced in Section 2.1, there are INTEGER, REAL, and CHARACTER variables. For example, if the variables Q, T, and K are to be real variables in a program and the variables N and B are to be integer variables, then the following lines contain the necessary declarations.

```
REAL Q, T, K
INTEGER N, B
```

If more significant digits are needed than your system keeps in type real, variables DPQ, X, and LONG may be declared double precision reals by the following declaration.

```
DOUBLE PRECISION DPQ, X, LONG
```

In the case of character variables, the variable name should be followed by an asterisk (*) and an integer indicating the number of characters in the character string. If the variable NAME is to be a string of 20 characters, it may be declared as follows.

```
CHARACTER NAME *20
```

Style Note: As a matter of good programming practice, every variable that is used in a Fortran program should be listed in a type declaration.

Default Variable Types

In its earliest days, the language Fortran did not have type declarations. Instead, variables were assigned a **default type** on the basis of the first letter of their names. Only real and integer variables were permitted. Variables whose names started with the letters I–N were type integer. All other variables were type real. Although it is now common practice to declare all variables, those that accidentally or intentionally remain undeclared are still assigned the default types.

IMPLICIT Statement

The default data types for a WATFIV program may be changed by an IMPLICIT statement. For example, the statement

```
IMPLICIT REAL (A-Z)
```

makes all variables type real by default, and the statement

```
IMPLICIT DOUBLE PRECISION (D, X-Z)
```

makes double precision any variable whose name starts either with letter D or with the letters X, Y, or Z. In many scientific applications, the overwhelming majority of variables are either all real or all double precision. By using an IMPLICIT REAL (A – Z) statement, the programmer has only to declare explicitly those variables that are not real. IMPLICIT statements should precede all explicit type declarations.

Supplying Input Data

The two input values 84 and 13 for the variables X and Y, shown in the sample execution of the program ADD2, did not appear in the computer by magic. They were typed in by the user in the WATFIV run file between the $ENTRY and $END lines. The data for this run of the program ADD2 consisted of the two data lines.

```
84
13
```

Echo of Input Data

In Fortran, as well as most other programming languages, it is a good programming practice for the user to provide an **echo** of the input data using PRINT statements, so that the output contains a record of the values used in the computation. Each READ statement in the program ADD2 is followed by an echo of the input data just read. Although the input WATFIV run file always contains the data, the printed output does not include the data values unless they are echoed by PRINT statements.

Style Note: It is good programming practice to echo all input data.

Rerunning a Program With Different Data

The program ADD2 contains echoes, whose importance is demonstrated when the program is rerun using different input data. The echoes of input data help identify which answer goes with which problem. Other important uses of input echoes will appear later. The program does not change; only the input data change. This time, the run file has the following two data lines.

The printed output consists of the same program listing as before and the following execution printout.

```
INPUT DATA  X:           4
INPUT DATA  Y:           7
X + Y =          11
```

The final PRINT statement of ADD2 refers to the variables X and Y. As the execution printout for the two sample runs shows, what actually is printed is the value of the character string constant 'X + Y = ' followed by the value of the expression X + Y at the moment the PRINT statement is executed.

The program ADD2R (add 2 reals) is obtained from the program ADD2 simply by changing the keyword INTEGER in the variable declaration to the keyword REAL, which causes the type of the variables X and Y to be REAL. The program ADD2R can be used to add two quantities that are not necessarily whole numbers. This execution of the program also illustrates that the input data values may be negative. The input data for this sample execution contains two lines

```
97.6
-12.9
```

```
C       PROGRAM ADD2R
        REAL X, Y
        READ, X
        PRINT, 'INPUT DATA  X:', X
        READ, Y
        PRINT, 'INPUT DATA  Y:', Y
        PRINT, 'X + Y =', X + Y
        STOP
        END
```

```
INPUT DATA  X:          97.6000000
INPUT DATA  Y:         -12.8999900
X + Y =            84.6999900
```

Reading Several Values

The READ statement may be used to obtain values for several variables at a time, as shown in the program AVG4V3, which calculates the average of any four numbers. Unlike the program AVG4V2 in the previous section, the four numbers to be averaged are supplied as data, rather than appearing as constants in the program. This permits the same program to be used to average different sets of four numbers.

```
C       PROGRAM AVG4V3
        REAL A, B, C, D
        READ, A, B, C, D
        PRINT, 'INPUT DATA  A:', A
        PRINT, '            B:', B
        PRINT, '            C:', C
        PRINT, '            D:', D
        PRINT, 'AVERAGE =', +(A + B + C + D) / 4
        STOP
        END
```

The input data file in the sample execution has one line

```
58.5 60 61.3 57
```

When we run the program AVG4V3 using this data file, the following output is produced.

```
INPUT DATA  A:          58.5000000
            B:          60.0000000
            C:          61.3000000
            D:          57.0000000
AVERAGE =         59.1999900
```

As shown in the sample execution, the data are supplied to the variables in the order in which they are listed in the READ statement. Note that the four variables in the READ statement are separated by commas and that there is a comma between the keyword READ and the first variable in the input list. Although it is not required by Fortran, it is often desirable to put all input data for a READ statement on one line in the input file, creating a correspondence between READ statements and data lines. However, the input data file

```
58.5
60
61.3
57
```

also would have produced the same execution output.

Execution of each READ statement reads data from a new line in the input file. Thus if four separate READ statements were to be used to read the variables A, B, C, and D, the four input values must be on four separate data lines in the input file.

Default Input Format

The comma immediately following the keyword READ in the READ statement indicates that the format of the input data is left to the preparer of the input file, except that the individual values must be separated by at least one blank character or a comma. It is easy to prepare input data for default READ formats. They tend to be very forgiving. The term "user-friendly" is also used.

Rules for Naming Variables

The **variable names** X and Y are used in the program ADD2, and the variable names A, B, C, and D are used in AVG4V3. Single letters of the alphabet are acceptable variable names in Fortran. However, greater variety is desirable, both to improve the readability of programs and to provide for programs with more than 26 variables. Fortran has the following rules for naming variables:

1. The first character of any variable name must be a letter.
2. The remaining characters may be any mixture of letters or digits.
3. There must be at most six-characters in a variable name.

These rules allow ordinary names like LISA, PAMELA, and JULIE to be used as variable names. They also allow ordinary English words like SUM, AREA, and BRAINS and more technical-looking names like X3J3 and W3KT as variable names.

Blanks are generally ignored in a Fortran program.

Style Note: It is a good idea to put blanks around variable names to make them more easily read by a human, but it is probably not advisable to put blanks in the middle of a variable name.

Subroutines, functions and other constructs to be described later are also assigned names. The rules for naming variables apply to all other names in a Fortran program.

Characters other than letters and digits are not allowed in Fortran names. Arithmetic symbols must be excluded to prevent ambiguity. For example, if minus signs were allowed in variable names, there would be no way to decide whether A − 1 was a single variable, A-one, or the result of subtracting 1 from the value of the variable A. Although some of the other characters available on computer input devices often could be allowed in names without causing ambiguity, some characters like the comma or decimal point have specific meaning, and it is simpler to exclude them all, since sufficient variety is already available. Tables 2.1 and 2.2 summarize what is and is not allowed in a name in Fortran.

Table 2.1 Acceptable Variable Names in Fortran.

LISA, PAMELA, JULIE	usual names
ANSWER, NUMBER, VALUE	English words
ANFANG, ESPRIT, MUCHO	foreign words
X3J9, W3KT, YHV93X, EXPO67	mixed alphabetic and numeric

Table 2.2 Unacceptable Variable Names in Fortran.

6AU8, 14U2	starting with a digit
E/L/O, MANY%, A − 1	characters other than letters or digits
SERENDIPITY, SITZMARK	more than six characters

Variable names should describe what the values of a variable represent. Although at one time, the six-character limit may have been considered generous, almost every program in this book contains variable names that could be more self-descriptive. Some Fortran systems have anticipated future Fortran standards by allowing longer variable names. However, such programs will not run on most Fortran systems. The original reason for the six-character limit was that precisely six characters could be stored in each word of main memory in the first computer to have a Fortran compiler.

The program SNDWCH (cost of a peanut butter and jelly sandwich) illustrates new features of Fortran.

```
C       PROGRAM SNDWCH
C       COMPUTES THE COST OF A PEANUT BUTTER
C       AND JELLY SANDWICH USING TWO SLICES OF BREAD,
C       .0625 JARS OF PEANUT BUTTER, AND .03125 JARS OF JELLY
C
        REAL LOFBRD, PBUTTR, JELLY, SLCBRD, CSTSND, SLICES
C
        LOFBRD = .59
        PBUTTR = 1.65
        JELLY = 1.29
        SLICES = 16.0
C
```

```
      SLCBRD = LOFBRD / SLICES
      CSTSND = 2 * SLCBRD + .0625 * PBUTTR + .03125 * JELLY
      PRINT, 'A PEANUT BUTTER AND JELLY SANDWICH COSTS $',
     +    CSTSND
      PRINT, 'PRICES ARE SUBJECT TO CHANGE AT ANY TIME'
      PRINT, '  WITHOUT WRITTEN NOTICE.'
      STOP
      END
```

```
A PEANUT BUTTER AND JELLY SANDWICH COSTS $             0.2171874
PRICES ARE SUBJECT TO CHANGE AT ANY TIME
  WITHOUT WRITTEN NOTICE.
```

Assignment Statements

Execution of the program SNDWCH begins with six **assignment statements**. For example, the fifth one assigns to the variable SLCBRD (slice of bread) the cost of one slice of bread, obtained by dividing the cost of a loaf of bread by the number of slices of bread in the loaf. The next statement is also an assignment statement; it assigns to the variable CSTSND the cost of a peanut butter and jelly sandwich. The value of any **arithmetic expression** can be assigned to a variable using an assignment statement.

In Fortran the **assignment operator** is an equal sign (=). In an assignment statement, the assignment operator is always preceded by the name of the variable to which the value is assigned.

The program concludes with three separate PRINT statements in order to produce three lines of output. The value printed represents a cost of approximately 22 cents. Your default format may print the answer in an equivalent, but slightly different form.

Important Rules About Assignment Statements

The Fortran statement

```
A = B
```

(pronounced "A is set equal to B") means *Set the value of the variable A to whatever the value of the variable B is.* It changes the value of A while leaving the value of the variable B fixed. It does not mean the same thing as

```
B = A
```

whose execution changes the value of B while leaving the value of the variable A fixed. A statement such as

```
4.7 = A
```

is absurd and unacceptable, because its left-hand side is a constant, whose value must not be changed.

The left-hand side of an assignment statement must be a variable (or as we will see later, an array element or substring), and the right-hand side must be something whose value can be assigned to that variable. The right-hand side may involve the same variable that appears on the left-hand side.

Descriptive Names for Variables

The use of appropriate variable and constant names helps make the program easier to understand, although the requirement to use at most six characters per variable name limits severely the amount of information that can be conveyed by the name. The meaning of some of the names would be much clearer if they were longer, such as COSTOFAJAROFJELLY in place of JELLY, but Fortran does not currently allow such long names.

> *Style Note:* The name of a variable should be chosen so that it describes what the value of the variable represents.

Comments

An additional feature that also helps clarify a program for the reader is the use of **comments**. Any line in a Fortran program that has a C in column one (the leftmost column) is a **comment line**. The explanations given in comments are reproduced every time a program is listed, but have absolutely no effect on the execution of the program. The comments in the program SNDWCH describe exactly what the program is supposed to do. This description makes it even easier for the reader to follow the rest of the program.

A comment line that is blank except for the C in column one also may be used to make the program easier to read.

Converting Meters to Inches

The program MTOIN (meters to inches), which converts a length in meters to the same length expressed in inches, illustrates again how an appropriate choice of variable and constant names can enhance the readability of a program.

```
C       PROGRAM MTOIN
C       CONVERTS LENGTH IN METERS TO LENGTH IN INCHES
C
        REAL METERS, INCHES, INPERM
C
        INPERM = 39.37
        READ, METERS
        INCHES = METERS * INPERM
        PRINT, METERS, 'METERS =', INCHES, 'INCHES.'
        STOP
        END
```

```
            2.0000000 METERS =            78.7399900 INCHES.
```

The assignment statement of the program MTOIN tells the computer to assign to the variable INCHES the value obtained by multiplying the value of the variable METERS by the constant 39.37, the conversion factor rounded to two decimal places.

The program MTOIN also gives some indication why the rules for naming variables are not more flexible. If just any combination of characters were allowed as a variable name, then the assignment statement in MTOIN might mean that the variable INCHES should be assigned the value of a variable called METERS*INPERM. While it is clear to persons who understand the problem that the context calls for multiplication, it is extremely difficult to design a workable computer language with even this much sensitivity to the context of human experience. A computer language must be unambiguous. Thus, variable names that look like arithmetic expressions cannot be allowed.

Reading and Writing Character Strings

Since computers can process character data as well as numeric information, computer languages provide for the reading and printing of character strings. The somewhat facetious program WHO shows how this is done in Fortran.

```
C       PROGRAM WHO
        CHARACTER WHATS *20
C
        PRINT, 'DO I REMEMBER WHATSHISNAME?'
        READ, WHATS
        PRINT, 'OF COURSE, I REMEMBER', WHATS
        STOP
        END
```

```
DO I REMEMBER WHATSHISNAME?
OF COURSE, I REMEMBER  ROGER KAPUTNIK
```

When the default input format is used to read a character string, the string must be enclosed in apostrophes, the same as a character constant used within a program. Apostrophes do not appear in the printed output when using the default output format. The input data for the execution of the program WHO shown above consists of one line.

```
'ROGER KAPUTNIK'
```

We close this section with a version of the program MTOINT (meters to inches, using a terminal) designed to be run on a WATFIV system in which input data is supplied for the READ statements by typing the data at a computer terminal during the execution of the program. This is called **interactive input**. The only change is to add a PRINT statement prompting the user about what data to type. This **input prompt** immediately precedes the READ statement.

```
C       PROGRAM MTOIN
C       CONVERTS LENGTH IN METERS TO LENGTH IN INCHES.
C       THE LENGTH IN METERS IS TYPED
C       WHEN PROMPTED DURING EXECUTION.
C
        REAL METERS, INCHES, INPERM
C
        INPERM = 39.37
        PRINT, 'ENTER A LENGTH IN METERS'
        READ, METERS
        INCHES = METERS * INPERM
        PRINT, METERS, 'METERS =', INCHES, 'INCHES.'
        STOP
        END
```

```
ENTER A LENGTH IN METERS
2
          2.0000000  METERS =          78.74399900  INCHES.
```

2.3 Introduction to Formatting and Roundoff

Fortran has extremely powerful, flexible, and easy-to-use capabilities for output formatting. This may seem surprising since Fortran is often considered a scientific programming language, but Fortran has always had better formatting facilities than many commercial languages. This section describes the basic formatting features that enable you to produce really good looking output, if you like. Of course, if the default PRINT format on your Fortran system is good enough, there is no necessity to learn PRINT formatting right away. This section appears early because most WATFIV systems do not have satisfactory default formats, especially for reals. On such systems, the techniques of this section are essential.

Section Preview

Format specification:

The format specification indicates the form that is to be taken by printed output.

Example:

```
(F5.1, A5, I4)
```

Format descriptor:

The format descriptor is a part of a format specification that indicates the form that is to be taken by one printed value.

Examples:

F5.1 for positional notation of real values
A5 for character (alphanumeric) values
I4 for integer values

Roundoff:

Roundoff occurs because most real numbers cannot be represented precisely in a computer.

Roundoff

Just as 1/3 cannot be represented exactly as a decimal, though .333333 comes very close, 1/10 and 1/100 cannot be represented exactly when the representation uses a number base sixteen instead of ten. Most computers use a **binary system** (base 2) or a **hexadecimal system** (base 16) of notation internally for storage and calculation of numeric values. As a result, when reals are converted from input represented in decimal notation to the computer's internal representation and back again during execution of a program, the original numbers may not be recovered precisely.

Perhaps you have already seen this in our output, in the form of a tell-tale sequence of 9s. For example, using the program ADD2R in Section 2.2, and the input data, 97.6 and −12.9, the following output resulted.

```
INPUT DATA  X:             97.6000000
INPUT DATA  Y:            -12.8999900
X + Y =           84.6999900
```

The value of the variable X prints as 97.6000000, which agrees with the value supplied in the input file. However, the printed value of the variable Y is 0.00001 too large at −12.89999 instead of −12.9. The difference between the intended and calculated values, 0.00001 in this case, is **roundoff** or **roundoff error**. It is normally of no consequence in practical calculations because it is virtually impossible to distinguish between such nearly equal values as −12.89999 and −12.9.

The printed value of X + Y is 84.6999900, differing by 0.00001 from the sum of the intended values and by 0.00002 from the sum of the printed values of X and Y, a hint to the expert that the computer being used probably does not use decimal arithmetic for its internal calculations.

Minor cases of roundoff are hidden easily by rounding values before printing. For example, if the unexpected echos of input data above are rounded to 4 decimal places before printing, the results will appear precisely as expected: 97.6000 + −12.9000 = 84.7000.

Depending in large measure on whether the default PRINT format for reals rounds answers to fewer decimal places than are actually calculated, you rarely see any trace of roundoff on many computer systems. These extra guard digits may actually contain roundoff, but rounding answers before printing guarantees that the user will not see small roundoff errors. We mention roundoff at this point to forewarn the beginner whose Fortran system shows it in output that roundoff is not a malfunction of the computer's hardware but a fact of life of type real arithmetic on computers.

In the remainder of this section we introduce the simplest forms of user-specified PRINT formatting, including the facility for rounding real values to a specified number of decimal places before printing.

Format Specifications

Extremely flexible and versatile control over the appearance of printed output is available in Fortran if you are willing to forego the convenience of the default PRINT format. A user-specified **format specification** is basically a list of **format descriptors**, separated by commas and enclosed in parentheses. An example is

```
(F5.1, A5, I4)
```

For each expression to be printed, one of the format descriptors in the format specification is used to determine the form of the output. For example if X = 6.3 is type real and N = −26 is type integer, then the two statements

```
      PRINT 15, X, ' AND ', N
15    FORMAT (F5.1, A5, I4)
```

would produce the output line

```
  6.3 AND  -26
```

This example shows the three most frequently used format descriptors, F (floating point) for positional notation printing of reals, A (alphanumeric) for character strings, and I (integer) for integers. The format descriptor F5.1 means that a total of 5 columns are reserved for printing a real value rounded to one place after the decimal point. The decimal point occupies a column and a minus sign, if needed, occupies another column, so the largest number printable in F5.1 format is 999.9 and −99.9 is the smallest. I4 format reserves 4 columns for printing an integer. The minus sign takes up one of the 4 columns. The A format descriptor reserves space for character output. The format descriptor A5 reserves 5 columns.

The FORMAT Statement

In WATFIV-S, the format specification is placed in a separate statement, a FORMAT statement. The digits 15 in the PRINT and FORMAT statements form a **statement label**. They identify the FORMAT statement so that the PRINT statement can refer to it. Labels may be one to five digits long. They are written in columns one to five of the first line of the statement they label.

As illustrated by the example above, the FORMAT statement consists of the keyword FORMAT followed by a format specification. FORMAT statements are not executable statements. Thus, they do not have to appear immediately following the PRINT statements that reference them. However, this is a reasonable place for FORMAT statements that are used only once. It is permissible for several PRINT statements to use the same FORMAT statement, in which case the FORMAT statement is still written only once. When this is done frequently in a program, many programmers collect all the FORMAT statements at the end of the program.

Tab and Line Feed Format Descriptors

The slash (/) format descriptor starts a new line in the printed output. Thus a single PRINT statement can produce several lines of output. For example

```
      PRINT 25, ' THESE CHARACTER STRINGS',
  +           ' ALL APPEAR', ' ON SEPARATE LINES'
25    FORMAT (A30, /, A30, /, A30)', 'THESE CHARACTER STRINGS',
```

produces the three lines of output

```
        THESE CHARACTER STRINGS
                     ALL APPEAR
              ON SEPARATE LINES
```

Each A30 format descriptor reserves 30 columns. Since each character string to be printed is shorter than 30 characters, they are right justified in the 30-column field and blanks are added at the left to fill the field. If a character string is too long for its A format descriptor, the rightmost characters are not printed. The next example shows one A format descriptor that is too long and one that is too short.

```
      PRINT 35, ' THESE CHARACTER STRINGS',
  +           ' ALL PRINT',
  +           ' ON ONE LINE'
35    FORMAT (A20, A20, A20)
```

which produces the output line

```
THESE CHARACTER STR           ALL PRINT           ON ONE LINE
```

Commas may be omitted around slash format descriptors.

The T (tab) format descriptor is used to skip to a specified column of the output line for precise control over the appearance of the output. Tabs may be either forward or backward on the current line. For example,

```
      PRINT 45, A, B, C
45    FORMAT (T30, I5, T50, I5, T10, I5)
```

will print the integer values of C in columns 10-14, A in columns 30-34, and B in columns 50-54. Some printing devices do not print column 1 of any output line. Instead, the character appearing in column 1 is used to control single and double spacing, overprinting, and skips to the top of a new page. If you have such a printer on your system, a T2 format descriptor will skip to column 2 to get single spacing, or a T1 format descriptor will skip to column 1 to use one of the line feed codes described in Appendix B.

Character Constant Format Descriptors

The A format descriptor can get to be quite a nuisance for printing character constants because the programmer must carefully count the number of characters to avoid either losing characters at the right or introducing unwanted blanks. As an alternative, Fortran permits character constant format descriptors for which the compiler counts the number of characters. Character constant format descriptors do not correspond to any item in the print list. For example, if X is 3.75, the statements

```
      PRINT 45, X
45    FORMAT (' THE ANSWER IS:  X =', F6.2)
```

will produce the output line

```
THE ANSWER IS:  X =  3.75
```

The first item in the print list, X, corresponds to the F6.2 format descriptor in this example.

Repeated Format Descriptors

If one or more format descriptors are to be repeated, they may be enclosed in parentheses and preceded by the positive integer representing the number of repetitions.

3(I4) is equivalent to 3I4 or I4,I4,I4
5(/) is equivalent to /,/,/,/,/ or /////
2(A4/T2) is equivalent to A4/T2,A4/T2 or A4,/,T2,A4,/,T2

The parentheses may be omitted if there is only one E, F, I, or A format descriptor inside the parentheses. The E format descriptor is used for printing reals in exponential notation.

Examples of Formatted Output

The following examples illustrate how formatted output works. If these lines are printed on many printers, such as the one used to produce the following output, the first character will not appear, but will affect the vertical spacing.

```
      REAL X
      INTEGER N
C
      X = 6.3
      N = -26
      PRINT 15, X, ' AND ', N
   15 FORMAT (F5.1, A5, I4)
      PRINT 25, ' THESE CHARACTER STRINGS',
     +          ' ALL APPEAR', 'ON SEPARATE LINES'
   25 FORMAT (A30, /, A30, /, A30)
      PRINT 35, ' THESE CHARACTER STRINGS',
     +          ' ALL PRINT',
     +          ' ON ONE LINE'
   35 FORMAT (A20, A20, A20)
      X = 3.75
      PRINT 45, X
   45 FORMAT (' THE ANSWER IS:  X =', F6.2)
      PRINT 55, 2, 3, 4
   55 FORMAT (3I2)
      X = 7.346E-9
      PRINT 65, ' THE ANSWER IS ', X
   65 FORMAT (A15, E10.3)
      Q1 = 5.6
      Q2 = 5.73
      Q3 = 5.79
      PRINT 75, 1, Q1, 2, Q2, 3, Q3
   75 FORMAT (' HERE COME THE ANSWERS--',
     +        3 (/, ' Q', I1, '=', F3.1) )
```

```
 6.3 AND  -26
```

```
      THESE CHARACTER STRINGS
                  ALL APPEAR
            ON SEPARATE LINES
THESE CHARACTER STR           ALL PRINT          ON ONE LINE
THE ANSWER IS:  X =  3.75
2 3 4
THE ANSWER IS  0.735E-08
HERE COME THE ANSWERS--
Q1=5.6
Q2=5.7
Q3=5.8
```

Note the following things about the resulting output:

1. The character strings are each right justified in either 20 or 30 columns.
2. The character string longer than 20 columns is truncated on the right.
3. The number 7.346E−9 is printed in a form in which the mantissa is between 0 and 1.

Formatted Input

A format specification can be used with the READ statement to indicate how the columns of the input line are to be interpreted. Formatted input is not as essential as formatted output because most natural arrangements of input data are accepted by the default READ formats. However, there are two major exceptions, which sometimes make the use of input formatting desirable. First, default formats for character input usually require apostrophes around the input strings. Character input read under an A format descriptor does not. Second, it is a small convenience not to have to separate numbers with commas or blanks when large amounts of data are read by a program. For example, it is much harder to type ten 1-digit integers on a line of input with separating commas than without them. Rather than discuss the rules in detail for using formatted input, one example is given.

```
      REAL X1, X2, X3
      INTEGER J1, J2, J3
      CHARACTER C *4
      READ 85, C, X1, J1, X2, J2, X3, J3
   85 FORMAT (A4, 3 (F2.1, I1))
```

If the input line is

```
1234567890123
```

then after executing the READ statement, the variables in the input list are assigned the following values. Notice that apostrophes for A format input data must be omitted and that decimal points for F format input data are assumed when they are omitted.

C = '1234'
X1 = 5.6
J1 = 7
X2 = 8.9
J2 = 0
X3 = 1.2
J3 = 3

Style Note: It is a good programming practice to use the default READ format whenever possible. Explicit input format specifications demand strict adherence to specified columns for each value in the input data. The slightest misalignment of the input data usually results in incorrect values assigned to the variables. By comparison, the default input format is usually relatively tolerant of variations in alignment and user-friendly.

2.4 Built-In Functions

Built-in functions increase the power of the Fortran language. They are supplied with every Fortran system and should be considered part of the language. **Built-in functions** are used in expressions in much the same way as the standard arithmetic operations (+, −, *, / and **). The only difference is that a function evaluation uses a mathematical notation in which the value to be operated on is enclosed in parentheses. For example, the statement

```
Y = SIN (X) + COS (X)
```

calculates a value for the variable Y by adding the sine of the angle X to the cosine of the angle X.

Section Preview

Built-in functions:

Built-in functions provide a collection of operations that can be performed on data of all types. The following table lists many of the commonly used built-in functions. Each is a representative of a family of built-in functions, designed to handle different data types.

1	INT	convert to integer
2	FLOAT	convert to real
3	ABS	absolute value
4	MIN	minimum
5	MAX	maximum
6	SQRT	square root
7	MOD	remainder
8	ALOG10	logarithm base 10
9	ALOG	logarithm base e
10	EXP	exponential
11	SIN	sine
12	COS	cosine
13	TAN	tangent
14	ASIN	arcsine
15	ACOS	arccosine
16	ATAN	arctangent
17	SINH	hyperbolic sine
18	COSH	hyperbolic cosine
19	TANH	hyperbolic tangent

Type Conversion

A value is converted to type integer by truncation, that is, eliminating the decimal part, if any. The integer part of a whole number is that number itself. For positive numbers that are not integers, the integer part of the number is less than the number, but for negative numbers that are not integers, as the fourth example in the following list shows, the integer part is algebraically greater than the number.

```
INT (4.23) = 4
INT (3.14159) = 3
INT (17.0) = 17
INT (-5.6) = -5
INT (2./3.) = INT (.666667) = 0
```

The expression in parentheses following the characters INT is called an argument. For the INT built-in function, the argument must be real. The built-in function IDINT converts from double precision to integer.

The built-in function FLOAT converts any integer value to its real equivalent. The function DFLOAT converts integer to double precision real.

Absolute Value

The **absolute value** of a number x is the number x itself if x is positive or zero, but the absolute value of a negative number x results from changing the sign of x to positive. Algebraically, this means that the absolute value of a negative number x is equal to the positive number $-x$. The built-in functions ABS and DABS are used to obtain the absolute value of a number. The value of the absolute value function is the same type as its argument for data types we've studied.

Minimum and Maximum

Fortran provides built-in functions MIN0, AMIN1, and DMIN1 whose values are the smallest of two or more values for types integer, real, and double precision, respectively. Similarly, the functions MAX0, AMAX1, and DMAX1 calculate the largest of two or more values. All of the arguments must be the same type. Any negative number, regardless of its absolute value, is considered less than zero, which in turn is considered less than any positive number. For example,

```
MIN0 (-99, -5) = -99
AMAX1 (-99.3, 3.6, 5.23) = 5.23
MIN0 (MAX0 (5, -7), 0) = MIN0 (5, 0) = 0
```

Square Root

The **square root** of a nonnegative number x is the unique nonnegative number y such that $y^2 = x$. The built-in function SQRT assigns the best possible approximate square root to a nonnegative number. The argument for the SQRT function must not be integer. SQRT (4) is not allowed, but SQRT (4.0) is permitted. The programmer should be prepared for an error message and possible program termination if the square root of a negative real value is requested. DSQRT is the function name for square roots of double precision real values.

Remaindering

A useful function is the built-in function MOD (modulus) that computes the remainder when the first argument is divided by the second. The two arguments must be the same type. The value produced is the same type as the arguments and is defined by

```
MOD (A1, A2) = A1 - INT (A1 / A2) * A2
```

For example,

```
MOD (17, 5) = 2
MOD (-17, 5)
   = -17 - INT (-17 / 5) * 5
   = -17 - (-3) * 5
   = -17 + 15
   = -2
MOD (17, -5)
   = 17 - (-3) * (-5)
   = 17 - 15
   = 2
AMOD (6.8, 2.1)
   = 6.8 - INT ( 6.8 / 2.1) * 2.1
   = 6.8 - 3 * 2.1
   = 6.8 - 6.3
   = 0.5
```

The remainder functions are named MOD for integer, AMOD for real, and DMOD for double precision.

Scientific Functions

The remaining built-in functions listed in the Section Preview may be used to calculate logarithms, exponentials, and various trigonometric and hyperbolic functions. Each of these has one real argument. Each has double precision version (with a D starting the function name), and the functions EXP, ALOG, SIN, and COS also have versions handling a complex argument. (See Tables 2.3 and 2.4.)

Table 2.3 Type Conversion Functions in WATFIV-S.

INT	IDINT	real and double precision to integer
FLOAT	DFLOAT	integer to real and double precision
SNGL	DBLE	double precision to real and vice versa
CMPLX	DCMPLX	two reals to complex (single and double precision)
REAL	AIMAG	real and imaginary parts of complex value

The Purpose of Built-In Functions

Built-in functions are augmentations of a computer language to improve its convenience to users. Some functions are built into the language by the designer of the compiler for that language. Others might be added by a local computer center. It makes no difference who builds a particular function into a language, except that the programmer can rely on the standard ones being available with any Fortran system. All a programmer needs to know to use a built-in function is its name and what it is supposed to do.

Built-in functions can be used to improve the readability of programs, even though other means exist for writing equivalent expressions. For example, the expression SQRT (2 * X + 1) might be used instead of the mathematically equivalent expression (2 * X + 1) ** 0.5 to make a program easier to write and easier to read.

Table 2.4 Names of Intrinsic (Built-In) Functions in WATFIV-S.

Function	Argument				
	Integer	Real	Double Precision	Complex	Double Precision Complex
Remainder	MOD	AMOD	DMOD		
Maximum	MAX0	AMAX1	DMAX1		
Minimum	MIN0	AMIN1	DMIN1		
Absolute value	IABS	ABS	DABS	CABS	CDABS
Square root		SQRT	DSQRT	CSQRT	CSSQRT
Sine		SIN	DSIN	CSIN	CDSIN
Cosine		COS	DCOS	CCOS	CDCOS
Tangent		TAN	DTAN		
e^x		EXP	DEXP	CEXP	CDEXP
Natural logarithm		ALOG	DLOG		
Common logarithm		ALOG10	DLOG10		
Arcsine		ARSIN	DARSIN		
Arctangent		ATAN	DATAN		
Arctan (y/x)		ATAN2	DATAN2		
Hyperbolic sine		SINH	DSINH		
Hyperbolic cosine		COSH	DCOSH		
Hyperbolic tangent		TANH	DTANH		
Normal error		ERF	DERF		
Error complemented		ERFC	DERFC		
Complex conjugate				CONJG	DCONJG

2.5 Running a Program

There are two fundamentally different ways of running a program. In **batch mode**, all the input data is prepared in advance of the program execution. In **interactive mode** input data is entered into the computer *during* the program execution. Some Fortran systems support batch execution, some support interactive execution, and some support both.

Section Preview

Batch systems:

Both program and data are prepared in advance. On shared systems, execution takes place at the central computer's convenience, often after a wait for the program's turn.

Interactive:

The computer responds relatively quickly to user requests.

Interactive execution:

The user is at a terminal when the program executes. The user may receive output at the terminal screen or printer, and may enter input data for the program execution during the program execution.

Interactive editing of programs and input data:

The computer maintains a copy of the text and modifies it under direction of the user. Some systems have interactive editing but batch execution, while other systems have both interactive editing and interactive execution.

Timesharing:

When many users share a central computer, timesharing is a way to make it seem as though each user has his or her own central computer.

Echo of input data:

When execution is in batch mode, input data are echoed to the printer or output file as soon as they are read. Echoes of input data are very useful in debugging.

Input prompts:

When execution is interactive, the user is prompted before execution of each READ statement with a message describing what input data are expected.

Batch Execution

Most of the sample executions shown so far have been in batch mode. Before running the program, we entered all the input data for the program immediately following the $ENTRY line. During execution there is no appreciable delay when a read statement is executed because the input data for that read statement is available in the input file.

In programs written for batch execution, we customarily echo all input data to the output file, which otherwise would have no record of this information.

Debugging Note: Batch execution has one major advantage: executing a program in batch mode does *not* destroy the input file. Since most programs are run many times before they are finally correct, we benefit from the fact that the input data, which may be extensive, have to be entered only once.

At large computer centers, more efficient use often can be made of the central computer if several programs in the same computer language are compiled and executed consecutively. These programs are batched together so they can run together. Input files, of course, must be prepared in advance or the benefits of batching would not be realized. This kind of batching has the disadvantage that the programs often are run at the computer's and not at the programmer's convenience.

As we use the term **batch execution**, it means only that input files are prepared and entered in advance, whether or not several jobs are grouped together. We even apply it to execution on a single-user, single-job microcomputer, as long as input comes from a prepared file.

Preparing and Specifying the Input File

It is easiest to prepare an input file with an editor, if one is available on your system. There are so many different editors that you will have to get instructions specific to the one you have available. It is not unusual that editing may be interactive while the eventual execution of your program will be in batch mode.

Another way to prepare an input file is to punch it in cards. Some systems copy this card file to a disk file before execution, while others read directly from the card file during execution. Also, the output files of one program can be used as input files to another program.

A computer system ordinarily has many files saved. The computer must be told which file to use as input and which file to use as output when a program is run. Methods vary among systems, so you must inquire locally to find out which method works on your computer. Some of the possibilities include additional information in the run command, default names for the input and output files related to the name of the program file, and specifying the file names in various ways inside the program.

In most WATFIV systems, the input data are typed at the end of the Fortran program file, after the $ENTRY line, identifying them as data.

Interactive Execution

When a program is run **interactively**, input data may be supplied to the program by a person as the program is running. This is usually done using a terminal. Whenever a READ statement is executed in the program, the user is expected to type some input data at the terminal. Whenever a PRINT statement is executed, the data are written to the terminal. This mode of running a program is **interactive execution**. The Waterloo Fortran systems for microcomputers run interactively.

> *Style Note:* When input data are expected from a terminal during an interactive execution of a program, it is a good programming practice to have the program send a **prompt**, an output message, giving the user at the terminal a clue as to what is supposed to be entered.

A good way to provide a prompt is to replace the PRINT statement that occurs in batch programs *after* each READ statement to provide the echo of input data with a prompt that occurs just *before* each READ statement. This is illustrated in the program SUB2.

```
C       PROGRAM SUB2
        INTEGER X, Y
        PRINT, 'INPUT DATA  X:'
        READ, X
        PRINT, 'INPUT DATA  Y:'
        READ, Y
        PRINT, 'X - Y = ', X - Y
        STOP
        END
```

```
INPUT DATA  X:
83
INPUT DATA  Y:
67
X - Y =    16
```

What happens during interactive execution of the program SUB2 is as follows. The computer types "INPUT DATA X: " as directed by the first PRINT statement and then waits for the user to supply a value for X to complete execution of the READ, X statement. When the user types a value, 83, followed by the carriage return, execution resumes, the computer types "INPUT DATA Y: " and pauses until the user supplies an input value to complete the READ, Y statement. When a value, 67, and a carriage return are typed by the user, execution resumes again and the answer, X – Y = 16, is written by the computer.

For interactive execution no input file is prepared prior to execution and the output file is written on the terminal. If the program is run again, the input data must be retyped. While this is not a serious problem with only two input values, its severity increases with the number of input values.

The advantages of interactive execution are that output is available to the user as soon as the statements that produce it are executed and that the user does not have to decide in advance what values are to be supplied as input. If the value that the user types as input depends on previous output, the user and computer interact during execution. Some applications, like editing and computer-assisted instruction, make sense only if executed interactively.

Compilers

A computer usually does not understand Fortran statements. It responds to very simple commands like "Add the number in memory location 740039 to the number in memory location 469983 and put the result in memory location 430988", or even simpler commands. A **compiler** is a program that translates Fortran programs into instructions that are more readily understood by a computer: the computer's machine language. A compiler usually is quite a complicated program. There are many things that a compiler must keep track of, such as the type of each variable, which names correspond to built-in functions, and the memory location assigned to store the value of each variable. Consider the Fortran statement

```
X = A + B * (C * D + E) + C * D
```

A compiler must recognize that the multiplication of C * D must be done before any of the other arithmetic operations. Optimizing compilers also recognize that the subexpression C * D appears twice and generate instructions to compute C * D only once when the expression is evaluated.

If you can observe the computer's activity when your program is run using a Fortran compiler, you may be able to distinguish several phases. First, your Fortran program is **translated** or **compiled** into machine language. Then, the result is **linked** to other machine language segments including code to implement the built-in functions and input/output formatting. Finally, your program is **run**, reading the input and writing the execution output. In WATFIV-S, these three phases are usually combined so the user is not ordinarily aware of the individual phases. However, if the $ENTRY line is omitted, the Fortran program is compiled, checked for syntax errors, but not run.

One of the interesting features of the Fortran language is that subprograms are entirely self-contained, so they may be compiled independently. There is no need for the compiler to know anything about a main program or any other subprograms that a particular subprogram may be used with in order to compile the subprogram. This permits programmers to work independently on parts of a large programming project and permits a part of a program to be changed and recompiled without the necessity of recompiling the entire program. WATFIV-S does not take advantage of independent subroutine compilation.

Interpreters

An **interpreter** is a program that decodes a Fortran program one statement at a time and immediately executes that statement. With an interpreter, there is no obvious delay for compilation before execution begins. However, execution will usually be much slower using a Fortran interpreter, since the apparent execution time includes the time necessary to decipher each statement each time it is executed.

Interpreters are particularly convenient for short programs or for debugging because many interpreters offer interactive debugging features. Sometimes, programs are debugged using an interpreter, and then compiled to achieve faster execution speed. The Waterloo Fortran systems for microcomputers are interpreters.

Operating Systems

Once the program is prepared, either by using an editor or by punching the program on cards, commands must be given to indicate that the program is to be run. These commands are actually instructions to the computer's **operating system**. The operating system is a complex program that controls the flow of information through the computer and schedules the use of the computer's hardware components. Different computer installations, even if they have exactly the same model of the same computer produced by the same manufacturer, may use different operating systems and consequently may require different commands. Upon arriving at a new installation, one of the first things a programmer needs to learn is a small amount of the command language used.

Figure 2.1 Mark I computer. *Courtesy International Business Machines Corporation.*

The Good Old Days of Computer Programming

There are programmers who can remember the good old days of personally reserving a whole computer, perhaps some time in the evening or after midnight. As recently as the early 1960s, it was common practice for programmers to place their cards in the card reader, put their feet up on the console, and sit back and watch the program run. Programmers shut the machine off during dinner or a coffee break and turned the power back on after returning. They could stop the execution of a program to see what was happening, or step through a program one instruction at a time. They could examine any location in memory and make corrections from the console. In those days, programmers dealt directly with the computer and spoke the machine's own language. At least some of these programmers are happy that the recent trend toward minicomputers and microcomputers is bringing back the good old days.

People who had the opportunity to work so intimately with a computer did not soon forget the experience, but in many places the environment has evolved to the point that a programmer might never see an actual computer. Advances in electronic technology have made this change desirable. Although earlier machines were still much faster than desk calculators or other computational devices, their computational speeds were slow enough that it was reasonable for a programmer to stop the machine, open up a program listing, try to locate what needed changing, and enter a correction or change before resuming execution of the program.

As computational speeds increased by more than several thousand-fold, however, it was no longer economically feasible for the computer to halt while the programmer monitored the execution of a program or made corrections from the console. A dozen complete programs could run while the computer waited for a programmer to make one correction. Machine operators took over the job of shuttling the cards, tapes, printouts, and other data into and out of the machine as efficiently as possible. Computer programmers from the good old days welcomed the improvements in computer speed and power, but they began to feel that computer programming was becoming depersonalized.

Even certain machine operations suffered a similar fate. The input and output operations, which are partly mechanical in nature, could not keep pace with the increases in electronic computational speeds. It became inefficient for the central processing unit, which performs the arithmetic and logical computations, to halt its operations while a card, or even a magnetic tape, was being read. The input and output operations were farmed out to satellite computers of limited computational ability, which signalled the central processing unit when the reading or writing was completed. This enabled the central processing unit to continue computing at the same time that data was being read or written.

Timesharing

The increased speed of computation which brought about separation of the computer programmer from the computer also can be used, paradoxically, to simulate the effect of giving each programmer a complete machine, by a process called **timesharing**. Imagine dining at a very well-run restaurant. You are met at the door and escorted immediately to a private booth from which no other diners can be seen. The waiter arrives with rolls and butter and fills the water glasses. He returns immediately with the menu and retires from sight to let you choose your dinner. When you are ready to order, he reappears to take your order. After a sufficient time for the preparation of each dish, the waiter

Figure 2.2 Apple IIe personal computer. *Courtesy Apple, Inc.*

returns to serve it. When the main course has been eaten, he returns in time to take dessert orders. When the service is good enough (remember that no other tables can be seen), it is impossible to determine whether there are any other diners in the restaurant. It doesn't matter if the waiter takes menus to another table on his way to the kitchen, or takes orders from a third table while your dinner is being cooked. As long as the waiter responds relatively quickly whenever you need his services, for all intents and purposes you have his undivided attention.

In timesharing, many users are connected simultaneously to a computer by means of relatively inexpensive input/output terminals. If the computational speeds of the central computer are fast enough so that no user needs all the computer's capabilities for very long, then all users have use of the computer almost as soon as they want it. All users have the illusion of being the only user and can program and operate from a terminal as though the computer were all their own. In addition, the capabilities of a much larger computer than could be reserved reasonably for one person's use are available when needed.

Operating Systems for Timesharing

With many users simultaneously connected to the computer, the operating system must be more complicated. It must handle many kinds of requests, from editing one line of a program to running a compiler or processing an input/output request from a running program. In scheduling these requests, the operating system must decide how long a wait is tolerable for each kind of request.

Figure 2.3 DEC VT100, a visual display terminal. *Courtesy Digital Equipment Corporation.*

Scheduling Algorithms

An operating system serving several users may receive requests requiring as little as several millionths of a second or as much as several hours of processing time. The operating system of a shared computer has a set of rules, the **scheduling algorithm** that determines which jobs are executed first, and when a particular job will be executed. The design of a satisfactory scheduling algorithm procedure is a complex task, very much the subject of active research and experimentation among computer scientists. In general, most **scheduling algorithms** provide for very short waiting times for requests demanding only a few central processing unit (CPU) cycles, and progressively longer waiting times for requests for greater usage. A request to enter a single line of a program from a terminal may be processed almost immediately, while a request to run a program may wait from several seconds to several minutes, and a request for a solid hour of computational time may have to wait until the end of the day or the end of the week.

Other factors are also taken into account. If a programmer is waiting at a terminal for the request to be completed, the priority may be higher than that given to a similar request when the programmer is not waiting. It is ordinarily more efficient for a computer to compile several consecutive programs written in the same computer programming language than to skip from one language to

Figure 2.4 DEC Correspondent, a hardcopy terminal with built-in modem. *Courtesy Digital Equipment Corporation.*

another. Some operating systems collect short jobs in the most popular programming languages over a period of perhaps 20 minutes and run the entire group at the end of the collection period. Such batch processing ordinarily is unacceptable if the user is waiting at a terminal. Another consideration is how long a request has been waiting for action. A sophisticated scheduling algorithm may permit a lower-priority request that has been waiting a relatively long time to be run ahead of higher-priority requests that have not been waiting nearly as long.

Requests specifying computer facilities that are already in use for another purpose or job must be delayed, although the importance of the job must be taken into account. A business might want to be sure that its payroll program is run by Friday afternoon. A student program may or may not be given priority over an accounting or record-keeping program, depending on whether the installation views its primary function as teaching programming or keeping records. Priorities may also vary with the time of day. Often shorter programs are given higher priority during the day, and longer programs are given elevated priority at night.

2.6 Case Study: Quadratic Formula

A quadratic equation is an equation involving the square of the unknown x and no higher powers of x. Algorithms for solution of quadratic equations equivalent to the quadratic formula are found in Old Babylonian texts dating to 1700 B.C. It is now routinely taught in high school algebra. In this section, we show how to write a Fortran program to evaluate and print the roots of a quadratic equation. We also discuss improving the efficiency of the calculation by isolating common subexpressions.

Section Preview

Quadratic equations:

A quadratic equation has two solutions, given by formulas. These formulas are expressible as Fortran expressions.

The Problem

The most general quadratic equation has the form

$$ax^2 + bx + c = 0$$

where a, b, and c are constants and x is the unknown. The quadratic formula says that the roots of the quadratic equation, that is, the values of x for which the equation is true, are given by the formula

$$x = \frac{-b \pm \sqrt{b^2 - 4ac}}{2a}$$

This means that one root is obtained by adding the square root term and the other root is obtained by subtracting the square root term.

The problem is to write a program that reads as input the three coefficients, a, b, and c, and prints as output the values of the two roots. Since there is very little input, and we wish to discuss the answers as they are computed, we write the program for interactive execution with input from a terminal keyboard and output to the display screen or printing element.

The Solution

Experienced programmers may regard the following pseudocode solution as obvious, as indeed it is, but the three steps of the pseudocode solution must be thought, if not necessarily written down.

```
Read the coefficients a, b, and c
Calculate the two roots by the quadratic formula
Print the two roots
```

It is but a small step to the Fortran program that implements the pseudocode solution.

```
      PROGRAM QUAD
C     CALCULATES AND PRINTS THE ROOTS OF A QUADRATIC EQUATION
C
C     VARIABLES:
C        A, B, C: COEFFICIENTS
C        X1, X2: ROOTS
C
      REAL A, B, C, X1, X2
C
C     READ THE COEFFICIENTS
      PRINT, 'ENTER A, THE COEFFICIENT OF X ** 2'
      READ, A
      PRINT, 'ENTER B, THE COEFFICIENT OF X'
      READ, B
```

```
      PRINT, 'ENTER C, THE CONSTANT TERM'
      READ, C
C
C     CALCULATE THE ROOTS BY THE QUADRATIC FORMULA
      X1 = (-B + SQRT (B ** 2 - 4 * A * C)) / (2 * A)
      X2 = (-B - SQRT (B ** 2 - 4 * A * C)) / (2 * A)
C
C     PRINT THE ROOTS
      PRINT, 'THE ROOTS ARE'
      PRINT 15, 'X1 =', X1
      PRINT 15, 'X2 =', X2
   15 FORMAT (T2, A4, F10.6)
      STOP
      END
```

In the input section, each READ statement is preceded by an input prompt, that is, a PRINT statement telling the user at the computer terminal what input is expected. In the calculation section, the quadratic formula illustrates the function SQRT (square root).

Program Testing

To test the program QUAD, we made up several quadratic equations with known roots. Since all variables are type real, our first test case has simple real roots. The solutions of the quadratic equation

$$x^2 - 5x + 6 = 0$$

are 2 and 3.

```
ENTER A, THE COEFFICIENT OF X ** 2
1
ENTER B, THE COEFFICIENT OF X
-5
ENTER C, THE CONSTANT TERM
6
THE ROOTS ARE
X1 =  3.000000
X2 =  2.000000
```

The next quadratic equation has negative and fractional roots to test whether the program will work in these cases. the solutions of the quadratic equation

$$4x^2 + 8x - 21 = 0$$

are -3.5 and 1.5, testing both possibilities.

```
ENTER A, THE COEFFICIENT OF X ** 2
4
ENTER B, THE COEFFICIENT OF X
8
ENTER C, THE CONSTANT TERM
-21
THE ROOTS ARE
X1 =  1.500000
X2 = -3.500000
```

Notice that X1 is always the greater of the two roots because its formula adds the square root term.

The next test case tests irrational roots of the quadratic equation. The golden ratio is a ratio famous from Greek mathematics. Renaissance artists thought that the golden ratio was the most pleasing ratio for the sides of a rectangular painting or the facade of a building. The spiral shells of snails and the arrangement of seeds in a sunflower are related to it. The two roots of the following equation are the golden ratio and the negative of its reciprocal.

$$x^2 - x - 1 = 0$$

```
ENTER A, THE COEFFICIENT OF X ** 2
1
ENTER B, THE COEFFICIENT OF X
-1
ENTER C, THE CONSTANT TERM
-1
THE ROOTS ARE
X1 =  1.618033
X2 = -0.618034
```

The exact solutions are $(1 + \sqrt{5}) / 2$ and $(1 - \sqrt{5} / 2$, which check with the output of the program using a hand calculator. The golden ratio has many interesting properties including the fact that $1 / 1.6180339 = .6180339$.

The quadratic equation

$$x^2 - 6x + 9 = 0$$

has only one solution, $x = 3$. You might wonder what a program designed to find two roots will do with this equation.

```
ENTER A, THE COEFFICIENT OF X ** 2
1
ENTER B, THE COEFFICIENT OF X
-6
ENTER C, THE CONSTANT TERM
9
THE ROOTS ARE
X1 =  3.000000
X2 =  3.000000
```

Mathematicians call the solution of this quadratic equation a double root. For this equation, the quantity $b^2 - 4ac$ is zero, so it doesn't matter whether its square root is added or subtracted in the calculation of a root. The answer is the same for both roots.

Finally, we try a test case which we know the program QUAD will not handle. The quadratic equation

$$x^2 + 1 = 0$$

has no real roots. Instead, the roots are $x = \pm\sqrt{-1}$, complex numbers with no real part. We still try it anyway, just to see what happens.

```
ENTER A, THE COEFFICIENT OF X ** 2
1
ENTER B, THE COEFFICIENT OF X
0
ENTER C, THE CONSTANT TERM
1
***ERROR***  X .LT. 0 FOR SQRT OR DSQRT OF X
```

Since $b^2 - 4ac$ is -4, the error message is right on the money. Two ways to cope with this situation are discussed in the next chapter.

Common Subexpressions

The arithmetic expressions for calculating the roots X1 and X2 both involve the same subexpression, SQRT (B ** 2 − 4 * A * C). As written, the program QUAD asks the computer to recalculate this subexpression as part of the calculation of X2. We can force the computer to calculate this subexpression only once by assigning it to a new intermediate variable SUBEXP, and then calculating both roots in terms of the variable SUBEXP.

```
      PROGRAM QUAD
C     CALCULATES AND PRINTS THE ROOTS OF A QUADRATIC EQUATION
C
C     VARIABLES:
C        A, B, C: COEFFICIENTS
C        X1, X2: ROOTS
C
      REAL A, B, C, X1, X2
C
C     READ THE COEFFICIENTS
      PRINT, 'ENTER A, THE COEFFICIENT OF X ** 2'
      READ, A
      PRINT, 'ENTER B, THE COEFFICIENT OF X'
      READ, B
      PRINT, 'ENTER C, THE CONSTANT TERM'
      READ, C
C
C     CALCULATE THE ROOTS BY THE QUADRATIC FORMULA
      SUBEXP = SQRT (B ** 2 - 4 * A * C)
      X1 = (-B + SUBEXP) / (2 * A)
      X2 = (-B - SUBEXP) / (2 * A)
C
C     PRINT THE ROOTS
      PRINT, 'THE ROOTS ARE'
      PRINT 15, 'X1 =', X1
      PRINT 15, 'X2 =', X2
   15 FORMAT (T2, A4, F10.6)
      STOP
      END
```

Some optimizing Fortran compilers will recognize that the program QUAD, in its original form, calls for the calculation of the same subexpression twice without change of any of the variables in the subexpression. Such a compiler would produce the more efficient machine language code corresponding to the second version, QUAD2, even when the programmer writes the less efficient first version.

2.7 Testing and Debugging: Syntax Errors

Using the techniques introduced in this chapter, we can write Fortran programs dealing with input, output, variables and calculations. In this section, and in similar sections in each chapter, we show some of the problems and pitfalls that might befall a programmer attempting to write and run a Fortran program. No programmer will make all of the mistakes we show and many programmers will make no mistakes in writing this program. However, students learning to program must become aware that when mistakes are made, it is not the end of the world, it is merely the beginning of the task of debugging, or identifying and correcting the mistake. Debugging is as important a skill to a programmer as writing the program in the first place.

The Problem

The time it takes a pendulum to complete one swing is virtually independent of the amplitude or maximum displacement of the pendulum at the height of its swing, as long as the swing is relatively small compared with the length of the pendulum. For this reason, pendulums have long been used to keep accurate time. The problem in this section is to write a program to calculate the frequency f (the number of swings per second) of a pendulum, and its period T (the time it takes to complete one swing). The input data is the length of the pendulum in meters.

The Formulas

The formula for the frequency of a pendulum is

$$f = \frac{1}{2\pi} \sqrt{\frac{g}{L}}$$

where g is the gravitational acceleration constant 9.80665 meters/sec^2 for bodies falling under the influence of gravity near the surface of the earth, L is the length of the pendulum in meters, and π is the mathematical constant 3.14159. In addition, the formula for the period T is

$$T = \frac{1}{f}$$

The Solution

This problem has everything we learned in this chapter: it has variables, input data, computational formulas, and even the built-in square root function. Nevertheless, it seems to be a straightforward calculation for which a Fortran program can be written.

```
C       PROGRAM PENDLM
C       CALCULATES THE FREQUENCY AND PERIOD
C       OF A PENDULUM OF LENGTH L
C
        REAL L, F, T, PI, G
        PI = 3.14159
        G = 9.80665
C
        READ, L
        PRINT, 'INPUT DATA L: ', L
        F = (1.0 / 2.0 * PI) SQRT (G / L)
        T = 1.0 / F
        STOP
        END
```

The First Compilation and Run

When this program is entered into the computer, it will not compile and run. The error messages we show below are illustrative approximations of the messages we get on actual Fortran compilers. The quality and amount of useful information contained in error messages varies widely. We suggest comparing the error messages shown here with the messages your system produces for the same errors. Good error messages are the programmer's best friend. The error messages your system produces are the ones you will have to live with, and you may as well begin getting used to them now.

```
C       PROGRAM PENDLM
C       CALCULATES THE FREQUENCY AND PERIOD
C       OF A PENDULUM OF LENGTH L
C
        REAL L, F, T, PI, G
        PI = 3.14159
        G = 9.80665
C
        READ, L
        PRINT, 'INPUT DATA L: ', L
        F = (1.0 / 2.0 * PI) SQRT (G / L)
***ERROR***  MISSING OPERATOR.UNEXPECTED ) BEFORE SQRT
***ERROR***  MISSING OPERATOR.UNEXPECTED ( BEFORE G
        T = 1.0 / F
        STOP
        END
```

The error message says that the compiler was expecting an operator when SQRT was found instead. Compiler error messages tend to use terms that were natural to the writers of the compiler, but which might not be familiar to the beginning programmer trying to use it. After you submit several dozen programs to a compiler, you begin to get a feeling for what the error messages really mean. In this case, the compiler seems to be telling us that it was expecting an operator, whatever that is, and the place it expected to find this operator was where the word SQRT appears in the statement. The rule is that the asterisk for multiplication cannot be omitted in Fortran in places where a multiplication sign can be omitted in ordinary algebraic notation. We correct this assignment statement to the following.

```
        F = (1.0 / 2.0 * PI) * SQRT (G / L)
```

The Second Compilation and Run

Since all known errors have been corrected, we rerun the program. This is what happens.

```
***ERROR***  CONTROL CARD ENCOUNTERED ON UNIT 5 AT EXECUTION.
             PROBABLE CAUSE:  MISSING DATA OR INCORRECT FORMAT.
```

What went wrong this time? First, let us remark that the situation is actually much improved over the first attempt. There are no syntax errors. This means that the current version is a syntactically correct Fortran program that compiled successfully and died during execution. Recalling that on WATFIV systems, the default input file is unit 5, the cause of the error message is clear. We never prepared the input file for this program.

Choice of Input Data for Testing

The data in the input file should consist of one number, the length of the pendulum in meters. Visualizing the size of a grandfather clock, and rounding the length of its pendulum to the nearest whole meter, we will use an input length of one meter. We now prepare an input data file with the single number

```
1
```

and run the program again.

The Third Compilation and Run

This time, there are no error messages.

```
INPUT DATA  L:                  1.0000000
```

Unfortunately, there is only one line of output, and that line is the echo of the input data. At least we know that the input data was read correctly. But why didn't the computer print the answers? The reason is very simple and embarrassing. The computer didn't print the answers because we didn't provide PRINT statements for them.

> *Debugging Note:* The computer does exactly what you tell it to do in the Fortran program, and nothing else. If you want the computer to print or calculate something, you must include Fortran statements directing the computer to print or calculate precisely the values you want printed or calculated.

It is clear to most people reading the program that we calculated values for the variables F and T for a purpose, but nothing is clear to the computer. It doesn't think. As much of a nuisance as it is, we must spell out every last detail for the computer. If we include statements to print the answers, we obtain the following version of the program PENDLM.

```
C        PROGRAM PENDLM
C        CALCULATES THE FREQUENCY AND PERIOD
C        OF A PENDULUM OF LENGTH L
C
         REAL L, F, T, PI, G
         PI = 3.14159
         G = 9.80665
C
         READ, L
         PRINT, 'INPUT DATA  L:', L
         F = (1.0 / 2.0 * PI) * SQRT (G / L)
         T = 1.0 / F
         PRINT, 'THE FREQUENCY OF THE PENDULUM IS',
     +          F, 'SWINGS / SEC.'
         PRINT, 'EACH SWING TAKES', T, 'SEC.'
         STOP
         END
```

The Fourth Compilation and Run

Assuming we have not introduced any syntax errors in the two new PRINT statements, we expect the program PENDLM to run, and this time, to print the correct answers. Here is what the fourth run produces.

```
INPUT DATA  L:                 1.0000000
THE FREQUENCY OF THE PENDULUM IS                  4.9190330 SWINGS / SEC.
EACH SWING TAKES                  0.2032920 SEC.
```

The program does run to completion; it prints the echo of the input data and the answers, but they are wrong! The pendulum of a grandfather clock does not make almost five complete swings per second.

One swing every two seconds is more like it, with each half of the swing producing a tick at one second intervals.

> *Debugging Note:* Just because the computer prints an answer, it doesn't necessarily mean that the answer is right. The computer's arithmetic is almost certainly perfect, but the formula it was told to compute might be in error.

All the evidence seems to be pointing a finger at the assignment statement to calculate the frequency F,

```
F = (1.0 / 2.0 * PI) * SQRT (G / L)
```

or, if that statement is correct, at the statements that assign values to the variables and constants that appear on the right in that statement. The assignment statement for F seems at first glance to be the Fortran equivalent of the algebraic formula for the frequency, so we shift our attention to the assignment of the constants PI and G, and the reading of the variable L. The echo of input data shows the L is correct. The assignment statements assigning PI and G seem to be correct, so we shift our attention back to the assignment statement calculating F. The error must be in this statement. If we still don't believe that it is wrong, we could print the values of PI and G just before this statement, to further narrow the focus.

Remember the rule that a sequence of multiplications and divisions is executed from left to right. Thus the assignment statement executes as though it were written

```
F = (( 1.0 / 2.0) * PI) * SQRT (G / L)
```

The correct Fortran version of the statement is

```
F = (1.0 / (2.0 * PI)) * SQRT (G / L)
```

This time, the answers look correct. We expected a pendulum one meter long to swing once every two seconds.

```
INPUT DATA   L:                1.0000000
THE FREQUENCY OF THE PENDULUM IS               0.4984031 SWINGS / SEC.
EACH SWING TAKES                2.0064070 SEC.
```

To check it we calculate the algebraic formulas on a hand calculator and get the same answers, and we could also try other pendulum lengths in the computer.

2.8 What You Should Know

1. A printed copy of a program is the program listing.
2. To get the computer to print the exact typographic characters specified, enclose them in apostrophes.
3. A sequence of typographic characters in apostrophes is a character string.
4. A real constant is a string of digits followed by a period, followed by another string of digits. Either of the strings, but not both, may be empty.
5. An integer constant is a string consisting only of the digits 0 to 9.
6. Exponential notation is the equivalent of scientific notation in a computer. For example, 2.3E5 means 2.3×10^5.
7. The symbols for the five arithmetic operations are +, −, *, /, and **.

8. READ, PRINT, STOP, and END are Fortran keywords. There are no reserved words in Fortran, as there are in other programming languages.
9. Each statement must begin on a new line.
10. A statement may be continued by placing a character other than zero or blank in column 6 of the next line.
11. Variable names start with a letter followed by any mixture of letters and digits. They must not be longer than six characters.
12. Every variable has a type describing what type of data is stored in it. Its type is declared in a type statement beginning with a keyword indicating the type.
13. The three most common intrinsic types are INTEGER, REAL, and CHARACTER.
14. Values that do not change during execution of a program may be assigned to parameters.
15. The rules for naming and declaring a parameter are the same as for variables.
16. It is good programming practice to provide an echo of the input data, so that the output contains a record of the values used in the computation.
17. For interactive execution, it is good programming practice to give the user an input prompt indicating what kind of data is expected.
18. The computer stores a fixed number of significant digits for each real value. All values are rounded to that number of digits.
19. The READ statement reads input values until it satisfies its input list. Then it skips to the beginning of the next line.
20. The PRINT statement prints a list of values to an output device, always beginning on a new line.
21. An assignment statement is another way to give a variable a value besides reading that value as input.
22. Constants, variables, and arithmetic expressions can be assigned as the values of a variable.
23. In Fortran, the assignment operator is an equal sign (=).
24. The name of a variable should be chosen so that it describes what the value of the variable represents.
25. Comments are placed in a program as explanation to a human reader of a program. Comments are placed on lines with C or * in column 1.
26. Input and output formats may be indicated by an asterisk (for default formatting), by a character expression whose value is a format specification, or by the label of a format statement.
27. The E and F format specifiers are used for real values.
28. The I format specifier is used for integer values.
29. The A format specifier is used for character values.
30. The T format specifier is used to tab to a certain column.
31. The / format specifier is used to start a new line.
32. Built-in operations, functions, and procedures increase the power of Fortran:

    a. INT takes the integer part of a real value.
    b. FLOAT converts a value to type real.
    c. IABS and ABS are the absolute value functions.
    d. MAX0 and AMAX1 find the maximum of several values.
    e. MIN0 and AMIN1 find the minimum of several values.
    f. SQRT extracts the square root of a number.
    g. MOD and AMOD give the remainder when one integer is divided by another integer.
    h. ALOG10 and ALOG are logarithm functions.

i. EXP means "*e* raised to the power".
j. SIN, COS, TAN, ASIN, ACOS, and ATAN are trigonometric functions.
k. SINH, COSH, and TANH are hyperbolic functions.

33. In batch mode, all the input data are prepared in advance of the program execution.
34. In interactive mode, input data are entered into the computer *during* the program execution.
35. A compiler translates Fortran programs into machine instructions.
36. An operating system interprets commands and schedules tasks and machine resources.
37. $JOB, $ENTRY, and $END are WATFIV control cards that separate parts of the WATFIV-S run deck.

2.9 Self-Test Questions

Section 2.1

1. For each line of the following program, tell whether it is correct Fortran or not.

```
C       PROGRAM DIVISION
        BEGIN
        PRINT, 243 / 11
        END.
```

2. Correct the errors in the Fortran program in Self-Test Question 1.
3. Which lines of the following Fortran program are correct?

```
        PROGRAM MULT
        PRINT 2 * 3 * 4 * 5
        STOP
        END PROGRAM
```

4. Write correct versions of the incorrect lines in the program MULT.
5. Is the following a legal WATFIV-S statement?

```
        PRINT, A + B, C - D, E * F
```

6. What is the command to run a program?
7. True/false:

   a. The symbol for division is /.
   b. The symbol for multiplication is ×.
   c. The symbol for raising to a power is ^.

8. What computer output might be expected when the following program is run?

```
C       PROGRAM CALC4
        PRINT, 1 + (201 + 55) * 4 - 2 * 10
        STOP
        END
```

9. The program CALC5 uses a confusing sequence of arithmetic operations whose meaning would be clearer if written with parentheses. What computer output might be expected when it is run? Insert parentheses in the PRINT statement in a way that does not change the value printed, but makes it easier to understand.

```
C       PROGRAM CALC5
        PRINT, 343 / 7 / 7 * 2
        STOP
        END
```

10. What computer output might be expected when CALC6 is run?

```
C       PROGRAM CALC6
        PRINT, 2 * (3 * (5 - 3))
        STOP
        END
```

11. Some computer programs have nothing to do with numerical computation. What computer output might be expected when the program WHEEEE is run?

```
C       PROGRAM WHEEEE
        PRINT, 'IT IS EASY TO DO CALCULATIONS ON A COMPUTER.'
        STOP
        END
```

12. What computer output might be expected when the program PWROF2 (power of 2) is run?

```
C       PROGRAM PWROF2
        PRINT, 2 * 2 * 2 * 2 * 2 * 2 * 2 * 2 * 2 * 2
        STOP
        END
```

13. What computer output might be expected when the following program is run?

```
C       PROGRAM SIMPLE
        PRINT, 1, 'AND', 1, 'MAKES', 1 + 1
        STOP
        END
```

14. Convert the following type real numbers from positional notation to exponential notation.

48.2613	−.00241	38499.0
.2717	−55.0	7.000001

15. Convert the following type real numbers from exponential notation to positional notation.

9.503E2	4.1679E+10	2.881E−5
−4.421E2	−5.81E−2	7.000001E0

Section 2.2

1. True/false:
   a. Any correct variable name is also a correct name for a program.
   b. Every variable has a type.
   c. It is a requirement of the Fortran language that every variable must appear in a type declaration.
2. Which of the following are valid names for variables?

NAME	ADDRESS	PHONE#	PHONEY	REAL
IOU	IOU2	4GOTTEN	PACKET	LAURIE

3. Which of the following variable declarations are correct? Correct the ones that are wrong.

```
INTEGER N = 6
REAL NUMBER
CHAR C
X: REAL
```

4. Which of the following assignment statements are correct? Correct the incorrect ones.

```
AVERAG = (A + B) / 2
SUM := A + B + C + D + E + F
RATE * TIME = DISTNC
ALPHABET = 'ABCDEFGHIJKLMNOPQRSTUVWXYZ'
N = 6.25
```

5. What is the output produced when the program SUB is run? The input data file contains the following two lines

```
27.93
14.65
```

```
C       PROGRAM SUB
        REAL A, B
C
        READ, A
        PRINT, 'INPUT DATA  A:', A
        READ, B
        PRINT, 'INPUT DATA  B:', B
        PRINT, A - B
        STOP
        END
```

6. What does the printout for the following computational program look like? The input data file contains the following line.

```
3 5 7
```

```
C       PROGRAM PROD3
        INTEGER X, Y, Z
C
        READ, X, Y, Z
        PRINT, 'INPUT DATA  X:', X
        PRINT, '            Y:', Y
        PRINT, '            Z:', Z
        PRINT, X * Y * Z
        STOP
        END
```

7. The program INTOFT (inches to feet) is similar to the program MTOIN described in Section 2.2. What output is produced when INTOFT is run using 110 inches as the input value?

```
C       PROGRAM INTOFT
        REAL INCHES, FEET, INPRFT
C
C       THERE ARE 12 INCHES PER FT (INPRFT)
        INPRFT = 12.0
        READ, INCHES
        FEET = INCHES / INPRFT
        PRINT, INCHES, 'INCHES =', FEET, 'FEET.'
        STOP
        END
```

8. From each of the following groups, pick out which combinations of characters are and which are not permissible names in Fortran. For those that are not permissible, tell which rule is violated.

7ELEVEN	SVN 11	SVN−11	SEVEN11
TWO+2	SIX FT TWO	6FT2	
FIRSTNUMBER	SECOND NUMBER	3RDNR	
JOHN'S	MARYSAGE	HIS/HER	PHOOEY
1STNAME	LAST NAME	MIDDLEINITIAL	
TIME	MINUTES	SECONDS	HR:MIN

9. Which of the following are permissible names for variables in Fortran? Explain your answers.

   PH PHD PH.D. DOCTOR OF PHILOSOPHY

10. Both the variables in the program RHYME are assigned their values by parameter statements in the program. What does a computer print when this program is run?

```
C       PROGRAM RHYME
        INTEGER JACK, JILL
        JACK = 1
        JILL = 2
        PRINT, JACK + JILL, 'WENT UP THE HILL.'
        STOP
        END
```

11. Does the choice of parameter names in the program RHYME distract the reader of the program with extraneous connotations?
12. What does the following program print? Its style is *not* recommended.

```
C       PRO  G    RAMUG  H
        PRIN
     +     T*       , 1
     +         2.0            + 34
     +       .6
        S             TOP
        END
```

Section 2.3

1. If the variable X has value 2.5, what does the output for the following statement look like? Show blank columns with a "b".

```
        PRINT 15, X, X ** 2
     15 FORMAT (F6.3, E11.1)
```

2. What are the largest and smallest values that can be printed by the statement

```
        PRINT 25, VALUE
     25 FORMAT (F8.3)
```

3. What does the following statement print? Use "b" for blank columns.

```
        PRINT 35, '|', 1.0/3.0, '|'
     35 FORMAT (T9, A1, F9.5, A1)
```

Section 2.4

1. Write an expression that rounds the value of the variable X to the nearest tenth.
2. When is INT (X /Y) equal to X / Y for real values X and Y?
3. What are the values of the following expressions?

```
ABS (5.3)
INT (-123.456)
ABS (-123.456)
SQRT (1.21)
```

4. Which of the following relationships is always true?

   SQRT (X * X) = X for all real X
   SQRT (X) ** 2 = X for all real X $\geq$ 0

5. Rewrite the following expression using the built-in function MOD. Assume N is type integer.

```
N - (N / 100) * 100
```

6. Write an expression using the built-in function MOD that has the value 1 when N is odd and 0 when N is even.
7. Write an expression using the built-in function MOD that is true if the value of the variable N is even and is false if N is odd.

Section 2.5

1. True/False:
   a. Timesharing is the same as interactive editing.
   b. In a batch system the program and input data must be on cards.
   c. In batch execution, input data must be prepared in advance.
   d. You can't have interactive editing without interactive execution.
   e. Interactive editing and execution require timesharing.
   f. Operating systems for large computers generally use timesharing.
2. True/false: which of the following are reasons for echoing input data?
   a. They are useful in debugging.
   b. Echoes keep input data from getting lost.
   c. They provide a record of which input data were used in a given execution.
   d. They provide a check that the right input data were read at the right time and assigned to the right variables.
   e. Input echoes are a good programming practice.
   f. Your instructor insists on them in all your programming projects.
3. What are the major differences between running a program from a terminal using prepared input files and running the same program from a terminal interactively?
4. When a program is run interactively, why is it desirable to have a prompting message printed before the user types each item of input data?
5. What difficulties might occur if a computer program with a large number of read statements did not give sufficient information to the user in its prompting messages or did not provide prompting messages at all?
6. When running a program interactively, is an echo of input data desirable after the user has entered a piece of data in response to an input prompting message?
7. Why are prompting messages superfluous when running a program from cards or from a terminal using prepared input files?

8. Why is an echo of input data desirable when running a program in batch mode?

Section 2.7

1. What effect would there be on the course of the debugging session if the real constants 1.0 and 2.0 in the assignment statement for the variable F were replaced with the integer constants 1 and 2, respectively? Why?
2. How would you modify the program PENDLM to accept the input data for the pendulum length L interactively?
3. How would the course of the debugging session differ if the interactive version of the program written in Question 2 were debugged?

2.10 Programming Exercises

1. **Purpose:** To write, enter, and successfully run a simple calculational program using READ, PRINT, and assignment statements.

   The problem: Near the surface of the earth, mass units such as the kilogram bear a constant relationship to weight units such as pounds. The problem is to write a Fortran program to convert from pounds to kilograms.

   Relevant information: Near the surface of the earth, 453.6 grams weigh one pound, as the packaging on many foods now informs us. Furthermore, our science teachers inform us that there are exactly 1000 grams in a kilogram, the roundness of this conversion factor being one of the beauties of the metric system. If *LB* is a weight in pounds, then the equivalent mass *KG* in kilograms is given by the formula

$$KG = LB \times \frac{453.6}{1000}$$

   Input data: The input data should consist of one number, a weight in pounds. Use the following input line:

```
2.2
```

   Sample output: The output should include an echo of the input data if your system is a batch system, or an input prompt if your system is interactive. Then, the answer should be printed with an identifying message. The following is satisfactory.

```
INPUT DATA  POUNDS:  2.2
2.200000 LBS =  .997920 KG
```

2. **Purpose:** To use format specifiers for rounding.

   The problem: The sample execution output of the program SNDWCH in Section 2.2 computes the cost of a peanut butter and jelly sandwich correctly, but it prints too many decimal places for a dollars and cents amount. On some systems, it even prints the answer in E format. The problem is to modify the program SNDWCH so that the answer is printed correctly rounded to the nearest penny.

   Input data: None. All values are assigned in the program.

Sample output:

```
A PEANUT BUTTER AND JELLY SANDWICH COSTS $0.22
PRICES ARE SUBJECT TO CHANGE AT ANY TIME
     WITHOUT WRITTEN NOTICE.
```

3. **Purpose:** To examine a pitfall of integer arithmetic.

   The problem: Calculate the number of seconds in a year.

   Background information: For purposes of this problem, assume there are exactly 365 days in the year.

   The pitfall: Although all of the conversion factors, 60 seconds in a minute, 60 minutes in an hour, etc., are relatively small integers, the answer is too large to be stored as an integer variable in most systems. If you get an overflow error, you will have to use type real for the calculation.

   Input data: None.

   Sample output:

```
A YEAR HAS 31536000. SECONDS
```

   Note that the answer shown has a decimal point since it was calculated in type real and printed using F format.

4. **Purpose:** To see if you can combine a programming project with some real-world research.

   The problem: The cost of the ingredients in the peanut butter sandwich calculated in the program SNDWCH in Section 2.2 were correct at the time the program was written. By now, all of the ingredients have gone up in price. This exercise has three parts:

   1. Go to the local supermarket or grocery store and find the current prices of the ingredients
   2. Rewrite the program SNDWCH to use the new prices.
   3. Calculate (and print, of course) the percent increase in each of the ingredients and for the whole sandwich.

   Input data: None.

   Sample output: (Your form should resemble this, but the percent increases will depend on the current prices you use.)

```
A PEANUT BUTTER SANDWICH USED TO COST $0.22
IT NOW COSTS $0.24
THE SANDWICH WENT UP 8.5%
BREAD WENT UP 7.3%
PEANUT BUTTER WENT UP 7.1%
JELLY WENT UP 10.1%
```

5. **Purpose:** To see if you can handle input and output of character strings using both default and programmer-defined print formats.

   The problem: The beginning of a dialog between the computer and the user in an interactive environment might begin by the computer saying "Hello, I am a computer. Who are You?" The name the user types should be stored in a variable and used in subsequent comments, such as "Glad to meet you, (fill in the name). Are you ready for today's session?" Write the program to carry out this three-line dialog two ways: first using default input and output formats for character strings, and second, using A formats.

Sample executions:

```
HELLO, I AM A COMPUTER. WHO ARE YOU?
'ICHABOD IGLOO'
GLAD TO MEET YOU, ICHABOD IGLOO.
ARE YOU READY FOR TODAY'S SESSION?
```

```
HELLO, I AM A COMPUTER. WHO ARE YOU?
ICHABOD IGLOO
GLAD TO MEET YOU, ICHABOD IGLOO
ARE YOU READY FOR TODAY'S SESSION?
```

DECISION STRUCTURES

The sequence of steps a computer follows in executing a program does not have to be the same every time the program is run. The computer is capable of choosing one of several computational alternatives. A company payroll is a situation in which such a choice is necessary to handle the possibility that some of the employees work overtime, for which they are paid time and a half instead of straight time. Calculating a graduated income tax also requires a choice among alternative computational procedures because the percentage of income paid as tax depends on the amount of taxable income.

In this chapter, the IF block is introduced and used to describe alternative sequences of instructions. The computer chooses one of the sequences depending on the results of a test or comparison. The form of the IF block shows clearly the parallel sequences of steps the computer might take.

Sometimes a single test is not enough to determine which course of action the computer should follow. Section 3.3 shows examples where IF statements are nested within other IF statements to implement multi-stage decisions. Also, two older Fortran IF constructs, the logical IF statement and the arithmetic IF statement are discussed briefly.

Section 3.5 discusses character strings and comparisons involving character string variables and constants.

3.1 IF Blocks

The IF block is a simple and elegant decision construct. This section introduces the IF block and uses it in programs both with and without the optional ELSE statement.

Section Preview

General form of an **IF Block:**

IF (*logical expression*) THEN DO
statements

ELSE DO
statements
END IF

The ELSE clause is optional and may be omitted. The END IF must not be omitted.

Examples:

```
IF (A .NE. B) THEN DO
   TEMP = A
   A = B
   B = TEMP
ELSE DO
   PRINT, 'THEY ARE THE SAME'
END IF
IF (A .EQ. B) THEN DO
   C = A
   PRINT, C
END IF
```

Caution: The comparison operator for equality (.EQ.) is not the same as the assignment operator (=).

Escape Velocity of a Rocket

If a rocket or other object is projected directly upward from the surface of the Earth at a velocity v, it will reach a maximum height h above the center of the Earth given by the formula

$$h = \frac{R_E}{1 - v^2 / 2gR_E}$$

where R_E is the radius of the Earth (6.6×10^6 meters) and g is the acceleration due to gravity at the surface of the Earth (9.80 meters/sec^2). This formula is not an unreasonable approximation since a rocket reaches its maximum velocity within a relatively short period of time after launching, and most of the air resistance is confined to a narrow layer near the surface of the Earth.

A close examination of this formula reveals that it cannot possibly hold for all velocities. For example, if the initial velocity v is such that $v^2 = 2gR_E$, then $1 - v^2/2gR_E$ is zero and the maximum height h is infinite. This velocity $v = 1.117 \times 10^4$ meters/sec (approximately 7 miles/sec) is called the escape velocity of the Earth. Any object, either rocket or atmospheric gas molecule, attaining this vertical velocity near the surface of the Earth will leave the Earth's gravitational field and not return. A particle starting at the escape velocity will continue rising to arbitrarily great heights above the Earth. As it does so, it will slow to practically, but not quite, zero velocity.

At initial velocities greater than the escape velocity, the particle or rocket's velocity will not drop toward zero. Instead it will escape from the Earth's gravitational field with a final velocity v_{final} given by the formula

$$v_{final} = \sqrt{v^2 - 2gR_E}$$

The original formula for the maximum height h gives negative answers in these cases and should not be used. The maximum height is infinite.

The Problem

We wish to write a computer program to which the input will be an initial velocity of a rocket or molecule (in meters/sec), and for which the output will be an appropriate printed description of the fate of the rocket or molecule. That is, if the rocket reaches a maximum height before falling back to Earth, the maximum height should be printed. On the other hand, if the rocket escapes the Earth's gravitational field, the final velocity with which it escapes should be printed.

The Solution in Pseudocode

From the preceding discussion, we see that the fate of the rocket or molecule can be determined by comparing the initial velocity to the escape velocity of the Earth, or equivalently, by comparing v^2 to $2gR_E$. If g or v is smaller, then a maximum height h is reached before the rocket or molecule falls back to Earth. If the initial velocity is greater, then the object in question escapes with a nonzero final velocity given by the second formula. In the pseudocode solution below, the control structure is modelled exactly on the Fortran IF block.

```
Read the initial velocity v
Echo the input data
IF (v² < 2gR_E) THEN DO
   Calculate maximum height h above center of Earth
   Print that the object attains maximum height h - R_E
         above the surface of the Earth
         before returning to Earth
ELSE DO
   Calculate the final velocity
   Print that the object escapes Earth
         with the calculated final velocity
END IF
```

The IF block extends from the keyword IF that begins the IF block to the keyword END IF that ends the block. The lines of pseudocode between the keyword THEN DO and the keyword ELSE DO are the THEN clause. They are executed if and only if $v^2 < 2gR_E$. The lines of pseudocode between the keyword ELSE DO and the keyword END IF are the ELSE clause. They are executed in case the preceding IF condition is false.

Arithmetic Comparison Operators

The pseudocode versions of the IF test in the IF block above uses the arithmetic comparison operators "is less than" (denoted "<" in mathematical usage). As a legacy of the days when Fortran was first invented and keypunches did not have the symbols "<" and ">", the six arithmetic comparison operators are each represented by a two-letter abbreviation surrounded by periods as shown in Table 3.1. The Fortran symbol "=" is the assignment operator used in arithmetic assignment statements. In standard Fortran and WATFIV, it is not interchangeable with the comparison operator .EQ.

The Fortran Solution

Little remains to be done to refine the pseudocode solution to an executable Fortran program except to choose names for the Fortran variables that most nearly resemble the variable names in the formulas, and to translate the pseudocode to Fortran nearly line by line. Three sample executions are shown.

Table 3.1 Fortran symbols for the comparison operators.

Mathematical symbol	Fortran symbol	English equivalent
$<$	.LT.	is less than
$>$	.GT.	is greater than
$=$	.EQ.	is equal to
$\leq$	.LE.	is less than or equal to
$\geq$	.GE.	is greater than or equal to
$\neq$	.NE.	is not equal to

```
      PROGRAM ESCAPE
C     ACCEPTS AS INPUT AN INITIAL VELOCITY V
C     PRINTS MAXIMUM HEIGHT ATTAINED,
C        IF OBJECT DOES NOT ESCAPE EARTH
C     PRINTS FINAL ESCAPE VELOCITY, VFINAL,
C        IF OBJECT ESCAPES
C
C     CONSTANTS
C        G  = ACCELERATION OF GRAVITY NEAR EARTH'S SURFACE
C                (IN METERS / SEC ** 2)
C        RE = RADIUS OF THE EARTH (IN METERS)
C
      REAL V, H, VFINAL, G, RE
C
      G = 9.80
      RE = 6.366E6
C
      READ, V
      PRINT, 'INITIAL VELOCITY OF OBJECT =', V, 'METERS / SEC'
      IF (V ** 2 .LT. 2 * G * RE) THEN DO
         H = RE / (1 - V ** 2 / (2 * G * RE))
         PRINT, 'THE OBJECT ATTAINS A MAXIMUM HEIGHT OF', H - RE, 'M'
         PRINT, 'ABOVE THE EARTH''S SURFACE BEFORE RETURNING TO EARTH.'
      ELSE DO
         VFINAL = SQRT (V ** 2 - 2 * G * RE)
         PRINT, 'THE OBJECT ESCAPES FROM EARTH WITH A VELOCITY OF',
     +         VFINAL, 'METERS / SEC.'
      END IF
      STOP
      END
INITIAL VELOCITY OF OBJECT =          1000.0000000 METERS / SEC
THE OBJECT ATTAINS A MAXIMUM HEIGHT OF        51432.0000000 M
ABOVE THE EARTH'S SURFACE BEFORE RETURNING TO EARTH.

INITIAL VELOCITY OF OBJECT =         20000.0000000 METERS / SEC
THE OBJECT ESCAPES FROM EARTH WITH A VELOCITY OF          16589.9400000 METERS / SEC.

INITIAL VELOCITY OF OBJECT =         11170.0000000 METERS / SEC
THE OBJECT ATTAINS A MAXIMUM HEIGHT OF 171153400000.0000000 M
ABOVE THE EARTH'S SURFACE BEFORE RETURNING TO EARTH.
```

Testing an IF Block

The goal in testing an IF block is to design test cases that exercise each alternative in the IF block. The first sample execution shows an initial velocity of 1.0×10^3 meters/sec (1 kilometer/sec), which is well below the escape velocity of the Earth. The sample execution shows that the rocket reaches a maximum height of 5.14×10^4 meters (51.4 kilometers) before falling back to Earth. Calculating the appropriate formula using a hand calculator gives the same answer.

The second sample execution shows an initial velocity of 2.0×10^4 meters/sec (20 kilometers/sec), which is well above the escape velocity. As expected, the printed output shows that the rocket will escape from the Earth's gravitational field, so the correct alternative in the IF block is executed. It may seem surprising at first that the final velocity upon escape is such a large fraction of the initial velocity. We rechecked it using a hand calculator and got the same answer. The explanation is that an initial velocity of nearly twice the escape velocity carries with it an initial kinetic energy (energy of motion) of nearly four times the energy of the escape velocity. So it is not really surprising that nearly ¾ of the initial kinetic energy is retained and carried away with the rocket in the form of a large final velocity.

The third sample execution is designed to test the program using the escape velocity 1.117×10^4 meters/sec (11.17 kilometers/sec) as the initial velocity. Unfortunately, there is a little bit of roundoff in the calculations, and the execution output does not show that the rocket escapes with final velocity zero. The printed answer is not bad. It says that the rocket will rise to a height of 1.69×10^{11} meters above the surface of the Earth before returning. Since this height is farther than the distance to either Mars or Venus at their nearest approach to Earth, for all practical purposes the program has reported that the rocket will escape.

You must expect some roundoff in any calculation using reals. The largest source of roundoff in this problem is the fact that the physical constants, the radius of the Earth and the gravitational acceleration, are given to only 3 or 4 significant digits, as is the escape velocity. Even if the physical constants were given and used to more digits, each arithmetic calculation in the computer is calculated to a fixed number of digits. If you run this program on your computer, you will probably notice that the last one or more digits of your computer's printed answers differ from the ones shown. This is to be expected. We suggest that you try initial velocities slightly larger than 1.117×10^4 meters/sec in an attempt to hit the escape velocity exactly on the nose. Quite likely there is no computer representable number on your machine to use as input which will cause the computer to print that the rocket escapes with final velocity zero. *Equality tests for reals are rarely satisfied.* The best you can reasonably expect is even larger maximum heights or extremely low final escape velocities.

Indentation of an IF Block

Since all blanks are ignored in columns 7 to 72 of a Fortran program, the indentation of an IF block is to improve readability and to make sense of the IF block to human readers of the program. The IF, ELSE, and END IF lines are clearly visible, and the clauses they separate are indented between them. Statements that are more than one line long are continued in the usual way by putting a nonblank, nonzero character in column 6 of each continuation line.

Style Note: As a matter of good programming style, the statements of the THEN clause of an IF block are indented beneath the IF test that determines whether they will be executed. The statements of the ELSE clause are similarly indented beneath the keyword ELSE DO. This indentation rule makes the structure of an IF block clearer.

Flowchart for an IF Block

In standard flowcharting conventions, a diamond-shaped box is used to indicate a decision or fork in the flow of the program execution. Most of the time, the decision can be made on the basis of the answer to a "yes/no" or "true/false" type question. Whenever possible, we will label a decision box with a "yes/no" question and place the arrow corresponding to the "yes" answer to the right. These conventions make our flowcharts correspond more nearly to our Fortran programs.

In an IF block, the statements of only one of its clauses are executed each time through the block. The clause that is executed is the THEN clause if the the test is true. If the test is false, the ELSE clause is executed. The flowchart in Figure 3.1 illustrates this flow of control.

Omitting the ELSE Statement

A second example is overtime pay. If an hourly worker works more than the standard 40 hours, the overtime formula is used to calculate pay; otherwise the regular formula is used. In pseudocode, this takes the form of an IF block.

```
IF (hours worked > 40) THEN DO
   Calculate pay by the overtime formula
ELSE DO
   Calculate pay by the regular formula
END IF
```

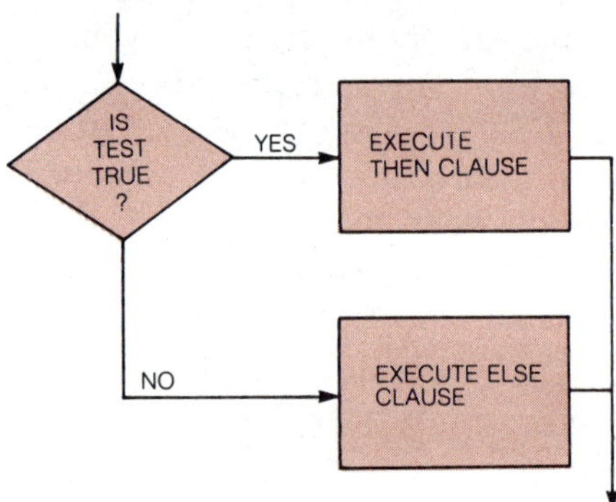

Figure 3.1 Flowchart for an IF block with two alternatives.

A shorter IF block results when there is nothing to be done in the ELSE clause. The IF block reduces to only an IF test, a THEN clause, and an END IF statement. For example, in the program XPOS (make X positive), there is nothing to do if X is already positive. In this case, the ELSE statement may be omitted. (See Figure 3.3.)

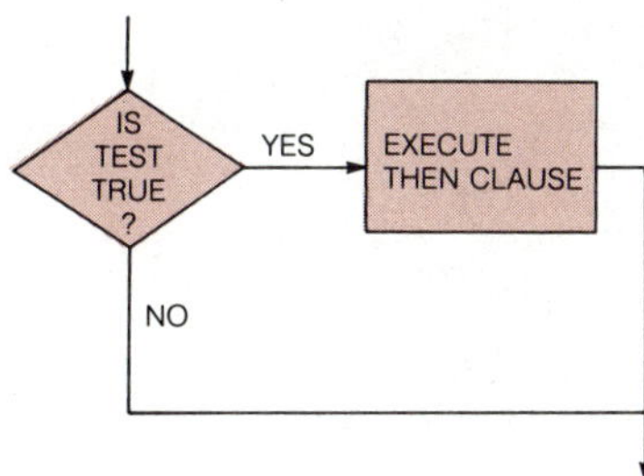

Figure 3.2 Flowchart for an IF block with no ELSE clause.

```
C       PROGRAM XPOS
        INTEGER X
        READ, X
        PRINT, 'INPUT DATA  X:', X
        IF (X .LT. 0) THEN DO
           X = -X
        END IF
        PRINT, 'ABSOLUTE VALUE =', X
        STOP
        END
INPUT DATA   X:             -5
ABSOLUTE VALUE =               5
INPUT DATA   X:               7
ABSOLUTE VALUE =                7
```

These executions are easy to follow if you remember that $-(-5) = 5$. When X is negative, $-X$ is positive, which is what X is changed to before printing.

Note: In Fortran 77, the keyword DO does not follow THEN or ELSE. Some WATFIV systems permit it to be omitted in these cases.

3.2 Case Study: Graduated Income Tax

The federal income tax is a graduated or progressive tax, which means that each income level is taxed at a different rate. After all deductions, progressively higher incomes are taxed at increasing rates. A program to calculate federal income tax uses a "multi-alternative IF block", constructed by nesting several IF blocks to select the correct tax computation formula for each income level.

Also in this section, the logical operators .AND., .OR., and .NOT. are used to form more flexible and powerful IF tests.

Section Preview

Decisions involving more than two alternatives are handled by an IF block with ELSE IF statements

The **logical operators** .AND., .OR., and .NOT. are used to formulate more complex conditions for IF tests.

Example:

```
IF (DICE .LE. 3 .OR. DICE .EQ. 12) THEN DO
   PRINT, 'YOU LOSE!'
ELSE DO
IF (DICE .EQ. 7 .OR. DICE .EQ. 11) THEN DO
   PRINT, 'YOU WIN!'
ELSE DO
   PRINT, 'YOU HAVE TO KEEP ROLLING UNTIL YOU GET'
   PRINT, 'EITHER A 7 OR A ', DICE
END IF
END IF
```

The way these IF blocks are nested, when several conditions are true, only the first true condition is acted upon.

The Problem

Federal income tax laws tax different income levels at different rates. To calculate a person's income tax liability, the income for the year is modified by various exclusions, deductions, and adjustments to arrive at a taxable income. The problem treated in this section is that of writing a program to compute the federal income tax liability for an unmarried taxpayer based on taxable income. Schedule X summarizes the applicable regulations. (See Table 3.2.)

Table 3.2 Tax Rate Schedule X for Computing Federal Income Tax.

IF TAXABLE INCOME IS

OVER	BUT NOT OVER	THEN INCOME TAX IS		
$0	$500		14% of taxable income	
$500	$1,000	$70 plus	15% of excess over	$500
$1,000	$1,500	$145 plus	16% of excess over	$1,000
$1,500	$2,000	$225 plus	17% of excess over	$1,500
$2,000	$4,000	$310 plus	19% of excess over	$2,000
$4,000	$6,000	$690 plus	21% of excess over	$4,000
$6,000	$8,000	$1110 plus	24% of excess over	$6,000
$8,000	$10,000	$1590 plus	25% of excess over	$8,000
.	.	.		
.	.	.		
.	.	.		

Input and Output

The input to the program is the person's taxable income, after all deductions and adjustments. The output is both the tax due on that taxable income and the person's tax bracket, that is, the rate at which the last dollar earned is taxed.

To avoid a very long program, only part of Tax Rate Schedule X is incorporated into the program TAX1. This program cannot be used to compute the tax on incomes over $10,000; however, it is not difficult to continue the pattern of program steps to incorporate all of Tax Rate Schedule X.

The Solution

The central section of the program TAX1 to solve this problem corresponds directly to the alternatives in Tax Rate Schedule X.

```
C       PROGRAM TAX1
        REAL INCOME, TAX
        INTEGER BRAKET
C
        READ, INCOME
        PRINT 15, 'INPUT DATA  INCOME:', INCOME
   15   FORMAT (T2, A21, F15.2)
C       FIND APPROPRIATE RANGE AND COMPUTE TAX
        IF (INCOME .EQ. 0) THEN DO
           TAX = 0
           BRAKET = 0
        ELSE DO
        IF (INCOME .GT. 0 .AND. INCOME .LE. 500) THEN DO
           TAX = 0.14 * INCOME
           BRAKET = 14
        ELSE DO
        IF (INCOME .GT. 500 .AND. INCOME .LE. 1000) THEN DO
           TAX = 70 + 0.15 * (INCOME - 500)
           BRAKET = 14
        ELSE DO
        IF (INCOME .GT. 1000 .AND. INCOME .LE. 1500) THEN DO
           TAX = 145 + 0.16 * (INCOME - 1000)
           BRAKET = 16
        ELSE DO
        IF (INCOME .GT. 1500 .AND. INCOME .LE. 2000) THEN DO
           TAX = 225 + 0.17 * (INCOME - 1500)
           BRAKET = 17
        ELSE DO
        IF (INCOME .GT. 2000 .AND. INCOME .LE. 4000) THEN DO
           TAX = 310 + 0.19 * (INCOME - 2000)
           BRAKET = 19
        ELSE DO
        IF (INCOME .GT. 4000 .AND. INCOME .LE. 6000) THEN DO
           TAX = 690 + 0.21 * (INCOME - 4000)
           BRAKET = 21
        ELSE DO
        IF (INCOME .GT. 6000 .AND. INCOME .LE. 8000) THEN DO
           TAX = 1110 + 0.24 * (INCOME - 6000)
           BRAKET = 24
        ELSE DO
        IF (INCOME .GT. 8000 .AND. INCOME .LE. 10000) THEN DO
           TAX = 1590 + 0.25 * (INCOME - 8000)
           BRAKET = 25
        END IF
        END IF
        END IF
        END IF
        END IF
        END IF
        END IF
```

```
      END IF
      END IF
C     END OF TAX COMPUTATION SECTION
C
      IF (INCOME .LE. 10000) THEN DO
         PRINT 25, 'THE TAX ON $', INCOME, ' IS $', TAX
25       FORMAT (T2, A12, F8.2, A5, F7.2)
         PRINT 35, 'THIS INCOME IS IN THE ', BRAKET, '% TAX BRACKET.'
35       FORMAT (T2, A22, I2, A14)
      ELSE DO
         PRINT, 'TAXABLE INCOME TOO HIGH FOR THIS PROGRAM.'
      END IF
      STOP
      END
```

Each line in Tax Rate Schedule X corresponds to an IF test and corresponding THEN clause in the tax computation section. If INCOME lies in the indicated range for that IF test, then the variables TAX and BRAKET are calculated by the formula in that IF block. The conditions describing the ranges for INCOME follow the form of Schedule X exactly. They guarantee that only one range and one tax computation formula applies for each possible value of INCOME less than or equal to $10,000.

To be more specific, let us look at a few sample executions of TAX1, in which the computer is supplied with different values as input for the variable income.

```
INPUT DATA   INCOME:          100.00
THE TAX ON $  100.00 IS $  14.00
THIS INCOME IS IN THE 14% TAX BRACKET.

INPUT DATA   INCOME:         1200.00
THE TAX ON $ 1200.00 IS $ 177.00
THIS INCOME IS IN THE 16% TAX BRACKET.

INPUT DATA   INCOME:         7500.00
THE TAX ON $ 7500.00 IS $1470.00
THIS INCOME IS IN THE 24% TAX BRACKET.

INPUT DATA   INCOME:        75000.00
TAXABLE INCOME TOO HIGH FOR THIS PROGRAM.
```

Consider the second run with a taxable income of $1200. The only condition in the tax computation section which this taxable income satisfies is

```
INCOME .GT. 1000 .AND. INCOME .LE. 1500
```

The first IF test fails, so control falls through to the first ELSE clause. This ELSE clause is itself an IF block headed by the second IF test, which is consequently made. Since the second IF test also fails for INCOME of $1200, the second ELSE clause is executed. This is the IF block headed by the third IF test. When this test fails, the ELSE clause starting with the fourth IF test is executed. This IF test succeeds. The tax is computed by the formula in the fourth THEN clause.

```
TAX = 145 + 0.16 * (INCOME - 1000)
    = 145 + 0.16 * 200
    = 145 + 32
    = 177
```

The second assignment statement of the fourth THEN clause assigns a tax bracket of 16 (percent) to the variable BRAKET.

What happens next takes longer to unravel than to execute. Since the fourth THEN clause has been executed, execution of the fourth IF block is now complete. Its long, nested ELSE clause is not to be executed. Since the fourth IF block is complete, the ELSE clause of the third IF block is completely executed, which completes execution of the third IF block. Similarly, we see that execution of the third IF block completes execution of the second ELSE clause and IF block, and execution of the second IF block completes execution of the first ELSE clause and IF block. In short, nothing else happens in the tax computation section. All of the remaining IF tests in the tax computation section are skipped, but even if they were made, none of the other conditions would be satisfied and so no other action would be taken for a taxable income of $1200.

The final IF test of the program controls the printout. Since the value of INCOME is $1200, which is less than $10,000, the two sentences giving the tax and the tax bracket are printed.

In the last of the sample executions, using a taxable income of $75,000, none of the conditions in the tax computation section is satisfied. Thus TAX and BRAKET are not assigned values at all. In this execution, the final IF test causes the computer to print a warning that the taxable income is too large for the program.

The Logical Operators .AND., .OR., and .NOT.

The logical operators .AND., .OR., and .NOT. may be used to specify conditions that cannot be described using only one comparison. In the program TAX1, most of the ranges for INCOME are described by two comparisons. For example,

```
      IF (INCOME .GT. 1000 .AND. INCOME .LE. 1500) THEN DO
      IF (INCOME .GT. 1500 .AND. INCOME .LE. 2000) THEN DO
      IF (INCOME .GT. 2000 .AND. INCOME .LE. 4000) THEN DO
```

Both comparisons must be true before the statements in the IF block are executed.

On the other hand, the program EXPOR (explain or) below helps explain under what circumstances an IF test consisting of two conditions connected by the operator .OR. is satisfied.

```
C     PROGRAM EXPOR
      INTEGER X, Y
      READ, X, Y
      PRINT, 'INPUT DATA  X:', X
      PRINT, '            Y:', Y
      IF (X .EQ. 0 .OR. Y .EQ. 0) THEN DO
         PRINT, 'AT LEAST ONE OF THE VARIABLES X OR Y IS ZERO.'
      ELSE DO
         PRINT, 'NEITHER X NOR Y IS ZERO.'
      END IF
      STOP
      END
```

```
INPUT DATA  X:          0
            Y:          0
AT LEAST ONE OF THE VARIABLES X OR Y IS ZERO.
```

```
INPUT DATA  X:         0
            Y:         1
AT LEAST ONE OF THE VARIABLES X OR Y IS ZERO.
INPUT DATA  X:         1
            Y:         0
AT LEAST ONE OF THE VARIABLES X OR Y IS ZERO.
INPUT DATA  X:         1
            Y:         1
NEITHER X NOR Y IS ZERO.
```

As can be seen from the sample executions, whenever X is zero or Y is zero the IF test is satisfied. Consequently, the PRINT statement in the IF block causes the computer to print AT LEAST ONE OF THE VARIABLES X OR Y IS ZERO. If both X and Y are zero, there are two reasons for printing the message. Only if X and Y are both nonzero is the PRINT statement in the ELSE block executed to print the sentence NEITHER X NOR Y IS ZERO.

The logical operator .NOT. applied to a logical value changes it. If it is true, it becomes false; if it is false, it becomes true.

Precedence of Operators

In expressions without parentheses, the .NOT. operator is applied first, then the .AND. operator, and finally the .OR. operator. Thus, as far as operator precedence goes, the logical operator .AND. resembles the arithmetic operator "*" and .OR. resembles "+".

All of the comparison operators are more binding than the logical operators, a fact which enables us to write the tests in TAX1 without added parentheses. Arithmetic operators have higher precedence still, so that the logical expression

```
X + Y .GT. Z ** 2 .OR. .NOT. A .LT. B
```

is evaluated as if parenthesized

```
((X + Y) .GT. (Z ** 2)) .OR. (.NOT. (A .LT. B))
```

If A, B, and C are logical expressions, then

```
A .AND. .NOT. B .OR C
```

would be evaluated as if it were the expression

```
(A .AND. (.NOT. B)) .OR. C
```

Logical Data Type

The **logical** data type in Fortran consists of constants, variables, parameters, and expressions that take on only the values true or false. The two constants in logical type are

```
.TRUE.
```

and

```
.FALSE.
```

Variables and parameters may be declared logical, and logical values assigned to them. For example, the statements

```
LOGICAL YES, NO, DONE, FOUND, MISSING, QUIT
INTEGER NEWX, OLDX, COUNT
```

```
YES = .TRUE.
NO = .FALSE.
DONE = .TRUE.
FOUND = (NEWX .EQ. OLDX)
MISSING = .NOT. FOUND
```

declare that a number of variables are of type logical. The variables YES and NO are assigned logical constant values in assignment statements. They will probably be used like named constants. The variable DONE is assigned a logical value in an assignment statement. The value for DONE is the logical constant .TRUE., a simple example of a logical expression. A more complicated example appears in the next statement.

The result of a comparison is a logical value, which may then be assigned to the logical variable FOUND. The quantities compared are not logical, but the result of the comparison is always a logical value. Logical values may be combined using the logical operators .OR., .AND., and .NOT. to form more complex logical expressions. The value assigned to the logical variable MISSING is a simple example.

Logical expressions may be assigned to variables, or they may be used in IF tests. For example, the assignment statement

```
QUIT = (NEWX .GT. OLDX) .AND. .NOT. FOUND
```

assigns the logical variable QUIT the value of a complex logical expression. The IF block

```
IF ((NEWX .EQ. OLDX) .OR. (COUNT .GT. 100)) THEN DO
   PRINT, 'QUITTING'
ELSE DO
   PRINT, 'CONTINUING'
END IF
```

tests a complex logical condition, and prints a value dependent on the result of the test.

Non-Exclusive IF Conditions

Because the tax computation IF block in the program TAX1 is based so closely on Tax Rate Schedule X, the alternative IF conditions are mutually exclusive. Just as one and only one line of Tax Rate Schedule X applies to each taxable income, one and only one condition in the tax computation nested IF blocks in TAX1 is true (up to $10,000).

The IF test conditions need not be mutually exclusive when IF blocks are nested in ELSE clauses. However, even if several IF conditions are true, only the first such condition selects its THEN clause for execution. The remaining conditions are not even tested. After the selected THEN clause is executed, control passes directly to the END IF statements that end the nested IF blocks.

Using this rule for breaking ties when several conditions are satisfied, we may rewrite the program TAX1 with shorter test conditions in the tax computation IF block. The program TAX2 is the result.

```
C       PROGRAM TAX2
        REAL INCOME, TAX
        INTEGER BRAKET
C
        READ, INCOME
        PRINT 15, 'INPUT DATA  INCOME:', INCOME
   15   FORMAT (T2, A21, F15.2)
```

```
C       FIND APPROPRIATE RANGE AND COMPUTE TAX
        IF (INCOME .EQ. 0) THEN DO
           TAX = 0
           BRAKET = 0
        ELSE DO
        IF (INCOME .LE. 500) THEN DO
           TAX = 0.14 * INCOME
           BRAKET = 14
        ELSE DO
        IF (INCOME .LE. 1000) THEN DO
           TAX = 70 + 0.15 * (INCOME - 500)
           BRAKET = 14
        ELSE DO
        IF (INCOME .LE. 1500) THEN DO
           TAX = 145 + 0.16 * (INCOME - 1000)
           BRAKET = 16
        ELSE DO
        IF (INCOME .LE. 2000) THEN DO
           TAX = 225 + 0.17 * (INCOME - 1500)
           BRAKET = 17
        ELSE DO
        IF (INCOME .LE. 4000) THEN DO
           TAX = 310 + 0.19 * (INCOME - 2000)
           BRAKET = 19
        ELSE DO
        IF (INCOME .LE. 6000) THEN DO
           TAX = 690 + 0.21 * (INCOME - 4000)
           BRAKET = 21
        ELSE DO
        IF (INCOME .LE. 8000) THEN DO
           TAX = 1110 + 0.24 * (INCOME - 6000)
           BRAKET = 24
        ELSE DO
        IF (INCOME .LE. 10000) THEN DO
           TAX = 1590 + 0.25 * (INCOME - 8000)
           BRAKET = 25
        END IF
        END IF
        END IF
        END IF
        END IF
        END IF
        END IF
        END IF
        END IF
C       END OF TAX COMPUTATION SECTION
C
        IF (INCOME .LE. 10000) THEN DO
           PRINT 25, 'THE TAX ON $', INCOME, ' IS $', TAX
   25      FORMAT (T2, A12, F8.2, A5, F7.2)',
           PRINT 35, 'THIS INCOME IS IN THE ', BRAKET, '% TAX BRACKET.'
   35      FORMAT (T2, A22, I2, A14)',
```

```
      ELSE DO
         PRINT, 'TAXABLE INCOME TOO HIGH FOR THIS PROGRAM.'
      END IF
      STOP
      END
INPUT DATA  INCOME:         1200.00
THE TAX ON $ 1200.00 IS $ 177.00
THIS INCOME IS IN THE 16% TAX BRACKET.
```

For a taxable income of $1200, as shown in the sample execution, the first three conditions in the tax computation IF block are false, and all of the remaining conditions are true. Thus the first IF test that is satisfied is the fourth IF test.

```
      IF (INCOME .LE. 1500) THEN DO
```

Consequently, the tax is computed as specified in the corresponding THEN clause

```
      TAX = 145 + 0.16 * (INCOME - 1000)
          = 145 + 0.16 * 200
          = 145 + 32
          = 177
```

Even though IF tests five through eight would be satisfied, they are not tested and only this THEN clause was executed.

Exclusive vs. Non-Exclusive IF Conditions

What is to be gained by shortening the IF tests? Certainly, there is less typing to enter the program. In addition, since the IF tests are simpler, they will execute more rapidly. Just how much more rapidly is not clear. Not only is the correspondence between the length of the Fortran source program and the speed of execution of the compiled machine language program rather loose, but input and output operations tend to be very time-consuming when compared to computational statements. Thus, it is possible that most of the execution time is spent in the READ and PRINT statements, and even a significant improvement in the speed of the IF tests produces very little change in the total execution time.

What is lost? The most important thing that is lost is the correspondence between the program and Tax Rate Schedule X. The program TAX1 obviously implements Tax Rate Schedule X. TAX2 also implements Tax Rate Schedule X, but less obviously so. Which program would you most trust?

Another difference is that the IF block in the program TAX2 is slightly more fragile. This means that although it works perfectly in its present form, it is slightly more likely to fail if it is modified at a later date. For example, if the order of the alternatives in the program TAX1 are scrambled, perhaps listed in decreasing rather than in increasing order of taxable income, the tax computation IF block in TAX1 still works properly. The alternatives in the tax computation IF block in the program TAX2 must remain in increasing order or the IF block will fail to compute taxes properly. Of course, we know better than to scramble the order of the alternatives, having just proved to ourselves that the IF block in TAX2 implements Tax Rate Schedule X precisely because the alternatives are tested in the given order. However, would this fact be remembered a year from now by a different programmer assigned to modify this program?

We chose TAX1 because we were not impressed with the slight gains expected in execution speed from TAX2. We preferred the increased clarity of TAX1 to the increased fragility of TAX2.

3.3 Nested IF Statements

Section Preview

Nested IF statements:

An IF block may contain almost any Fortran statements, including other IF statements. The inner blocks are **nested** within the outer block.

Three Related Decision Procedures

We open this section with three related examples of programs using IF statements. In each of the three applications, an exam has been given. The exam contains not only the regular questions, which are marked normally, but also three bonus questions. The input data for all the programs consists of four items. The first item is a numerical exam score for the regular questions. Each of the remaining three items is either the character R, for "right", or W, for "wrong", depending on which of the bonus questions are answered correctly. There is no partial credit for the bonus questions. The comparison operator equals (.EQ.) may be used to compare two characters.

```
C       PROGRAM EXTRA1
C       FIVE EXTRA POINTS FOR EACH QUESTION ANSWERED CORRECTLY
        CHARACTER RIGHT *1, BONUS1 *1, BONUS2 *1, BONUS3 *1
        INTEGER SCORE
        RIGHT = 'R'
C
        READ, SCORE, BONUS1, BONUS2, BONUS3
        PRINT, 'INPUT DATA  SCORE:', SCORE
        PRINT, '            BONUS1:', BONUS1
        PRINT, '            BONUS2:', BONUS2
        PRINT, '            BONUS3:', BONUS3
C
        IF (BONUS1 .EQ. RIGHT) THEN DO
           SCORE = SCORE + 5
        END IF
        IF (BONUS2 .EQ. RIGHT) THEN DO
           SCORE = SCORE + 5
        END IF
        IF (BONUS3 .EQ. RIGHT) THEN DO
           SCORE = SCORE + 5
        END IF
C
        PRINT, 'ADJUSTED EXAM SCORE =', SCORE
        STOP
        END
```

```
INPUT DATA  SCORE:           83
            BONUS1: R
            BONUS2: W
            BONUS3: R
ADJUSTED EXAM SCORE =           93
```

In the program EXTRA1, the variable SCORE is increased by 5 every time a bonus question is answered correctly. Thus an adjusted test score can be as much as 15 points higher than the score on the regular questions if all three bonus questions were answered correctly.

In the next example, the instructor has decided to adjust the regular exam score only if all three bonus questions are answered correctly. No adjustment is to be made if only one or two bonus questions are answered correctly.

```
C       PROGRAM EXTRA2
C       FIVE EXTRA POINTS IF ALL THREE BONUS QUESTIONS ANSWERED CORRECTLY
        CHARACTER RIGHT *1, BONUS1 *1, BONUS2 *1, BONUS3 *1
        INTEGER SCORE
        RIGHT = 'R'
C
        READ, SCORE, BONUS1, BONUS2, BONUS3
        PRINT, 'INPUT DATA  SCORE:', SCORE
        PRINT, '            BONUS1:', BONUS1
        PRINT, '            BONUS2:', BONUS2
        PRINT, '            BONUS3:', BONUS3
C
        IF (BONUS1 .EQ. RIGHT .AND.
     +      BONUS2 .EQ. RIGHT .AND.
     +      BONUS3 .EQ. RIGHT) THEN DO
           SCORE = SCORE + 5
        END IF
C
        PRINT, 'ADJUSTED EXAM SCORE =', SCORE
        STOP
        END
INPUT DATA  SCORE:          83
            BONUS1:   R
            BONUS2:   W
            BONUS3:   R
ADJUSTED EXAM SCORE =          83
```

The IF test has three comparisons separated by the .AND. operator. Commas or other punctuation that might be used if this were an English sentence are not used in Fortran.

In the next example, test scores are to be adjusted by five points if any bonus question is answered correctly. There is no additional credit for a second or third bonus question that is also answered correctly.

```
C       PROGRAM EXTRA3
C       FIVE EXTRA POINTS IF AT LEAST ONE BONUS QUESTION ANSWERED CORRECTLY
        CHARACTER RIGHT *1, BONUS1 *1, BONUS2 *1, BONUS3 *1
        INTEGER SCORE
        RIGHT = 'R'
C
        READ, SCORE, BONUS1, BONUS2, BONUS3
        PRINT, 'INPUT DATA  SCORE:', SCORE
        PRINT, '            BONUS1:', BONUS1
        PRINT, '            BONUS2:', BONUS2
        PRINT, '            BONUS3:', BONUS3
C
```

```
      IF (BONUS1 .EQ. RIGHT .OR.
     +    BONUS2 .EQ. RIGHT .OR.
     +    BONUS3 .EQ. RIGHT) THEN DO
         SCORE = SCORE + 5
      END IF
C
      PRINT, 'ADJUSTED EXAM SCORE =', SCORE
      STOP
      END
INPUT DATA  SCORE:            83
            BONUS1:   R
            BONUS2:   W
            BONUS3:   R
ADJUSTED EXAM SCORE =           88
```

This program is identical to the previous program, except that .AND. has been changed to .OR. The regular exam score thus is increased by five points if one, two, or three of the bonus questions are answered correctly and is unchanged only if none of the bonus questions is answered correctly.

Nesting

We now show how to program the last two applications without using either .AND. or .OR. The programs become somewhat longer and probably less clear.

```
C     PROGRAM XTRA2B
C     FIVE EXTRA POINTS IF ALL THREE BONUS QUESTIONS ANSWERED CORRECTLY
      CHARACTER RIGHT *1, BONUS1 *1, BONUS2 *1, BONUS3 *1
      INTEGER SCORE
      RIGHT = 'R'
C
      READ, SCORE, BONUS1, BONUS2, BONUS3
      PRINT, 'INPUT DATA  SCORE:', SCORE
      PRINT, '            BONUS1:', BONUS1
      PRINT, '            BONUS2:', BONUS2
      PRINT, '            BONUS3:', BONUS3
C
      IF (BONUS1 .EQ. RIGHT) THEN DO
         IF (BONUS2 .EQ. RIGHT) THEN DO
            IF (BONUS3 .EQ. RIGHT) THEN DO
               SCORE = SCORE + 5
            END IF
         END IF
      END IF
C
      PRINT, 'ADJUSTED EXAM SCORE =', SCORE
      STOP
      END
INPUT DATA  SCORE:            83
            BONUS1:   R
            BONUS2:   W
            BONUS3:   R
ADJUSTED EXAM SCORE =           83
```

In this program, there are three IF blocks, one nested within the next. The last IF statement corresponds with the first END IF and vice versa. The third IF block is entirely contained within the second IF block, which in turn is entirely contained in the first IF block. None of these IF blocks contains an ELSE statement, so if any one of the three tests is not satisfied, the computer proceeds to the PRINT statement (see Figure 3.4). The program XTRA2B is grammatically correct and executes properly, but it is more confusing than EXTRA2, which is therefore preferred.

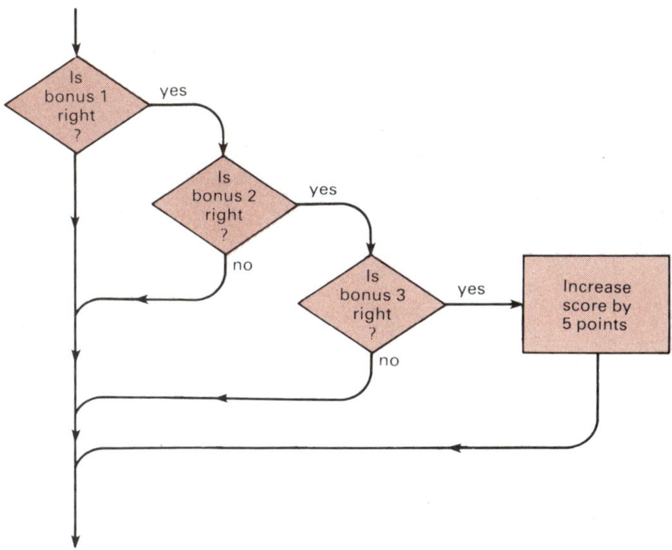

Figure 3.3 Nested IF block structure of the program XTRA2B. All three IF conditions must be satisfied to earn the 5-point bonus.

In order to eliminate the operator .OR. from the program EXTRA3, successive IF blocks are nested in the ELSE clause of the previous IF block, as in the program TAX1. Recall that with this kind of nesting, called ELSE IF nesting, only the first IF test satisfied has its THEN clause executed.

```
C       PROGRAM XTRA3B
C       FIVE EXTRA POINTS IF AT LEAST ONE BONUS QUESTION ANSWERED CORRECTLY
        CHARACTER RIGHT *1, BONUS1 *1, BONUS2 *1, BONUS3 *1
        INTEGER SCORE
        RIGHT = 'R'
C
        READ, SCORE, BONUS1, BONUS2, BONUS3
        PRINT, 'INPUT DATA  SCORE:', SCORE
        PRINT, '           BONUS1:', BONUS1
        PRINT, '           BONUS2:', BONUS2
        PRINT, '           BONUS3:', BONUS3
C
```

```
      IF (BONUS1 .EQ. RIGHT) THEN DO
         SCORE = SCORE + 5
      ELSE DO
         IF (BONUS2 .EQ. RIGHT) THEN DO
            SCORE = SCORE + 5
         ELSE DO
            IF (BONUS3 .EQ. RIGHT) THEN DO
               SCORE = SCORE + 5
            END IF
         END IF
      END IF
C
      PRINT, 'ADJUSTED EXAM SCORE =', SCORE
      STOP
      END
INPUT DATA  SCORE:          83
            BONUS1:          R
            BONUS2:          W
            BONUS3:          R
ADJUSTED EXAM SCORE =          88
```

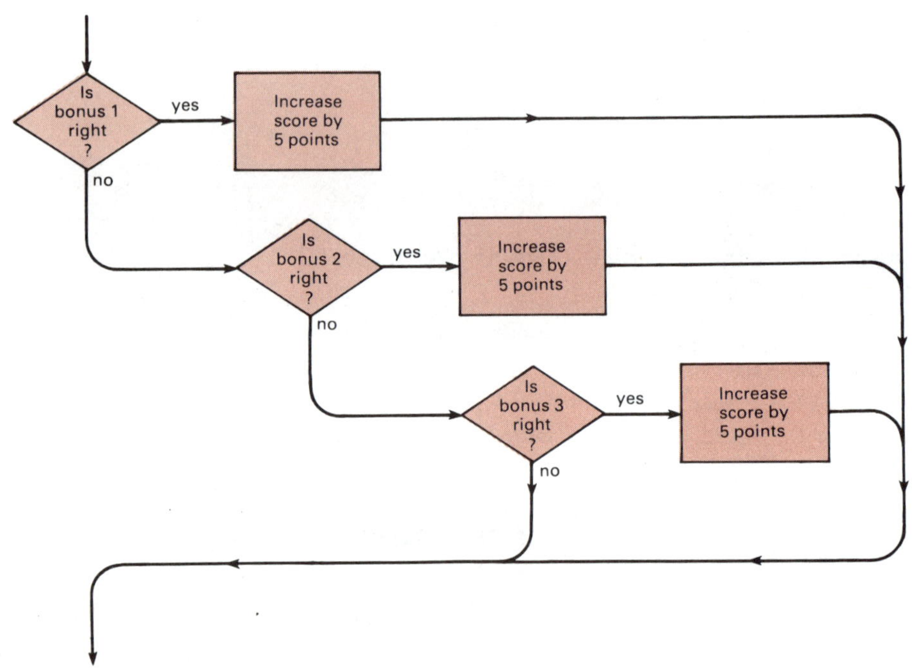

Figure 3.4 IF block structure of the program XTRA3B. The 5-point bonus is awarded if any of the three bonus questions is answered correctly.

With effort, it can be verified that this program is correct (see Figure 3.5). However, the program using the operator .OR. is clearly preferable.

The Logical IF Statement

The logical IF statement in Fortran IV permitted test conditions of the same kind as the IF block, but the action to be taken when the test succeeded was limited to one statement. This restriction can be a nuisance if more than one statement must be executed conditionally. Nevertheless, the logical IF statement, introduced in Fortran IV in the early 1960s, was a tremendous improvement over the earlier arithmetic IF statement which permitted only one form of test condition, a test of an arithmetic expression against zero.

The general form of the logical IF statement shows that it is a single statement, rather than a block of statements like the IF block.

IF (*logical condition*) *Fortran statement*

The logical conditions acceptable in a logical IF statement are precisely those acceptable in the IF test of an IF block. The WATFIV-S compiler distinguishes between the two statement types by noting that the logical condition in an IF block is followed by the keyword THEN DO and nothing else on that line, while the logical condition in a logical IF statement is not followed by THEN DO. Instead, a complete Fortran statement completes the logical IF statement. The following examples illustrate the difference. The lines

```
IF (X .GT. XMAX) THEN DO
   X = XMAX
END IF
```

form an IF block. The single line

```
IF (X .GT. XMAX) X = XMAX
```

is a logical IF statement specifying the same test and outcome. The conditional structure of this statement is better displayed in the program listing if the conditionally executed statement is placed on a continuation line.

```
      IF (X .GT. XMAX)
     +          X = XMAX
```

Although this typographic layout of the logical IF statement makes it look more like an IF block, it is still one statement written on several lines. Thus, the continuation character may not be omitted in column 6 of each continuation line. The giveaway is that the logical IF statement does not use the keyword THEN DO.

Since a logical IF statement can sometimes say in one line what it takes an IF block three lines to say, although the total number of characters is nearly the same for both methods, the logical IF statement is still sometimes used as an abbreviation for the corresponding IF block. We don't use the logical IF statement much in this book because we believe that for beginners, one good way to do things is enough.

The Arithmetic IF Statement

There is an even older version of the IF statement, called the arithmetic IF statement. It was the only IF statement in the first version of Fortran delivered in 1957. It is based on an IBM 704 machine instruction that compared an arithmetic quantity to zero and made a transfer of control to one of three places, depending upon whether the quantity was negative, zero, or positive. For example, the following statement causes a transfer to the statement with label 40 if X − Y is negative, that is, if X < Y. If X − Y is zero, that is, X = Y, the statement with label 50 is executed next. If X − Y is positive, that is, X > Y, then there is a transfer to the statement with label 60.

```
IF (X - Y) 40, 50, 60
```

Programmers don't use the arithmetic IF statement much any more because it is difficult to understand when reading the program, and it is hard to remember which of the three labels corresponds to the three different conditions being tested. We include this discussion of the arithmetic IF statement so that, if you see one in an old program, you will know what it means.

3.4 Case Study: Complex Roots of a Quadratic Equation

In Section 2.6, the quadratic formula was used in a program QUAD to calculate the roots of a quadratic equation. QUAD worked well when the two roots were real, but it failed in the test case of a quadratic whose roots were imaginary. In that case, the quadratic formula calls for taking the square root of a negative number, a function evaluation with no real answer. In this section, we show how to use an IF block to distinguish between the cases and to print the correct answer whether the roots of the quadratic are real or complex.

Section Preview

An IF test can be used to prevent evaluation of a function at a value of its argument for which the function is undefined.

The Problem

A quadratic equation is an equation of the form

$$ax^2 + bx + c = 0$$

The quadratic formula, described in Section 2.6, says that the two roots may be calculated by the formula

$$x = \frac{-b \pm \sqrt{b^2 - 4ac}}{2a}$$

The subexpression

$$d = b^2 - 4ac$$

is called the **discriminant** because it discriminates between the cases of two real roots, a double real root, and two complex roots. If d is positive, then there is a real square root of d, and the quadratic formula gives two real roots, one calculated by adding the square root of d and the other by subtracting it. If d is zero, then so is its square root. Consequently, when d is zero the quadratic formula gives only one real root, $-b/2a$.

When d is negative, on the other hand, its square root is imaginary. The complex square root of a negative number is obtained by taking the square root of its absolute value and multiplying the result by i, the basis of the complex number system. For example, if $d = -4$, then $\sqrt{d} = 2i$. Thus when d is negative, the two roots of the quadratic equation are given by the formulas

$$x_1 = \frac{-b}{2a} + \frac{\sqrt{|d|}}{2a}\, i$$

and

$$x_2 = \frac{-b}{2a} - \frac{\sqrt{|d|}}{2a}\, i$$

The problem now is to write a program that will select the proper set of formulas and calculate the roots of a quadratic equation, even if the roots are complex. The input is the three coefficients a, b, and c.

The following pseudocode version expresses the solution.

```
Read the coefficients
Calculate the discriminant d = b² - 4ac
IF d >= 0 THEN DO
   Calculate and print the roots using the quadratic formula
         for real valued solutions
ELSE DO
   Calculate and print the roots using the quadratic formula
         for complex valued solutions
END IF
```

The case of two equal real roots is not singled out as a separate alternative clause because the quadratic formula for reals works in this case also. The Fortran program QUAD2 results from refining the pseudocode by substituting the appropriate Fortran expressions for the formulas.

```
C       PROGRAM QUAD2
C
C       CALCULATES AND PRINTS THE ROOTS OF A QUADRATIC FORMULA
C       EVEN IF THEY ARE COMPLEX
C
C       VARIABLES:  A, B, C = COEFFICIENTS
C                   X1, X2 = REAL ROOTS
C                   D = DISCRIMINANT
C                   REALX, IMAGX = REAL AND IMAGINARY PARTS
C                                  OF COMPLEX ROOTS
C
        REAL A, B, C, X1, X2, D, REALX, IMAGX
C
C       READ THE COEFFICIENTS
        READ, A, B, C
        PRINT 15, 'ECHO OF INPUT DATA  A:', A
        PRINT 15, '                    B:', B
        PRINT 15, '                    C:', C
   15   FORMAT (T2, A22, F12.6)
C
C       CALCULATE THE ROOTS
        D = B ** 2 - 4 * A * C
        IF (D .GE. 0) THEN DO
C          USE REAL FORM OF QUADRATIC FORMULA FOR THE ROOTS
           X1 = (-B + SQRT (D)) / ( 2 * A)
           X2 = (-B - SQRT (D)) / ( 2 * A)
           PRINT, 'THE ROOTS ARE REAL'
           PRINT 25, 'X1 =', X1
           PRINT 25, 'X2 =', X2
   25      FORMAT (T2, A4, F12.6)
```

```
      ELSE DO
C        USE COMPLEX FORM OF QUADRATIC FORMULA FOR ROOTS
         REALX = -B / (2 * A)
         IMAGX = SQRT (ABS (D)) / (2 * A)
         PRINT, 'THE ROOTS ARE COMPLEX'
         PRINT 35, 'X1 = ', REALX, ' + ', IMAGX, 'I'
         PRINT 35, 'X2 = ', REALX, ' - ', IMAGX, 'I'
   35    FORMAT (T2, A5, F12.6, A3, F12.6, I1)
      END IF
      STOP
      END
```

Program Testing

It is standard practice when testing a program with an IF block to use test data that forces the program execution into each alternative of the IF block. The first test case is the quadratic equation

$$x^2 + 1 = 0$$

that caused an execution error in the previous quadratic formula program QUAD. We may as well find out as quickly as possible whether the program QUAD2 in this section solves the problem.

```
ECHO OF INPUT DATA  A:     1.000000
                    B:     0.000000
                    C:     1.000000
THE ROOTS ARE COMPLEX
X1 =      0.000000 +      1.000000I
X2 =      0.000000 -      1.000000I
```

This test case is doubly successful: not only are the two complex roots, $+i$ and $-i$ found correctly, but the program does not terminate with an execution error while trying to take the square root of a negative number.

We must also test that the new program QUAD2 will work in the cases handled properly by the previous program QUAD. Accordingly, the next test case is one of QUAD's successes.

$$4x^2 + 8x - 21 = 0$$

```
ECHO OF INPUT DATA  A:     4.000000
                    B:     8.000000
                    C:   -21.000000
THE ROOTS ARE REAL
X1 =      1.500000
X2 =     -3.500000
```

Even though it is not represented by a separate alternative in the IF block, the case when the discriminant is zero deserves to be tested. The quadratic equation

$$x^2 - \frac{2}{3}x + \frac{1}{9} = 0$$

has the double real root, $x = 1/3$, and zero discriminant. We suggest that you try the program QUAD2 on this equation using your computer. There are three possible things that might happen.

1. The discriminant D will be calculated exactly as zero and two equal real roots will be printed.

2. Because of roundoff, the discriminant D will be calculated as a very small positive number. As a result, the roots printed will be two different, but nearly equal real numbers.
3. Because of roundoff, the discriminant D will be calculated as a very small negative number. As a result, the roots printed will be two complex numbers with the same real part and very small imaginary parts of opposite signs.

We cannot predict which of these possibilities will happen on your machine, so you will just have to try it to find out.

The Complex Data Type

A more elegant way to find solutions of quadratic equations that may have complex roots is to use the Fortran **complex** data type. Variables may be declared to be type complex and arithmetic may be performed on complex quantities in much the same way that it is done with real values. The program QUAD3 illustrates the use of complex values to compute the roots of any quadratic equation, whether its roots are real or complex. It also illustrates several syntactic features of complex data types. A **complex constant** is written as two real constants separated by a comma and enclosed in parentheses. For example the complex constant $2 - 3.7i$ would be written

```
(2.0, -3.7)
```

If anything more complicated than a constant is needed as either the real or imaginary part of a complex value, the built-in conversion function CMPLX is needed. It takes two real arguments and forms a complex value. The first argument becomes the real part of the complex number, and the second becomes the coefficient of i. For example, to convert a real value X to its complex equivalent $Z = X + 0i$, you use the statement

```
Z = CMPLX (X, 0.0)
```

To recover the real and imaginary parts of a complex value Z, you use the statements

```
X = REAL (Z)
Y = AIMAG (Z)
```

Complex conjugates are computed by the built-in function CONJG which reverses the sign of the imaginary part of a complex value.

```
ZBAR = CONJG (Z)
```

The magnitude of a complex value Z is calculated by the built-in function CABS which returns a nonnegative real answer. The following two statements produce the same answer, the magnitude of Z.

```
MAGZ = CABS (Z)
MAGZ = SQRT(REAL (Z) **2 + AIMAG (Z) **2)
```

Most of the standard scientific built-in functions have COMPLEX and double precision complex versions. (See Tables 2.3 and 2.4 in Section 2.4.)

The default input and output formats for complex values consist of a pair of real values enclosed in parentheses. In the first sample execution, the first root is $0 + 1i$, which is printed as (0.000000E+00, 0.100000E+01); in the second execution the value for Z1 is $1.5 + 0i$, which is printed as (0.150000E+01, 0.000000E+00). If input is needed for a default formatted READ statement, the same form is used.

```
C       PROGRAM QUAD3
C
C       CALCULATES AND PRINTS THE ROOTS OF A QUADRATIC FORMULA
C       EVEN IF THEY ARE COMPLEX
C
C       VARIABLES:  A, B, C = COEFFICIENTS
C                   CA, CB, CC = COMPLEX COEFFICIENTS
C                   Z1, Z2 = ROOTS
C
        REAL A, B, C
        COMPLEX CA, CB, CC, Z1, Z2
C
C       READ THE COEFFICIENTS
        READ, A, B, C
        PRINT 15, 'ECHO OF INPUT DATA  A:', A
        PRINT 15, '                    B:', B
        PRINT 15, '                    C:', C
   15   FORMAT (T2, A22, F12.6)
C
C       CONVERT COEFFICIENTS TO TYPE COMPLEX
        CA = CMPLX (A, 0.0)
        CB = CMPLX (B, 0.0)
        CC = CMPLX (C, 0.0)
C
C       CALCULATE THE ROOTS
        Z1 = (-CB + CSQRT (CB ** 2 - 4 * CA * CC)) / (2 * CA)
        Z2 = (-CB - CSQRT (CB ** 2 - 4 * CA * CC)) / (2 * CA)
C
C       PRINT THE ROOTS
        PRINT, 'THE ROOTS ARE:'
        PRINT, 'Z1 =', Z1
        PRINT, 'Z2 =', Z2
        STOP
        END
```

```
 ECHO OF INPUT DATA  A:    1.000000
                     B:    0.000000
                     C:    1.000000
 THE ROOTS ARE:
 Z1 =  (  0.0000000E 00,   0.100000E 01)
 Z2 =  (  0.0000000E 00,  -0.100000E 01)
 ECHO OF INPUT DATA  A:    4.000000
                     B:    8.000000
                     C:  -21.000000
 THE ROOTS ARE:
 Z1 =  (  0.150000E 01,   0.0000000E 00)
 Z2 =  ( -0.350000E 01,   0.0000000E 00)
```

3.5 Character String Comparisons

Character string values may be compared in IF tests. This section explains how comparisons work for this type.

Section Preview

Comparison of Characters and Character Strings:

For single characters, the character with lower position in the collating sequence is considered smaller. For character strings, the relative positions of the first characters that differ determine which will be considered the smaller character string. This ordering extends ordinary alphabetic order.

Character strings to be compared or assigned need not have exactly the same length. The shorter one is assumed to be padded at the end with blanks.

The following example illustrates declaration, assignment, and comparison of character strings in Fortran.

```
C       PROGRAM EXAMPL
        CHARACTER FIRST *4, NAME *5, NAME2 *5

        FIRST = 'LISA'
        NAME = 'PAM'
        IF (NAME .LT. FIRST) THEN DO
           NAME2 = NAME
        ELSE DO
           NAME2 = 'JULIE'
        END IF
C
        PRINT, NAME2
        STOP
        END
```

Character Sets

A variable may be declared to be type character as illustrated in the following example, which declares the character variables C1, Q23, and NAME.

```
CHARACTER C1 *1, Q23 *9, NAME *20
```

Each character variable has a declared length which follows its name in the declaration. The value of such a variable may be any sequence of computer-representable characters, whose length is the same as the declared length. If fewer characters than the declared length are assigned, blanks are added on the right until the correct length is reached; if more characters are assigned, characters are automatically deleted from the right until the string is the declared length. If several character variables have the same length, an abbreviated form of length declaration is permitted. The two following declarations are equivalent.

```
CHARACTER A *10, B *10, C *10
CHARACTER *10 A, B, C
```

Most computers use either the 128-character **ASCII character set** or the 256-character **EBCDIC character set**. The acronym ASCII stands for "American Standard Code for Information Interchange", and the acronym EBCDIC stands for "Extended Binary Coded Decimal Interchange Code". Both character sets include uppercase and lowercase letters, numerals, standard punctuation signs, and all the characters on the keyboard of your computer terminal or keypunch. Tables 3.3 and 3.4 list most of the printable characters in the ASCII and EBCDIC character codes.

Character Collating Sequence

The 128 possible characters of the ASCII character set or the 256 possible characters of the EBCDIC character set have an intrinsic ordering derived from the most usual ways of storing or representing character data in a computer. This ordering is the **collating sequence** for the character set. As Tables 3.3 and 3.4 show, the collating sequences for the ASCII and EBCDIC character sets do not agree on important particulars. However, they do agree that both uppercase and lowercase letters are in alphabetic order and that the digits are in numeric order.

Table 3.3 The collating sequence for a selection of printable ASCII characters.

---

blank ! " # $ % & ' ( ) * + , - . /
0 1 2 3 4 5 6 7 8 9 : ; < = > ? @
A B C D E F G H I J K L M N O P Q R S T U V W X Y Z [ ] ^ _ `
a b c d e f g h i j k l m n o p q r s t u v w x y z { | } ~

Table 3.4 The collating sequence for a selection of printable EBCDIC characters.

---

blank] . < (+ ! & [$ *) ; ^ - / , % _ > ? : # @ ' = "
a b c d e f g h i j k l m n o p q r s t u v w x y z
A B C D E F G H I J K L M N O P Q R S T U V W X Y Z
0 1 2 3 4 5 6 7 8 9

Character Comparisons

In Fortran, the six comparison operators

.LT. .GT. .LE. .GE. .EQ. .NE.

may be used to compare character values according to the intrinsic ordering of the character set used. If the first character of one character string precedes the first character of the second character string in the collating sequence, then we say the first character string is less than the second. If the first characters are equal, the second characters are used to decide which character string is smaller. If the second characters match also, the third characters are used to decide, and so on. The character string with the smaller character in the first position where the two disagree is considered the smaller character string. When character strings of different lengths are compared, the shorter one is treated as if it were padded with enough blanks at the end to make it the same length as the longer one.

For example

```
'APPLE' .LT. 'BUG' .LT. 'CACOPHONY' .LT. 'DOLDRUMS'
'EARACHE' .LT. 'ELEPHANT' .LT. 'EMPATHY' .LT. 'EQUINE'
'PHLEGMATIC' .LT. 'PHONOGRAPH' .LT. 'PHOTOSYNTHETIC'
'DIPOLE' .LT. 'DUPLICATE' .EQ. 'DUPLICATE    ' .LT. 'DYNAMIC'
```

In the first line of comparisons, decisions are made on the basis of the first letter of the strings. In the second line, since each string has first letter "E", decisions are made on the basis of the relative collating position of the second letters. In the third set of comparisons, third or fourth letters differ.

From these examples, it is clear that the natural order of character strings corresponds exactly to ordinary alphabetic order when the character strings are words written either entirely in uppercase or entirely in lowercase letters.

String ordering does not take meaning into account. For example, although

```
'1' < '2' < '3' < '4'
```

as expected, it is also true that

```
'FOUR' < 'ONE' < 'THREE' < 'TWO'
```

and, worse yet

```
'12' < '2'
```

String ordering is also sensitive to upper and lower case. The two character strings

```
'word'
'WORD'
```

are not equal. Moreover, the ASCII and EBCDIC collating sequences do not agree on which comes first.

3.6 Testing and Debugging: Debugging an IF Block

In an IF block, one of the alternatives is executed once, and the other alternatives are not executed at all. Part of the challenge of debugging an IF block is to determine which alternative is executed and why it is chosen.

Section Preview

Debugging an IF Block: There are four major techniques used:

1. Design test cases that execute all alternatives.
2. Insert PRINT statements in each alternative to see which alternative is executed.
3. Print the values of the variables involved in the IF tests before the test is made to determine why an alternative is accepted or rejected.
4. Insert a PRINT statement immediately after the END IF statement to see what values were assigned by the IF block.

The Problem

Floppy disks for microcomputers are sold in boxes containing 10 disks. At the Mail Order Computer Supply Shop, boxes of 10 disks can be purchased for $21.50 per box plus $1.50 for shipping and handling. If you buy ten or more boxes at one time, the price drops to $16.60 per box. If you buy five or more, the price is $19.30 per box. The $1.50 shipping and handling charge applies to orders of any size.

The program we wish to write should accept as input the number of floppy disks being purchased. It should check that the number of disks is a multiple of ten, printing an error message if it isn't. Then it should calculate the price of the disks, adding the shipping and handling charge of $1.50. Tax is not charged because the orders are being shipped out of state.

The Solution

The principal feature of the program BUYDSK (buy disks) will be an IF block to determine which price applies to an order. The program is straightforward; however, this does not mean that we can't make mistakes in writing the program. The main focus of this section is to design test cases to demonstrate the correctness of the program.

```
C       PROGRAM BUYDSK
C       CALCULATES THE COST OF FLOPPY DISKS ORDERED BY MAIL
C
        INTEGER DISKS, BOXES
        REAL PRICE, PRCBOX, SHIPNG
        SHIPNG = 1.50
C
        READ, DISKS
        PRINT, 'INPUT DATA  DISKS:', DISKS
        IF (MOD (DISKS, 10) .NE. 0) THEN DO
           PRINT, 'NOT AN EXACT NUMBER OF BOXES'
           PRINT, 'ORDER CANCELLED'
        ELSE DO
           BOXES = DISKS / 10
C
C          DETERMINE PRICE PER BOX
           IF (BOXES .GE. 10) THEN DO
              PRCBOX = 16.60
           ELSE DO
           IF (BOXES .LT. 10) THEN DO
              PRCBOX = 19.30
           ELSE DO
           IF (BOXES .LT. 5) THEN DO
              PRCBOX = 21.50
           END IF
           END IF
           END IF
C
C          CALCULATE PRICE OF DISKS (INCLUDING SHIPPING AND HANDLING)
           PRICE = BOXES * PRCBOX + SHIPNG
C
           PRINT 15, 'THE DISKS COST $', PRICE
   15      FORMAT (T2, A16, F6.2)
           PRINT, 'INCLUDING SHIPPING AND HANDLING'
        END IF
        STOP
        END
```

Testing the Program

The structure of the program BUYDSK is a three-alternative IF-ELSE IF construct nested within the ELSE clause of the two-alternative IF block. To test the program, we must design test data that test each of the alternatives. The first decision the program makes is whether the number of disks requested is a whole number of boxes. We must therefore have at least one test case with a whole number of boxes and one without. Second, if the number of disks is a whole number of boxes, the program decides which of the three prices per box applies to the order. We should supply test data with whole numbers of boxes in each of the three price ranges. An order of 36 disks should test the error message for incomplete boxes. An order of 20 disks should test the highest price. An order of 110 disks should test the lowest price, and an order of 70 disks should test the middle price. Then we should test the breakpoints in the decision process, exactly 5 and 10 boxes of disks.

```
INPUT DATA  DISKS:  36
NOT AN EXACT NUMBER OF BOXES
ORDER CANCELLED

INPUT DATA  DISKS:  20
THE DISKS COST $ 40.10
INCLUDING SHIPPING AND HANDLING

INPUT DATA  DISKS:  110
THE DISKS COST $184.10
INCLUDING SHIPPING AND HANDLING

INPUT DATA  DISKS:  70
THE DISKS COST $136.60
INCLUDING SHIPPING AND HANDLING

INPUT DATA  DISKS:  50
THE DISKS COST $ 98.00
INCLUDING SHIPPING AND HANDLING

INPUT DATA  DISKS:  100
THE DISKS COST $167.50
INCLUDING SHIPPING AND HANDLING
```

The program correctly rejects 36 disks as expected. Next we take a hand calculator and calculate prices for the other test cases for verification. The price for 20 disks should be $44.50 because 2 boxes falls in the highest price category of $21.50 per box plus $1.50 for handling. All the other test cases are correct.

In order to find the bug with great certainty and efficiency, we insert debugging PRINT statements in the three-alternative IF-ELSE IF nested blocks. These debugging statements are of three kinds: PRINT statements in each alternative to let the computer tell you for certain which alternative is executed; PRINT statements preceding each IF test to tell you for certain what the computer thinks is the value of each of the variables involved in the test; and a PRINT statement at the conclusion of the nested IF blocks to tell you what value was assigned to the variable PRCBOX.

```
C     DETERMINE PRICE PER BOX
      PRINT, 'BEFORE THE FIRST IF TEST, BOXES =', BOXES
      IF (BOXES .GE. 10) THEN DO
         PRINT, 'EXECUTING ALTERNATIVE 1'
         PRCBOX = 16.60
      ELSE DO
      PRINT, 'BEFORE THE SECOND IF TEST, BOXES =', BOXES
      IF (BOXES .LT. 10) THEN DO
         PRINT, 'EXECUTING ALTERNATIVE 2'
         PRCBOX = 19.30
      ELSE DO
      PRINT, 'BEFORE THE THIRD IF TEST, BOXES =', BOXES
      IF (BOXES .LT. 5) THEN DO
         PRINT, 'EXECUTING ALTERNATIVE 3'
         PRCBOX = 21.50
```

```
      END IF
      END IF
      END IF
C
      PRINT, 'AFTER THE IF BLOCKS, PRCBOX =', PRCBOX
```

Keeping the rest of the program unchanged, we now rerun the test case that failed to get additional information about what happened during execution.

```
INPUT DATA  DISKS:  20
BEFORE THE FIRST IF TEST, BOXES =  2
BEFORE THE SECOND IF TEST, BOXES =  2
EXECUTING ALTERNATIVE 2
AFTER THE IF BLOCKS, PRCBOX =          193.0000000
THE DISKS COST $ 40.10
INCLUDING SHIPPING AND HANDLING
```

Now we know what happened during this incorrect execution. First, BOXES was set to 2, and it remains 2 just before the first IF test. The first IF test fails as expected, and the value of BOXES is still 2 when the second IF test is executed. Next we can tell that this IF test succeeded because the printout shows that the second alternative is executed. This is a surprise because two boxes of disks should fall in the highest price alternative and not in the middle one. Something is wrong. The IF test that controls the second alternative

```
      IF (BOXES .LT. 10) THEN DO
```

certainly will succeed when BOXES is two. So would the IF test that controls the third alternative

```
      IF (BOXES .LT. 5) THEN DO
```

The problem is that we intended the third alternative to be executed in case BOXES is two, and not the second. We have fallen prey to the dangers of non-exclusive conditions in an IF-ELSE IF construct. Such nested IF blocks are extremely fragile, and the order in which the IF and ELSE IF tests are made is critical.

There are two ways to fix this bug. We could make the test conditions mutually exclusive so that their order does not matter, or we could change the order of the tests to make the IF block work when BOXES is two. We prefer the first method because if the second method is used to make the IF block work in this case, changing the order of the tests might cause it to fail in cases that had worked properly in the previous order. We rewrite the IF block as follows

```
C        DETERMINE PRICE PER BOX
         IF (BOXES .GE. 10) THEN DO
            PRCBOX = 16.60
         ELSE DO
         IF (BOXES .LT. 10 .AND. BOXES .GE.5) THEN DO
            PRCBOX = 19.30
         ELSE DO
         IF (BOXES .LT. 5) THEN DO
            PRCBOX = 21.50
         END IF
         END IF
         END IF
```

The conditions are now mutually exclusive and the change was so minor that it is unlikely to upset the correct execution of the other test cases. In fact, it doesn't upset them, as we find out when we rerun *all* of the test cases against the corrected program. These executions are omitted in the book to save space.

3.7 What You Should Know

1. The IF block is built using other statements.
2. The condition in the IF test is a logical expression.
3. The only values a logical expression can have are true and false, written .TRUE. and .FALSE. in a Fortran program.
4. The THEN clause of an IF block is executed if the logical condition tested is true.
5. The ELSE clause of an IF block is executed if the tested IF condition is false.
6. The ELSE clause may be omitted if no action is required when the condition is false.
7. The THEN clauses of an IF block may be any legal sequences of Fortran statements. The same is true for the ELSE clause.
8. When one of the clauses of an IF block is itself an IF statement, the IF statements are said to be nested.
9. A nested sequence of IF tests with mutually exclusive conditions can handle a decision with more than two alternatives.
10. The logical operators .AND., .OR., and .NOT. may be used to build more complex logical expressions.
11. The six arithmetic comparison operators may be used to construct logical conditions. They are .GT., .LT., .GE., .LE., .EQ., and .NE.
12. The same six comparison operators may be used to compare character strings.
13. String ordering is an extension of alphabetic ordering. One character string is less than a second character string if it precedes the second character string in alphabetic order.
14. Character strings may be compared even if they have different lengths; the shorter one is considered to be padded at the end with blanks.
15. The two most used character sets are the ASCII (American Standard Code for Information Interchange) character set, and the EBCDIC (Extended Binary Coded Decimal Interchange Code) character set.
16. A flowchart is a way of depicting the sequence in which instructions are executed. It is particularly useful for analyzing the effect of IF statements and nested IF statements.
17. When a program is tested, there should be at least one set of test data to test each alternative in the program.
18. It is good programming practice to warn the user when a situation occurs that the program is not designed to handle.
19. The value of type CHARACTER may be any sequence of computer-representable characters.
20. Character comparisons are based on the collating sequence for the character set. Characters with lower positions are considered less than characters with higher positions.

3.8 Self-Test Questions

Section 3.1

1. Which of the following WATFIV-S IF blocks are syntactically incorrect? Which are syntactically correct, but probably meaningless?

```
IF (HOUR .GT. 12) THEN DO
   PRINT, 'IT IS LATE.'

IF (X = Y) THEN DO
   PRINT, X
   Z = X
ELSE DO
   Z = 5
END IF

IF (5 .EQ. 5) THEN DO
   X = 6
END IF

IF (A .GT. 0) THEN DO
   B = A
ELSE DO
   B = -A
END IF

IF (A .LT. 0) THEN DO A = -A

IF (YOU .EQ. ME) THEN DO
   WE = 'YES'
END IF

IF (X + 1 = Y - 1) THEN DO
   BEGIN
   Z = X
   PRINT, Y - 1
   END
```

2. Correct the IF blocks in Question 1 that are either syntactically incorrect or probably meaningless.

Section 3.2

1. Find and correct all syntax errors in the following IF blocks.

```
IF (N .EQ. 1) THEN DO
   X = 1
ELSE IF (N .LE. 4) THEN DO
   X = 2
   Y = 1
ELSE DO
   Y = 2
END

IF (N .GE. N) THEN DO
END IF
```

2. Write an IF block that prints the word VOWEL if the value of the variable LETTER is a vowel (i.e., A, E, I, O, or U) and the word CONSONANT if

the value of LETTER is any other letter of the alphabet. Only uppercase letters can appear as values of LETTER.

Section 3.3

1. To test your understanding of the syntax of IF blocks, hand simulate the programs EXMPL1 to EXMPL4 using the values 45, 75, and 95 as input data (12 simulations in all). Check your answers with a computer, if possible, as well as against the answers in the book. *Caution:* These simulations are tricky, but each program is syntactically correct. No indentation has been used in order not to give any hints about the structure of the IF blocks.

```
C       PROGRAM EXMPL1
        INTEGER X
        READ, X
        IF (X .GT. 50) THEN DO
        IF (X .GT. 90) THEN DO
        PRINT, X, ' IS VERY HIGH.'
        ELSE DO
        PRINT, X, ' IS HIGH.'
        END IF
        END IF
        STOP
        END
C       PROGRAM EXMPL2
        INTEGER X
        READ, X
        IF (X .GT. 50) THEN DO
        IF (X .GT. 90) THEN DO
        PRINT, X, ' IS VERY HIGH.'
        ELSE DO
        END IF
        PRINT, X, ' IS HIGH.'
        END IF
        END
C       PROGRAM EXMPL3
        INTEGER X
        READ, X
        IF (X .GT. 50) THEN DO
        IF (X .GT. 90) THEN DO
        PRINT, X, ' IS VERY HIGH.'
        END IF
        ELSE DO
        PRINT, X, ' IS HIGH.'
        END IF
        STOP
        END
C       PROGRAM EXMPL4
        INTEGER X
        READ, X
        IF (X .GT. 50) THEN DO
        END IF
```

```
IF (X .GT. 90) THEN DO
PRINT, X, ' IS VERY HIGH.'
ELSE DO
PRINT, X, ' IS HIGH.'
END IF
STOP
END
```

Section 3.5

1. Which of the following character declaration and assignment statements are correct? Correct the incorrect ones.

```
CHARACTER SIGNAL *3, BEE *1
SIGNAL = 'STOP'
BEE = 'B'

CHARACTER WORD *4 PUNCT *1
WORD = 'DONE'
PUNCT = ''''

CHARACTER *5, WING, DING
WING = 'ONE'
DING = 'TWO'
```

2. Which of the following variable declarations are correct?

```
CHAR FIRSTNAME *4, LAST *9
CHAR HUM *4, DRUM *3
```

3. Which of the following assignment statements are correct? Use the variable declaration

```
CHARACTER SEE *1, WORD *4, YES *2

SEE = 'C'
WORD := 'CERTAINLY'
'YES' = 'NO'
```

4. Which of the following comparisons are valid and, if valid, which are true?

```
IF ('ONE' .LT. 'TWO') THEN DO
IF ('TWO' .LT. 'THREE') THEN DO
IF ('FIVE' .LT. 6) THEN DO
IF ('FIVE' .LT. '6') THEN DO
IF ('a' .LT. 'A') THEN DO
IF ('ALBATROSS' .LT. 'ALBUMEN ') THEN DO
```

5. Compare the two character strings 'ABC' and '123' using the ASCII and the EBCDIC collating sequences given in Tables 3.3 and 3.4. Which string comes first (i.e., collates low) in ASCII? Which in EBCDIC?

3.9 Programming Exercises

1. **Purpose:** To write a simple program with two alternatives based on values in the input data.

   The problem: The Old Fashioned Department Store offers its cash customers a 7 percent discount but makes charge customers pay full price. The problem is to automatically compute the appropriate price based on the customer's mode of payment. Although the natural mode of execution in this application is interactive, you may write the program for batch input if interactive input is not available.

Input data: The input data will consist of two parts: first the letter "C" for cash or "P" for charge (plastic), and second the amount of the purchase. A sample input line might be the following.

```
'C' 50.00
```

Sample output: The printed output should echo the input data and print the customer price. For the input data above the output might be

```
CASH PURCHASE OF $50.00
CUSTOMER PRICE IS $46.50
```

2. **Purpose:** To program a slightly more difficult set of alternatives, including one subcase within an alternative.

   The problem: A toll bridge charges $1.50 for passenger cars, $2.00 for busses, $3.00 for trucks under 10,000 pounds, and $5.00 for trucks over 10,000 pounds. The problem is to write a program to compute the toll. Use interactive input if it is available.

   Input data: First the letter C, B, or T for car, bus, and truck respectively. If the class is T (truck) then prompt the user for another character which is either "<" (meaning less than 10,000 pounds) or ">" (meaning greater than 10,000 pounds)

   Sample executions:

```
  ENTER VEHICLE CLASS (C, B, OR T)
T
  ENTER < OR > TO INDICATE WEIGHT CLASS
<
  THE TOLL IS $3.00

  ENTER VEHICLE CLASS (C, B, OR T)
C
  THE TOLL IS $1.50
```

3. **Purpose:** To practice comparison of character strings and formatted input of alphabetic information.

   The problem: Many computer systems require the user to enter a password when signing on the system to prevent unauthorized persons from using the system. The program to be written for this exercise should read a 3-character password from input and test it against the correct 3-character password "CHG" assigned in the program.

   Input data: A 3-character password, without enclosing apostrophes.

   Sample executions:

```
WELCOME TO THE SUPER SIMULATED COMPUTER SYSTEM
PLEASE TYPE YOUR SECRET PASSWORD
WSB
I AM SORRY. THAT IS NOT THE CORRECT PASSWORD.
GOODBYE.

WELCOME TO THE SUPER SIMULATED COMPUTER SYSTEM
PLEASE TYPE YOUR SECRET PASSWORD
CHG
HELLO CHG. WHAT SHALL WE DO TODAY?
```

4. **Purpose:** To get a lot of practice typing IF tests with long, compound conditions.

The problem: For nonresident married persons earning income in New York State who elect to file a joint federal income tax return but separate New York State returns, Table 3.6 shows the progressive tax rate schedule on taxable income. The problem is to write a program to calculate the tax owed on a given taxable income according to this schedule.

Table 3.5 New York State Tax Rate Schedule for Certain Persons

IF TAXABLE INCOME IS

OVER	BUT NOT OVER	THEN INCOME TAX IS		
$0	$1,000		2% of taxable income	
$1,000	$3,000	$20 plus	3% of excess over	$1,000
$3,000	$5,000	$80 plus	4% of excess over	$3,000
$5,000	$7,000	$160 plus	5% of excess over	$5,000
$7,000	$9,000	$260 plus	6% of excess over	$7,000
$9,000	$11,000	$380 plus	7% of excess over	$9,000
$11,000	$13,000	$520 plus	8% of excess over	$11,000
$13,000	$15,000	$680 plus	9% of excess over	$13,000
$15,000	$17,000	$860 plus	10% of excess over	$15,000
$17,000	$19,000	$1,060 plus	11% of excess over	$17,000
$19,000	$21,000	$1,280 plus	12% of excess over	$19,000
$21,000	$23,000	$1,520 plus	13% of excess over	$21,000
$23,000	$25,000	$1,780 plus	14% of excess over	$23,000
$25,000		$2,060 plus	15% of excess over	$25,000

Input data: One number, the taxable income.

Sample execution:

```
INPUT DATA  TAXINC:  16000
THE TAX IS $960.00
```

5. **Purpose:** To program a simpler 3-alternative situation.

   The problem: The Enlightened Corporation is pleased when its employees enroll in college classes. It offers them an 80 percent rebate on the first $500 of tuition, a 60 percent rebate on the second $400, and a 40 percent rebate on the next $300. The problem is to compute the amount of the rebate.

   Input data: One number, the amount of tuition paid by the employee.

   Sample execution:

```
INPUT DATA  TUITON:  600
THE EMPLOYEE'S REBATE IS $  460
```

6. **Purpose:** To program nested IF blocks.

   The problem: The price of an issue of a popular computing magazine is given in the following table:

	Subscription	Newsstand
U. S.	$1.75	$3.50
Canada	$1.95	$3.95

   The problem is to write a program to print the correct price based on input data telling whether it is bought by subscription (S) or at a newsstand (N), and the country in whose funds the price is paid.

   Input data: Two enquoted character strings, subscription code ('S' or 'N') and country ('US' or 'CANADA'). For example,

```
'S' 'CANADA'
```

   Sample output:

```
INPUT DATA  CODE:  S
INPUT DATA  CNTRY:  CANADA
THE PRICE IS $  1.95
```

7. **Purpose:** To understand the complex data type.

   The problem: As an exercise in the use of built-in functions and other features of complex data type, write a program to compute the quantity $e^{i}\pi$.

   Background information: The constant π can be computed by the formula $\pi = 4 * \text{ATAN}(1.0)$ since $\tan(\pi/4) = 1$. The complex constant i can be written (0, 1) The built-in function EXP (X) is used for raising the mathematical constant e to a power.

   Input data: None.

   Sample output:

```
THE VALUE OF E TO THE POWER I*PI IS ___
```

   We are not going to give away the answer to this one.

4 LOOP STRUCTURES

The value of a variable may change not only from one run to the next as a result of different values of the input data, but also during the course of a single run. The reassignment of new values to a variable during execution is a crucial feature of many programs, particularly of those containing a **loop**, which is a sequence of instruction to be executed repeatedly.

All of the programs so far suffer from the defect that each instruction is executed exactly once. At the enormous speed at which computers execute instructions, it would be difficult to keep a computer busy for very long using this type of program. By the simple expedient of having the computer execute some instructions more than once, perhaps a large number of times, it is possible to produce a computer program that takes longer to execute than to write. More important, a loop increases the difficulty of writing a program very little, while it greatly increases the amount of useful data processing and calculation done by the program.

There are two loop structures in WATFIV-S: the **DO loop**, or **DO block**, which is introduced in Section 4.1, and the **WHILE loop** introduced in Section 4.2. Since some variables repeatedly have their values changed during execution of a loop, this chapter provides an opportunity to take a closer look at the underlying nature of a variable in a computer program.

The remainder of the chapter treats the use of a loop to calculate a sum and average, and the special problems involved in debugging a program that contains a loop.

4.1 DO Blocks

Quite frequently, the successive values taken by a variable follow a simple pattern, like 1, 2, 3, 4, 5, 6, 7, 8, 9, 10, or 3, 5, 7, 9. Because these sequences occur so often in programming, there is a simple means of assigning successive values to a variable in Fortran, the DO statement.

Section Preview

DO Block:

General Form:

```
        DO label variable = expression, expression, expression
           statement
              .
              .
              .
           statement
label   CONTINUE
```

Note: The only kinds of expressions permitted in a DO statement are integer variables or constants.

Examples:

```
      DO 18 N = 1, 20
         PRINT, N
   18 CONTINUE
      DO 28 VALUE = 100, ULIMIT, 4
         SUM = SUM + VALUE
   28 CONTINUE
```

Step Size:

In Fortran, successive values of a DO variable may increase by any positive integer amount. The step size is one if none is given in the DO statement.

Counting Forward

The program TENLIN tells a computer to print the numbers from 1 to 10, one per line. It uses a DO block to print the numbers.

```
C     PROGRAM TENLIN
C     PRINT THE NUMBERS FROM 1 TO 10
C
      INTEGER NUMBER
      DO 18 NUMBER = 1, 10
         PRINT, NUMBER
   18 CONTINUE
      STOP
      END
```

```
         1
         2
         3
         4
         5
         6
         7
         8
         9
        10
```

The three statements beginning with the DO statement are called a **DO block**. A DO block begins with a DO statement and ends with a CONTINUE statement having the label given in the DO statement. The statements between these two statements form the **body** of the DO loop. They are executed repeatedly.

Style Note: Actually, it is the label and not the CONTINUE statement that signals the bottom of a DO block. However, some restrictions apply and modern programming practice is to end all DO blocks with CONTINUE statements.

In the program TENLIN, the body of the DO loop consists of a single PRINT statement. The first time the PRINT statement is executed, the **DO variable** NUMBER has the value of 1, and this number is printed as the the first output line. Then the DO variable NUMBER takes on the value 2, which is printed on the next line. Then the DO variable takes on the values 3, 4, 5, 6, 7, 8, 9, and 10 for successive repetitions of the PRINT statement. At this point, the possible values for the DO variable NUMBER specified in the DO statement are exhausted and the program execution terminates.

The DO Statement

The values of a DO variable may either increase by one, or increase by any fixed integer amount, as in later examples. The general forms of a DO statement are

DO *label variable* = *expression*, *expression*, *expression*
DO *label variable* = *expression*, *expression*

The three expressions specifying the starting value, the stopping value, and the step size between successive values of the DO variable may be integer constants or integer variables. The step size must be positive. The DO statement in the program TENLIN used constants 1 and 10 for the starting and stopping values. When the step size expression is omitted, as it is in the program TENLIN, a step size of one is used.

Labels

The number 18 in front of the CONTINUE statement is called a **label**. We encountered labels previously on FORMAT statements in Section 2.3. A label consists of one to five digits and is written in columns one to five. As with other parts of Fortran statements, blanks in a label are ignored, but we do not recommend using blanks in a label because they make it difficult to read. We suggest that all labels be right justified so that the last digit of the label is in column 5. Leading zeros in labels also are ignored, with the result that 18, 018, and 00018 are all the same label.

A label serves to uniquely identify the statement it labels. Ordinarily, labels are used only on those statements that must be referenced or referred to by another statement in the program. FORMAT statements carry labels so that a PRINT statement can specify which FORMAT statement is to be used. CONTINUE statements that end DO blocks carry labels so that the DO statement that heads the block can specify where the block ends. In this book, all DO blocks end with a CONTINUE statement that has a label ending with the digit 8. There is no requirement that the label end with 8, but it is good practice to be consistent in assigning these labels. There is also no requirement that a DO block end with a CONTINUE statement, but this is considered good programming practice and it avoids the difficulty of learning which kinds of statements must not end a DO block.

A Table of Squares and Square Roots

A structurally minor modification of the program TENLIN can produce a program SQUARS to print a table of squares and square roots of numbers from 1 to 10.

```
C       PROGRAM SQUARS
C       PRINTS A TABLE OF SQUARES AND SQUARE ROOTS
C
        INTEGER NUMBER
C
        PRINT 15, 'NUMBER', 'SQUARE', 'SQUARE ROOT'
   15   FORMAT (2A10, A15)
C
        DO 28 NUMBER = 1, 10
           PRINT 25, NUMBER, NUMBER ** 2, SQRT (FLOAT (NUMBER))
   25      FORMAT (2I10, F15.3)
   28   CONTINUE
        STOP
        END
```

```
    NUMBER    SQUARE    SQUARE ROOT
         1         1          1.000
         2         4          1.414
         3         9          1.732
         4        16          2.000
         5        25          2.236
         6        36          2.449
         7        49          2.646
         8        64          2.828
         9        81          3.000
        10       100          3.162
```

Eleven lines of output are printed by the program SQUARS. The first PRINT statement that prints the heading of the columns is executed only once, because it is not within the DO block. Indenting the body of a DO block makes it easier to see which instructions are to be repeated. After the headings are printed, the PRINT statement within the DO block prints a number, its square, and its square root, for each value of the variable NUMBER from 1 to 10. Using a format for all output expressions forces proper placement on the print line, so the headings are positioned directly above the columns of numbers they identify. Notice also that the built-in function SQRT cannot accept a type integer argument, so the type conversion function FLOAT is applied first.

Counting By Twos

In Fortran, the differences between successive values of a DO variable need not be 1, as they have been in the previous examples. However, these differences must be constant, as is illustrated by the program TWOS.

```
C       PROGRAM TWOS
C       COUNTS BY TWOS
C
        INTEGER NUMBER
C
```

```
      DO 18 NUMBER = 2, 10, 2
         PRINT, NUMBER
   18 CONTINUE
      STOP
      END
```

```
        2
        4
        6
        8
       10
```

The new feature of this program is the third number following the equal sign in the DO statement, indicating the **step size** or **increment** for the DO variable. Since the step size is 2 in this example, each time the DO block is repeated, the next value assigned to the DO variable NUMBER is 2 more than the previous value. Thus the successive values of the DO variable NUMBER are 2, 4, 6, 8, and 10.

In WATFIV, it is not possible to have a DO variable count backwards. However, a simple trick allows an auxiliary variable calculated from the iteration count (DO variable) to count backward. If the DO variable ITER (short for iteration) takes on successive values 1, 2, 3, ..., 99, then the variable

```
      N = 100 - ITER
```

takes on successive values 99, 98, 97, ..., 1. Thus it is possible to print the complete words to the popular camp song "Ninety-Nine Bottles of Beer on the Wall" with a WATFIV program. The program BEER, which tells the computer to print the verses, is given below, in pseudocode form in Figure 4.1 and then in WATFIV using the auxiliary DO variable trick. In the program, a PRINT statement is used to print a blank line between verses.

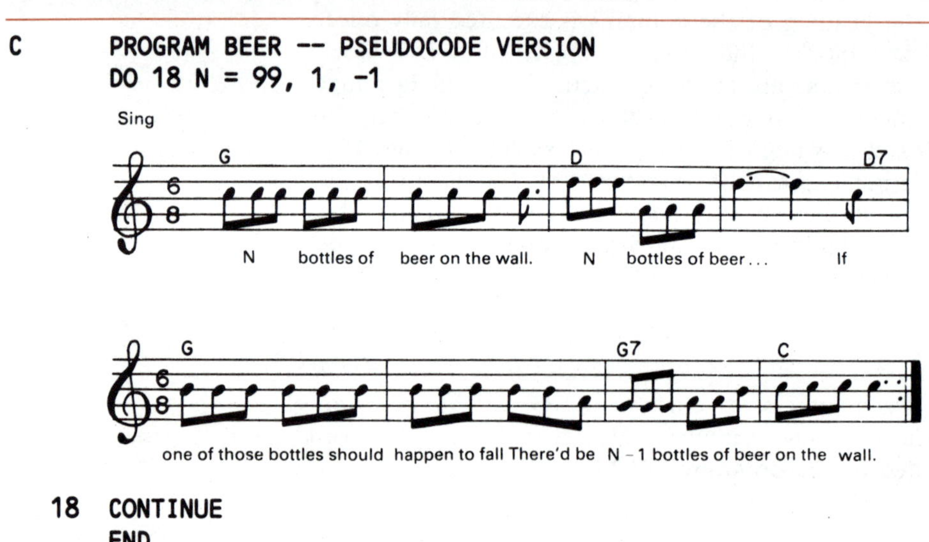

Figure 4.1 A musical DO block for a 5-mile hike.

```
C     PROGRAM BEER
C     PRINTS THE WORDS OF A CAMP SONG
C
```

```
      INTEGER N, ITER
C
      DO 18 ITER = 1, 99
         N = 100 - ITER
         PRINT, ' '
         PRINT, N, 'BOTTLES OF BEER ON THE WALL.'
         PRINT, N, 'BOTTLES OF BEER.'
         PRINT, 'IF ONE OF THOSE BOTTLES SHOULD HAPPEN TO FALL,'
         PRINT, 'THERE''D BE', N - 1, 'BOTTLES OF BEER ON THE WALL.'
   18 CONTINUE
      STOP
      END
```

```
          99 BOTTLES OF BEER ON THE WALL.
          99 BOTTLES OF BEER.
IF ONE OF THOSE BOTTLES SHOULD HAPPEN TO FALL,
THERE'D BE          98 BOTTLES OF BEER ON THE WALL.

          98 BOTTLES OF BEER ON THE WALL.
          98 BOTTLES OF BEER.
IF ONE OF THOSE BOTTLES SHOULD HAPPEN TO FALL,
THERE'D BE          97 BOTTLES OF BEER ON THE WALL.

          97 BOTTLES OF BEER ON THE WALL.
          97 BOTTLES OF BEER.
IF ONE OF THOSE BOTTLES SHOULD HAPPEN TO FALL,
THERE'D BE          96 BOTTLES OF BEER ON THE WALL.
      .
      .
      .
           1 BOTTLES OF BEER ON THE WALL.
           1 BOTTLES OF BEER.
IF ONE OF THOSE BOTTLES SHOULD HAPPEN TO FALL,
THERE'D BE           0 BOTTLES OF BEER ON THE WALL.
```

A short name N is chosen for the auxiliary variable to make it easier to sing the program listing. The execution printout shown is abbreviated after three full verses, with the last verse also given to show how the loop ends.

Note that the last line of each verse of the song contains an apostrophe. Because apostrophes are used to delimit a character string within a Fortran program, the apostrophe in "THERE'D" would normally be taken as the end of the character string. To avoid this difficulty two consecutive apostrophes in a program listing stand for a single apostrophe in a character string.

Variable Limits for a DO Block

For users who do not need or want all the lyrics of the popular camp song printed, the modified program ANYBER allows a choice of which verses to print. The starting value and the stopping value need not be constants, but may also be given as the values of variables. Of course, if a variable is used in specifying the starting value or stopping value for a DO variable, it must be assigned a value before the DO statement is reached. In the program ANYBER, the variable NRITER (number of iterations) has its value calculated from the input values FIRST and LAST before it is used as the upper limit in the DO block.

```
C       PROGRAM ANYBER
C       PRINTS SELECTED VERSES OF A CAMP SONG
C
        INTEGER FIRST, LAST, N, ITER, NRITER
C
        READ, FIRST, LAST
        PRINT, 'INPUT DATA  FIRST:', FIRST
        PRINT, '            LAST:', LAST
C
        NRITER = FIRST - LAST + 1
        DO 18 ITER = 1, NRITER
           N = FIRST + 1 - ITER
           PRINT, ' '
           PRINT, N, 'BOTTLES OF BEER ON THE WALL.'
           PRINT, N, 'BOTTLES OF BEER.'
           PRINT, 'IF ONE OF THOSE BOTTLES SHOULD HAPPEN TO FALL,'
           PRINT, 'THERE''D BE', N - 1, 'BOTTLES OF BEER ON THE WALL.'
   18   CONTINUE
        STOP
        END
```

```
INPUT DATA  FIRST:           83
            LAST:           81

      83 BOTTLES OF BEER ON THE WALL.
         .
         .
         .
THERE'D BE           80 BOTTLES OF BEER ON THE WALL.
```

DO Blocks That Are Executed No Times

Sometimes, you might want the body of a DO block to execute no times at all. For instance, the loop

```
        DO 18 N = 1, MAX
           PRINT, N
   18   CONTINUE
```

could be used to print all the numbers from one to MAX. When MAX is 0, this loop reduces to

```
        DO 18 N = 1, 0
           PRINT, N
   18   CONTINUE
```

In WATFIV, this DO block still executes once, as does the DO block

```
        DO 18 N = 1, 1
           PRINT, N
   18   CONTINUE
```

because the test for completion of a DO block is performed at the bottom of the DO block body. Thus a WATFIV DO block always executes at least once, no matter what value the starting and stopping expressions have. If you wish to allow for the possibility of zero iterations, you must nest the DO block in an IF block. For example, the statements

```
      IF (MAX .GT. 0) THEN DO
         DO 18 N = 1, MAX
            PRINT, N
18       CONTINUE
      END IF
```

will print the numbers from 1 to MAX if MAX is greater than zero, and will print nothing if MAX is less than or equal to zero.

Flowchart for a DO Block

The sequence of steps a computer performs when it executes a DO block are summarized in the flowchart in Figure 4.2. First, the DO variable is initialized, then the body of the DO loop is executed, after which the DO variable is incremented and tested. If the value of the DO variable is less than or equal to the stopping value, the body of the loop is repeated; if not, execution of the DO block is complete and control passes (normally) to the next statement after the DO block. Since the test for completion follows each iteration, even the first iteration, it is clear that in a DO block where the starting value for the DO variable already exceeds the stopping value, the body of the loop is executed once.

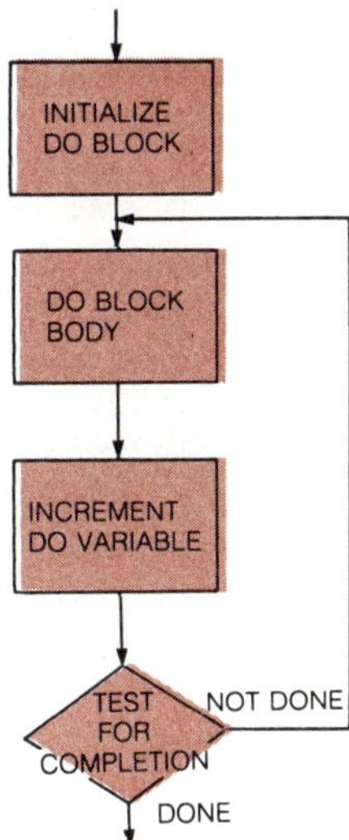

Figure 4.2 Flowchart for a DO Block.

DO Blocks Whose Upper Limit is not Attained Exactly

The DO statement

```
      DO 18 N = START, FINISH, STEP
```

considered as pseudocode, seems to imply that after a sufficient number of steps, the DO variable N will finally take on the value FINISH for the last iteration of the loop. However, Fortran does not require this. In some programs, the programmer never intends the upper limit to be reached exactly. Although it may be easy to describe a criterion to distinguish between the last desired value of a DO variable and the first excluded value, it may be more difficult to write a formula to express the last desired value exactly. For example, if we want to print all multiples of 13 that are less than or equal to 500 using a DO block, it might not be obvious what the last desired multiple of 13 is. However, as shown in the program MULT13, it is unnecessary to know the final value in advance.

```
C       PROGRAM MULT13
C       PRINTS ALL MULTIPLES OF 13 THAT ARE <= 500
C
        INTEGER N
C
        DO 18 N = 13, 500, 13
           PRINT, N
   18   CONTINUE
        STOP
        END
```

```
          13
          26
          39
           .
           .
           .
         481
         494
```

The sample execution printout from the program MULT13 shows that the value of the DO variable N is 13 for the first iteration of the DO block. Then it increases by 13 for each subsequent iteration. On the final iteration, the value of N is 494. There is no iteration with N = 494 + 13 = 507 because this value of the DO variable exceeds the stopping value 500.

> *Style Note:* Originally, the value of a DO variable was only defined within the DO block. On normal exit, it was *undefined* and *inaccessible*. The WATFOR, WATFIV series of compilers specified that the value of the DO variable on normal exit is the first value in the sequence not used in an iteration of the body of the loop, a practice later adopted by the 1977 Fortran standards.
>
> Because as pseudocode, the DO statement seems to imply that the final value of the DO variable is the value of the stopping expression, and because of the earlier differing standards, we recommend never using the value of a DO variable after normal exit from a DO block.

Nesting an IF Block in a DO Block

The **body** of a DO block may contain most Fortran statements; however, if the block contains an IF statement, the entire IF block must be contained within the DO block. The program MULT5 uses an IF block **nested** within a DO block to print only those multiples of 5 less than or equal to 45 that are not also multiples of 3. Each time a multiple of 3 is reached (recognized because MOD (N, 3) is zero), the value of N is not printed.

```
C       PROGRAM MULT5
C       PRINTS ALL MULTIPLES OF 5
C       THAT ARE <= 45 AND NOT MULTIPLES OF 3
C
        INTEGER N
```

```
C
      DO 18 N = 5, 45, 5
         IF (MOD (N, 3) .NE. 0) THEN DO
            PRINT, N
         END IF
   18 CONTINUE
      STOP
      END
```

```
         5
        10
        20
        25
        35
        40
```

4.2 WHILE Blocks

Although a DO block is very convenient when it applies, by itself it is often too specialized for many applications. The number of times a DO block is to execute must be known, if not when the program is written, at least before the DO block is entered during program execution. This restriction can be circumvented by using a WHILE block or a DO block with **exit**. They can be used when termination of a loop depends on testing a calculated value or on recognizing a signal value in the input data.

Section Preview

WHILE Block:

General Form:

WHILE (*condition*) DO
statements
END WHILE

Example:

```
READ, NUMBER
WHILE (NUMBER .NE. SIGNAL) DO
   PRINT, NUMBER
   READ, NUMBER
END WHILE
```

A WHILE Loop With Calculated Exit Condition

Suppose we wish to write a program to find the first (smallest) power of 2 that exceeds 1000. Successive powers of 2 may be calculated by starting with a small power of 2, say $2^0 = 1$, and repeatedly doubling that number. Doubling is repeated until a power of 2 is found that exceeds 1000. That power of 2 is printed and the program BIGPWR (big power) ends.

This sequence of values 1, 2, 4, 8, 16, 32, ..., does not have a constant difference between successive values, so a DO loop is not immediately applicable to generate these values. Instead, we use a more general and more flexible WHILE loop block.

In a WHILE loop, any logical condition can be used in the repetition-versus-exit test that controls the loop's execution. Moreover, the initialization and incrementing of a variable are not built into the loop control structure, so they may be replaced by any kind of initialization and periodic change of values whatsoever.

The key step that makes a WHILE loop work well in this application is the statement

```
POWER = POWER * 2
```

to calculate successive values of the critical variable POWER. The initialization

```
POWER = 1
```

and the WHILE test

```
WHILE (POWER .LE. 1000) DO
```

closely mirror the computational strategy outlined above. Note that the WHILE test lists the condition for **continuing** the loop. Where this condition fails, that is, when POWER is greater than 1000, the WHILE loop block is exited.

```
C       PROGRAM BIGPWR
C       FINDS FIRST POWER OF 2 > 1000
        INTEGER POWER
C
C       INITIALIZE POWER AS 2 ** 0 = 1
        POWER = 1
C
        WHILE (POWER .LE. 1000) DO
C          DOUBLE POWER TO GET NEXT POWER OF 2
           POWER = POWER * 2
        END WHILE
C
        PRINT, POWER, 'IS THE FIRST POWER OF 2 THAT EXCEEDS 1000.'
        STOP
        END
```

```
 1024 IS THE FIRST POWER OF 2 THAT EXCEEDS 1000.
```

WHILE Loops Terminated By Special Data

Many kinds of input data ordinarily come in groups whose exact size or length cannot be predicted in advance at the time the program is written. Although the amount of data actually present can be counted by the user at the time the input file is prepared, people are not particularly good at counting more than a few items. The computer, on the other hand, is very good at repetitive tasks like counting.

The next program shows how to make a computer count the number of lines in the input data. In this example, the input data consists of a sequence of integer test scores, one score per line, with an integer -1 on the last line. It is presumed that -1 is not a valid score on this test. The programs will count the number of scores. The -1 on the last line is not to be considered a score and so is not counted. Also the scores are echoed to the output, which makes good sense if the program is not run interactively. If execution is interactive, the echo of input data should be replaced with a prompt requesting the user to type a score.

The First WHILE Block Solution

The basic strategy of the solution is to continue reading data **until** an end-of-data signal is encountered. The WHILE construct phrases the exit test backwards: Continue reading data **while** the last item read was not an end-of-data signal. The following pseudocode version describes the algorithm using the WHILE construct.

```
Set count to 0
Read a number
Echo the number to the printer
WHILE the number isn't an end-of-data signal DO
   Increase the count by 1
   Read another number
   Echo it to the printer
Print the final count
```

The WATFIV-S version of the program SCORE1 is practically a line-by-line translation of the pseudocode. The sample input data for the execution include enough scores to give the program a little exercise, followed by the signal value −1.

```
C       PROGRAM SCORE1
C       COUNT THE NUMBER OF SCORES IN THE INPUT FILE
C       DO NOT COUNT THE SIGNAL AT THE END OF THE INPUT
C
        INTEGER NUMBER, COUNT, SIGNAL
C
        SIGNAL = -1
        COUNT = 0
        READ, NUMBER
        PRINT, 'INPUT DATA  NUMBER:', NUMBER
C
        WHILE (NUMBER .NE. SIGNAL) DO
C       EXIT WHEN A SIGNAL VALUE IS READ
           COUNT = COUNT + 1
           READ, NUMBER
           PRINT, 'INPUT DATA  NUMBER:', NUMBER
        END WHILE
C
        PRINT, ' '
        PRINT, 'THERE ARE', COUNT, 'SCORES.'
        STOP
        END
```

```
INPUT DATA  NUMBER:          62
INPUT DATA  NUMBER:          45
INPUT DATA  NUMBER:          89
INPUT DATA  NUMBER:          50
INPUT DATA  NUMBER:           4
INPUT DATA  NUMBER:          99
INPUT DATA  NUMBER:          -1

THERE ARE  6  SCORES.
```

Critique of the First WHILE Block Solution

The first comment that needs to be made about the program SCORE1 is that it works! It even works when there are no scores before the signal value −1. Try it, or use hand simulation. It prints that there are 0 scores when indeed there are none except the signal.

The second comment is that the program uses no statement labels. A WHILE block begins with a WHILE statement and ends with its matching END WHILE statement. This kind of self-evident structure adds clarity to the program listing.

In fairness to the DO block, it should be mentioned that although it uses statement labels, with the modern convention of ending all DO blocks with CONTINUE statements, it no longer uses statement labels in an essential way. If we think of the CONTINUE statement that ends a DO block as an END DO statement, the statement labels are superfluous. In fact, some Fortran preprocessors accept DO blocks without statement labels and insert the labels required by current Fortran syntax in the obvious way.

What is not entirely desirable about the program SCORE1 is that the statements to read and echo a number must appear in two different places in the program. They must appear once above the WHILE statement to read the first input number because the WHILE test makes no sense until the variable NUMBER has a value. They must appear a second time at the bottom of the WHILE loop body so that subsequent WHILE tests test subsequent data values.

The practical problems of two separate but identical sections of code are twofold. First, there is the effort involved in ensuring that the two sections of code are indeed identical. While this is a mere nuisance when the program is first written, it is a major source of errors when such a program is modified at a later date, long after it has been forgotten that these two sections of code must be identical, or even that these steps are performed in two different places. By comparison, the second problem is minor, a tendency to skimp on user-friendly niceties such as echoes of input data in the duplicated sections because they must be written twice.

In spite of these faults, many programmers prefer this style of WHILE loop. So that you can make up your own mind, we present two alternative ways of solving the same problem.

Flags

A **flag**, also called a **semaphore** or **switch**, is a logical variable set at one time in a program execution and used to control a decision at a later time in the execution. In the second solution of the counting problem, the flag MORDAT (more data) is used to control repetition of a WHILE loop. The variable MORDAT is initialized to true, and remains until the end-of-data signal is read. It is then set to false. The program SCORE2 implements this strategy.

```
C       PROGRAM SCORE2
C       COUNT THE NUMBER OF SCORES IN THE INPUT FILE
C       DO NOT COUNT THE SIGNAL AT THE END OF THE INPUT
C
        INTEGER NUMBER, COUNT, SIGNAL
        LOGICAL MORDAT
C
        SIGNAL = -1
        COUNT = 0
        MORDAT = .TRUE.
```

```
      WHILE (MORDAT) DO
C     EXIT WHEN A SIGNAL VALUE IS READ
         READ, NUMBER
         PRINT, 'INPUT DATA  NUMBER:', NUMBER
         IF (NUMBER .EQ. SIGNAL) THEN DO
            MORDAT = .FALSE.
         ELSE
            COUNT = COUNT + 1
         END IF
      END WHILE
C
      PRINT, ' '
      PRINT, 'THERE ARE', COUNT, 'SCORES.'
      STOP
      END
INPUT DATA  NUMBER:          62
INPUT DATA  NUMBER:          45
INPUT DATA  NUMBER:          89
INPUT DATA  NUMBER:          50
INPUT DATA  NUMBER:           4
INPUT DATA  NUMBER:          99
INPUT DATA  NUMBER:          -1

THERE ARE  6  SCORES.
```

Critique of the Second WHILE Block Solution

Again, our first comment is that the program SCORE2 works, even if there are no numbers preceding the signal value. The second comment is that the major flaw of the first method, the duplicated code, has been eliminated. The statements to read and echo the input data appear only once, in the middle of the WHILE loop where they handle all input data equally, the first input value as well as all subsequent values.

The price we pay for this improvement is an IF block nested within the WHILE block. It is in the nature of the problem that the basic loop in any solution must be executed "*n* and a half" times. By this we mean that if there are *n* valid input scores plus a termination signal, the "half" of the loop that does the counting must execute *n* times, while the "half" of the loop that includes the READ statement must execute $n + 1$ times, *n* times for the valid scores and one extra time to read the signal value.

The IF block serves two functions. First, it prevents execution of the counting "half" of the WHILE loop when a signal value is read. Second, it sets the flag MORDAT to false so that the WHILE block will be exited at the next execution of the WHILE statement.

The principal fault with the structure of the program SCORE2, in the opinion of many programmers, is that "half" of the body of the WHILE block is moved to the ELSE clause of the enclosed IF block. Since this part of the loop contains the computational statements to handle the usual case of valid, nonsignal data, they would rather see these steps nested only in a WHILE block.

Style Note: At this point we advise keeping an open mind. After you have written a sufficient number of "*n* and a half" iteration loops both ways, you can make an informed choice.

DO Block With Exit

The third solution of the counting problem uses a new and very powerful program structure called a **DO block with exit**.

In order to exit from the DO block, a new statement, the GO TO statement, is used. It consists of the keywords GO TO followed by a statement label, and when executed causes the statement with the named label to be executed next.

> *Style Note:* In this book, the only use of a GO TO statement will be to exit from a DO block and in that case, the transfer always will be made to the first statement after the end of the block. We will use the convention of labelling such a statement with a label that is one more than the label of the CONTINUE statement just preceding it so that all such labels will end with the digit 9. DO blocks with exits constructed this way are well-structured in the sense that they have one entrance and essentially one exit destination for both normal and early exits.

When a DO loop is terminated by an early exit, the value of the DO variable is available for further use, and it carries the value it had at the time the loop was exited. This was also true in the original Fortran language.

Since the exit test and GO TO statement can be placed anywhere in the loop, and control passes directly to the statement with the specified label without passing either the top or the bottom of the loop, no flag is necessary in this version. The flow of control is quite explicit and quite clear.

```
C       PROGRAM SCORES
C       COUNT THE NUMBER OF SCORES IN THE INPUT FILE
C       DO NOT COUNT THE SIGNAL AT THE END OF THE INPUT
C
        INTEGER LINE, NUMBER, COUNT, SIGNAL
C
        SIGNAL = -1
        COUNT = 0
        DO 18 LINE = 1, 10000
C       EXIT WHEN A SIGNAL VALUE IS READ
           READ, NUMBER
           PRINT, 'INPUT DATA  NUMBER:', NUMBER
           IF (NUMBER .EQ. SIGNAL) THEN DO
              GO TO 19
           ELSE DO
              COUNT = COUNT + 1
           END IF
     18 CONTINUE
C
     19 PRINT, ' '
        PRINT, 'THERE ARE', COUNT, 'SCORES.'
        STOP
        END
```

The computer repeats the body of the DO block until the the number -1 is encountered. The maximum number of iterations, 10000, is set so high that we do not expect the DO block to repeat this often without encountering -1. For nonnegative values, the steps are to read a number, echo it to the printer or screen, test for -1, and increase the count by one. The assignment statement

```
COUNT = COUNT + 1
```

directs the computer to take the previous value of the variable COUNT, add one to it, and to store the result as the new value of the variable COUNT. When the input value of NUMBER is −1, the THEN clause is taken instead of the ELSE clause and the computer goes to the PRINT statement labelled 19 for its next instruction.

Critique of the DO Block With Exit Solution

Again, this version works, even if the input data consists of only a signal value. The most obvious fault is the dummy upper limit 10000 on the DO loop variable LINE. This number number, 10000, is obviously larger than any amount of data one can reasonably enter in a student job in WATFIV, but nevertheless, it is esthetically unpleasing to have to enter any such meaningless limit in the Fortran source program.

Fortran does not have a DO FOREVER loop block, although you could construct one using a WHILE block with true condition

```
WHILE (.TRUE.) DO
```

We do not do so for two reasons. First, the DO FOREVER construct is misleading in this problem. The loop is not expected to execute forever; only until a signal value is read. The second reason is that we wish this third solution to run in standard Fortran 77, which does not have a WHILE loop construct.

The second "fault" of the DO block with exit solution is its use of statement labels and GO TO statements. In the early days of computer programming, statement labels and GO TO statements acquired a very bad reputation because they were used to create all kinds of chaotic program structures. This unsavory reputation was richly deserved because programs with chaotic flows of control are very difficult to debug, modify, and maintain. In time, this wisdom became oversimplified to the slogan, "GO TOs are bad" and programming languages were designed to eliminate GO TO statements.

In fact, it is the orderly flow of control that makes a program "structured", not the presence or absence of statement labels. The flow of control is more explicit and more clearly stated in the DO block with exit solution SCORE3 than either WHILE block solution SCORE1 or SCORE2. All three versions are well structured in the sense that their loop blocks have exactly one entrance and exactly one statement to which control flows on exit from the loop. They merely differ on how explicitly the exit statement is named in the program.

4.3 Case Study: Calculating Averages

An average is found by dividing a total by the number of items added to form the total. Calculating the total of a column of numbers is basically a repetitive task: each new number is added to the running total. In this case study, we examine how a DO block is used to calculate a total and how the values of the variables change during the execution of a loop.

Section Preview

Accumulating Totals:

The statement

```
SUM = SUM + SCORE
```

increases the value of the variable SUM by the value of the variable SCORE. Used repeatedly in a loop, this kind of statement forms the key step in programs to calculate the sum (and subsequently, the average) of many quantities.

Example:

```
           SUM = 0
           DO 18 I = 1, 10
              READ, SCORE
              SUM = SUM + SCORE
      18   CONTINUE
```

Hand Simulation:

This is a technique in which you put yourself in the role of the computer and perform by hand the steps which the computer is directed to perform by its program. It is important for understanding and debugging programs.

The Problem

An instructor wishes to find the average of the test scores that the 27 students in a class earned on their first examination.

The First Solution

The instructor could write a program AVG27 using 27 constants. However, if the instructor knows that there will be several more examinations during the semester, it might be desirable to write a program that can be used for subsequent examinations as well. The program AVG27 uses variables instead of specific numbers written in the program, so that it can find the average of any 27 numbers. Recall that Fortran statements that do not fit on one line may be continued on subsequent lines by placing a symbol in column 6 of the continuation line.

```
C       PROGRAM AVG27
C       FINDS THE AVERAGE OF 27 TEST SCORES
C
        REAL A, B, C, D, E, F, G, H, I, J
        REAL K, L, M, N, O, P, Q, R, S, T
        REAL U, V, W, X, Y, Z, AA
C
        READ, A, B, C, D, E, F, G, H, I, J,
     +           K, L, M, N, O, P, Q, R, S, T,
     +           U, V, W, X, Y, Z, AA
C
        PRINT, + (A + B + C + D + E + F + G + H + I + J +
     +               K + L + M + N + O + P + Q + R + S + T +
     +               U + V + W + X + Y + Z + AA) / 27
        STOP
        END
```

```
           82.2962900
```

The fact that more than 26 variables are needed is not a problem since the name of a variable can be more than one letter long. The first plus sign in the PRINT statement is necessary because in WATFIV, a PRINT list item cannot start with a left parenthesis.

Critique of the First Solution

The absence of input echoes makes it impossible to tell whether 82.29629 is indeed the correct answer, because it is impossible to tell what input data was used. Despite the extra trouble, input echoes would have been added if this program were not going to be replaced immediately with a better one. Our fundamental objection is that the program AVG27 does not exploit the basic repetitiveness of the process of adding the 27 test scores.

The Second Solution: Using a Loop to Calculate the Average

The program AVG27B (average of 27, version 2), however, uses a DO block to reflect in the program the repetitiveness of the task. A side benefit is reducing the number of variables needed to two, namely SUM and SCORE. Now it is reasonable to echo print the input data for the program.

```
C       PROGRAM AVG27B
C       CALCULATE THE AVERAGE TEST SCORE
C       IN A CLASS WITH 27 STUDENTS
C
        INTEGER NUMSCR, COUNT
        REAL SUM, SCORE
C
        NUMSCR = 27
        SUM = 0
        DO 18 COUNT = 1, NUMSCR
           READ, SCORE
           PRINT 15, 'INPUT DATA  SCORE:', SCORE
   15      FORMAT (T2, A18, F9.4)
           SUM = SUM + SCORE
   18   CONTINUE
C
        PRINT 25, 'AVERAGE TEST SCORE =', SUM / NUMSCR
   25   FORMAT (T2, A20, F9.4)
        STOP
        END
```

The first assignment statement of the program AV27V2 gives the variable SUM its initial value of zero. The next five lines, which comprise a DO block, tell the computer to read and to add up the test scores, and the final PRINT statement tells the computer to print the answer.

Execution of a DO Block

The DO block of the program AVG27B is executed as if the 81 statements

```
        READ, SCORE
        PRINT, 'INPUT DATA  SCORE: ', SCORE
        SUM = SUM + SCORE
        READ, SCORE
        PRINT, 'INPUT DATA  SCORE: ', SCORE
        SUM = SUM + SCORE
        READ, SCORE
        PRINT, 'INPUT DATA  SCORE: ', SCORE
        SUM = SUM + SCORE
        .
        .
        .
```

```
READ, SCORE
PRINT, 'INPUT DATA  SCORE: ', SCORE
SUM = SUM + SCORE
```

were written instead of the 5-line DO block. Since the READ and PRINT statements are executed 27 times, the execution printout is much longer than the actual program.

```
INPUT DATA  SCORE:  85.0000
INPUT DATA  SCORE:  97.0000
INPUT DATA  SCORE:  68.0000
INPUT DATA  SCORE:  86.0000
INPUT DATA  SCORE:  75.0000
INPUT DATA  SCORE:  90.0000
INPUT DATA  SCORE:  82.0000
INPUT DATA  SCORE: 100.0000
INPUT DATA  SCORE:  87.0000
INPUT DATA  SCORE:  63.0000
INPUT DATA  SCORE:  79.0000
INPUT DATA  SCORE:  85.0000
INPUT DATA  SCORE:  93.0000
INPUT DATA  SCORE:  62.0000
INPUT DATA  SCORE:  88.0000
INPUT DATA  SCORE:  76.0000
INPUT DATA  SCORE:  38.0000
INPUT DATA  SCORE:  70.0000
INPUT DATA  SCORE:  87.0000
INPUT DATA  SCORE:  93.0000
INPUT DATA  SCORE:  98.0000
INPUT DATA  SCORE:  81.0000
INPUT DATA  SCORE:  95.0000
INPUT DATA  SCORE:  72.0000
INPUT DATA  SCORE:  89.0000
INPUT DATA  SCORE:  99.0000
INPUT DATA  SCORE:  84.0000
AVERAGE TEST SCORE =   82.2963
```

The echo of input data is extremely useful in checking that all the test scores were entered correctly.

Increasing the Value of a Variable

The meaning of the assignment statement

```
SUM = SUM + SCORE
```

is: "Add the values of the variables SUM and SCORE and assign their sum as the new value of the variable SUM". The value of the variable SCORE is not changed by this statement.

The assignment statement is *not* a mathematical equation in which the variable SUM can be cancelled on both sides of the assignment operator to "solve" the assignment statement for the variable SCORE = 0. Each variable on the right of the assignment operator has its value determined before execution of the assignment statement begins, while the variable on the left is assigned a new value as a result of the statement.

Hand Simulation

To show in more detail how a DO block works, we follow the steps, one at a time, that a computer performs during the execution of the program AVG27B. Since the statements inside the block are executed 27 times and the statements outside the block are executed only once, almost all the steps of the execution correspond to instructions in the DO block. Of particular interest are the changing values of the variables SCORE and SUM. Following the steps in this manner is **hand simulation** because the computer's computations are simulated by hand. It is perfectly acceptable to use a hand calculator to do the arithmetic when hand simulating a program.

The second statement of the program AVG27B assigns the variable SUM its initial value of 0. The other variable SCORE does not yet have a value. The DO block is then started. In each of the 27 repetitions of the block, the computer reads a number and assigns that number to the variable SCORE. Then it prints an echo of the value that it read. Finally, it adds the value of SCORE to the current value of the variable SUM to obtain a new value for the variable SUM.

During the first pass through the body of the DO loop, that is, the repeated statements, the number 85.0 is read and assigned to the variable SCORE. The first echo of input data line

```
INPUT DATA  SCORE:    85.0000
```

of the printout confirms that the first number supplied as input data is indeed 85.0000. Then the value 85.0000 of SCORE is added to the current value, 0.0000, of the variable SUM to obtain a new sum 0.0000 + 85.0000 = 85.0000, which is assigned as the new value for SUM. Thus the values of the variables SCORE and SUM after the first pass through the repeated instructions are 85.0000 and 85.0000. Table 4.1 shows the values of these variables after each of the 27 passes.

After 27 complete passes, the loop body is not repeated and the computer execution proceeds to the final PRINT statement. By then, all of the test scores have been added to yield the sum 2222.0, which is the final value of the variable SUM. When the final PRINT statement specifies printing the expression SUM/27, the average of all 27 test scores is printed.

Critique of the Second Solution

The program AVG27B is better in all respects than the program AVG27. The input values are echoed. The basic repetitiveness of the task of accumulating the sum is represented by a loop, the DO block. The number of variables is greatly reduced, and several very long Fortran statements are eliminated.

So what could be wrong with the second solution? It does solve the stated problem. But what if one student is absent the day of the test? The program AVG27B, as it stands, cannot find the average of 26 test scores.

> *Programming Note:* In the real world, the original statement of a problem is rarely complete, and may be inaccurate and oversimplified or undersimplified. The true nature of the problem the user needs solved is often clear only after a solution of the original problem is attempted.

Clearly, the instructor needs a program that can also find the average of 26 test scores, and so might try to change AVG27B into a program AVG26B, that would find it. Because we have followed good programming practice, *only one line* would change: the assignment statement for the variable NUMSCR (number of scores). This is one of the advantages of using named constants.

Table 4.1 Values of the variables SCORE and SUM during execution of the program AVG27B using data from the sample run.

SCORE	SUM	PASS THROUGH THE DO BLOCK
undefined	0.0	before the 1st pass
85.0	85.0	after the 1st pass
97.0	182.0	after the 2nd pass
68.0	250.0	after the 3rd pass
86.0	336.0	after the 4th pass
75.0	411.0	after the 5th pass
90.0	501.0	after the 6th pass
82.0	583.0	after the 7th pass
100.0	683.0	after the 8th pass
87.0	770.0	after the 9th pass
63.0	833.0	after the 10th pass
79.0	912.0	after the 11th pass
85.0	997.0	after the 12th pass
93.0	1090.0	after the 13th pass
62.0	1152.0	after the 14th pass
88.0	1240.0	after the 15th pass
76.0	1316.0	after the 16th pass
38.0	1354.0	after the 17th pass
70.0	1424.0	after the 18th pass
87.0	1511.0	after the 19th pass
93.0	1604.0	after the 20th pass
98.0	1702.0	after the 21st pass
81.0	1783.0	after the 22nd pass
95.0	1878.0	after the 23rd pass
72.0	1950.0	after the 24th pass
89.0	2039.0	after the 25th pass
99.0	2138.0	after the 26th pass
84.0	2222.0	after the 27th pass

However, the program AVG26B won't work if all 27 students take the test, and another program AVG25B is needed if two are absent. What is needed is a solution of greater generality, a program that can find the average of any number of test scores.

The Third Solution: A More General Program for Averaging

Fortunately, it is easy to change the program AVG27B into a program AVGSCR (average of scores) that can compute the average of any number of test scores. All that is needed is to read the value of the variable NUMSCR (number of scores) from the input file before the DO block is entered.

```
C       PROGRAM AVGSCR
C       FINDS THE AVERAGE OF ANY NUMBER OF SCORES
C
        INTEGER NUMSCR, COUNT
        REAL SCORE, SUM
C
```

```
      READ, NUMSCR
      PRINT, 'INPUT DATA  NUMSCR:', NUMSCR
C
      SUM = 0
      DO 8 COUNT = 1, NUMSCR
         READ, SCORE
         PRINT 15, 'INPUT DATA  SCORE:', SCORE
   15    FORMAT (T2, A18, F9.4)
         SUM = SUM + SCORE
    8 CONTINUE
C
      PRINT, 'AVERAGE TEST SCORE =', SUM / NUMSCR
   25 FORMAT (/, T2, A20, F9.4)
      STOP
      END
```

The new feature in this program is that the number of times the DO block is repeated is a variable. Of course, a value for this variable NUMSCR must be assigned before the DO block can be started. The statement

```
      READ, NUMSCR
```

obtains this value from an input device before any of the test scores are read. Thus the data for the more general program AVGSCR must consist of a first number giving the number of test scores to be averaged, and then an appropriate number of test scores.

The sample run of AVGSCR uses only 6 scores to be averaged, although the program would work just as well with 60 or 600.

> *Debugging Note:* It is a great convenience to be able to test a program on a small number of data items, because the results can be checked more easily by hand.

```
INPUT DATA  ENROLL:           6
INPUT DATA  SCORE:  82.0000
INPUT DATA  SCORE:  78.0000
INPUT DATA  SCORE:  93.0000
INPUT DATA  SCORE:  91.0000
INPUT DATA  SCORE:  52.0000
INPUT DATA  SCORE:  72.0000

AVERAGE TEST SCORE =  78.0000
```

The program AVGSCR can be used by any instructor for a class of any size. Even an instructor who does not know how to program can be told how to prepare input data for AVGSCR.

Critique of the Third Solution

Again the solution solves the stated problem. The program AVGSCR works for any class size. It echoes the input data so we can see if any test score is mistyped. What more could we want? All you have to do is count the number of test scores and place that number before any scores in the input file.

In Section 4.2, we saw how to write a program to count a variable number of data items. To make the program even more user-friendly, a solution that also counts the number of test scores could be written. We leave this fourth solution as an exercise. There is always something you can do to improve a program.

4.4 Testing and Debugging: Debugging a Loop

The practice of detecting and removing errors from a program is **debugging**. Loops pose special problems in debugging. Since each statement in the body of a loop is executed many times, a statement that executes correctly on one iteration may still be in error and fail on another iteration.

Section Preview

Debugging:

Removing bugs, that is, errors, from a program. Two case studies show the use of **echoes of input data** in debugging.

Discovering Mistakes in a Program

The usual cause of a disappointing program execution is a mistake in the program. When a programmer means to write one thing but accidentally writes another, the computer executes the program it actually sees, not the one that would have made sense. The program ATTAVG (attempt average) contains a mistake of this kind.

```
C       PROGRAM ATTAVG
C       THIS AVERAGING PROGRAM CONTAINS A BUG!
C
        INTEGER ENROLL, COUNT
        REAL SCORE, SUM
C
        READ, ENROLL
        PRINT, 'INPUT DATA  ENROLL:', ENROLL
C
        SUM = 0
        DO 8 COUNT = 1, ENROLL
           READ, SCORE
           PRINT 15, 'INPUT DATA  SCORE:', SCORE
   15      FORMAT (T1, A18, F9.4)
           SUM = SCORE
    8   CONTINUE
C
        PRINT 25, 'AVERAGE TEST SCORE =', SUM / ENROLL
   25   FORMAT (/, T2, A20, F9.4)
        STOP
        END
```

```
INPUT DATA  ENROLL:           5
INPUT DATA  SCORE:  72.0000
INPUT DATA  SCORE:  46.0000
INPUT DATA  SCORE:  93.0000
INPUT DATA  SCORE:  86.0000
INPUT DATA  SCORE:  75.0000

AVERAGE TEST SCORE =  15.0000
```

A programmer usually can determine whether or not there is an error in a program by carefully choosing test data and independently calculating what results to expect. The actual average of the five test scores in the illustrative test run is 74.4. The value 15 for the average test score shown in the execution printout is obviously wrong, because it is smaller than any of the supplied test scores.

In a program this short, there is not much room for an error to hide. Once one is known to exist, the programmer usually can find it by critically rereading the program. Examination of the echoes of input data in the execution output indicates that the value for enrollment was read correctly, as were each of the five test scores. This means that the loop was executed the correct number of times. Very little of the program is left to check for possible errors. In this case, the statement

```
SUM = SCORE
```

should be changed to

```
SUM = SUM + SCORE
```

After making this change, which seems to explain the erroneous execution, the program should be rerun, first with the same test data and then with a representative range of reasonable test scores, including extreme values such as 100 and 0, if these are the limits of valid input data. We ran such tests and they show the bug was corrected.

Mistakes in the Input Data

Even after exercising considerable care in writing a program, a programmer may sometimes still find the execution printout disappointing. Even a correct program cannot be expected to give correct results if there is a mistake in the input data. This is illustrated using the program AVGSCR. Suppose the data for this program consists of the seven test scores 45, 98, 77, 64, 38, 86, and 53, but the first required data item, the enrollment, is inadvertently omitted, a common mistake.

```
INPUT DATA  ENROLL:              45
INPUT DATA  SCORE:  98.0000
INPUT DATA  SCORE:  77.0000
INPUT DATA  SCORE:  64.0000
INPUT DATA  SCORE:  38.0000
INPUT DATA  SCORE:  86.0000
INPUT DATA  SCORE:  53.0000
***ERROR***  CONTROL CARD ENCOUNTERED ON UNIT 5 AT EXECUTION.
             PROBABLE CAUSE:  MISSING DATA OR INCORRECT FORMAT.
```

The control card was the $END card that follows all the data. Unit 5 is the internal name for the standard input data file in WATFIV.

> *Warning:* On many WATFIV systems, this end-of-file error message does not appear if the $END control card is missing. Instead the execution terminates suddenly at this point with no message whatsoever.

Because the sample execution printout contains clearly identified echoes of all input data, the cause of the erroneous program execution is not hard to find. The program AVGSCR tells the computer that the first number it reads is the value for the variable NUMSCR. Accordingly, when the first number in the input data is 45, the computer anticipates 45 test scores in the data. When it finds only 6 more numbers before the $END line, it is unable to continue with the program execution and prints an error message saying that it has run out of data, that is, that it has come to the end of the input file without having found all the numbers that it needs. The cure is simply to rerun the program with the enrollment value included. A similar execution error occurs if the signal value is omitted from the input file in a program to count the number of data items.

In the absence of an exit triggered by recognition of the signal value, the computer continues reading, only to fail when the data runs out.

Overconfidence Fed By Undertesting

The commutative law of addition states that it doesn't matter in what order numbers are added; the result is the same. The program TWOSUM attempts to test whether the commutative law holds for computer addition by showing whether the sum $1 + 2 + 3 + \cdots + N$ gives the same result as the sum $N + (N - 1) + (N - 2) + \cdots + 1$. If you think that equality of the two sums is a foregone conclusion, try it also using a step size of 1/10 instead of 1. You may be surprised.

As a start for this debugging study, we give the program TWOSUM and two sample executions.

```
C       PROGRAM TWOSUM
C       TESTS WHETHER THE ASCENDING SUM 1+2+3+...+N
C       IS EQUAL TO THE DESCENDING SUM N+(N-1)+...+2+1
C
        INTEGER N, J, SUM, SUM2
C
        READ, N
        PRINT, 'INPUT DATA  N:', N
C
        SUM = 0
        DO 18 J = 1, N
           SUM = SUM + J
   18   CONTINUE
        PRINT, 'THE ASCENDING SUM IS', SUM
C
        DO 28 J = N, 1
           SUM2 = SUM + J
   28   CONTINUE
        PRINT, 'THE DESCENDING SUM IS', SUM
        STOP
        END
```

```
INPUT DATA  N:          5
THE ASCENDING SUM IS          15
THE DESCENDING SUM IS          15
```

```
INPUT DATA  N:          100
THE ASCENDING SUM IS          5050
THE DESCENDING SUM IS          5050
```

The first test case is easily checked by hand. $1 + 2 + 3 + 4 + 5 = 15$, and both calculated sums print as 15. In the second test case, both sums again print as equal. Thus they are either both correct or both wrong. A formula from our high school algebra textbook tells us that the sum of the first n integers is $\frac{n \times (n + 1)}{2}$. When N is 100, the sums should be 5050, which they are.

But is the program TWOSUM correct? Additional tests using different values for N all give the same result: The two sums printed are equal and they are correct. However, since we are first learning about loops, let us put PRINT statements in the middle of the two DO loops to let the computer show us what is happening in the middle of each loop, how each variable changes from iteration to iteration, and why the correct sums are calculated. The important variables are J and SUM, so we put the following PRINT statement at the bottom of each loop body, just before each CONTINUE statement.

```
PRINT, 'J =', J, '   SUM =', SUM
```

The program TWOSUM is then rerun using the first test value N = 5.

```
INPUT DATA  N:              5
J =             1      SUM =            1
J =             2      SUM =            3
J =             3      SUM =            6
J =             4      SUM =           10
J =             5      SUM =           15
THE ASCENDING SUM IS                15
J =             5      SUM =           15
THE DESCENDING SUM IS               15
```

The sums are still fine, but where is the rest of the debugging output from the second DO block? It would seem that the body of the second DO loop is executed only once. Appearances are not deceiving. The second DO loop is executed only once. In the DO statement

```
DO 28 J = N, 1
```

the initial value for J is the value of N, namely 5. Thus the initial value of J already exceeds the stopping value, 1. What was intended was for J to count backward, and that requires an auxiliary variable in WATFIV.

```
DO 28 ITER = 1, N
   J = N + 1 - ITER
```

It is also possible to rewrite this DO loop as a WHILE loop.

```
J = N
WHILE (J .GE. 1) DO
   SUM2 = SUM + J
   PRINT, 'J =', J, '   SUM =', SUM
   J = J - 1
END WHILE
```

The debugging printout must come before the value of J is decremented in the WHILE loop block.

We make either correction and rerun the program TWOSUM, keeping in the debugging PRINT statements.

```
INPUT DATA  N:              5
J =             1      SUM =            1
J =             2      SUM =            3
J =             3      SUM =            6
J =             4      SUM =           10
J =             5      SUM =           15
THE ASCENDING SUM IS                15
J =             5      SUM =           15
J =             4      SUM =           15
J =             3      SUM =           15
J =             2      SUM =           15
J =             1      SUM =           15
THE DESCENDING SUM IS               15
```

Now the second DO loop is obviously executing the correct number of times, 5, and the DO variable J is taking on the proper value during each iteration. However, all printed intermediate answers are wrong!

Of course they are wrong. The debugging PRINT statement that prints these intermediate sums reads

```
PRINT, 'J =', J, '  SUM =', SUM
```

but the accumulating sum in the second loop is named SUM2. The correct debugging PRINT statement is

```
PRINT, 'J =', J, '  SUM =', SUM2
```

We rerun the program with this change and get the following output.

```
INPUT DATA   N:              5
J =            1      SUM =          1
J =            2      SUM =          3
J =            3      SUM =          6
J =            4      SUM =         10
J =            5      SUM =         15
THE ASCENDING SUM IS            15
J =            5      SUM =         20
J =            4      SUM =         19
J =            3      SUM =         18
J =            2      SUM =         17
J =            1      SUM =         16
THE DESCENDING SUM IS            15
```

With apologies to those readers who are skilled at debugging and already know what the error is, we plod on, unravelling the mystery step by step. Since the intermediate sums are wrong, we look at the statement that accumulates them

```
SUM2 = SUM + J
```

Of course, this statement should be

```
SUM2 = SUM2 + J
```

so that new values of SUM2 are based on previous values of SUM2, not on previous values of the first sum SUM. We make this change and rerun the program.

```
INPUT DATA   N:              5
J =            1      SUM =          1
J =            2      SUM =          3
J =            3      SUM =          6
J =            4      SUM =         10
J =            5      SUM =         15
THE ASCENDING SUM IS            15
***ERROR***  VALUE OF  SUM2  IS UNDEFINED
```

This error message usually means that a variable has not been assigned an initial value. Since the only two variables on the right side of the offending assignment statement are SUM2 and J, and J has just been assigned a value, the uninitialized variable is SUM2. We insert the initialization

```
SUM2 = 0
```

above the second loop and obtain the following (WATFIV-S) source program and execution.

```
C       PROGRAM TWOSUM
C       TESTS WHETHER THE ASCENDING SUM 1+2+3+...+N
C       IS EQUAL TO THE DESCENDING SUM N+(N-1)+...+2+1
C
        INTEGER N, J, SUM, SUM2
C
```

```
      READ, N
      PRINT, 'INPUT DATA  N:', N
C
      SUM = 0
      DO 18 J = 1, N
         SUM = SUM + J
         PRINT, 'J =', J, '    SUM =', SUM
   18 CONTINUE
      PRINT, 'THE ASCENDING SUM IS', SUM
C
      SUM2 = 0
      DO 28 ITER = 1, N
         J = N + 1 - ITER
         SUM2 = SUM2 + J
         PRINT, 'J =', J, '    SUM =', SUM2
   28 CONTINUE
      PRINT, 'THE DESCENDING SUM IS', SUM
      STOP
      END
INPUT DATA  N:              5
J =             1     SUM =            1
J =             2     SUM =            3
J =             3     SUM =            6
J =             4     SUM =           10
J =             5     SUM =           15
THE ASCENDING SUM IS            15
J =             5     SUM =            5
J =             4     SUM =            9
J =             3     SUM =           12
J =             2     SUM =           14
J =             1     SUM =           15
THE DESCENDING SUM IS            15
```

What is to be learned from this example? First, you can never test a program too much! Some programs show new bugs even after years of successful and bug-free executions. To put this another way, testing by itself is not sufficient to instill confidence in a program. The inherent believability of the program listing is an important factor in convincing those who can read it that a program does what it is intended to do. This requires readable program listings, good, self-explanatory variable names, and clear program structure.

Second, strategically placed PRINT statements can tell you precisely what value the computer has calculated for a variable, which may not be the same as the value you get by hand simulation. Humans are fallible at long and tedious tasks, making long hand simulations prone to error. Moreover, when hand simulating, you are likely to simulate the statements you intended to write rather than the statements you actually entered into the computer. Having the computer print the actual values calculated helps determine just how far the computer program got before the calculations began differing from what you intended.

As a parting shot, we remark that, appearances to the contrary, the program TWOSUM is still not debugged. For one thing, we were lucky that the default type for the DO variable ITER is integer. We did not remember to declare it. Second, in spite of the apparent correctness of the debugging output, there is still a small, but serious error in the WATFIV-S source program. We leave its discovery as a challenge. The answer is at the end of this chapter.

4.5 Case Study: Approximating a Definite Integral

WATFIV-S does not allow a DO variable to be type real or double precision. Like earlier Fortrans, it restricts DO variables to type integer. In this case study, a WHILE block is used to simulate a DO block with type real DO variable to approximate the area of a region bounded by three straight lines and a curve $y = f(x)$. A new Fortran feature, the one-line function definition statement, is used to define the function $f(x)$ in the Fortran program.

Section Preview

Real DO Variables:

The DO variable in a DO block must not be type real or double precision. When such a construct appears in pseudocode, a WHILE block is used to refine it.

variable = *starting value*
WHILE (*variable* .LE. *stopping value*) DO
  body of loop
  variable = *variable* + *step size*
END WHILE

Statement Function:

General Form:

function name (list of dummy variables) = *expression*

Examples:

```
F (X) = X ** 2 - 1
GLOP (Y, Z) = SQRT (Y - F (Z))
```

The Problem

The value of a definite integral is the area of an "almost rectangular" region of the plane bounded by the three straight lines. $x = a$, $y = 0$, $x = b$, and the curve $y = f(x)$. (See Figure 4.3.) The better part of a semester in any calculus sequence is spent seeking analytic solutions to the area problem, that is, expressing the area by an algebraic or trigonometric expression. At the conclusion, the calculus student acquires a modest repertoire of useful functions that can be integrated in "closed form".

It turns out to be easier to approximate the area of such "almost rectangular" regions numerically, if you have a computer available. Moreover, the numerical approximation method works even for functions that cannot be integrated algebraically. If we replace the curve $y = f(x)$ by a straight line with the same endpoints, we convert the region in question to a trapezoid, a simple four-sided figure whose area is given by the formula

$$A = (b - a) \times \frac{(f(a) + f(b))}{2}$$

Of course, the area of this trapezoid is not exactly equal to the area of the original region with curved boundary, but the smaller the width of the trapezoid, the better the approximation.

Specifically, the problem we wish to solve is to find the area of one arch of the curve $y = \sin(x)$, that is the area under this curve for x from 0 to π radians (180°). We will do it by writing a program to calculate trapezoidal approximations to the area, choosing a number of trapezoids sufficient to give the answer to three decimal places.

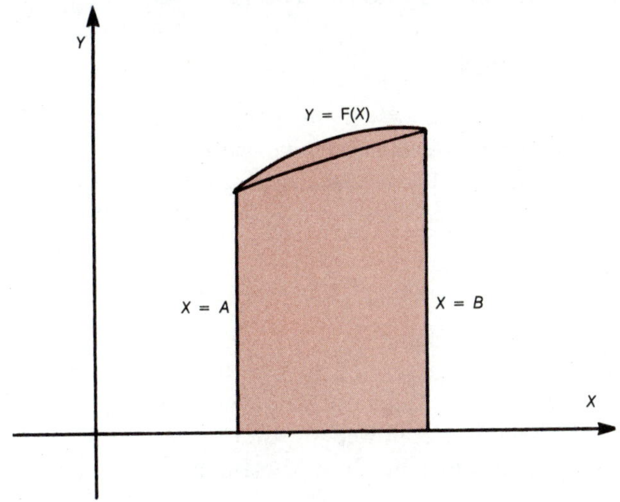

Figure 4.3 A region approximated by a trapezoid.

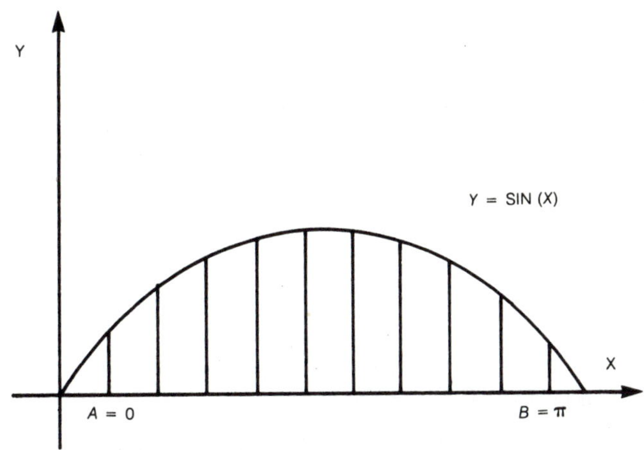

An area divided into n trapezoids.

If in Figure 4.4 we call the width of each trapezoid h, we have the relationship

$$h = (b - a) / n$$

After a little algebra, the sum of the areas of the n trapezoids may be expressed by the formula

$$T_n = h(\tfrac{1}{2} f(a) + f(a+h) + f(a+2h) + \cdots + f(b-h) + \tfrac{1}{2} f(b))$$

Since the main difficulty in this formula is a sum similar to those calculated in Sections 4.3 and 4.4, the program to calculate the trapezoidal approximation will undoubtedly resemble the programs written in those sections. The new feature is the sequence of values

$$a, a+h, a+2h, \cdots b-h, b$$

to be taken on by the DO variable. Although these will in general be noninteger real values, the fact that the difference between successive values is constant enables us to use a DO block to run through this sequence of values, at least as pseudocode.

The Statement Function

Nearly every term in the formula for T_n involves the function $f(x)$. Fortran provides a simple way to define functions that can be described in one line of code. A **statement function** consists of the name of the function followed by a parenthesized list of its dummy arguments or variables, followed by the assignment operator (=), followed by the expression that describes how the function is evaluated. For example, the function definition

```
F (X) = X ** 2 - 1
```

defines a function named F by the formula $X^2 - 1$. As in algebra, the variable X is merely a dummy variable or place holder that allows you to specify simply how the function value is calculated. The names of the function and of the dummy variable follow the usual naming convention in Fortran, and their types must be declared above the function definition statement. Moreover, function definition statements must precede all executable statements in a Fortran program.

Function definition expressions may use any of the arithmetic operators or built-in functions. They may also use any statement functions, defined in previous lines. For example, the following sequence of function definitions

```
DISCR (A, B, C) = B ** 2 - 4 * A * C
ROOT1 (A, B, C) = (-B + SQRT (DISCR (A, B, C)) / (2 * A)
ROOT2 (A, B, C) = (-B - SQRT (DISCR (A, B, C)) / (2 * A)
```

are valid, assuming all variables are properly declared. These functions are useful in solving quadratic equations.

The Program

```
C     PROGRAM TRAP
C     CALCULATES A TRAPEZOIDAL APPROXIMATION TO AN AREA
C     USING N TRAPEZOIDS.
C     N IS READ FROM THE INPUT FILE.
C
C     THE REGION IS BOUNDED BY LINES X = A, Y = 0, X = B,
C     AND THE CURVE Y = SIN (X).
C     A AND B ALSO ARE READ FROM THE INPUT FILE.
C
      REAL X, A, B, H, SUM, TN, F
      INTEGER N
C
      F (X) = SIN (X)
```

```
      READ, N
      PRINT, 'INPUT DATA  N:', N
      READ, A, B
      PRINT 15, 'INPUT DATA  A:', A
      PRINT 15, '            B:', B
   15 FORMAT (T2, A14, F9.4)
      H = (B - A) / N
C     CALCULATE THE SUM 1/2 F(A) + F(A+H) +...+ F(B-H) + 1/2 F(B)
      SUM = 0.5 * F (A)
C     DO 18 X = A + H, B - H, H  --PSEUDOCODE
      X = A + H
      WHILE (X .LE.B - H) DO
         SUM = SUM + F(X)
         X = X + H
      END WHILE
      SUM = SUM + 0.5 * F(B)
C
      TN = H * SUM
      PRINT 25, 'TRAPEZOIDAL APPROXIMATION TO THE AREA =', TN
   25 FORMAT (T2, A39, F9.5)
      STOP
      END
```

```
INPUT DATA  N:          100
INPUT DATA  A:    0.0000
            B:    3.1416
TRAPEZOIDAL APPROXIMATION TO THE AREA = 1.99986
INPUT DATA  N:         1000
INPUT DATA  A:    0.0000
            B:    3.1416
TRAPEZOIDAL APPROXIMATION TO THE AREA =   1.99987
```

Since these two answers differ by only one in the fifth decimal place, we may conclude that there is no need to rerun the program using more trapezoids to meet the limits of accuracy specified in the problem statement. Both calculated answers round to 2.00 to three decimal places.

4.6 What You Should Know

1. The DO block consists of a DO statement, a body, and a CONTINUE statement. The same statement label appears in the DO statement and on the CONTINUE statement.
2. The body of a DO block may contain any other Fortran statements, subject to the rules for proper nesting of IF blocks and DO blocks.
3. The DO statement specifies how many times the block will be executed and what the values of the DO variable will be in each repetition.
4. The values of the DO variable can increase by any integer constant amount between iterations.
5. To execute the body of a DO block no times at all, the DO block is enclosed in an IF block.
6. Variable length input data is handled by loops that terminate when a programmer-defined signal value is recognized.

7. A WHILE block consists of a WHILE statement, a body, and an END WHILE statement.
8. Hand simulation means putting yourself in the place of the computer and simulating the steps the computer would take in executing the program.
9. Echoes of input data are extremely useful in debugging. They tell whether the input has been prepared and read correctly.
10. You should know how to write a loop to accumulate a sum and calculate an average.
11. You should know how to read variable length input data and count how many values were read.

4.7 Self-Test Questions

Section 4.1

1. Which of the following DO blocks are syntactically correct?

```
      DO 18 N = 1, 10
         PRINT, N * N
   18 CONTINUE

      DO 28 N = 10, 1
         PRINT, N
   28 CONTINUE

      DO 38 X = 10, 3, -2
         PRINT, X
   38 CONTINUE

      DO 48 YEAR := 1960 TO 1984
         READ, PROFIT
   48 CONTINUE

      DO 58 ITER = 10, 20
         READ, VALUE
         PRINT, VALUE
   58 CONTINUE

      DO 68 TIME = 1, 3
         TOTAL = TOTAL + 1
   68 CONTINUE

      DO 78 N = 1, 100
         IF (N .LT. 50) THEN DO
            PRINT, N
         ELSE DO
            CONTINUE
   78    END IF
```

```
      DO 87 N = 1, 10
         PRINT, N * N
   87 CONTINUE
```

2. Correct those DO blocks in Question 1 that have syntax errors.
3. Hand simulate the execution of the following statements, keeping track of the value of N and PROD after the execution of each statement.

```
      PROD = 1
      DO 68 N = 2, 4
         PROD = PROD * N
   68 CONTINUE
```

4. What output is produced by the following program?

```
C     PROGRAM EX4
      INTEGER M
      DO 78 M = 1, 20
         IF (MOD (M, 2) .NE. 0) THEN DO
            PRINT, M
         END IF
   78 CONTINUE
      STOP
      END
```

Section 4.2

1. Which of the following DO blocks are syntactically correct? Which have problems with uninitialized variables? Which have other problems? What is the final value of the integer variable RESULT that is printed when the program segment ends?

```
      DO 18 N = 1, 1000
         RESULT = N
         IF (N .GE. 10) THEN DO
            GO TO 19
         END IF
   18 CONTINUE
   19 PRINT, RESULT

      RESULT = 1
      DO 28 N = 1, 1000
         IF (RESULT .LE. 1) THEN DO
            GO TO 29
         END IF
   28 CONTINUE
   29 PRINT, RESULT

      DO 38 N = 1, 1000
         RESULT = RESULT + 1
         IF (RESULT .GT. 10) THEN DO
            GO TO 39
         END IF
   38 CONTINUE
   39 PRINT, RESULT
```

```
      DO 48 N = 1, 1000
         IF (RESULT .EQ. 0) THEN DO
            GO TO 19
         ELSE DO
            READ, RESULT
         END IF
   48 CONTINUE
   49 PRINT, RESULT

      DO 58 N = 1, 1000, 2
         RESULT = RESULT + N
         IF (RESULT .GT. 100) THEN DO
            GO TO 58
         END IF
   58 CONTINUE
   59 PRINT, RESULT
```

2. Correct the mistakes in the DO blocks of Question 1.

Section 4.3

1. What is the meaning of the statement

```
      SUM = SUM + 1
```

2. What is the value of the variable SUM at the conclusion of the following blocks?

```
      SUM = 0
      DO 18 N = 1, 10
         SUM = SUM + 1
   18 CONTINUE
      SUM = 0
      DO 28 N = 1, 5
         SUM = SUM + N * N
   28 CONTINUE

      SUM = 0
      DO 38 N = 1, 14, 2
         SUM = SUM + N * N
   38 CONTINUE

      SUM = 0
      DO 48 N = 5, 1, -1
         SUM = SUM + N
   48 CONTINUE
```

3. Hand simulate the execution of the following statements recording the values of N and PROD after the execution of each statement.

```
      PROD = 1
      DO 58 N = 2, 4
         PROD = PROD * N
   58 CONTINUE
```

4. Which of the following blocks are syntactically correct? Which require initialization not shown? Give a plausible initialization statement. If a sum is accumulated, what is its final value?

```
      DO 68 N = 1, 9
         SUM = SUM + N
   68 CONTINUE

      SUM = 1
      DO N = 2, 9, 2
         SUM = SUM + N

      SUM = 0
      DO 78 COUNT = 1, N
         READ, SCORE
         SUM = SUM + SCORE
   78 CONTINUE

      DO 88 COORD = 1, 3
         READ (VECTOR (COORD))
   88 CONTINUE
```

Section 4.4

1. Find the bug in the following program to add the numbers from 1 to 5. If you have a computer available, type the program in as given below and debug from the output. If no computer is available, hand simulate the execution of the program, especially the PRINT statements, and debug from the simulated output.

```
C     PROGRAM BUG1
      INTEGER N, SUM

      SUM = 0
      DO 28 N = 1, 5
         SUM = SUM + 1
         PRINT, 'N = ', N, '  SUM = ', SUM
   28 CONTINUE

      PRINT, 'FINAL SUM = ', SUM
      STOP
      END
```

2. Discuss the following programs from the point of view of clarity, self-documentation, and ease of debugging. They all were intended to have the same execution, except for input echoes and identification of output. Which one or ones of these contain bugs? Can you be certain? Which one is the hardest to verify that it is correct or to debug in case it is not? You may use a computer if you have one. What conclusions can you draw from this?

```
C     PROGRAM AVGSCR
C     FINDS THE AVERAGE OF ANY NUMBER OF SCORES
C
      INTEGER NUMSCR, COUNT
      REAL SCORE, SUM
C
      READ, NUMSCR
      PRINT, 'INPUT DATA  NUMSCR:', NUMSCR
C
```

```
      SUM = 0
      DO 8 COUNT = 1, NUMSCR
         READ, SCORE
         PRINT 15, 'INPUT DATA  SCORE:', SCORE
   15    FORMAT (T2, A18, F9.4)
         SUM = SUM + SCORE
    8 CONTINUE
C
      PRINT, 'AVERAGE TEST SCORE =', SUM / NUMSCR
   25 FORMAT (/, T2, A20, F9.4)
      STOP
      END

C     PROGRAM T
      INTEGER N, C
      REAL R, S
C
      READ, N
      PRINT, 'INPUT DATA  N:', N
C
      S = 0
      DO 8 C = 1, N
         READ, R
         PRINT, 'INPUT DATA  R:', R
         S = S + R
    8 CONTINUE
C
      PRINT, ' '
      PRINT, 'AVERAGE TEST SCORE =', S / N
      STOP
      END

C     PROGRAM CONFUS
      INTEGER DINNER, PLATE
      REAL ABOOK, WINE
C
      READ, DINNER
      PRINT, 'INPUT DATA  DINNER:', DINNER
C
      WINE = 0
      DO 8 PLATE = 1, DINNER
         READ, ABOOK
         PRINT, 'INPUT DATA  ABOOK:', ABOOK
         WINE = WINE + ABOOK
    8 CONTINUE
C
      PRINT, ' '
      PRINT, 'A DELIGHTFUL MEAL =', WINE / DINNER
      STOP
      END
```

4.8 Programming Exercises

1. **Purpose:** To test proficiency at writing a simple DO loop.

   The problem: Print a table of the numbers from 1 to 10 and their cubes.

   Input data: None.

   Sample output:

```
NUMBER    CUBE
     1       1
     2       8
     3      27
     4      64
     5     125
     6     216
     7     343
     8     512
     9     729
    10    1000
```

2. **Purpose:** To test methods of varying the upper limit in a DO block.

   The problem: The program TENLIN in Section 4.1 prints the numbers from 1 to 10 on ten separate lines. a) Modify the program TENLIN to print the numbers from 1 to 25 on twenty-five separate lines. Use a variable for the upper limit in the DO statement. b) Modify the program TENLIN so that the number of lines is a value read from input.

   Input data: For the second part, the input consists of a single integer, the number of lines to be printed.

   Sample execution:

```
INPUT DATA  NRLINS:  4
1
2
3
4
```

3. **Purpose:** To write a short DO block with a long, and possibly tricky PRINT statement in the loop body.

   The problem: Print the numbers from 1 to 100 using 10 lines, with the numbers from 1 to 10 going down the first column, the numbers from 11 to 20 going down the second column, etc.

   Input data: None.

   Sample output:

```
 1  11  21  31  41  51  61  71  81  91
 2  12  22  32  42  52  62  72  82  92
 3  13  23  33  43  53  63  73  83  93
 4  14  24  34  44  54  64  74  84  94
 5  15  25  35  45  55  65  75  85  95
 6  16  26  36  46  56  66  76  86  96
 7  17  27  37  47  57  67  77  87  97
 8  18  28  38  48  58  68  78  88  98
 9  19  29  39  49  59  69  79  89  99
10  20  30  40  50  60  70  80  90 100
```

```
 8 18 28 38 48 58 68 78 88  98
 9 19 29 39 49 59 69 79 89  99
10 20 30 40 50 60 70 80 90 100
```

4. **Purpose:** to write a program with an IF block nested in a DO block.

   The problem: An integer is a perfect square if it is the square of another integer. For example, 25 is a perfect square because it is 5 × 5. For this problem, you should write a program to selectively print those numbers less than 100 that are not perfect squares. Hint: One way to see if a number is a perfect square is to see if its square root is an integer. Using Fortran built-in functions, you can test whether INT (SQRT (REAL (X))) has the same value as SQRT (REAL (X)).

   Input data: None.

   Sample output:

```
2
3
5
6
7
8
10
 .
 .
 .
99
```

5. **Purpose:** To illustrate the principle of reading input data into a temporary location, called an input buffer, and examining the input value before passing it on to its intended variable.

   The problem: In real life, directions such as, "Watch where I get off the bus and get off one stop sooner" are paradoxical. In computer programming, it is possible to look ahead and, if the new input value is a termination signal, still recover the previous value. The trick is to keep the new input value in a different variable than the previous, nonsignal value. The problem is in two parts, which can be combined in one program, if you like. a) Read integers from input until the signal value zero is read. Then print the last nonzero value in the input data. b) Read integers from input until the signal value zero is read. Then print the average of all the nonzero values that preceded the value zero.

   Input data: A file of integers with zero as the last line.

```
3
7
1
10
0
```

   Sample output:

```
INPUT DATA  BUFFER:  3
INPUT DATA  BUFFER:  7
INPUT DATA  BUFFER:  1
INPUT DATA  BUFFER:  10
INPUT DATA  BUFFER:  0
THE LAST NONZERO VALUE IS 10
THE AVERAGE OF THE NONZERO VALUES IS 5.25000
```

6. **Purpose:** To write a WHILE block for which the number of iterations before early exit cannot easily be predicted in advance.

   The problem: The successive powers of three are $3^0 = 1$, $3^1 = 3$, $3^2 = 9$, ... The problem is to calculate successively higher powers of three, and to print only the first power of three that exceeds 1000.

   Input data: None.

   Sample output: Since you are not supposed to know what the answer is when you write the program, we show the form of the output, but not the value that is calculated.

```
___ IS THE FIRST POWER OF 3 THAT EXCEEDS 1000
3 ** ___ = ___
```

7. **Purpose:** To write a WHILE block or a DO block with exit in which the number of iterations before exit is predictable only by running the program. This problem also tests conversion of area from one measuring unit to another.

   The problem: In 1970, the population of New Jersey was 7,168,192 and it was increasing at the rate of 18% per decade. The area of New Jersey is 7521 square miles. On the basis of the 18% growth rate continuing indefinitely into the future, predict the population of New Jersey every decade from 1980 on. Stop the predictions when the average number of square feet per person is less than 100. Print out all estimates.

   Input data: None.

   Sample execution:

```
YEAR      POPULATION     SQ FT / PERSON
1980        8458466.            24789.6
1990        9980990.            21007.3
  .             .                   .
  .             .                   .
  .             .                   .
```

8. **Purpose:** To test writing a WHILE block that simulates a pseudocode DO block with DO variable of type REAL.

   The problem: Find the sum of the numbers 0., 0.1, 0.2, 0.3, ..., 10..

   Input data: None.

   Sample output:

```
THE SUM OF THE NUMBERS 0.0 + 0.1 + 0.2 + 0.3 + ... + 10.0 = 505.000
```

9. **Purpose:** To test writing a WHILE block or DO block with early exit based on a calculated value.

   The problem: A number GUESS is the square root of a number N if and only if the value of N/GUESS is equal to GUESS. Furthermore, if GUESS is bigger than the square root of N, then N/GUESS is smaller than GUESS, and vice versa. The problem is to find the square root of an input integer, or the two integers closest to the square root in case it is not an integer.

   The method of solution: Test all integers from 1 to the input number N by seeing if N/GUESS and GUESS are equal. If the square root of N is an integer, it will be found by this test. If the square root of N is not an integer, testing should continue until GUESS exceeds N/GUESS. At that time GUESS and GUESS -1 are the two integers surrounding the square root of N.

Input data: One positive integer. For example,

```
72
```

Sample output:

```
INPUT DATA  N:  72
THE SQUARE ROOT OF  72  IS BETWEEN  8  AND  9
```

10. **Purpose:** To calculate a scientifically useful sum using a DO loop.

The problem: A 3-dimensional vector v is a quantity described by means of 3 components, v_1, v_2, and v_3. The magnitude of a vector is the quantity

$$\sqrt{v_1^2 + v_2^2 + v_3^2}$$

Calculate the magnitude of a vector for the three component values given in the input file. Use a DO block executed 3 times and a variable VSUBI to hold each component when it is read and SUM to accumulate the sum of the squares of the components.

Input data: Three real numbers, representing the components of a 3-dimensional vector. For example,

```
5.0 12.0 13.0
```

Sample output:

```
INPUT DATA  VSUBI:  5.00000
INPUT DATA  VSUBI:  12.0000
INPUT DATA  VSUBI:  13.0000
THE MAGNITUDE OF THE VECTOR IS  18.3848
```

5 SUBPROGRAMS, MODULARITY, AND STEPWISE REFINEMENT

Subroutines and functions collectively are called **subprograms**. Original Fortran did not have independent subprograms, but within a year, six new statements were added to the language, all having to do with subroutines and function subprograms. Thus, as early as 1958, it was realized that large programs were extremely difficult to debug unless they could be split into independent modules. Modern programming practice has gone even further. Even relatively short programs are greatly improved when their component parts are refined as subprograms. Subprograms provide a simple way to specify a possibly complex sequence of steps in a program.

A large part of this chapter is the complete top-down analysis, in Sections 5.2 to 5.4, of a large problem, from the initial statement of the problem to the final executable Fortran program of over 100 lines. Programmer-defined subroutines provide the key for doing this.

In the first examples of the use of subprograms, calling programs communicate with a subroutine by putting exactly the same list of names in the parentheses of the CALL statement as appear in the parentheses of the SUBROUTINE statement. This method is easy to learn and permits modularization. However, it is possible to communicate values between a calling program and a subroutine in a much more general way.

The twin themes of the second half of this chapter are

1. Subprograms are independent from each other and from the main program.
2. Arguments provide a flexible and reliable channel for passing information to and from a subprogram.

In Fortran, all variables used in a subprogram are **local** to that subprogram. Even if a variable in another subprogram or in a calling program happens to have the same name as a local variable, Fortran considers the two to be different. Changes in a local variable cannot *ever* cause side effects by changing the value of a variable with the same name in another subprogram.

Fortran has two **argument passing** conventions. In one convention, information is passed from the supplied argument to the corresponding dummy argument, but no information may be returned from that dummy argument. In the other argument-passing convention, information may flow in both directions. The form of the supplied argument determines which convention applies.

A function is a subprogram closely resembling a subroutine. When the purpose of a programming process is to obtain a single value, that process may be written as a function rather than as a subroutine. Finding the average of a list of numbers is such a process. Arguments may be passed to functions as well as to subroutines.

When a program is planned from the top down, the steps that appear in a high-level analysis of the problem often will take many Fortran statements to refine. One good way to prevent the high-level organization of the problem from becoming submerged in a sea of details is to refine these steps as calls to subroutines. The subroutine call preserves the organization, and the subroutine supplies the details. In this section, we discuss how to write subroutines.

Local Variables:

With the exception of its dummy arguments, all variables in a subroutine are local variables. A local variable is known only in one subroutine and may have the same name as a variable in another subroutine or in the main program.

The CALL and SUBROUTINE Statements

One way to find class averages for several classes is to repeat several times the process of finding the class average for one class. The program AVGSEV (average of several) implements this strategy, refining the step of finding the class average for one class by a **subroutine call**

```
CALL AVGONE
```

to a **subroutine** named AVGONE (average of one). A subroutine is **called** by writing its name after the keyword CALL in a CALL statement. Subroutines enable a programmer to write a program in larger conceptual units, making it easier to keep from getting lost in the mass of details.

Refining a step in the program by a subroutine call does not relieve the programmer of responsibility for supplying the details for that step. It just moves the details from the main program to a separate subroutine.

```
C       PROGRAM AVGSEV
        INTEGER NRCLAS, CLSCNT
C
C       MAIN PROGRAM TO FIND THE AVERAGE TEST SCORES
C       FOR SEVERAL CLASSES
C
        READ, NRCLAS
        PRINT, 'INPUT DATA  NRCLAS:', NRCLAS
        DO 18 CLSCNT = 1, NRCLAS
           CALL AVGONE
   18   CONTINUE
        STOP
        END
C
C
        SUBROUTINE AVGONE
C       FIND THE CLASS AVERAGE FOR ONE CLASS
C
        INTEGER ENROLL, COUNT
        REAL SUM, SCORE
C
        PRINT, ' '
        PRINT, ' '
        READ, ENROLL
        PRINT, 'INPUT DATA  ENROLL:', ENROLL
C
        SUM = 0
        DO 18 COUNT = 1, ENROLL
           READ, SCORE
           PRINT 15, 'INPUT DATA  SCORE:', SCORE
   15      FORMAT (T2, A18, F10.4)
           SUM = SUM + SCORE
   18   CONTINUE
C
```

```
      PRINT, ' '
      PRINT 25, 'AVERAGE TEST SCORE =', SUM / ENROLL
   25 FORMAT (T2, A20, F10.4)
      RETURN
      END
```

```
INPUT DATA  NRCLAS:              3


INPUT DATA  ENROLL:              6
INPUT DATA  SCORE:   73.0000
INPUT DATA  SCORE:   68.0000
INPUT DATA  SCORE:   94.0000
INPUT DATA  SCORE:   88.0000
INPUT DATA  SCORE:   75.0000
INPUT DATA  SCORE:   79.0000

AVERAGE TEST SCORE =    79.5000


INPUT DATA  ENROLL:              2
INPUT DATA  SCORE:   76.0000
INPUT DATA  SCORE:   83.0000

AVERAGE TEST SCORE =    79.5000


INPUT DATA  ENROLL:              4
INPUT DATA  SCORE:   99.0000
INPUT DATA  SCORE:   77.0000
INPUT DATA  SCORE:   64.0000
INPUT DATA  SCORE:   73.0000

AVERAGE TEST SCORE =    78.2500
```

The details of the subroutine AVGONE appear after the main program AVGSEV. In some Fortran systems, a subroutine and its calling program may go in either order, or in fact, be compiled completely separately from one another. However, top-down design is based on planning the main program first and looking at the details later. From this point of view it is clearer and more natural to put the highest level executive or main program first and the details later.

END, RETURN, and STOP Statements

Each program or subprogram segment must end with an END statement. Thus the program AVGSEV has two END statements, one at the end of the main program, and one at the end of the subroutine AVGONE. In WATFIV, the last statement executed in a subroutine must be a RETURN statement consisting only of the keyword RETURN. Similarly, main programs must end with STOP statements. If the STOP or RETURN statements are omitted, WATFIV prints the error message

```
END STATEMENT NOT PRECEDED BY A TRANSFER
```

The meaning of this error message is that END statements are not executable in WATFIV, and the absence of a STOP or RETURN statement at the end of a program or subroutine would allow control to flow to the END statement. A

RETURN statement is considered a transfer back to the calling program and a STOP statement is a transfer back to the WATFIV-S operating system.

Arguments

The relationship between the main program AVGSEV and the subroutine AVGONE is particularly simple because there are no values that must be available to both modules. The values NRCLAS (number of classes) and the counter CLSCNT (class count) are used in the main program and the values ENROLL, COUNT, SCORE, and SUM are used in the subroutine. (See Table 5.1.)

Table 5.1 Accessibility of variables in the program AVGSEV.

Main program	Subroutine AVGONE
NRCLAS	ENROLL
CLSCNT	COUNT
	SCORE
	SUM

It is more often the case that values need to be shared. Suppose a test consists of three parts, each worth a maximum of 50 points. A student's grade on this test is the sum of the two highest part scores. We now write a program AVG3 that finds the class average for this test. For clarity, we use a subroutine GETONE to read the three part scores and to determine the test score for one student, so that these details do not appear in the main program. In particular, the main averaging program does not need to know the three part scores for a student, but it does need to share access to the value of SCORE, the test score determined from them. For this reason, SCORE appears as an argument for the subroutine GETONE. (See Table 5.2.)

Table 5.2 Accessibility of variables in the subroutine GETONE.

Main program	Both	Subroutine AVGONE
NRSTDT	SCORE	S1
STUDNT		S2
SUM		S3
SIGNAL		

```
C       PROGRAM AVG3
C       COUNT THE NUMBER OF STUDENTS AND
C       CALCULATE THE CLASS AVERAGE TEST SCORE
C       A NEGATIVE TEST SCORE IS A TERMINATION SIGNAL
C
        INTEGER NRSTDT, STUDNT, SUM, SCORE, SIGNAL
        LOGICAL MORSTD
C
```

```
      SIGNAL = -1
      SUM = 0
      NRSTDT = 0
C
      MORSTD = .TRUE.
      WHILE (MORSTD) DO
         CALL GETONE (SCORE)
C        A NEGATIVE SCORE IS A TERMINATION SIGNAL
         IF (SCORE .GT. SIGNAL) THEN DO
            PRINT, 'SCORE =', SCORE
            SUM = SUM + SCORE
            NRSTDT = NRSTDT + 1
         ELSE DO
            MORSTD = .FALSE.
         END IF
      END WHILE
C
      IF (NRSTDT .GT. 0) THEN DO
         PRINT, ' '
         PRINT, 'THE NUMBER OF STUDENTS IS', NRSTDT
         PRINT 15, 'THE AVERAGE SCORE IS', FLOAT (SUM) / NRSTDT
   15    FORMAT (T2, A20, F10.4)
      ELSE DO
         PRINT, 'THERE ARE NO STUDENTS'
      END IF
      STOP
      END
C
      SUBROUTINE GETONE (SCORE)
C     A STUDENT'S TEST SCORE IS THE SUM
C     OF THE TWO LARGEST PART SCORES
C
      INTEGER S1, S2, S3, SCORE
C
      READ, S1, S2, S3
      PRINT, 'INPUT DATA  SCORES:', S1, S2, S3
C     ADD UP THE SCORES, BUT EXCLUDE THE SMALLEST ONE
      SCORE = S1 + S2 + S3 - MIN0 (S1, S2, S3)
      RETURN
      END
```

```
INPUT DATA  SCORES:           40           30           35
SCORE =          75
INPUT DATA  SCORES:           45           45           30
SCORE =          90
INPUT DATA  SCORES:           35           37           48
SCORE =          85
INPUT DATA  SCORES:           -1           -1           -1

THE NUMBER OF STUDENTS IS              3
THE AVERAGE SCORE IS   83.3333
```

The quantities listed in parentheses after the subroutine name both in the CALL statement and in the SUBROUTINE statement are **arguments**. These are the values that need to be shared between the main program and the subroutine. The subroutine GETONE has only one argument SCORE, because that is the only value needed by both the subroutine and the main program. In this case the subroutine computes the value of SCORE and the main program uses it. Notice that the variable SCORE needs to be declared in both the main program and the subroutine.

The argument mechanism is a very powerful one in Fortran, but for now we use it only in this simple way: all values shared by a subroutine and main program are listed as arguments both in the CALL statement in the main program and the SUBROUTINE statement in the subroutine. If there is more than one argument, they are separated by commas.

5.2 Case Study: Grade Reports for a College

The time has come to put all the pieces together for a full-scale test. We have at our disposal most of the major programming features of Fortran: input, output, arithmetic calculations, assignment, character strings, IF blocks, DO blocks, WHILE blocks, and subroutines. We have the methodology for attacking complex problems described in Chapter 1: top-down design with stepwise refinements. We are now in a position to trace the solution of a problem from its initial statement to the final executable Fortran program which solves it.

Section Preview

Top-Down Analysis:

A problem is attacked first at a high conceptual level that is natural to the human program planner and close to the statement of the problem.

Successive Refinement:

Each level of solution of the problem is refined by replacing relatively higher-level descriptions of steps by more detailed, lower-level descriptions of the same steps. Ultimately, an executable program is produced.

Modularity:

Readability of the final program is maintained by breaking it into modules called **subroutines**. This method also retains a record of the top-down analysis of the problem.

Arrays:

An **array** is a list or collection of similar data items. The array name specifies which collection and the subscript specifies which data item within the collection.

Array Declarations:

General Form:

type arrayname (largest subscript)

Examples:

```
REAL GNP (25), PROFIT (25)
CHARACTER TITLE *25 (12)
```

The Problem: Preparation of Grade Reports

South Mountain College is a liberal arts school with 1037 students presently enrolled. Although some administrative tasks are done by the computer, until recently each student's grade report was prepared by hand and typed. Gradepoint averages were computed on hand calculators and typed into the report as well. In the fall of last year as a senior project, computer science major Rena Little prepared an analysis of the system then in effect and the extent to which it might be automated. We follow her analysis.

She observed that the registrar maintains a file of index cards prepared during registration, one for each student, with the student's roster of courses written on the card. This roster includes the name of each course and the number of credits that each course is worth. In most courses, the number of credits equals the number of hours per week that a course meets.

At the end of a semester, the instructors send copies of the grades to the registrar, and the registrar's assistants transfer the grades to these index cards. The grade reports are prepared from these index cards. For instance, Figure 5.1 shows a report for a student named Gordon Grimswell.

Name: Gordon Grimswell — Class: 1989
Semester: Fall, 1985 — GPA: 3.06

Course	*Credits*	*Grade*
Applications Programming for Turing Machines 105	3	B
Survey of Inca Music 321	2	A
Phrenology 294	4	A
Conversational Aztec 308	5	C
Precambrian Art & Architecture 220	4	B

Figure 5.1 A grade report for a student at South Mountain College.

To calculate a gradepoint average (abbreviated GPA) at South Mountain College, the first step is to convert letter grades A, B, C, D, and F to the respective numerical values 4, 3, 2, 1, and 0, which are called number grades. The product of the number grade for a course and the number of credits is the student's gradepoint score in the course. For example, Gordon Grimswell has a gradepoint score of $3 \times 3 = 9$ in Applications Programming for Turing Machines 105 and a score of $2 \times 4 = 8$ in Survey of Inca Music 321. Overall, he earned a total gradepoint score of

$$3 \times 3 + 2 \times 4 + 4 \times 4 + 5 \times 2 + 4 \times 3 = 55$$

in the fall semester of 1983.

The gradepoint average is calculated by dividing the total gradepoint score by the total number of credits taken. Since Grimswell took

$$3 + 2 + 4 + 5 + 4 = 18$$

credits and earned 55 gradepoints, his GPA is

$$55 / 18 = 3.055555...$$

The gradepoint average is rounded to two decimal places and recorded on the grade report.

How to Begin Writing a Program

We are faced with the task of constructing a program complex enough that it might not be obvious where to begin programming. Top-down programming means to begin to write a program in a form understandable to humans, almost as though you were writing for a much smarter computer than you actually have available. Then you go back over the program and refine it.

If some of the steps happen to be in a computer-executable language, so much the better. If not, the refinement process continues until they are. Even in parts of the program description that are not yet computer-executable, choose constructions that resemble keywords and phrases of the target language, Fortran. This makes the task of converting preliminary descriptions into executable statements a little easier.

The following version of the program GRADES might be a suitable beginning for the refinement process.

```
C       PROGRAM GRADES
C       PROCESS GRADE REPORTS FOR ENTIRE COLLEGE
        Read the input data that is common to all students
        DO for every student in the college
           Process the grade report for that student
        CONTINUE
        STOP
        END
```

Although this initial version of the program might appear vague or even ambiguous because of its lack of detail, it is a small but definite step in the right direction. It expresses quite clearly the undeniable fact that the way to do grade reports for the entire college is to do them one student at a time until they are all done.

The structure of this initial version makes some token gestures in the direction of Fortran syntax, but the statements are really designed to be read by people, and then only by people who understand the procedures of the registrar's office.

Choice of Loop Structure

Although South Mountain College has exactly 1037 students, it would be unwise to carve this enrollment figure in stone in the program. (Note: Neolithic computers supported carved stone; modern computers do not. Babylonian computers could read clay tablets, however.) Thus, we reject a DO block with a fixed number of iterations and choose a WHILE block with duplicated initialization to run through all the students in the college. This choice also permits processing the entire college's grade reports in several smaller batches.

```
C       PROGRAM GRADES
C       REFINEMENT 1:  WHILE LOOP CHOSEN
C       PROCESS GRADE REPORTS FOR ENTIRE COLLEGE
        Read the input data that is common to all students
        Inquire if there are more students this run
        WHILE (there are more students) DO
           Process the grade report for one student
           Inquire if there are more students this run
        END WHILE
        STOP
        END
```

The top-down analysis has been partially successful; we now have two simpler problems to solve (see also Figure 5.2). They are:

1. How do we read the input data common to all students?
2. How do we process a grade report for one student?

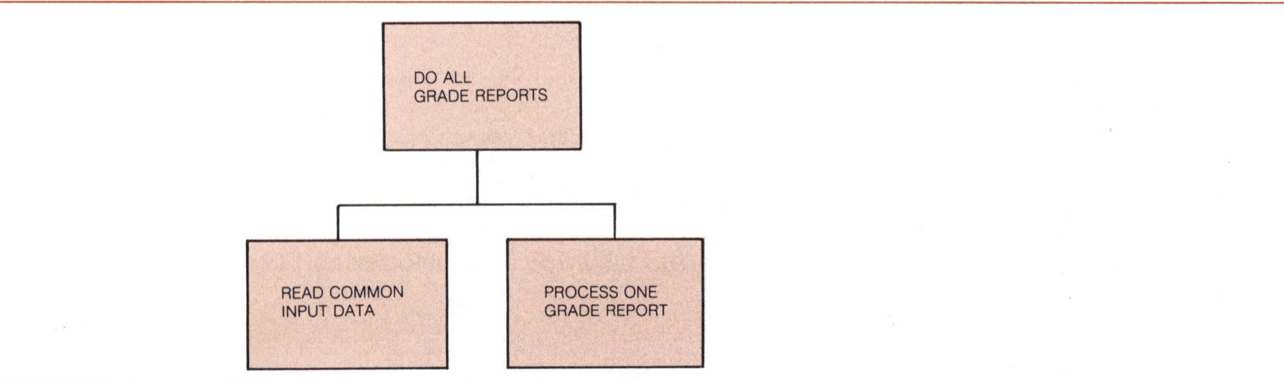

Figure 5.2 A breakdown of the gradepoint problem into two parts.

Knowing that initialization statements are best refined last, we pass over Step 1 and refine Step 2:

```
        Process one grade report
```

Modularity

Processing the grade report for one student has all the hallmarks of a **modular subprocess:**

1. It is reasonably self-contained.
2. It is described easily. (We just did it in seven words.)
3. It is a meaningful conceptual unit to the designer and reader of the program.

Therefore we refine this subprocess into a subroutine call.

```
        CALL ONEREP
```

and supply the details in the subroutine ONEREP (one grade report). Drawing on our analysis of how gradepoint averages and hence grade reports are prepared, we may write the following refinement of the subroutine ONEREP.

```
        SUBROUTINE ONEREP
C       FOR ONE STUDENT ONLY
        Read all the input data for this student
        Convert letter grades to number grades
        Calculate the gradepoint average (GPA)
        Print the finished grade report
        RETURN
        END
```

Even though more details have been supplied, we are still asking too much of a computer. It would have to be able to read and understand the preceding pages of this section. It would have to know that the input data consists of the information found on the registrar's index cards. It would have to know how to convert letter grades to number grades and how to calculate a gradepoint average. And it would have to know what information belongs in the finished grade report and how to print it.

Although it is easy to find humans who understand these instructions (for example, the clerical staff in the registrar's office), a computer will not understand them without further elaboration of the details. Therefore, we continue with the process of refining the program, making its meaning more explicit by spelling out some of the steps in greater detail. We may measure our progress, as shown in Figure 5.3, by the fact that we have broken up the subproblem of processing one grade report into four still smaller problems:

1. Reading all the input data for one student.
2. Converting letter grades to number grades.
3. Calculating the gradepoint average.
4. Printing the final report for the one student.

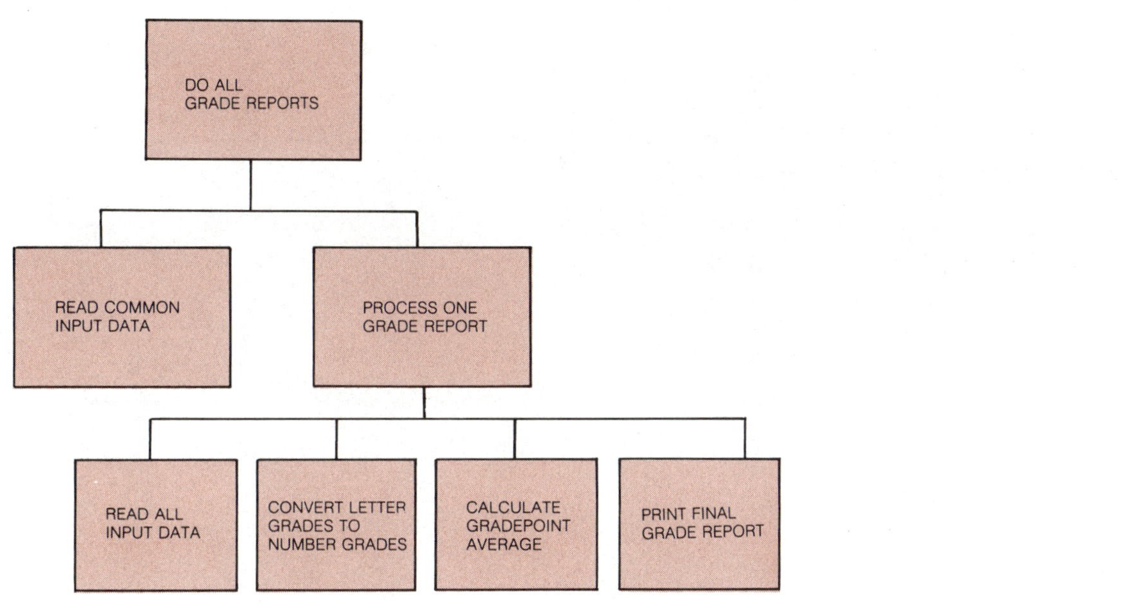

Figure 5.3 A further breakdown: one part of the gradepoint problem is decomposed into four subparts.

Refining the Output Statement

Since we do not have a super-smart computer that can execute this version of the procedure ONEREP, we must refine the program by replacing one or more of its statements by other statements describing the same part of the program in greater detail. Each refinement is a little bit further along the way toward converting the program into Fortran.

Often, a good place to start refining a program is either with the input or output statement. Such a refinement will make explicit exactly what answers we want the program to print and what input data must be supplied to the computer so that it has enough information to calculate these answers. In the process, we also will make explicit the names of some of the variables that appear in the input and output sections of the program.

In this program as in most programs, the output section is easier to refine first because the form of the output is specified in the problem description. Stated simply, the registrar would like the output to look like the grade report shown earlier in Figure 5.1. With a copy of Figure 5.1 in front of us, it is not hard to write a procedure that produces output resembling it. Don't worry too much now about the exact spacing of the fields in the gradc report. All we want to do is to get close to the specified appearance of the grade report, and then we will hash out the final details with the registrar later. A sample grade report, done on graph paper, was used to get the format descriptors used below.

```
      SUBROUTINE PRINT (NAME, CLASS, SEMSTR, GPA,
     +                  NRCORS, MAXCRS, TITLE, CREDIT, LETTER)
C     PRINT GRADE REPORT FOR ONE STUDENT
C
      CHARACTER  NAME *35, SEMSTR *15
      REAL GPA
      INTEGER CLASS, NRCORS, MAXCRS, CREDIT (MAXCRS), COURSE
      CHARACTER TITLE *25 (MAXCRS), LETTER *1 (MAXCRS)
C
      PRINT, ' '
      PRINT 15, 'NAME:  ', NAME, 'CLASS:  ', CLASS
   15 FORMAT (T2, A7, A35, T40, A8, I4)
      PRINT 25, 'SEMESTER AND YEAR:  ', SEMSTR, 'GPA:  ', GPA
   25 FORMAT (T2, A20, A15, T40, A6, F6.2)
      PRINT, ' '
      PRINT 35, 'COURSE', 'CREDIT', 'GRADE'
   35 FORMAT (T2, A15, A30, A15)
C
      DO 18 COURSE = 1, NRCORS
         PRINT 45,
     +         TITLE (COURSE), CREDIT (COURSE), LETTER (COURSE)
   45 FORMAT (T2, A25, I18, A15)
   18 CONTINUE
C
      PRINT, ' '
      RETURN
      END
```

Notice that the subroutine PRINT is written entirely in Fortran. (The Fortran features, some new, are explained in the next several pages.) This branch of the top-down design process has produced a refinement that is an executable subroutine.

Variable Names

The name of the subroutine, PRINT, is identical with the keyword used in PRINT statements. This is no problem. Fortran keywords are not reserved.

Following the subroutine name is a list of variables shared between the subroutine PRINT and its calling program. Since every variable to be printed is calculated in another part of the program, each appears in this list of dummy arguments.

In order to write executable Fortran code, it was necessary to choose names for the variables whose values will be printed on the final grade report. The student's name will be in a character string of length 35 called NAME. Few names are longer than 35 characters, so this should be enough room.

```
      CHARACTER NAME *35
```

The student's graduating class will be kept in an integer type variable called CLASS, the semester will be in a character string of length 15 called SEMSTR, and the student's gradepoint average will be the value of a real type variable called GPA. All of these variable names are **self-documenting**, that is, each variable name, in large measure, explains what its values will represent.

```
INTEGER CLASS
CHARACTER SEMSTR *15
REAL GPA
```

Arrays

Collections of any type of data can be organized into **arrays**, which are subscripted lists of values. For instance, suppose that the author of a popular textbook wants to write a program concerned with the number of copies her book sold in the first ten years and her royalties in those years. The declarations

```
INTEGER SALES (10)
REAL ROYLTY (10)
```

would enable her to use the integer-valued quantities SALES (1), SALES (2), ..., SALES (10) and real-valued quantities ROYLTY (1), ROYLTY (2), ..., ROYLTY (10) in her program.

A DO block can tell the computer to read the sales figures and royalties one year at a time, as follows:

```
      DO 18 YEAR = 1, 10
         READ, SALES (YEAR), ROYLTY (YEAR)
   18 CONTINUE
```

These fragmentary examples barely hint at the possible uses of DO blocks in conjunction with arrays, treated in detail in Chapter 6. An array allows a number of related values of the same kind to be stored in memory locations with the same array name, but with different relative locations. The relative location of an individual element in an array is indicated by its **subscript** value written in parentheses after the array name. Subscripts must be type integer.

A DO block allows all of the data items in an array to be processed simply. The DO variable is used as the array subscript. Thus, when a statement containing such an array reference is executed repeatedly in a DO block, the subscript changes each time, until it runs through all the values indicated in the DO statement.

Programming Note: An array is used to hold several values of the same kind simultaneously. If the values are not needed simultaneously, a simple variable should be used.

In the program for processing grade reports, some of the variables must be arrays because there is more than one piece of data of that type. For example, there is ordinarily one letter grade for each course, and a student usually takes more than one course per semester. Assuming that no student takes more than 12 courses in a semester and that MAXCRS is assigned the value 12 in the calling program, we make the following declarations for the variable MAXCRS (maximum number of courses) and the variable LETTER (letter grade).

```
INTEGER MAXCRS
CHARACTER LETTER *1 (MAXCRS)
```

The declaration

```
CHARACTER LETTER *1 (MAXCRS)
```

which is valid only if MAXCRS is an integer-valued dummy argument of the subroutine, specifies that the valid subscripts for the array LETTER go from 1 to MAXCRS, which is 12. Each array element will hold one character. The array element LETTER (1) will hold the letter grade for the first course the student took, the array element LETTER (2) will hold the letter grade for the second course the student took, and so forth. If the value of the integer type variable NRCORS is the number of courses the student took in the semester of the grade report, the array element LETTER (NRCORS) will hold the letter grade for the last course the student took. All array elements with higher subscripts will have either undefined values or values left over from the grade report of some previous student. In any event, they will not be used in the current grade report because the DO variable in the subroutine PRINT runs only from 1 to NRCORS.

Note that in the declaration of the array of character strings, the description of the string length precedes the allowable subscripts. Fortran 77 uses the opposite order.

Since the number of credits for each course is always an integer (at least at South Mountain College), the following declaration for the array credit is suitable.

```
      INTEGER CREDIT (MAXCRS)
```

If South Mountain College ever introduces fractional credit for courses, we simply change INTEGER to REAL.

Two additional variables, whose values do not appear in the printed output, were necessary to write the subroutine PRINT. They are the DO variable COURSE and its upper limit NRCORS, both of type integer. Since neither the variable NRCORS nor any of the printed variables is assigned a value in the subroutine PRINT, using and printing these values in the subroutine imposes an obligation on the rest of the program to assign values to them before the subroutine PRINT is executed. Also, these variables must appear in the list of dummy arguments so their values can be shared.

Converting Letter Grades to Number Grades

For those who are keeping track of our progress, we are working on the subproblem "Process one grade report", which was refined to four subproblems. The score is one down ("Print final grade report"), three to go. We even have some executable Fortran code to show for our efforts, although the planning that went into the preliminary version actually represents more progress than the executable code.

We shift to high gear and look for another subproblem to conquer. If success with the output problem suggests attempting the input subproblem, we suppress the idea because reading input is a kind of initialization, and we still do not know for sure exactly what values must be read until we have explored the details of the calculations that will be done on them.

So we write a subroutine to convert letter grades to number grades. The task is straightforward and there are no difficulties. We need another array NUMBER to hold the number grades. Nesting of IF blocks is useful for doing the actual conversion of individual letter grades to the equivalent number grades.

```
      SUBROUTINE CONVRT (NRCORS, MAXCRS, LETTER, NUMBER)
C     CONVERTS LETTER GRADES TO NUMBER GRADES
C
      INTEGER NRCORS, MAXCRS, NUMBER (MAXCRS), COURSE
      CHARACTER LETTER *1 (MAXCRS), L *1
C
      DO 18 COURSE = 1, NRCORS
         L = LETTER (COURSE)
         IF (L .EQ. 'A') THEN DO
            NUMBER (COURSE) = 4
```

```
           ELSE DO
           IF (L .EQ. 'B') THEN DO
              NUMBER (COURSE) = 3
           ELSE DO
           IF (L .EQ. 'C') THEN DO
              NUMBER (COURSE) = 2
           ELSE DO
           IF (L .EQ. 'D') THEN DO
              NUMBER (COURSE) = 1
           ELSE DO
              NUMBER (COURSE) = 0
           END IF
           END IF
           END IF
           END IF
   18   CONTINUE
        RETURN
        END
```

All of the cases in the nested IF blocks are distinguished on that basis of the possible values for a single variable, L, the letter grade being converted. This kind of decision structure is called the **case construct** in other programming languages. WATFIV-S has a CASE statement, but the selector variable must take on small integer values starting with 1. This is a severe and awkward restriction, so we always use the more flexible and powerful IF block constructions that can handle more varied ways of selecting the proper case.

Calculating the Gradepoint Average

Two down and two to go! We now write a subroutine to calculate a gradepoint average. Each course contributes to the total gradepoint score a number of gradepoints equal to credit for the course × the numbergrade for the course. The gradepoint average is the quotient of the total gradepoint score and the total credits for courses taken in the semester. A first pseudocode version of the subroutine CLCGPA (calculate gpa) follows immediately.

```
SUBROUTINE CLCGPA
Calculate total gradepoint score
Calculate total credits
GPA = totalgradepoints / totalcredits
RETURN
END
```

As Figure 5.4 shows, CLCGPA is refined using three subproblems, one of them already solved.

The two remaining subproblems are solved easily with DO blocks that accumulate the appropriate sums. Since the details are so short, we do not refine these subproblems into additional subroutine calls. Instead, we place the initial version of the subproblem statement as a comment and place the DO block that implements the accumulation of the sum below it.

```
      SUBROUTINE CLCGPA (NRCORS, MAXCRS, NUMBER, CREDIT, GPA)
C     CALCULATE GRADE POINT AVERAGE (GPA)
C
      INTEGER NRCORS, MAXCRS, NUMBER (MAXCRS), CREDIT (MAXCRS)
      REAL GPA
      INTEGER POINTS, CREDTS, COURSE
C
```

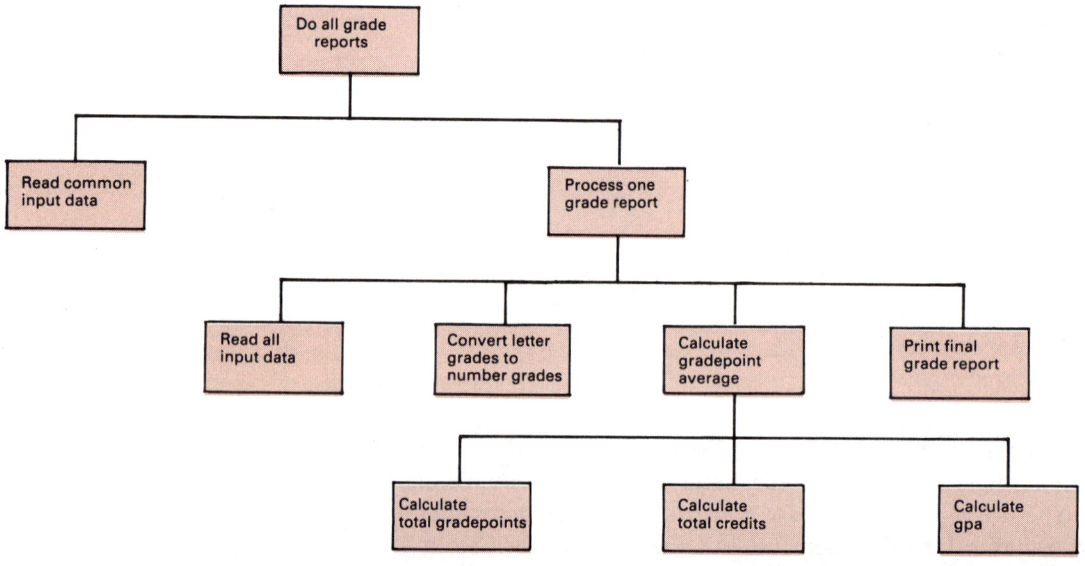

Figure 5.4 Refining the gradepoint average calculation to three subproblems.

```
C       CALCULATE TOTAL GRADE POINTS
        POINTS = 0
        DO 18 COURSE = 1, NRCORS
           POINTS = POINTS + NUMBER (COURSE) * CREDIT (COURSE)
   18   CONTINUE
C
C       CALCULATE TOTAL CREDITS
        CREDTS = 0
        DO 28 COURSE = 1, NRCORS
           CREDTS = CREDTS + CREDIT (COURSE)
   28   CONTINUE
C
C       CALCULATE GPA
        GPA = FLOAT (POINTS) / FLOAT (CREDTS)
        RETURN
        END
```

Three down, one to go! We refine the remaining level 3 subproblem, "read all input data for one student", in the next section. It consolidates some techniques used to handle the fact that the number of courses taken, and thus the amount of input data, will vary from one student to another.

5.3 Refining Input Procedures

Refinement of the gradepoint average program continues in this section. The input subroutine refined here uses a programmer-defined signal to terminate reading of variable length data.

Section Preview

Programmer-Defined Termination Signals:

A program can recognize certain input responses of the programmer's choosing as signals that no more data of the current kind will be forthcoming. Recognition of termination signal data can be used to trigger termination of a DO block.

Refining the Input Subroutine

We have left the input subroutine for last because it is the hardest. First of all, until we had refined all the other subproblems, we couldn't be sure exactly what information these subroutines would require, so we couldn't write the input subroutine to supply it. Second, the amount of input data in each category is variable. The number of courses taken is not the same for all students.

Since we now know what data is absolutely needed to calculate and print a grade report for one student, we may write a first version of the subroutine GETDAT (read one student's data). The character string SEMSTR (semester) is not read in this subroutine because it is information common to all students. Therefore it will be read in a subroutine GETCOM (get common information), called outside the loop that runs through all the students.

```
      SUBROUTINE GETDAT
C     READ ALL INPUT DATA FOR ONE STUDENT
C     FIRST VERSION

      Read the student's name
      Read the student's graduating class
      DO for every course this student took this semester
         Read title of course
         Read credit for course
         Read letter grade for course
      CONTINUE
      RETURN
      END
```

If the registrar's record-keeping operations had been computerized for some time, it would be likely that the input information would already be available in some file that contains not only the relevant information read above, but also lots of other information about the student and the courses. Since the only way to skip information in an input file is to read it, the input subroutine would then have to read both relevant and extraneous information for each student so that subsequent calls to the subroutine GETDAT would be able to read information for the next student. The rest of the program simply would ignore the extraneous information.

Interactive vs. Batch Input

We have to decide whether reading input will be interactive, with input entered during execution, or whether an input data file will be prepared for all students in advance. The decision was an easy one. South Mountain College ran only WATFIV-S in batch mode.

Counting the Number of Courses

The number of courses varies from one student to the next. We therefore use a programmer-defined end-of-data signal to terminate input for each student. The **termination signal** we choose is a course title of "NO MORE COURSES".

We have a choice of three loop structures to handle the variable amount of input data: WHILE loop with duplicated initialization, WHILE loop with flag, and DO block with exit. We choose the DO block with exit for this subroutine because the DO variable COURSE that counts the iterations has a natural interpretation and even more important, a natural use in the loop as the subscript in the arrays TITLE, LETTER, and CREDIT to distinguish data for one course from data for another course. The final value of the DO variable COURSE also indicates how many courses the student took.

```
      SUBROUTINE GETDAT (NAME, CLASS, TITLE, CREDIT,
     +                   LETTER, NRCORS, MAXCRS)
      INTEGER CLASS, MAXCRS, CREDIT (MAXCRS), NRCORS, COURSE, UPLIM
      CHARACTER NAME *35, TITLE *25 (MAXCRS), LETTER *1 (MAXCRS)
      CHARACTER TTLBUF *25
C
      READ 15, NAME
   15 FORMAT (A35)
      PRINT, 'NAME: ', NAME
C
      READ, CLASS
      PRINT, 'CLASS: ', CLASS
C
      UPLIM = MAXCRS + 1
      DO 18 COURSE = 1, UPLIM
         PRINT, 'ENTER NEXT COURSE TITLE:'
         READ 25, TTLBUF
   25    FORMAT (A25)
         IF (TTLBUF .NE. 'NO MORE COURSES' .AND.
     +       COURSE .LE. MAXCRS) THEN DO
            TITLE (COURSE) = TTLBUF
            READ, CREDIT (COURSE)
            PRINT, 'CREDIT: ', CREDIT (COURSE)
            READ, LETTER (COURSE)
            PRINT, 'GRADE: ', LETTER (COURSE)
         ELSE DO
            NRCORS = COURSE - 1
            GO TO 19
         END IF
   18 CONTINUE
C
   19 RETURN
      END
```

Progress Report

Four down and none to go! Or at least, so it seems. In our elation at writing executable Fortran for all four subproblems of processing one grade report, we may have momentarily lost sight of the fact that this completely solves only one part of the main problem "Do all grade reports".

Refining the Main Program

Since we are ready to solve the remaining level 2 subproblems, we reproduce the latest version of the main program GRADES for reference.

```
C       PROGRAM GRADES
C       REFINEMENT 1:  WHILE LOOP CHOSEN
C       PROCESS GRADE REPORTS FOR ENTIRE COLLEGE
        Read the input data that is common to all students
        Inquire if there are more students this run
        WHILE (there are more students) DO
           Process the grade report for one student
           Inquire if there are more students this run
        END WHILE
        STOP
        END
```

The input data common to all students turns out to consist only of the semester, so this step is refined by the single statement

```
        READ, SEMSTR
```

This statement will appear in the subroutine GETCOM (get common information). The subroutine ONEREP (do one grade report), with all its subordinate subroutines, was the result of completely refining the subproblem of processing the grade report for one student. All that is left to do is to refine the details of the WHILE loop structure that repeats the subroutine ONEREP for every student in the college.

In a batch execution "inquiring if there are more students this run" can only mean reaching an item of data that answers this question. We will use the character string 'MORE' to indicate more students and the string 'DONE' to indicate no more students. The variable MORSTD (more students) will receive one of these two values to control the WHILE loop repetition vs. exit test. A graceful termination permits the printing of summary statistics, or at least a polite GOODBYE to the user.

```
C       PROGRAM GRADES
C       FINAL VERSION
C       PROCESS GRADE REPORTS FOR THE ENTIRE COLLEGE
C
        CHARACTER SEMSTR *15, MORSTD *4
        INTEGER STUDNT
C
        CALL GETCOM (SEMSTR)
        READ 15, MORSTD
   15   FORMAT (A4)
        WHILE (MORSTD .EQ. 'MORE') DO
           CALL ONEREP (SEMSTR)
           READ 15, MORSTD
           PRINT, MORSTD
        END WHILE
C
```

```
      PRINT
      PRINT, 'GOODBYE.  HAVE A NICE DAY.'
      STOP
      END
```

The planning process is now complete. We leave the tasks of assembling the pieces and testing the program to the next section.

5.4 Combining and Testing the Subroutines

In this section, we put together all the pieces of the solution of the gradepoint averaging program for the registrar's office at South Mountain College. These pieces have emerged from the top-down analysis of the problem in Sections 5.2 and 5.3. Then we test the program.

Section Preview

Final Synthesis:

The complete, executable Fortran program for the gradepoint average problem is shown and tested.

Subroutines:

Subroutines and the main program may be placed in any order, but it is recommended that subroutines follow the main program and lower level subroutines follow higher level subroutines.

Documentation:

A program should be supplied with internal and external documentation and a manual for its use by nonprogrammers.

Placement of Subroutines

In Fortran, the main program and subroutines may be placed in any order. However, in accordance with the objective of having the top-down design of the program highly visible to a reader of a program, the highest level component of the problem solution, the main program, should come first.

Following this reasoning down the line, all level 2 subroutines should follow the main program and all level 3 subroutines should follow the level 2 subroutines that call them. Thus the subroutines with the most specific details come last.

The Complete Fortran Program GRADES

To get the complete, executable, final version of the program, we have to do the straightforward but time-consuming job of collecting all the final executable versions of the subroutines written in Sections 5.2 and 5.3. They must be arranged in order of their generality, and declarations must be written for all the variables and parameters used in the program.

We can now see what we have accomplished. We have written a Fortran program of over a hundred lines. One point still needs to be clarified about the declaration of the highest subscript in an array. In the highest level subroutine that declares a particular array, the upper subscript bound must be an integer constant. In lower level subroutines called from this subroutine, the declared upper subscript bound may be an integer constant or an integer valued dummy argument of the subroutine. Thus in the subroutine ONEREP, where these arrays originate, the declared upper bounds for the subscript of the arrays TITLE, LETTER, CREDIT, and NUMBER are the constant 12. In lower level subroutines, the upper bound is the dummy argument MAXCRS, passed down from the originating subroutine ONEREP. Confining the constant 12 to only one subroutine makes it very easy to change this maximum subscript bound, should such a change prove necessary or desirable.

```
C     PROGRAM GRADES
C     FINAL VERSION
C     PROCESS GRADE REPORTS FOR THE ENTIRE COLLEGE
C
      CHARACTER SEMSTR *15, MORSTD *4
      INTEGER STUDNT
C
      CALL GETCOM (SEMSTR)
      READ 15, MORSTD
   15 FORMAT (A4)
      WHILE (MORSTD .EQ. 'MORE') DO
         CALL ONEREP (SEMSTR)
         READ 15, MORSTD
         PRINT, MORSTD
      END WHILE
C
      PRINT, ' '
      PRINT, 'GOODBYE.  HAVE A NICE DAY.'
      STOP
      END
C
C
      SUBROUTINE GETCOM (SEMSTR)
C     GET INFORMATION COMMON TO ALL STUDENTS
C
      CHARACTER SEMSTR *15
C
      READ 15, SEMSTR
   15 FORMAT (A15)
      PRINT, 'SEMESTER AND YEAR: ', SEMSTR
      RETURN
      END
C
C
      SUBROUTINE ONEREP (SEMSTR)
C     FINAL VERSION
C     DOES REPORT FOR ONE STUDENT ONLY
C
      CHARACTER SEMSTR *15
      CHARACTER NAME *35, TITLE *25 (12), LETTER *1 (12)
      INTEGER CLASS, CREDIT (12), NRCORS, NUMBER (12), MAXCRS
      REAL GPA
C
C     INITIALIZE ARRAY SIZE FOR ALL LOWER-LEVEL SUBROUTINES
      MAXCRS = 12
C
```

```
      CALL GETDAT (NAME, CLASS, TITLE, CREDIT, LETTER,
     +             NRCORS, MAXCRS)
      CALL CONVRT (NRCORS, MAXCRS, LETTER, NUMBER)
      CALL CLCGPA (NRCORS, MAXCRS, NUMBER, CREDIT, GPA)
      CALL PRINT (NAME, CLASS, SEMSTR, GPA,
     +            NRCORS, MAXCRS, TITLE, CREDIT, LETTER)
      RETURN
      END
C
C
      SUBROUTINE GETDAT (NAME, CLASS, TITLE, CREDIT, LETTER,
     +                   NRCORS, MAXCRS)
C     READS ALL THE DATA FOR ONE STUDENT
C     COUNTS THE NUMBER OF COURSES (NCORS) TAKEN
C
      INTEGER MAXCRS, UPLIM
      CHARACTER NAME *35, TITLE *25 (MAXCRS), LETTER *1 (MAXCRS)
      INTEGER CLASS, CREDIT (MAXCRS), NRCORS, COURSE
      CHARACTER TTLBUF *25
C
      READ 15, NAME
   15 FORMAT (A35)
      PRINT, 'NAME: ', NAME
C
      READ, CLASS
      PRINT, 'CLASS: ', CLASS
C
      UPLIM = MAXCRS + 1
      DO 18 COURSE = 1, UPLIM
         READ 25, TTLBUF
   25    FORMAT (A25)
         IF (TTLBUF .NE. 'NO MORE COURSES' .AND.
     +        COURSE .LE. MAXCRS) THEN DO
            TITLE (COURSE) = TTLBUF
            READ, CREDIT (COURSE)
            PRINT, 'CREDIT: ', CREDIT (COURSE)
            READ 35, LETTER (COURSE)
   35       FORMAT (A1)
            PRINT, 'GRADE: ', LETTER (COURSE)
         ELSE DO
            NRCORS = COURSE - 1
            GO TO 19
         END IF
   18 CONTINUE
C
   19 RETURN
      END
C

      SUBROUTINE CONVRT (NRCORS, MAXCRS, LETTER, NUMBER)
C     CONVERTS LETTER GRADES TO NUMBER GRADES
      INTEGER NRCORS, MAXCRS, NUMBER (MAXCRS), COURSE
      CHARACTER LETTER *1 (MAXCRS), L *1
C
```

```
      DO 18 COURSE = 1, NRCORS
         L = LETTER (COURSE)
         IF (L .EQ. 'A') THEN DO
            NUMBER (COURSE) = 4
         ELSE DO
         IF (L .EQ. 'B') THEN DO
            NUMBER (COURSE) = 3
         ELSE DO
         IF (L .EQ. 'C') THEN DO
            NUMBER (COURSE) = 2
         ELSE DO
         IF (L .EQ. 'D') THEN DO
            NUMBER (COURSE) = 1
         ELSE DO
            NUMBER (COURSE) = 0
         END IF
         END IF
         END IF
         END IF
   18 CONTINUE
      RETURN
      END
C
C
      SUBROUTINE CLCGPA (NRCORS, MAXCRS, NUMBER, CREDIT, GPA)
C     CALCULATE GRADE POINT AVERAGE (GPA)
      INTEGER NRCORS, MAXCRS, NUMBER (MAXCRS), CREDIT (MAXCRS)
      REAL GPA
      INTEGER POINTS, CREDTS, COURSE
C
C     CALCULATE TOTAL GRADE POINTS
      POINTS = 0
      DO 18 COURSE = 1, NRCORS
         POINTS = POINTS + NUMBER (COURSE) * CREDIT (COURSE)
   18 CONTINUE
C
C     CALCULATE TOTAL CREDITS
      CREDTS = 0
      DO 28 COURSE = 1, NRCORS
         CREDTS = CREDTS + CREDIT (COURSE)
   28 CONTINUE
C
C     CALCULATE GPA
      GPA = FLOAT (POINTS) / FLOAT (CREDTS)
      RETURN
      END
C
C
      SUBROUTINE PRINT (NAME, CLASS, SEMSTR, GPA,
     +                  NRCORS, MAXCRS, TITLE, CREDIT, LETTER)
C     PRINT GRADE REPORT FOR ONE STUDENT
      CHARACTER NAME *35, SEMSTR *15
      REAL GPA
      INTEGER CLASS, NRCORS, MAXCRS, CREDIT (MAXCRS), COURSE
      CHARACTER TITLE *25 (MAXCRS), LETTER *1 (MAXCRS)
```

```
C
      PRINT, ' '
      PRINT 15, 'NAME:  ', NAME, 'CLASS:  ', CLASS
   15 FORMAT (T2, A7, A35, T40, A8, I4)
      PRINT 25, 'SEMESTER AND YEAR:  ', SEMSTR, 'GPA:  ', GPA
   25 FORMAT (T2, A20, A15, T40, A6, F6.2)
      PRINT, ' '
      PRINT 35, 'COURSE', 'CREDIT', 'GRADE'
   35 FORMAT (T2, A7, A30, A15)
C
      DO 18 COURSE = 1, NRCORS
         PRINT 45,
     +         TITLE (COURSE), CREDIT (COURSE), LETTER (COURSE)
   45    FORMAT (T2, A25, I13, A15)
   18 CONTINUE
C
      PRINT, ' '
      RETURN
      END
```

```
SEMESTER AND YEAR:  FALL 1985
MORE
NAME:  GORDON GRIMSWELL
CLASS: 1989
CREDIT:                3
GRADE:  B
CREDIT:                2
GRADE:  A
CREDIT:                4
GRADE:  A
CREDIT:                5
GRADE:  C
CREDIT:                4
GRADE:  B

NAME:  GORDON GRIMSWELL                CLASS:  1989
SEMESTER AND YEAR:  FALL 1985          GPA:    3.06

COURSE                       CREDIT         GRADE
PROG. TURING MACHINES 105              3              B
SURVEY OF INCA MUSIC 321               2              A
PHRENOLOGY 294                         4              A
CONVERSATIONAL AZTEC 308               5              C
PRECAMBRIAN ART ARCH. 220              4              B

MORE
NAME: JEANNE ADAMS
CLASS: 1987
CREDIT:                4
GRADE:  A
CREDIT:                3
GRADE:  B
CREDIT:                5
GRADE:  A
```

```
NAME:  JEANNE ADAMS                          CLASS:  1987
SEMESTER AND YEAR:  FALL 1985                GPA:    3.75

COURSE                           CREDIT          GRADE
PHYSICS 300                                4              A
CALCULUS 320                               3              B
CHEMISTRY 210                              5              A

MORE
NAME: TOM TAYLOR
CLASS: 1987
CREDIT:                5
GRADE:  C
CREDIT:                3
GRADE:  F

NAME:  TOM TAYLOR                            CLASS:  1987
SEMESTER AND YEAR:  FALL 1985                GPA:    1.25

COURSE                           CREDIT          GRADE
ARTS AND LEISURE 101                       5              C
COMPUTER SCIENCE 105                       3              F

DONE

GOODBYE.  HAVE A NICE DAY.
```

Documentation

This first test of the program looks correct. Other tests would then be conducted to satisfy the registrar that the program is reliable and correct. Perhaps, for a full semester's grade reports, this program would be used in parallel with the old, hand method of preparing grade reports and the results compared.

However, before the program is released for use by the clerks in the registrar's office, the program must be **documented**. Three types of documentation are usually required:

1. **Internal documentation:** this is documentation in the program listing for the benefit of programmers who will read the program later to modify it, to verify its correctness, or to fix a bug that shows up after the program has been released.

   Internal documentation includes the use of self-explanatory variable and subroutine names, which this program has in abundance, and comments to explain its few potentially puzzling steps. The better the variable and subroutine names, the fewer comments a program needs. Straightforward, top-down design minimizes the number of puzzling steps.

   Most beginners and experts alike need to be encouraged to include more comments, and to include them when the program is first written to aid in the debugging, but it is possible to overdo comments by explaining what is already clear in the program. Use your good judgment to decide what is necessary and useful.
2. **External documentation:** a programmer should record what algorithms and methods were used in the solution. The statement of the problem and the method of calculating gradepoint averages at South Mountain College, as given in Section 5.2, should be included. Figures 5.2 to 5.4 showing the organization of the main modules would be helpful.

Sometimes a condensed version of this information also is included in comments in the program listing.

Important strategic decisions, like the choice to make the program execution interactive, should be chronicled, and the reasons for the decision documented. Options considered but not implemented in code should be described to make it easier to implement them later. For example, the programmer might discuss in the documentation how the program might be modified so that even though input remains interactive, the finished grade reports are written to a file for later printing.

3. A **manual** for use of the program: this manual should describe, *in terms understandable to nonprogrammers*, how to start the program, how to enter data at the appropriate times during the execution, and how to terminate the execution. It should describe all error halts (there are none in this program), what to do if data is entered incorrectly, limitations on permissible data (like the maximum number of courses, or the maximum length of a student name or course title), and a description of any quirks in the use of the program.

   A transcript of a typical program execution, like the one shown in this section, is an important adjunct to the verbal description of the program use and should be included in the documentation. The execution transcript, perhaps annotated with comments at pivotal points in the execution, is often clearer and easier for the user to follow than verbal instructions, but including both in the documentation is best.

5.5 Argument Passing

There are two aspects of modularization: isolation and communication. Variables in a subprogram are ordinarily local variables, and as such can have no effect whatsoever on another subprogram. The programmer can then control how much information is to be exchanged between modules. Communication channels are established with **argument lists**. A one-to-one correspondence is set up between **actual argument** in the calling program and **dummy argument** in the subprogram. The corresponding arguments need not have the same name, and the correspondence is temporary, lasting only for the duration of the subprogram call.

This section describes how to write and use subroutines with arguments. It introduces the extremely useful programmer-defined subroutines named SWAPR, READLI (read list of integers), and PRNTLI (print list of integers) that reappear several times in this book. The section also contains a discussion of the local nature of subroutine variables, which guarantees that a subroutine does not create undesirable side effects by accidentally revaluing a variable used in the calling program.

Section Preview

Dummy Argument List:

In a subroutine statement, the subroutine name may be followed by a list of dummy arguments.

Supplied Argument List:

In a subroutine call, the subroutine name is followed by a list of supplied arguments. Each supplied argument is associated with the corresponding dummy argument for the duration of the subroutine call. Supplied arguments also are called actual arguments.

Reference Arguments:

A dummy argument whose actual argument is a variable, an array name, or an array element, is called by reference. Any reference to the dummy argument in the subroutine causes the computer to behave as if the reference were to the corresponding supplied argument. Statements in the subroutine causing changes to such a dummy argument cause the same changes to the corresponding supplied argument.

Value Arguments:

A dummy argument whose actual argument is a constant or expression more complex than a single variable name can only pass a value to the corresponding dummy argument. The dummy argument then must not have its value changed during execution of the subroutine.

Local Variables:

Variables in a subroutine must be declared in that subroutine (or accept default types). Except for dummy arguments, these variables are local to the subroutine in which they are used and declared; that is, they are known within the subroutine in which they are used, but they are distinct from any variable of the same name declared in the main program or in any other subprogram.

Compatibility of Supplied Arguments and Dummy Arguments:

Corresponding actual and dummy arguments must be the same type.

Example:

```
C       PROGRAM POWERS
        INTEGER S, C, FOURTH, SIXTH, NINTH
        REAL INVERS
C
        CALL SQRCUB (2, S, C)
        CALL SQRCUB (C, SIXTH, NINTH)
C
C       ASSIGN TO MAIN PROGRAM VARIABLE
        INVERS = 1.0 / FLOAT (SIXTH)
C
        CALL SQRCUB (S, FOURTH, SIXTH)
        REAL INVERS
        PRINT, SIXTH * INVERS, 'SHOULD BE 1'
        STOP
        END
C
C
        SUBROUTINE SQRCUB (N, SQUARE, CUBE)
        INTEGER N, SQUARE, CUBE
        FLOAT INVERS
C
C       COMPUTE THE SQUARE AND THE CUBE OF N
        SQUARE = N * N
C
```

```
C       ASSIGN TO LOCAL VARIABLE
        INVERS = 1.0 / FLOAT (N)
C
C       INT (X + 0.5) IS X ROUNDED TO THE NEAREST INTEGER
        CUBE = INT (SQUARE * SQUARE * INVERS + 0.5)
        RETURN
        END
```

Swapping the Values of Two Variables

The purpose of the subroutine SWAPR (swap reals) presented here is to exchange two real values, a fairly common programming operation. Although the program SWAPR contains only four executable statements, there is a good deal of merit in keeping these four lines from continually cluttering up the many programs that need this common operation.

```
      SUBROUTINE SWAPR (P, Q)
C     SWAPS TWO REAL VALUES
      REAL P, Q, TEMP
      TEMP = P
      P = Q
      Q = TEMP
      RETURN
      END
```

Dummy Arguments and Actual Arguments

The listing for the subroutine SWAPR looks like the listings of subroutines in previous sections. In the SUBROUTINE statement, the subroutine name SWAPR is followed by a list (P, Q) of variables enclosed in parentheses. The variables P and Q in that list are the **dummy arguments** of the subroutine SWAPR. The new feature in this section is that the **actual arguments** that appear in the CALL statement will not be named P and Q. The term **argument passing** refers to establishing correspondences between actual and dummy arguments and sharing values between these sets of variables.

An Application: Growth of Exponential Functions

The Problem: Functions having the general form

$$y = c_1 e^{ax} + c_2 e^{bx}$$

arise throughout mathematics, physics, chemistry, and engineering because they are the most general solution of the second-order differential equations that govern the behavior of systems in the case that the coefficients are constant. Such functions might represent current in an electrical circuit, vibrations of a mechanical system, population growth or decline, approach to equilibrium of a chemical reaction, or growth of roundoff error in an iterated computational algorithm. We wish to write a program to demonstrate that in the long run, the most important factor affecting the growth or decay of the values of such a function is the larger of the two coefficients a and b. The program will read the four coefficients c_1, c_2, a, and b, and determine which of the two coefficients a or b is larger. If necessary, it will interchange the two terms, that is, swap coefficients a for b and c_1 for c_2, so that the first term $c_1 e^{ax}$ has the larger coefficient in the power. It will then print the values of the full function and of this principal term for $x = 0.1$, 1, 10, and 100.

```
C       PROGRAM GROWTH
C       DEMONSTRATES THE RELATIVE IMPORTANCE
C       OF THE PRINCIPAL TERM IN AN EXPONENTIAL FUNCTION
C          Y = C1 * EXP (A * X) + C2 * EXP (B * X)
C
        REAL X, Y, C1, C2, A, B
C
        READ, C1, C2, A, B
        PRINT, 'INPUT DATA  C1:', C1
        PRINT, '            C2:', C2
        PRINT, '             A:', A
        PRINT, '             B:', B
C
        IF (A .LT. B) THEN DO
           CALL SWAPR (A, B)
           CALL SWAPR (C1, C2)
        END IF
C
        PRINT 15, 'X', 'Y', 'YPRIN'
    15  FORMAT (T12, A1, T36, A1, T58, A5)
C
        X = 0.1
        WHILE (X .LE. 100) DO
           Y = C1 * EXP (A * X) + C2 * EXP (B * X)
           YPRIN = C1 * EXP (A * X)
           PRINT, X, Y, YPRIN
           X = X * 10
        END WHILE
        STOP
        END
        SUBROUTINE SWAPR (P, Q)
C       SWAPS TWO REAL VALUES
        REAL P, Q, TEMP
        TEMP = P
        P = Q
        Q = TEMP
        RETURN
        END
```

Suppose the input data for an execution of the program GROWTH consists of the following line.

```
7, 5, 0.1, 0.2
```

The computer reads these four values and assigns the values 7 to C1, 5 to C2, 0.1 to A and 0.2 to B. The values are then echoed to the output listing. Since the value of A is less than the value of B, the IF test succeeds and the THEN clause is executed.

We now examine in detail what happens when the first CALL statement

```
CALL SWAPR (A, B)
```

is executed. During execution of the subroutine SWAPR, it is as if every occurrence of the dummy argument P in SWAPR were replaced by the variable A, and every occurrence of the dummy argument Q in SWAPR were replaced by the variable B. The top half of Figure 5.5 shows this replacement. In executing the statement

```
TEMP = P
```

of the subroutine SWAPR, the computer assigns to the variable TEMP the value 0.1 of the variable A in the program GROWTH, just as if the statement were written

```
TEMP = A
```

In executing the statement

```
P = Q
```

of the subroutine SWAPR, the computer assigns to the variable A the value 0.2 of the variable B, as though the statement were written

```
A = B
```

Finally, the value 0.1 that is saved as the value of the variable TEMP is assigned to the variable B by the statement

```
Q = TEMP
```

as though it were written

```
B = TEMP
```

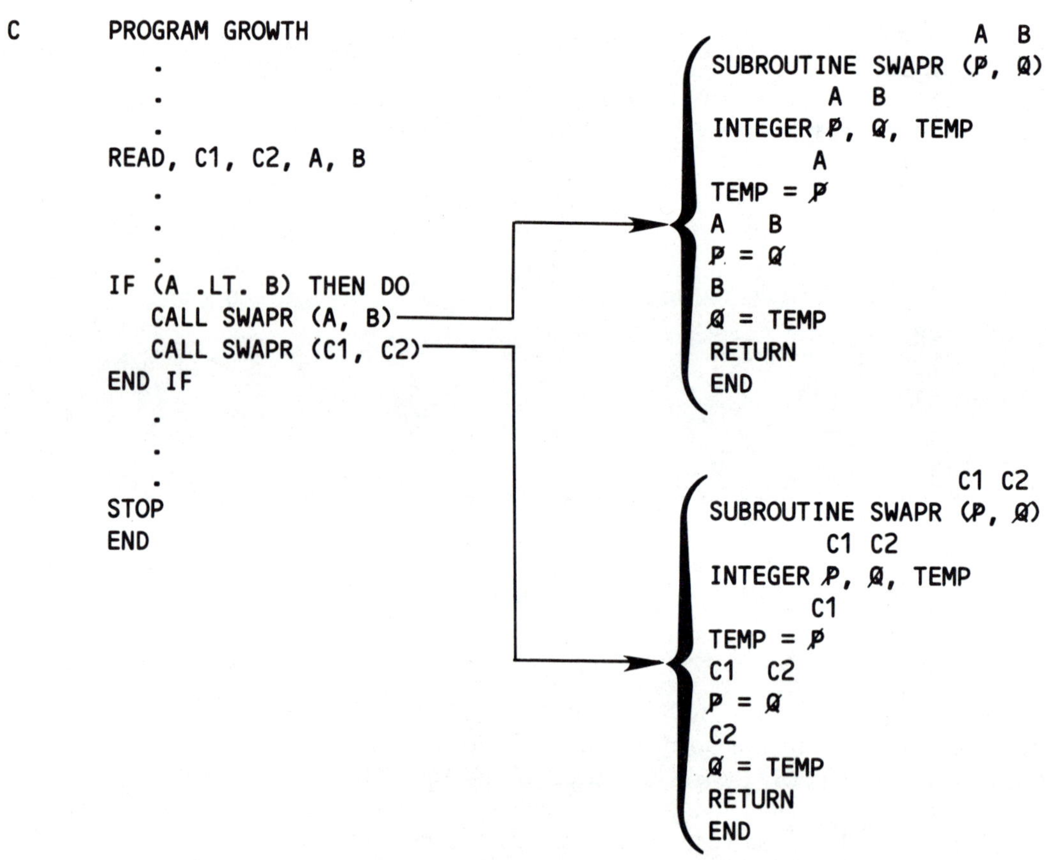

Figure 5.5 Supplying arguments to a subroutine.

Supplied Arguments

The variables A and B in the statement

```
CALL SWAPR (A, B)
```

are the **supplied arguments** or **actual arguments** of the subroutine call. There is no need for the supplied arguments to have names different from the dummy arguments. Whatever the names of the dummy arguments, during the execution of the subroutine, it is always as if the names of the supplied arguments were copied in place of the dummy arguments. This is why the supplied arguments are declared in the calling program to have the *same types* as declared for the dummy arguments in the subroutine.

The Second Call of the Subroutine SWAPR

The full power of Fortran's argument-passing convention begins to be felt when control returns to the main program to execute a second call to the subroutine SWAPR

```
CALL SWAPR (C1,C2)
```

This time allowing the dummy arguments in the subroutine to have different names from the supplied arguments in the calling program is not just a convenience, it is a necessity. The supplied arguments are different in the second call from those in the first. It is the possibility of using differing names that allows a subroutine to be general purpose, to function in many contexts. As the lower half of Figure 5.5 shows, this time the subroutine SWAPR swaps the values of the coefficients C1 and C2.

Table 5.3 Accessibility of variables in a subroutine call.

Main Program		Subroutine SWAPR
X		TEMP
Y		
A, C1	◄———	P
B, C2	◄———	Q

Local Variables

It would not matter if a calling program happened to use variables whose names coincided with those of the dummy arguments P and Q of SWAPR. When SWAPR is called, it is executed as if the supplied arguments were written in place of the dummy arguments. This leaves leave no opportunity for the execution of SWAPR to affect calling program variables named A or B, unless those variables are supplied arguments.

The same rules apply to other variables in the subroutine. Whenever the variable TEMP appears in the subroutine, it is to be regarded as a private variable for that subroutine, and not as a variable in the calling program that happens to have the same name. (See Table 5.4.)

The program LOCAL illustrates more fully how some of these concepts work. Note that two variable or parameter names in different subroutines may not only have different values, but may have different data types as well. In the

Table 5.4 Variable references in a subroutine call. In the first call, any reference to the dummy argument P in the subroutine SWAPR is resolved as a reference to the corresponding supplied argument A in the calling program GROWTH. Similarly, any reference to Q is treated as a reference to B. The variables X and Y are local to the main program GROWTH and the variable TEMP is local to the subroutine SWAPR.

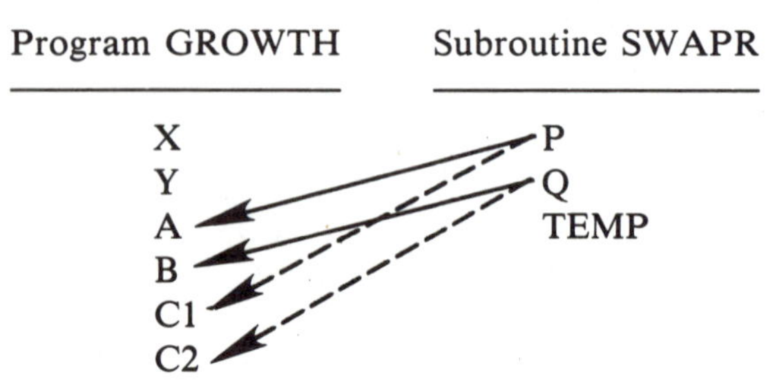

main program LOCAL, the variable TEMP is a character, but it is type real in the subroutine SWAPR. A name could represent a simple variable in the main program and an array in a subroutine called by the program. Note also that although the dummy arguments P and Q of the subroutine SWAPR have the same names as variables in the calling program LOCAL, the values of the variables P and Q in the main program are unaffected by execution of the subroutine SWAPR.

```
      PROGRAM LOCAL
      REAL P, Q, R, S
      CHARACTER TEMP *1
      P = 1
      Q = 2
C
      TEMP = 'X'
      R = 3
      S = 4
      CALL SWAPR (R, S)
      PRINT, TEMP, P, Q, R, S
      STOP
      END
C
C
      SUBROUTINE SWAPR (P, Q)
C     SWAPS TWO REAL VALUES
      REAL P, Q, TEMP
      TEMP = P
      P = Q
      Q = TEMP
      RETURN
      END
X          1.0000000          2.0000000          4.0000000          3.0000000
```

Compatibility of Supplied Arguments With Dummy Arguments

For a subroutine call to be correct, the calling program must supply the same number of arguments specified in the SUBROUTINE statement. The data type of each supplied argument and its corresponding dummy argument must agree. For example, if the dummy argument is type CHARACTER, then the supplied argument must be type CHARACTER. One consequence of this rule is that a different subroutine must be written to swap two integer values, since SWAPR swaps two real values. The subroutine SWAPI (swap two integers) is the same as SWAPR except that all variables in SWAPI are declared to be type integer.

```
      SUBROUTINE SWAPI (P, Q)
C     SWAPS TWO INTEGER VALUES
      INTEGER P, Q, TEMP
      TEMP = P
      P = Q
      Q = TEMP
      RETURN
      END
```

Array Arguments

The subroutine READLI (read a list of integers) reads a list of integer values from an input file, stopping when it reads a signal value. What makes the subroutine READLI particularly flexible and useful is that the array name, its declared maximum size, and even the termination signal value are dummy arguments of the subroutine. They may therefore be associated with any appropriate actual arguments in the calling program. The subroutine PRNTLI (print a list of integers) is similarly flexible, but requires only the actual count of numbers to be printed. To test the subroutines, we write a main program RDPRNT (read and print) that calls them.

```
C     PROGRAM RDPRNT
C     TESTS THE SUBROUTINES READLI (READ LIST OF INTEGERS)
C                       AND PRNTLI (PRINT LIST OF INTEGERS)
C
      INTEGER MAX, HOWMNY, ENDSIG, NUMBRS (100)
C
      MAX = 100
      ENDSIG = -1
      PRINT, 'READING THE LIST'
      CALL READLI (NUMBRS, MAX, ENDSIG, HOWMNY)
      PRINT, ' '
      PRINT, 'PRINTING THE LIST'
      CALL PRNTLI (NUMBRS, HOWMNY)
      STOP
      END
C
C
      SUBROUTINE READLI (LIST, MAXSUB, SIGNAL, COUNT)
C     READ A LIST OF INTEGERS
C     STOP WHEN THE VALUE SIGNAL IS READ,
C     AND RETURN THE COUNT
C
      INTEGER LIST (MAXSUB), SIGNAL, COUNT, I, BUFFER
C
```

```
      DO 18 I = 1, MAXSUB
         READ, BUFFER
         PRINT, 'INPUT DATA  BUFFER:', BUFFER
         IF (BUFFER .NE. SIGNAL) THEN DO
            LIST (I) = BUFFER
            COUNT = I
         ELSE DO
            GO TO 19
         END IF
   18 CONTINUE
   19 RETURN
      END
C
C
      SUBROUTINE PRNTLI (LIST, COUNT)
C     PRINT A LIST OF INTEGERS
C
      INTEGER COUNT, LIST (COUNT), I
C
      DO 18 I = 1, COUNT
         PRINT, LIST (I)
   18 CONTINUE
      RETURN
      END
READING THE LIST
INPUT DATA  BUFFER:            5
INPUT DATA  BUFFER:           10
INPUT DATA  BUFFER:           15
INPUT DATA  BUFFER:           20
INPUT DATA  BUFFER:           -1

PRINTING THE LIST
5
10
15
20
```

In the subroutine READLI, the first dummy argument, LIST, is an array. In order to coordinate the range of subscripts for the dummy argument LIST with that of the actual argument, the array NUMBRS, the second dummy argument MAXSUB will receive as value the maximum permitted subscript. In a subroutine, the declared subscript bounds for an array can be an integer-valued dummy argument.

Changing the Value of a Dummy Argument

For dummy arguments whose values are not changed during the execution of the subroutine, the corresponding supplied arguments may be constants and expressions of all kinds (including a single variable). The types of the supplied arguments must be the same as the types of the corresponding dummy arguments. If a dummy argument may be changed by reading, assignment, or another subroutine call, the supplied argument must be a variable or array element and must be declared to be the same type.

Forbidden Supplied Arguments

Constants may be supplied to a subroutine as arguments if the program that results from simultaneously replacing every occurrence of each dummy argument in the subroutine by its corresponding supplied argument is executable.

For example, the statement

```
CALL SWAPI (2, 3)
```

is a mistake, because replacement of the dummy arguments A and B of the subroutine SWAPI by the supplied arguments 2 and 3 changes the perfectly reasonable statements

```
TEMP = A
A = B
B = TEMP
```

into the statements

```
TEMP = 2
2 = 3
3 = TEMP
```

The first of these three resulting statements makes sense, but the other two are nonsense. For this reason, constants and arbitrary expressions should not be supplied arguments for dummy arguments whose value might be changed. If you violate this rule, the WATFIV system will produce an error message similar to the following:

```
***ERROR***  SUBPROGRAM SWAPI  REDEFINES A CONSTANT, EXPRESSION, DO PARAMETER
                               OR ASSIGNED GOTO INDEX (ARGUMENT NUMBER   1)
```

Why the Simpler Argument-Passing Convention Works

Our preliminary rule for forming argument lists, described in Section 5.1, was that all variables whose values are shared by the calling program and the subroutine should appear in the argument list. Moreover, the argument lists in the CALL and SUBROUTINE statements should be identical and all relevant declarations the same. We can now see that this simplified convention is consistent with the need for compatibility between actual and dummy arguments.

5.6 Function Subprograms

A **function** is a construction that looks a lot like a subroutine but is used like a built-in function to compute a single value. It is a programmer's way of augmenting a language to include functions that are not built in.

Section Preview

Function:

General Form:

FUNCTION *functionname* (*dummyvariable*, ..., *dummyvariable*)
declarations
statement
...
C AT LEAST ONE SUCH ASSIGNMENT
functionname = *expression*
...

statement;
RETURN
END

Example:

```
      FUNCTION SMALST (FIRST, SECOND, THIRD)
C     DETERMINES SMALLEST OF THE THREE INTEGER ARGUMENTS
      INTEGER SMALST, FIRST, SECOND, THIRD, SMALER
C
      IF (FIRST .LT. SECOND) THEN DO
         SMALER = FIRST
      ELSE DO
         SMALER = SECOND
      END IF
C
      IF (SMALER .LT. THIRD) THEN DO
C        FUNCTION VALUE ASSIGNMENT
         SMALST = SMALER
      ELSE DO
C        FUNCTION VALUE ASSIGNMENT
         SMALST = THIRD
      END IF
      RETURN
      END
```

Function Call:

A function is called by using it in an expression.

Example:

```
      SUM = SMALST (A, B, C) + SMALST (X, Y, Z)
```

Side Effects:

A function ordinarily is designed to compute one single value, the function value, on the basis of the values of the supplied arguments. Any other effect on the calling program is usually considered a side effect and is usually avoided by not reassigning the values of any of the dummy arguments. *Note:* There are exceptions to these rules and not all experienced programmers agree 100% with these conventions.

Functions and Subroutines

Like a subroutine, a function has a title line that might list some dummy arguments, followed by declarations, executable statements, a RETURN and an END statement. Like a subroutine, a function is executed as if supplied arguments were copied in place of the dummy arguments. One difference, however, is that a subroutine is called *explicitly* by a CALL statement, while a function is called *implicitly* whenever the computer executes a program statement that uses the function's name. A **subprogram** is either a function subprogram or a subroutine.

Rounding

Our first example of a function is concerned with rounding a number to a specified precision. The first argument is the number to be rounded and the second argument specifies the precision. The driver program TSTRND (test round) tests the function ROUND.

```
C       PROGRAM TSTRND
        REAL ROUND
        PRINT, ROUND (6.789, 0.1), ROUND (-2.6, 0.5)
        STOP
        END
C
C
        FUNCTION ROUND (NUMBER, PRECSN)
C       ROUNDS NUMBER TO GIVEN PRECISION
        REAL ROUND, NUMBER, PRECSN
        INTEGER WHOLE, NINT
        WHOLE = NINT (NUMBER / PRECSN)
        ROUND = WHOLE * PRECSN
        RETURN
        END
            6.8000010           -2.5000000
```

The function ROUND has two dummy arguments, NUMBER and PRECSN, both declared to be type real. The value of the function also is type real, indicated by the declaration of ROUND in the function. The type of the value of the function also must be declared in each program or subprogram that uses the function ROUND.

Assigning a Function Value

Most of the assignment statements in a function are executed exactly as if they were in a subroutine. The first assignment statement assigns to the integer variable WHOLE the number of whole times that PRECSN goes into NUMBER. The second assignment statement

```
ROUND = WHOLE * PRECSN
```

however, is a **function value assignment**, found only in functions. The only difference is that the name on the left of the assignment is the same as the name of the function. This instruction is executed by evaluating the expression on the right of the assignment symbol and assigning it to the variable named. The last value assigned is the one returned to the calling program as the value of the function.

```
                          6.789    0.1
        FUNCTION ROUND (NUMBER, PRECSN)
C       ROUNDS NUMBER TO GIVEN PRECISION
        REAL ROUND, NUMBER, PRECSN
        INTEGER WHOLE, NINT
                          6.789     0.1
        WHOLE = NINT (NUMBER / PRECSN)
                             0.1
        ROUND = WHOLE * PRECSN
        RETURN
        END
```

Figure 5.6 Supplying arguments to a function program.

Returning a Function Value to the Calling Program

When the execution of the function is completed, the function value is returned to the calling program, and the computer continues with the execution of the calling program.

Suppose, for example, that a program includes the calling statement

```
PRINT, ROUND (6.789, 0.1)
```

As illustrated in Figure 5.6, the value 6.789 is supplied to the function ROUND to replace the dummy argument NUMBER, and the value 0.1 is supplied to replace the dummy argument PRECSN. When the first assignment statement is executed, the local integer variable WHOLE is assigned the value NINT (6.789 / 0.1) = NINT (67.89) = 68. The second assignment statement assigns 68 * 0.1 = 6.8 as the value of the function.

Since execution of the function is now completed, the function value is returned to the calling program, and execution of the calling program resumes. In this case, the computer continues execution of the PRINT statement that called ROUND by printing the function value just calculated.

A function program is written in much the same manner as a subroutine. Functions and subroutines may be placed in a program in any order. Execution of any program that calls an available function proceeds exactly as if the function were built in.

The function NINT, which rounds its real argument to the nearest integer, is not available in WATFIV. Writing the function NINT is left as an exercise.

What Day of the Week is New Year's Day?

The function subprogram NEWYR (New Year's Day) calculates the day of the week on which the new year begins for every year in the twentieth century.

```
      FUNCTION NEWYR (YEAR)
C     COMPUTES THE DAY OF THE WEEK OF NEW YEAR'S DAY
C
      INTEGER NEWYR, YEAR, LEPYRS, ADVANC
      LEPYRS = (YEAR - 1901) / 4
      ADVANC = YEAR - 1901 + LEPYRS
C     1901 JAN 1 WAS TUESDAY, DAY 2 IN THE WEEK (SUN = 0)
      NEWYR = MOD (2 + ADVANC, 7)
      RETURN
      END
```

Advancing of Calendar Dates and Days of the Week

Division of the number of days in an ordinary calendar year, 365, by the number of days in a week, 7, yields a quotient of 52 weeks and a remainder of 1 day. If New Year's Day of an ordinary year falls on a Thursday, for example, the remainder of 1 day will push New Year's Day of the following year to a Friday. In an ordinary year beginning on a Monday, December 30, which is the last day of the 52nd week, will be on Sunday. Therefore, December 31 will be Monday and January 1, New Year's Day, will be Tuesday.

A leap year of 366 days has 52 whole weeks and two extra days. Leap year causes New Year's Day to advance two days of the week. It follows that, if New Year's Day of a leap year falls on a Wednesday, the year after it will fall on a Friday.

A similar progression occurs for other fixed dates in the calendar year. In successive years a fixed calendar date advances 1 day of the week unless a February 29 intervenes, in which case it advances 2 days.

Finding the Julian Date

Any day of the year can be assigned a number from 1 to 365 or 1 to 366, which is known as its Julian date. The function JULIAN computes the Julian date for any month, day, and year.

```
      FUNCTION JULIAN (YEAR, MONTH, DAY)
C     COMPUTES DAY NUMBER FROM 1 TO 365 OR 366
C
      INTEGER JULIAN, YEAR, MONTH, DAY, PRVMON
      INTEGER JDATE, M, DPERMO (12)
C
      DPERMO (1) = 31
      DPERMO (2) = 28
      DPERMO (3) = 31
      DPERMO (4) = 30
      DPERMO (5) = 31
      DPERMO (6) = 30
      DPERMO (7) = 31
      DPERMO (8) = 31
      DPERMO (9) = 30
      DPERMO (10) = 31
      DPERMO (11) = 30
      DPERMO (12) = 31
C
      JDATE = 0
      PRVMON = MONTH - 1
      IF (PRVMON .GT. 0) THEN DO
         DO 18 M = 1, PRVMON
            JDATE = JDATE + DPERMO (M)
C           ADD FEB 29 FOR LEAP YEARS
            IF (M .EQ. 2 .AND. MOD (YEAR, 4) .EQ. 0) THEN DO
               JDATE = JDATE + 1
            END IF
   18    CONTINUE
      END IF
C
      JULIAN = JDATE + DAY
      RETURN
      END
```

It adds the number of days in each of the months preceding the specified month to the specified day and adds an extra day for February 29 if the year is divisible by four.

Some Background Information For Calendar Computations

The twentieth century began on January 1, 1901, a Tuesday, and will end on December 31, 2000. It is a mistake to think that it began in 1900 and will end in 1999, because the first century began in the year 1 (there never was a year 0) and every century is 100 years long.

The only additional information needed to understand the calculations employed by the program NEWYR is which years of the twentieth century are leap years. Although most calendar years are 365 days long, the earth requires nearly 365¼ days to orbit the sun. In order to compensate for the extra fraction of a day beyond 365, nearly every fourth year is designated a leap year, during which the calendar is lengthened to 366 days by adding one day to February's normal 28.

It was arbitrarily decided long ago that, if the number 4 evenly divides the year number, or equivalently, if it evenly divides the last two digits of the year number, then the year is a leap year, except for one special case, the last year of a century. Although the year number of the last year of any century is always divisible by 4, such a year is not a leap year unless its year number is also divisible by 400. For example, the years 1800 and 1900 were not leap years, and the years 2100, 2200, and 2300 will not be leap years. On the other hand, 2000 and 2400 will be leap years.

The reason for this complication in the last year of a century is that the earth's orbiting time is about 365.24219879 days, a shade under 365¼ days, and the general goal of the rule for designating leap years is to keep the average length of the calendar year nearly equal to the earth's orbiting time.

Testing the Program DAYWK

The execution printouts for the executable refinement of the program DAYWK (day of the week) show that it is being tested with years whose starting dates are verified easily. An almanac is a convenient source of calendars for the past few and the next few years.

```
C       PROGRAM DAYWK
C       COMPUTES DAY OF THE WEEK
C       OF ANY DAY IN THE 20TH CENTURY
C
        INTEGER YEAR, MONTH, DAY
        INTEGER DAYNR
        INTEGER JAN1, JDATE, NEWYR, JULIAN
        CHARACTER DAYNAM *9 (7)
C
        DAYNAM (1) = 'SUNDAY'
        DAYNAM (2) = 'MONDAY'
        DAYNAM (3) = 'TUESDAY'
        DAYNAM (4) = 'WEDNESDAY'
        DAYNAM (5) = 'THURSDAY'
        DAYNAM (6) = 'FRIDAY'
        DAYNAM (7) = 'SATURDAY'
C
        READ, YEAR, MONTH, DAY
        PRINT, 'INPUT DATA  YEAR:', YEAR
        PRINT, '           MONTH:', MONTH
        PRINT, '             DAY:', DAY
        IF (YEAR .GE. 1901 .AND. YEAR .LE. 2000) THEN DO
           JAN1 = NEWYR (YEAR)
           JDATE = JULIAN (YEAR, MONTH, DAY)
           DAYNR = MOD (JAN1 + JDATE - 1, 7) + 1
           PRINT, 'THE DAY OF THE WEEK WAS OR WILL BE',
     +               DAYNAM (DAYNR)
        ELSE DO
           PRINT, 'THE YEAR MUST BE AN INTEGER',
     +              'FROM 1901 TO 2000.'
        END IF
        STOP
        END
```

```
INPUT DATA  YEAR:         1984
            MONTH:           1
            DAY:           1
THE DAY OF THE WEEK WAS OR WILL BE SUNDAY
INPUT DATA  YEAR:         1984
INPUT DATA  MONTH:          10
INPUT DATA  DAY:          26
THE DAY OF THE WEEK WAS OR WILL BE FRIDAY
INPUT DATA  YEAR:         1985
INPUT DATA  MONTH:           3
INPUT DATA  DAY:          15
THE DAY OF THE WEEK WAS OR WILL BE FRIDAY
```

In the function NEWYR the variable LEPYRS (number of leap years) is assigned a value equal to the number of occurrences of February 29 between New Year's Day, 1901, and New Year's Day of the given year. The variable ADVANC is then assigned as its value the total number of advances of New Year's Day from 1901 to the given year.

For example, the number of leap years from 1901 to 1984 is 20, the result of dividing 83 by 4 and ignoring the remainder. The number of advances, therefore, is 103, one day's advance for each of the 83 years from the base date January 1, 1901, to the objective date January 1, 1984, plus one additional day's advance for each of the 20 leap years between those two dates. If the day of the week is advanced 7 times, there is no change, so when the number of advances is added to 2, the day number for Tuesday, all multiples of 7 are removed from the result. This is accomplished by taking the remainder when the result is divided by 7. For 1984, this is MOD (2 + 103, 7) = 0, so the day of the week is Sunday.

Since January 1 is the first day of the year, the Julian date makes no contribution in the first sample execution, so January 1, 1984 is day 0, a Sunday. In the second execution, the Julian date of October 26 is 300 because 1904 is a leap year, so that the day of the week is MOD (0 + 300 − 1, 7) = MOD (299, 7) = 5, a Friday.

Since, unlike Fortran 77, WATFIV arrays may not be subscripted using the integer 0, Sunday is stored as day 1, Monday as day 2, etc. Thus, just before the character string representing the day of the week is determined, the value one must be added to the day number.

Expressions as Supplied Arguments

In general, a supplied argument to a subprogram may be an expression. With a built-in function, the only restriction is that the function value be defined for the value of the supplied argument. However, in order for a subprogram call to be executed when an expression is supplied as an argument, it is necessary that it makes sense to substitute the expression itself for each occurrence of the corresponding dummy argument. In particular, a dummy argument that receives an expression as a supplied argument should not be changed. For instance, the following calls to the function ROUND are both executable, because the substitutions they specify all make sense if Y is type real.

```
PRINT, ROUND (Y + 5, 0.001)
PRINT, ROUND (Y, 10.0 ** INT (ALOG10 (Y) - 2))
```

The mathematically inclined may be able to show that the second of these statements rounds Y to 3 significant digits.

Comparison of Functions and Subroutines

A function listing looks so much like a subroutine listing that one might wonder why both structures are included in a programming language. The reason is largely a matter of programming style.

The concept of a function is borrowed from mathematics, in which a function f assigns a value $f(x)$ or $f(x_1, x_2, ..., x_n)$ to each allowable value of its argument or list of arguments. To avoid confusion, Fortran functions should be reserved for precisely this usage. A subroutine can be used for any other kind of subtask.

The guiding principle in deciding whether to isolate a part of the whole program as a function or as a subroutine is that, if its purpose is to produce a single value, then usually a function is used. Otherwise a subroutine is used. Beyond this guiding principle, however, there are some important conventions to be obeyed in writing functions.

Avoidance of Side Effects

The most important convention for writing functions is that a function should have no side effects. A statement like

```
XR = ROUND (X, 0.01)
```

tells the computer to calculate the value of the function ROUND and assign this value to the variable XR. If there is any other effect of executing this statement, a person reading the program in which the statement is contained would be totally unaware of it. Therefore, if execution of a function causes side effects, it is very difficult to determine the behavior of a program that calls that function.

Execution of a function should not change the values of its dummy arguments. If other effects on the calling program are necessary or desirable, the programmer should write a subroutine instead of a function.

Any effect of a subroutine on a calling program not related to the subroutine's stated computational purpose is a side effect and also should be avoided. However, subroutines commonly are used to achieve numerous effects on the calling program, including changing the values of some variables in the calling program. For example, the entire point of the subroutine SWAPR is to change the values of its arguments. Thus such a change in the arguments is not a side effect.

Supplied Arguments Outside the Function Domain

It is a serious mistake to attempt to pass to a subprogram a supplied argument that is incompatible with the corresponding dummy argument. For instance, supplying character strings to the function ROUND won't work.

Even if a supplied argument is of the correct type, its value might still be outside the function domain. If, for example, the supplied argument to the built-in function ALOG were -1, the function could not produce a value, because the logarithm of a negative number is not defined. Many computer systems would terminate execution of the program if this were attempted.

When a supplied argument is of the right type, it is still possible that the value might represent something of a nonstandard case. Under such circumstances, the function may return a special, recognizable signal instead of doing the usual calculations and returning their result.

For instance, a function to search a given list looking for the presence of a specific value might return as function value the location of that value in the list, if it is found. It might return a special signal function value in case the specific value is not in the list. Although the inability to find a particular entry in a list might be a disaster for one calling program, it might be merely a mild setback for another, and possibly a routine occurrence for a third calling program. Returning the special signal value enables the calling program to react according to its individual needs. The calling program is free either to test for the signal value or to continue computing without testing, at its own possible peril.

The burden of screening the values of supplied arguments does not always fall completely on the subprogram. Sometimes the calling program screens them itself in order to avoid meaningless computations or possible program termination.

Style Rule: Avoid Reassigning a Function Value

It is a good programming practice to assign a function value exactly once in each execution of a function subprogram. If no function value is assigned, the function might return no value at all or a value unrelated to the current supplied arguments. For instance, it might return the function value computed for the supplied arguments in the previous call, or perhaps still worse, the garbage left by another program or programmer.

If several function value assignments are executed, the last one determines the value of the function. However, a function program is easier to read when not more than one function value assignment is made during a single function execution. When a function value assignment is encountered in the function program listing, it is then possible to conclude that at least one case of the computation is finally settled.

Nesting Subroutine Calls and Function Calls

It is permissible for a function to call a subroutine and for a subroutine to call a function. Supplied arguments may pass through several levels of such mixed calls.

5.7 Testing and Debugging: Agreement of Arguments

Section Preview

Subroutine Calls:

A subroutine may be called more than once in the same program.

Function Calls:

A function call, F (X), and an array element reference, A (I), are identical in form in Fortran. Only the declarations distinguish between them.

The Application

In analytical geometry or physics, a 3-dimensional vector A is a triplet of real numbers (a_1, a_2, a_3). A vector is also described as an arrow in 3-dimensional coordinate space. In that case, the vector A extends from the origin of the coordinate system (0, 0, 0) to the point (a_1, a_2, a_3). The dot product of two vectors a and b is the sum

$$a \cdot b = a_1 \times b_1 + a_2 \times b_2 + a_3 \times b_3$$

There is a more geometric definition of the dot product of two vectors involving their lengths and the angle between them, but the computational definition above is all we need. Curiously, many nonphysical calculations also take the form of a dot product: one is the sum that defines the total gradepoints earned by a student in Section 5.2. We wish to write a program that reads two 3-dimensional vectors a and b, then calculates and prints their dot product.

The Solution

Since a 3-dimensional vector is just a list, we will modify the subroutine READLI (read a list of integers) to create a subroutine READLR (read a list of reals) by changing the declarations and use READLR to read the two vectors. Then we will write a new function program DOT to calculate the dot product. We have calculated such sums before so this one should be easy. We pass directly to a Fortran version because the main program is so straightforward that pseudocode seems unnecessary.

```
C       PROGRAM DOTVEC
C       READS TWO 3-DIMENSIONAL VECTORS
C       AND FINDS THEIR DOT PRODUCT
C       CONTAINS BUGS
C
        INTEGER MAXSIZ
        REAL A (100), B (100), DOT, D
C
        MAXSIZ = 100
C
        PRINT, 'THE VECTOR A'
        CALL READLR (A, MAXSIZ, -1, 3)
        PRINT, 'THE VECTOR B'
        CALL READLR (B, MAXSIZ, -1, 3)
C
        D = DOT (A, B)
        PRINT, 'THEIR DOT PRODUCT =', D
        STOP
        END
C
C
        SUBROUTINE READLR (LIST, MAXSIZ, SIGNAL, COUNT)
C       READ A LIST OF REALS
C       STOP WHEN THE VALUE SIGNAL IS READ
C       AND RETURN THE COUNT
C
        INTEGER MAXSIZ, COUNT, I
        REAL LIST (MAXSIZ), SIGNAL, BUFFER
C
```

```
      DO 18 I = 1, MAXSIZ
         READ, BUFFER
         PRINT, 'INPUT DATA  BUFFER:', BUFFER
         IF (BUFFER .NE. SIGNAL) THEN DO
            LIST (I) = BUFFER
            COUNT = I
         ELSE DO
            GO TO 19
         END IF
   18 CONTINUE
   19 RETURN
      END
C
C
      FUNCTION DOT (A, B, SIZE)
C     FINDS THE DOT PRODUCT OF TWO VECTORS,
C     EACH OF GIVEN SIZE
C
      REAL A, B, DOT, SUM
      INTEGER SIZE, I
C
      SUM = 0
      DO 18 I = 1, SIZE
         SUM = SUM + A (I) * B (I)
   18 CONTINUE
      DOT = SUM
      RETURN
      END
THE VECTOR A
***ERROR***  INVALID TYPE FOR ARGUMENT NUMBER   3
             IN REFERENCE TO SUBPROGRAM READLR
```

The problem is that there is a type mismatch between the supplied argument and the dummy argument SIGNAL. This is fixed easily by changing the supplied argument from -1 to -1.0. While making that change, let's do what should have been done in the first place and make the supplied termination signal a variable.

There is another error in the program DOTVEC that is subtle enough that it might not be caught by your WATFIV system. The fourth actual arguments in the subroutine calls

```
      CALL READLR (A, MAXSIZ, -1, 3)
      CALL READLR (B, MAXSIZ, -1, 3)
```

are integer constants. The corresponding dummy argument, COUNT, is of type integer also, but it is assigned a value in the subroutine READLR. Therefore it should not correspond to a constant actual argument. Some systems report the error. Others miss the error, but do not return the value of COUNT to the actual argument, which causes little harm in this program. Still others return the value of COUNT, thereby modifying the value of the constant 3. With correct data for this example, even this unsatisfactory practice would go unnoticed because the correct value of COUNT is also 3. However the subroutine call

```
      CALL SWAPI (2, 3)
```

would permanently interchange the values of the constants 2 and 3 for the rest of the program execution on such a system. The results could be quite puzzling.

Those errors are corrected and the program is run again.

```
C       PROGRAM DOTVEC
C       READS TWO 3-DIMENSIONAL VECTORS
C       AND FINDS THEIR DOT PRODUCT
C       STILL CONTAINS BUGS
C
        INTEGER MAXSIZ, SIZE
        REAL A (100), B (100), DOT, D, SIGNAL
C
        MAXSIZ = 100
        SIGNAL = -1.0
C
        PRINT, 'THE VECTOR A'
        CALL READLR (A, MAXSIZ, SIGNAL, SIZE)
        PRINT, 'THE VECTOR B'
        CALL READLR (B, MAXSIZ, SIGNAL, SIZE)
C
        D = DOT (A, B, SIZE)
        PRINT, 'THEIR DOT PRODUCT =', D
        STOP
        END
C
C
        SUBROUTINE READLR (LIST, MAXSIZ, SIGNAL, COUNT)
C       READ A LIST OF REALS
C       STOP WHEN THE VALUE SIGNAL IS READ
C       AND RETURN THE COUNT
C
        INTEGER MAXSIZ, COUNT, I
        REAL LIST (MAXSIZ), SIGNAL, BUFFER
C
        DO 18 I = 1, MAXSIZ
           READ, BUFFER
           PRINT, 'INPUT DATA  BUFFER:', BUFFER
           IF (BUFFER .NE. SIGNAL) THEN DO
              LIST (I) = BUFFER
              COUNT = I
           ELSE DO
              GO TO 19
           END IF
   18   CONTINUE
   19   RETURN
        END
C
C
```

```
      FUNCTION DOT (A, B, SIZE)
C     FINDS THE DOT PRODUCT OF TWO VECTORS,
C     EACH OF GIVEN SIZE
C
      REAL A, B, DOT, SUM
      INTEGER SIZE, I
C
      SUM = 0
      DO 18 I = 1, SIZE
         SUM = SUM + A (I) * B (I)
   18 CONTINUE
      DOT = SUM
      RETURN
      END
THE VECTOR A
INPUT DATA  BUFFER:              1.0000000
INPUT DATA  BUFFER:              2.0000000
INPUT DATA  BUFFER:              3.0000000
INPUT DATA  BUFFER:             -1.0000000
THE VECTOR B
INPUT DATA  BUFFER:              4.0000000
INPUT DATA  BUFFER:              5.0000000
INPUT DATA  BUFFER:              6.0000000
INPUT DATA  BUFFER:             -1.0000000
***ERROR***  INVALID TYPE FOR ARGUMENT NUMBER    1
             IN REFERENCE TO SUBPROGRAM DOT
```

The error message indicates that there is now something wrong with the first argument for the function DOT. If we look at the statement

```
SUM = SUM + A (I) * B (I)
```

we know that A and B should be vectors. In fact, they are declared as such in the main program.

```
REAL A (100), B (100), DOT, D
```

However, it is not the main program variables A and B that are causing the problem. The function subprogram DOT also uses arrays A and B, its dummy arguments, and they are declared

```
REAL A, B, SUM, DOT
```

without subscript bounds. When the Fortran compiler encounters the expressions A (I) and B (I) in the function subprogram DOT, it also expects A and B to be declared as arrays. The correction is to declare A and B as arrays in the subprogram DOT.

Before showing the corrected program DOTVEC and its execution, we point out that the subroutine READLR is called twice in this program. However, the subroutine READLR appears only once in the program listing. This economy of space resulting from listing the details only once, although they are executed more than once, was at one time considered the major virtue of subroutines. Now, however, the importance of subroutines in top-down design has eclipsed this virtue.

```
C       PROGRAM DOTVEC
C       READS TWO 3-DIMENSIONAL VECTORS
C       AND FINDS THEIR DOT PRODUCT
C
        INTEGER MAXSIZ, SIZE
        REAL A (100), B (100), DOT, D, SIGNAL
C
        MAXSIZ = 100
        SIGNAL = -1.0
C
        PRINT, 'THE VECTOR A'
        CALL READLR (A, MAXSIZ, SIGNAL, SIZE)
        PRINT, 'THE VECTOR B'
        CALL READLR (B, MAXSIZ, SIGNAL, SIZE)
C
        D = DOT (A, B, SIZE)
        PRINT, 'THEIR DOT PRODUCT =', D
        STOP
        END
C
C
        SUBROUTINE READLR (LIST, MAXSIZ, SIGNAL, COUNT)
C       READ A LIST OF REALS
C       STOP WHEN THE VALUE SIGNAL IS READ
C       AND RETURN THE COUNT
C
        INTEGER MAXSIZ, COUNT, I
        REAL LIST (MAXSIZ), SIGNAL, BUFFER
C
        DO 18 I = 1, MAXSIZ
           READ, BUFFER
           PRINT, 'INPUT DATA  BUFFER:', BUFFER
           IF (BUFFER .NE. SIGNAL) THEN DO
              LIST (I) = BUFFER
              COUNT = I
           ELSE DO
              GO TO 19
           END IF
   18   CONTINUE
   19   RETURN
        END
C
C
        FUNCTION DOT (A, B, SIZE)
C       FINDS THE DOT PRODUCT OF TWO VECTORS,
C       EACH OF GIVEN SIZE
C
        INTEGER SIZE, I
        REAL A (SIZE), B (SIZE), DOT, SUM
C
        SUM = 0
```

```
      DO 18 I = 1, SIZE
         SUM = SUM + A (I) * B (I)
   18 CONTINUE
      DOT = SUM
      RETURN
      END
THE VECTOR A
INPUT DATA  BUFFER:               1.0000000
INPUT DATA  BUFFER:               2.0000000
INPUT DATA  BUFFER:               3.0000000
INPUT DATA  BUFFER:              -1.0000000
THE VECTOR B
INPUT DATA  BUFFER:               4.0000000
INPUT DATA  BUFFER:               5.0000000
INPUT DATA  BUFFER:               6.0000000
INPUT DATA  BUFFER:              -1.0000000
THEIR DOT PRODUCT =              32.0000000
```

5.8 What You Should Know

1. The high-level analysis of a problem is preserved in the final program by making subprocesses subprograms.
2. Programmer-defined subprograms enable a programmer to write a program in larger conceptual units.
3. Top-down programming means to first write a program in a form understandable to humans, almost as though you had a much smarter computer than you actually have available. Then you go back over the program, describing in more detail those processes that the available computer cannot understand.
4. Even in parts of the program description that are not yet computer-executable, choose constructions that resemble keywords and phrases for the target language, Fortran.
5. The hallmarks of a modular process are:
   a. It is reasonably self-contained.
   b. It is described easily.
   c. It is a meaningful conceptual unit to the designer and reader of the program.
6. A self-documenting variable name explains, in large measure, what its values will represent.
7. Arrays are used to store a list of similar values. The value of the subscript indicates which item in the list is being referenced.
8. A programmer can define a termination signal, which the program tests for, to end reading of data.
9. Internal documentation appears in the program listing for the benefit of programmers who will read the program later to modify it, to verify its correctness, or to fix a bug.
10. External documentation includes a record of the analysis of the problem, the strategic choices made, the algorithms chosen, and charts showing the organization of the main modules.
11. A manual for using the program should be written in terms a nonprogrammer can understand.

12. A subprogram is either a function or a subroutine.
13. Subprograms should follow the main program in the top-down programming style.
14. A local variable is a variable known only within the main program or within one subprogram.
15. All variables used in a subprogram are declared in the subprogram.
16. A subroutine is called by writing its name following the keyword CALL as a statement in a program.
17. Every subprogram should have a specific and well-defined task to do.
18. Side effects, peripheral effects of one subprogram on another, are effects unrelated to the task of the offending subprogram.
19. Except for dummy arguments, all variables in a subprogram are local to that subprogram.
20. Changes in a local variable cannot *ever* cause side effects in another subprogram.
21. A subprogram may have a list of arguments through which it communicates with the calling program.
22. Supplied and dummy arguments must have exactly the same type.
23. If a supplied argument is a variable, an array element, or a character substring, all references to the corresponding dummy argument are replaced with references to the supplied argument.
24. Dummy arguments that have corresponding supplied arguments that are expressions other than variables, array elements, or character substrings are assigned the value of the supplied argument before subprogram execution begins. The value of the dummy argument must not be changed.
25. A function subprogram is a construction like a subroutine, with two major differences:

    a. A function returns a function value whose type is declared.
    b. A function is called implicitly by being written in an expression.

26. In general, a function should have no effect other than computing its function value.
27. In a function, the function values should be assigned exactly once in each execution.

5.9 Self-Test Questions

Section 5.1

1. How do you call a subroutine?
2. Should the subroutine go before or after the main program?
3. What is the minimum number of arguments for a subroutine?
4. True/false:

    a. The main program must not use the same variable names as the subroutine.
    b. Subroutines enable a programmer to think and write a program in terms of larger, more natural conceptual units.
    c. Subroutines augment the vocabulary of Fortran.

Section 5.2

1. Why did we refine the output procedure first?
2. What is a modular subprocess?
3. True/false: The first real progress was made when we wrote executable Fortran code for the output routine.

Section 5.3

1. What is a termination signal?
2. What do you think the user of the program should be instructed to do in case a mistake is made in typing the input data?

Section 5.4

1. In what order do the subroutines for subtasks appear in the final program listing?
2. What are the three major kinds of documentation that should accompany a program? Give examples of what is included under each heading.
3. How many times should you test a program?
4. What happens in the program GRADES in this section if a student takes no courses this semester? Will the program crash (a) always, or (b) only if the user handles this case the wrong way? What should the user be told to do to handle this case?

Section 5.5

1. True/false:

   a. A dummy argument must have the same name as its supplied argument.
   b. A supplied argument must have the same type as its dummy argument.
   c. A constant may be used as a supplied argument.
   d. When you write a Fortran subroutine, you do not have to declare a variable that has the same name as one in the main program.

2. Why are local variables used?
3. When are dummy arguments called by reference, and when are they called by value?
4. Suppose that the value of the integer variable I is 1, that the value of A (1) is 2, and that the value of A (2) is 3. The array A is type integer. What are the values of these variables after the execution of the following statement? Test your answer on a computer, if possible.

```
CALL SWAPI (I, A (I))
```

Section 5.6

1. How does a function differ from a subroutine?
2. True/false:

   a. The dummy arguments of a function do not all have to be of the same type.
   b. Subroutines and functions may be mixed in any order.
   c. The first value assigned to a function inside the function body is the value returned to the calling program.

3. Hand simulate the execution of the function ILLDEF (ill-defined) for the supplied arguments −3.14, 8, and 6.4. Why is this function ill-defined? What kind of remedy is needed to make it well?

```
      FUNCTION ILLDEF (A, B, C)
      LOGICAL ILLDEF
      REAL A, B, C

      IF (B .LE. A) THEN DO
         ILLDEF = .FALSE.
      ELSE DO
      IF (B .GT. A .AND. B .LE. C) THEN DO
         ILLDEF = .TRUE.
      END IF
      END IF
      RETURN
      END
```

4. Compute the value of

```
      ROUND (X, 10.0 ** INT (ALOG10 (X) - N + 1))
```

for X = 27.6 and X = 4,827,674, and N = 3, N = 1, and N = −2. Describe the value of this expression for an arbitrary real X and integer N.

5.10 Programming Exercises

1. **Purpose:** To illustrate the use of subprograms in top-down design to clarify the main program. The program is of modest size. User-specified output and input formats are required.

   The problem: An input file contains a list of one month's transactions for a checking account, represented as follows. First comes an integer, giving the number of transactions for the month. Next come pairs of entries, each consisting of a one-character transaction code and the amount of the transaction. Valid transaction codes are I for initial balance brought forward from the previous month, C for check, D for deposit, and S for service charge.

   The problem is to write a program to read this input file and to print a monthly statement for the checking account. Handle the processing for each transaction type in a separate subroutine and let the main program decide which subroutine to called. The program should print the final balance.

   Sample input file:

```
8
I 378.16
C 110.00
D 25.03
C 221.82
D 50.00
C 36.39
S 3.00
```

   Sample output:

```
                     DEPOSIT  WITHDRAWAL  BALANCE
INITIAL BALANCE                            378.16
CHECK                             110.00   268.16
CHECK                              57.76   210.40
DEPOSIT                25.03               235.43
CHECK                             221.82    13.61
```

```
DEPOSIT             50.00              63.61
CHECK                         36.39    27.22
SERVICE CHARGE                 3.00    24.22

FINAL BALANCE                          24.22
```

2. **Purpose:** To modify the program in Exercise 1 to add variable-length input terminated by an end-of-data signal.

   The problem: Modify the program written for Exercise 1 so that service charges do not appear in the input file, but are calculated automatically on the basis of the other transactions. Service charges are 10 cents per check, $3 per month for maintaining the account, and a $15 overdraft charge each time a check leaves a balance below $0.00 during the month. Also introduce a new transaction type E for end-of-month, and use this input line to terminate reading instead of the count of the number of transactions previously entered by the user. The end-of-month input line should not have an amount.

   Input data Similar to Exercise 1, except the first line is omitted and a new last line is added.

```
I 378.16
C 110.00
C 57.76
D 25.03
C 221.82
D 50.00
C 36.39
S 3.00
E
```

   Sample output: Similar to Exercise 1.

3. **Purpose:** To modify an existing program so as to move details out of the main program and into subprograms.

   The problem: The quadratic equation $ax^2 + bx + c = 0$ has two real roots, two complex roots, or one real root depending on whether the quantity $b^2 - 4ac$ is positive, negative, or zero, respectively. The program QUAD2 in Section 3.4 handles these case with an IF block with the details in each case written into the main program. Rewrite the program QUAD2 to use a separate subroutine call to handle each of the cases.

   Input data: The same as to QUAD2, the three coefficients a, b, and c.

```
1 -5 6
```

   Sample execution:

```
INPUT DATA A:   1.00000
           B:  -5.00000
           C:   6.00000
THE ROOTS ARE REAL
X1 = 3.00000
X2 = 2.00000
```

4. **Purpose:** To modify a large existing program. The top-down design of the large program will make it easier to modify it and still have it work.

   The problem: When using the program GRADES, written in Sections 5.2–5.4, the user could accidentally type a letter other than the standard letter grades A, B, C, D, and F. First, find out what the program GRADES would do when this happens. Then modify the program GRADES so that it checks if a letter grade entered during execution is one of these five standard grades. If one or more of the entered letter grades for a student is illegal, print an error message instead of a grade report.

Hint: Use a variable ERRCNT (error count) to count how many such errors there are in the input.

Input data: Input is interactive. The input data will appear in the sample output.

Sample output:

```
SEMESTER: FALL 1985
MORE
NAME: GEORGE GLITCH
CLASS: 1987
COURSE: QUAD FORM IN BABYLONIA
CREDIT: 3
GRADE: E
COURSE: SURVEY 19TH CENT COMPUT
CREDIT: 2
GRADE: A
COURSE: NO MORE COURSES

*** ILLEGAL LETTER GRADE -- NO GRADE REPORT GENERATED FOR GEORGE GLITCH ***
```

5. **Purpose:** To modify a large existing program.

   The problem: North Mountain College uses a different grading scale than South Mountain College. At North Mountain College, the possible grades are A+, A, A−, B+, B, B−, C+, C, C−, D+, D, D−, and F. The numeric equivalents of these grades range from 1 for A+ down to 13 for F. Modify the program GRADES in Section 5.4 to handle the grading scale at North Mountain College.

   Input data: Interactive input similar to that of Exercise 4.

   Sample output: Similar to that of the program GRADES in Section 5.4.

6. **Purpose:** To modify a large existing program.

   The problem: Most colleges also have grades of W (withdrawn), P (passing), and I (incomplete). Although their effects on the total number of credits accumulated toward a degree differ, all three grades of W, P, and I have the same effect on the current semester's gradepoint average; that is, the courses for which they are given are excluded from the gradepoint average calculation. Modify the program GRADES in Section 5.4 so that grades of W, P, and I are accepted and printed in the grade reports, but not used in the calculation of a student's gradepoint average.

   Hint: Use an array EXCLUD (MAXCRS) of type character or logical to keep track of which courses are to be excluded from the gradepoint average calculations.

   Input data: Similar to the program GRADES, but also including at least one course with a grade of W, a course with a grade of P, and a course with a grade of I.

   Sample output: If there are no grades of W, P, or I in the input for a student, the output for this exercise should look exactly like that of the program GRADES. For students with grades of W, P, or I, the sample output will look very similar.

7. **Purpose:** To convert a program that uses interactive input into a program that uses batch input.

   The problem: To modify the program GRADES in Section 5.4 so that it runs in batch mode with input data in a prepared file. You must modify the program GRADES, plan and document the format of the input file, and debug the modified program.

8. **Purpose:** To get practice hand simulating an execution in a situation where there are subprograms and local variables.

   The problem: The purpose of the program MAXOF4 is to determine the maximum of four numbers supplied as input. Hand simulate its execution.

```
C       PROGRAM MAXOF4
C       ILLUSTRATES THE USE OF LOCAL VARIABLES
C       NOT THE BEST WAY TO FIND THE LARGEST OF FOUR NUMBERS
        INTEGER N1, N2, N3, N4, TEMP, LARGST
C
        READ, N1, N2, N3, N4
        PRINT, 'INPUT DATA  N1:', N1
        PRINT, '            N2:', N2
        PRINT, '            N3:', N3
        PRINT, '            N4:', N4
C
C       SET TEMP = LARGER OF N1 AND N2
        IF (N1 .GE. N2) THEN DO
           TEMP = N1
        ELSE DO
           TEMP = N2
        END IF
C
C       MAKE SURE THAT N3 IS NOT LESS THAN N4
        IF (N3 .LT. N4) THEN DO
           CALL SWAPI (N3, N4)
        END IF
C
C       NOW PICK THE LARGER OF TEMP AND N3
        IF (N3 .GT. TEMP) THEN DO
           LARGST = N3
        ELSE DO
           LARGST = TEMP
        END IF
C
        PRINT, LARGST, 'IS THE LARGEST.'
        STOP
        END
C
C
        SUBROUTINE SWAPI (P, Q)
        INTEGER P, Q, TEMP
        TEMP = P
        P = Q
        Q = TEMP
        RETURN
        END
```

Input data:

```
23 7 3 14
```

Sample execution: Hand simulation.

9. **The problem:** Rewrite the program MAXOF4 in Exercise 8 using the built-in function MAX. It will, of course, be considerably shorter.

Input data:

```
23 7 3 14
```

Sample output:

```
23 IS THE LARGEST
```

10. **Purpose:** To write a useful mathematical function subprogram.

The problem: The quantity $n!$, called *n factorial*, is the number 1 if $n = 0$, and is the product

$$n \times (n-1) \times \cdots \times 3 \times 2 \times 1$$

if n is a positive integer. When n is a positive integer the quantity $n!$ is the number of ways of arranging n different items in a row.

a) Write a function subprogram FACT (N) that returns the function value N! if the argument N is a nonnegative integer, and the value -1 to signal an improper supplied argument otherwise.

b) Write a main program to input a value for N and to test the function subprogram FACT (N) using the input value N.

Input data: One number, the input value for the argument N of FACT.

Sample output:

```
INPUT DATA N:  5
5 FACTORIAL =  120
```

11. **Purpose:** To learn about side effects of a subprogram.

The problem: The function YRINT calculates the total interest accumulating in 1 year for a savings account that pays interest monthly. The initial amount and the annual rate are supplied as arguments.

```
      PROGRAM TSTINT
C     ONE YEAR'S COMPOUND INTEREST ON $1000
C     AT 5% AND 6% ANNUAL RATE, COMPOUNDED MONTHLY
      REAL RATE, PRINC, YRINT
C
      PRINC = 1000
      RATE = 0.05
      PRINT, 'ONE YEAR''S COMPOUND INTEREST ON $', PRINC
      PRINT, '    AT 5%, COMPOUNDED MONTHLY:', YRINT (PRINC, RATE)
C
      RATE = RATE + 0.01
      PRINT, 'ONE YEAR''S COMPOUND INTEREST ON $', PRINC
      PRINT, '    AT 6%, COMPOUNDED MONTHLY:', YRINT (PRINC, RATE)
      END

      FUNCTION YRINT (PRINC, RATE)
C     CAUSES POSSIBLE UNDESIRABLE SIDE EFFECTS
      REAL YRINT, PRINC, RATE
      REAL BALANC
      INTEGER MONTH
C
      BALANC = PRINC
C     CONVERT ANNUAL INTEREST RATE TO A MONTHLY RATE
      RATE = RATE / 12
C
      DO 18 MONTH = 1, 12
         BALANC = BALANC + BALANC * RATE
   18 CONTINUE
C
```

```
      YRINT = BALANC - PRINC
      RETURN
      END
```

The two parts of this exercise are concerned with diagnosing and curing possible side-effects of the poorly written function YRINT.

a) Hand simulate the execution of the driver program TSTINT to find the undesirable side effect of the function subprogram YRINT. What is it?

b) Rewrite the function subprogram YPRINT so that it has no side effect on any calling program.

Input data: None.

Sample output: Hand simulated.

Purpose: The purpose of Exercises 12 – 19 is to do a major programming project involving many subroutines.

12. **The problem:** A library allows books to be borrowed for a period of 2 weeks and charges a fine of 5 cents a day for the first week a book is overdue, 10 cents a day for the second week, and 25 cents a day thereafter. The following program is for computing the amount of the fine, if any, on a borrowed book:

```
      PROGRAM FINES
      Read withdrawal and return dates
      Calculate number of days overdue
      Determine fine, if any
      Print fine or message saying that none is due
      STOP
      END
```

Refine the program FINES to an executable Fortran program, using subroutines and subroutine calls for program steps that involve too much detail. An answer to this exercise is acceptable if the main program is entirely in Fortran, but some of the subroutines still require further refinement.

13. The amount of the fine on an overdue book depends only on the number of days the book is overdue. One way to calculate the number of days the book is overdue is based on numbering the days of a year from 1 for January 1 to 365 (or 366 in leap years) for December 31. For days in the same year, simple subtraction suffices to determine the number of days for which a book is borrowed. For borrowing periods that start in one year and end in another year, the formula is only slightly more complex.

    Refine the subroutine or program steps that determine this fine on an overdue book to an executable program. For this exercise, it is not necessary to refine the step that converts a month and day of the month to a day-of-the-year number from 1 to 365 (or 366), if it is done in a subroutine. This is saved for Exercise 14.

14. January 1 is the first day of the year, and December 31 is the 365th day of an ordinary year or the 366th day of a leap year. It is easy to convert a month and day of the month to a day of the year for ordinary years using the information contained in Table 5.5.
    For example, October 26 is the 273 + 26 = 299th day of an ordinary year. Write a program to convert a given month and day of the month to a day of the year and refine it to an executable subroutine. For this exercise, you may make the simplifying assumption that all years are ordinary years; that is, ignore leap years.

15. For the years from 1901 to 2099, any year that is exactly divisible by 4 (with remainder 0) is a leap year and has a twenty-ninth day in February. Improve the subroutine written in Exercise 14 to work correctly for leap

Table 5.5 Converting a month and day of the month to a day of the year for ordinary (nonleap) years.

	MONTH	DAY OF THE YEAR
1	January	0 + day of the month
2	February	31 + day of the month
3	March	59 + day of the month
4	April	90 + day of the month
5	May	120 + day of the month
6	June	151 + day of the month
7	July	181 + day of the month
8	August	212 + day of the month
9	September	243 + day of the month
10	October	273 + day of the month
11	November	304 + day of the month
12	December	334 + day of the month

years also. To refine this program to an executable Fortran subroutine, use the built-in function MOD. The value of the function MOD is the integer remainder when two integers are divided. Thus a year from 1901 to 2099 is a leap year if and only if

```
MOD (YEAR, 4) .EQ. 0
```

16. Include a leap year correction in the subroutine for Exercise 13.
17. Refine the subroutine or program steps written for Exercise 12 that read the withdrawal date and the return date. You must make sure that all the information required to calculate the number of days overdue is obtained or calculated. Otherwise the program FINES will not work when all the subroutines are included in the program. This is why the refinement of this step is saved for last. The answer to this exercise depends on whether the subroutine written for Exercise 14 to calculate the day of the year uses the full names January, February, and so on, or abbreviations such as Jan, Feb, and so on, for the months, or requires the month to be specified as a number from 1 to 12.
18. What effect would it have on the program FINES if the withdrawal and return dates were entered as numbers from 1 to 365 (or 366)? Are there any problems with this from the standpoint of a user of the program FINES?
19. What is the effect on the program FINES of entering the withdrawal and return dates as days of the century, from 1 to 36525? Is this desirable?
20. Write a function NINT that rounds its real argument to the nearest integer. Make sure it works for negative numbers. Hint: Use the built-in function INT.

6 ARRAYS

When a programming application requires the processing of a number of different pieces of information of the same kind, it is natural to organize the data in an array. For example, in taking an average of test scores, each test score may be different, but they are all data of the same kind and each is to be treated in the same way by the program. The existence of a conceptual list of test scores, however, does not mean that the computer program must use an array.

In Section 4.3, an average of test scores was calculated without using an array by arranging the calculation so that only one test score is needed at a time in the computer. Each test score was read, echoed, added to the sum, and then discarded. It is fortunate that a discarded test score was not needed again later in the program execution, because it was no longer available. It was replaced by the next test score read into the same variable. In some sense, this program to average test scores is harder than one using arrays, because it distorts the natural organization of the data to make the computation possible.

The fundamental syntax and interpretation of arrays in Fortran are introduced in this chapter. Then the chapter discusses the extremely important applications of searching and sorting that fully exploit the systematic organization of an array.

6.1 Lists, Subscripts, and Index Variables

In ordinary usage, a **list** is a sequence of values, usually all representing data of the same kind, or otherwise related to one another. A list of students registered for a particular course and a list of all students enrolled at a college are examples. The roster of active players on an athletic team and the names of all the presidents of the United States are also lists. So are grocery lists and lists of entrants in a jousting tournament. Synonyms for the same concept are **one-dimensional array** and **vector**.

In Fortran, a collection of values of the same type is called an **array**. We will also refer to a one-dimensional array as a list. This section is concerned mainly with introducing the programming techniques associated with lists, including the concepts of **subscripts** and **index variables**.

Section Preview

Array:

An array is a list of values of the same type.

Array Declaration:

General Form:

type arrayname (*constant*)

Example:

```
      REAL BATAVG (9), FREQ (10)
      CHARACTER NAMLST *25 (100)
      CHARACTER *5 LISTA (25), LISTB (25)
      INTEGER NUMBER (10)
```

Subscript:

The relative position within an array, written between parentheses, is the subscript of the array element.

Index Variables:

A subscript may be a variable! Indeed, there would hardly be any use for arrays if a subscript couldn't vary. A variable that appears as a subscript of an array is an index variable.

Example:

```
C     READS VALUES FOR THE 3 COMPONENTS OF VECTOR
      REAL VECTOR (3)
      INTEGER I
      DO 18 I = 1, 3
         READ, VECTOR (I)
   18 CONTINUE
```

Implied DO Loop:

The implied DO construction is used to create a list of expressions, indexed by a variable increasing by constant increments.

General Form:

(*expression*, ..., *expression*, *variable* = *expression*, *expression*, *expression*)

Example:

```
      PRINT, (A (I), B (I+1), I = 2, 6, 2)
```

A Credit Card Checking Application

As an example of a problem concerned with a list, suppose that a company maintains a computerized list of credit cards that either have been reported lost or stolen or are greatly in arrears in payments. The company needs a program to determine quickly whether a given credit card, presented by a customer wishing to charge a purchase, is on this list of credit cards that can no longer be honored.

Suppose that a company has a list of 8,262 credit cards reported lost or stolen, as illustrated in Table 6.1.

Since all of the 8,262 numbers in the list must be retained simultaneously in the computer's main memory for efficient searching, each number must be assigned as the value of a variable with a different name so that the computer can be instructed to compare each account number of a lost or stolen card against the account number of the card offered in payment for goods and services.

Table 6.1 List of the Account Numbers of Credit Cards Reported Lost or Stolen.

Account number of 1st lost credit card	2718281
Account number of 2nd lost credit card	7389056
Account number of 3rd lost credit card	1098612
Account number of 4th lost credit card	5459815
Account number of 5th lost credit card	1484131
.	.
.	.
.	.
Account number of 8262nd lost credit card	1383596

Subscripts

It is possible to use the 8262 Fortran variable names

```
LC1
LC2
LC3
 .
 .
 .
LC8262
```

(lost card 1, lost card 2, lost card 3, ... , lost card 8262). Unfortunately, the Fortran language does not recognize the intended relationship between these variable names. The form used for designating the items in a Fortran list is the following:

```
LSTCRD (1)
LSTCRD (2)
LSTCRD (3)
         .
         .
         .
LSTCRD (8262)
```

This seemingly minor modification of otherwise perfectly acceptable variable names opens up a new dimension of programming capabilities. All the programs in this chapter, and a large number of the programs in succeeding chapters, cannot be written without this form. The numbers in parentheses that specify the location of an item within a list are **subscripts**, a name borrowed from mathematics. Although mathematical subscripts are usually written below the line (hence the name), such a form of typography is impossible on most computer input devices. A substitute notation, enclosing the subscript in parentheses or brackets, is adopted in most computer languages. It is customary to read the expression X (3) as "X sub 3", just as if the number 3 were written below the line.

Why Use Subscripts?

The advantage of this method of naming the quantities over using the variable names LC1, LC2, ..., LC8262 springs from the following programming language capability: *the subscript of an array variable may itself be a variable, or an even more complicated expression.*

The consequences of this simple statement are much more profound than would appear at first sight. In fact, it is one of the most important principles in modern computer programming. This entire chapter, and much of the rest of this book, is devoted to exploring some of the uses of this facility.

For a start in describing the uses of a subscript that is itself a variable, the two statements

```
I = 1
PRINT, LSTCRD (I)
```

produce exactly the same output as the single statement

```
PRINT, LSTCRD (1)
```

namely, 2718281, the account number of the first lost credit card on the list. Similarly, the account numbers of the first three lost credit cards may be written by the statements

```
I = 1
PRINT, LSTCRD (I)
I = 2
PRINT, LSTCRD (I)
I = 3
PRINT, LSTCRD (I)
```

The effect is the same as executing the three statements

```
PRINT, LSTCRD (1)
PRINT, LSTCRD (2)
PRINT, LSTCRD (3)
```

Based on the data in Table 6.1, the sample output in both cases would be

```
2718281
7389056
1098612
```

In fact, the entire list of account numbers of lost credit cards can be written by the subroutine PRTLST (print lost cards).

```
      SUBROUTINE PRTLST (LSTCRD)
      INTEGER LSTCRD (8262)
      INTEGER I
C
      DO 18 I = 1, 8262
         PRINT, LSTCRD (I)
18    CONTINUE
      RETURN
      END
```

```
2718281
7389056
1098612
   .
   .
   .
1383596
```

The sample output resembles Table 6.1 without the names. The important thing to keep in mind when following the execution of the subroutine PRTLST is that, each time the PRINT statement is executed, there is a different value for the subscript I, and consequently a different item in the list is printed. Figure 6.1 shows another example of how the value of the subscript distinguishes between elements of an array.

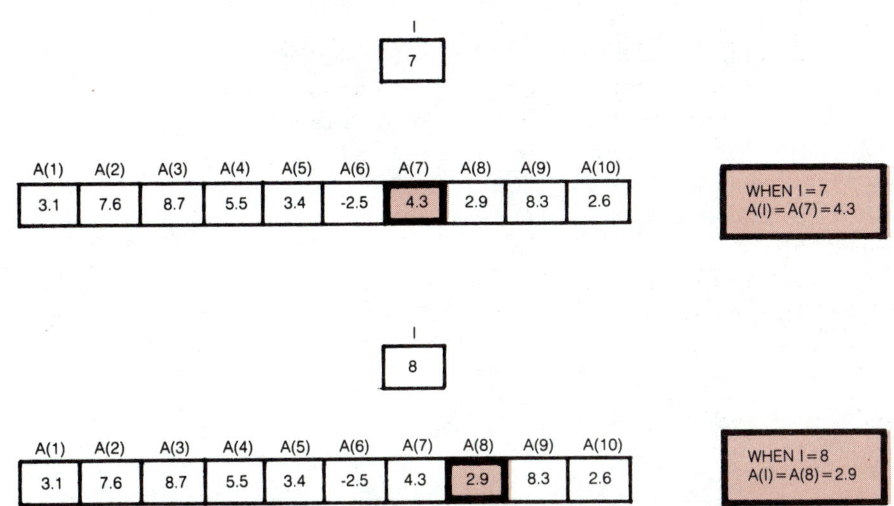

Figure 6.1 The effect of changing the value of the subscript I on the array element A (I).

Index Variables

A variable used to indicate which item in a list is being referenced is an **index**. The variable subscript I in the subroutine PRTLST is such an **index variable**. Traditionally, the name "I" is a very popular one for index variables, partly because it is the first letter in the word "index", and partly because the letter "I" is commonly used in mathematics for a variable subscript. The names "J" and "K" are popular also.

Array Declarations

The name of an array must obey the same rules as an ordinary variable name. Each array must be declared in the declaration section of the program. A name is declared to be an array by putting it in a type statement and following the name with a range of subscripts, enclosed by parentheses. For example,

```
REAL X (9), Y (9)
LOGICAL YESNO (99)
```

declares that X and Y are lists of 9 real values and that YESNO is a list of 99 logical values. This declaration implies that a subscript for X or Y must be an integer expression with a value from 1 to 9 and that a subscript for YESNO must be an integer expression whose value is from 1 to 99.

A list of character strings may be declared in a form like the following.

```
CHARACTER CHRLST *8 (17)
```

In this example, the variable CHRLST is a list of 17 character strings, each of length 8.

Note: Since the string length appears in a different place in a WATFIV-S character array declaration than it does in Fortran 77, people expecting to use both dialects might want to use the declaration

```
CHARACTER *8 CHRLST (17)
```

which is accepted in both dialects.

Variable-Length Lists

It is clearly absurd to assume that a company will always have exactly 8,262 credit cards reported lost or stolen. However, Fortran requires *fixed constant limits* for the range of subscripts in an array declaration for any array that is not a dummy argument. The way around this restriction is to have one variable MAXNR with a value of, say, 10,000 to be used as the upper bound in array declarations and a variable NRCRDS (actual number of cards), whose current value would be 8,262.

In this light, we rewrite the subroutine PRTLST and show the relevant declarations in the main program that uses the subroutine PRTLST, defining everything in terms of the single parameter MAXNR. In the main program, there would be declarations

```
      INTEGER MAXNR, NRCRDS, LSTCRD (10000)
      MAXNR = 10000
```

and the subroutine itself would be rewritten as follows.

```
      SUBROUTINE PRTLST (LSTCRD, NRCRDS)
      INTEGER I, NRCRDS, LSTCRD (NRCRDS)

      DO 18 I = 1, NRCRDS
         PRINT, LSTCRD (I)
   18 CONTINUE
      END
```

Although an array declared in the main program must have constant subscript bounds, the declaration of a *dummy argument* may use subscript ranges involving variables provided that those variables also are dummy arguments. The dummy variables used to indicate the subscript ranges must have a value that is *no bigger than* the declared size of the corresponding actual argument. In the example above, the value of NRCRDS must be less than or equal to 10,000.

Use of an Array When a Simple Variable Will Do

Some programs may be written either with or without arrays. The process is illustrated again by comparing the program AVGSC2, which does not use an array, with the program AVGSC3, which does. Both programs accept varying numbers of test scores in the input data and count the number of test scores.

```
C     PROGRAM AVGSC2
C     AVERAGE TEST SCORES
C     DOES NOT USE AN ARRAY
C
      INTEGER ENROLL, COUNT
      REAL SIGNAL, DATUM, SUM
      LOGICAL MORSCR
C
      SIGNAL = 9999
      ENROLL = 0
      SUM = 0
```

```
      MORSCR = .TRUE.
      WHILE (MORSCR) DO
         READ, DATUM
         PRINT, 'INPUT DATA  DATUM: ', DATUM
         IF (DATUM .EQ. SIGNAL) THEN DO
            MORSCR = .FALSE.
         ELSE DO
            ENROLL = ENROLL + 1
            SUM = SUM + DATUM
         END IF
      END WHILE
C
      PRINT, ' '
      PRINT, 'THERE ARE', ENROLL, 'TEST SCORES.'
      PRINT, 'AVERAGE TEST SCORE =', SUM / ENROLL
      STOP
      END
```

This program shows a typical use of the simple variables DATUM and SUM in a loop. On each iteration, a new value of the variable DATUM is read, and except when the termination signal card is read, a new value of the running total SUM is computed. Of course, the previous values of these variables are lost.

In contrast, the preliminary version of the program AVGSC3 cannot be refined without using an array, because all the test scores are stored simultaneously in the computer's memory after the reading step.

```
C     PROGRAM AVGSC3
C     PRELIMINARY VERSION
      Read and count all the test scores
      Calculate the average
      Print the results
      STOP
      END
```

In refining the program AVGSC3, the programmer must recognize that the role filled by the simple variable DATUM in the program AVGSC2 now requires a list, SCORE (MAXENR). The simple variable DATUM is retained as a buffer for holding the next score while the program tests whether this score value is the termination signal. The variable SUM does not need to be a list, because only one value for sum is needed at a time.

```
C     PROGRAM AVGSC3
C     AVERAGE TEST SCORES
C     USES AN ARRAY
C
      INTEGER ENROLL, COUNT
      REAL SIGNAL, SCORE (100), DATUM, SUM, AVG
      LOGICAL MORSCR
C
C     READ AND COUNT ALL THE TEST SCORES
      SIGNAL = 9999
      ENROLL = 0
      SUM = 0
```

```
      MORSCR = .TRUE.
      WHILE (MORSCR) DO
         READ, DATUM
         PRINT, 'INPUT DATA  DATUM: ', DATUM
         IF (DATUM .EQ. SIGNAL) THEN DO
            MORSCR = .FALSE.
         ELSE DO
            ENROLL = ENROLL + 1
            SCORE (ENROLL) = DATUM
         END IF
      END WHILE
C
C     CALCULATE THE AVERAGE
      SUM = 0
      DO 28 COUNT = 1, ENROLL
         SUM = SUM + SCORE (COUNT)
   28 CONTINUE
      AVG = SUM / ENROLL
C
C     PRINT THE RESULTS
      PRINT, ' '
      PRINT, 'THERE ARE', ENROLL, 'TEST SCORES.'
      PRINT, 'AVERAGE TEST SCORE =', AVG
      STOP
      END
```

The difference between these two programs is twofold. First, the reading of the scores and the calculating of the sum can be separate loops when the test scores are stored in a list. The calculation of the sum is particularly clear when it is done separately from the reading. For this problem, the increase in computer time needed for separate loops is a cheap price to pay to obtain clarity. Second, the program using a list requires more memory locations for storing values. When a computer with thousands of memory locations is used, this may be of no consequence. However, when a very small computer is used, there may not be enough room to run the program using subscripts. This is probably why many programmable desk calculators do not have the instructions needed to implement arrays.

Implied Do-Loops

As we have seen earlier, the first three elements of an array A may be printed by the DO block

```
      DO 18 I = 1, 3
         PRINT, A (I)
   18 CONTINUE
```

However, since this loop is the equivalent of the three PRINT statements

```
      PRINT, A (1)
      PRINT, A (2)
      PRINT, A (3)
```

the output is on three separate lines. Each new PRINT statement starts a new output line. To put all three values on one output line, we must use one PRINT statement

```
      PRINT, A (1), A (2), A (3)
```

Although the print list has a form that should be describable by a DO loop, an ordinary DO block cannot be used. For this purpose, Fortran provides the **implied DO loop**. The PRINT statement

```
PRINT, (A (I), I = 1, 3)
```

is considered the equivalent of the previous PRINT statement. This parenthesized expression is the implied DO loop. It stands for the list formed by taking array elements A (I) for all values of I from 1 to 3. More complex implied DO loops are possible. For example, the PRINT statement

```
PRINT, (A (I), B (I), I = 1, 3)
```

is equivalent to the statement

```
PRINT, A (1), B(1), A (2), B (2), A (3), B (3)
```

A step size is also permitted in an implied DO loop. Thus the statement

```
PRINT, (I, A (I), I = 2, 6, 2)
```

is equivalent to the statement

```
PRINT, 2, A (2), 4, A (4), 6, A (6)
```

The implied DO loop construction may be used in PRINT and READ statements, and in other statements (discussed later) in which a list of variables or expressions is expected. The program VECSUM (vector sum) further illustrates the reading and printing of lists using implied DO loops.

```
C      PROGRAM VECSUM
       INTEGER SIZE,  A (100), B (100), C (100), I
C
       SIZE = 3
C
       PRINT, 'INPUT DATA', SIZE, 'COMPONENTS OF A:'
       READ, (A (I), I = 1, SIZE)
       PRINT, (A (I), I = 1, SIZE)
C
       PRINT, 'INPUT DATA', SIZE, 'COMPONENTS OF B:'
       READ, (B (I), I = 1, SIZE)
       PRINT, (B (I), I = 1, SIZE)
C
       DO 88 I = 1, SIZE
          C (I) = B (I) + A (I)
   88  CONTINUE
C
       PRINT, ' '
       PRINT, 'THE VECTOR SUM IS:', (C (I), I = 1, SIZE)
       STOP
       END
```

```
INPUT DATA             3 COMPONENTS OF A:
          1             4           9
INPUT DATA             3 COMPONENTS OF B:
          5            12          13

THE VECTOR SUM IS:            6           16           22
```

Keeping Track of the Size of a List

Since the programmer must always declare one fixed size for each array, it is necessary to keep track of the actual number of values that have been put in the array at any time during execution of the program. This is usually done by using an integer variable that has a value in the range from zero to the declared size of the list. The variable ENROLL in the program AVGSC3 and the variable NRCRDS in the final version of the subroutine PRTLST are used to keep track of the actual size of a variable-length list.

An Array as an Argument

There is no restriction that an argument of a subroutine must be a simple variable. Lists and tables are permitted. Many of the subprograms in this chapter use arguments that are arrays.

6.2 Sequential Searching

The previous section describes the appropriate terminology and some of the Fortran rules concerning lists and subscripts. This section makes a start toward illustrating the power of lists and subscripts as they are used in meaningful programs. The application throughout this section is that of checking a given credit card account number against a list of account numbers of lost or stolen cards. Increasingly more efficient programs are presented here and compared.

Section Preview

Sequential Search:

In sequential search, the elements of an array are examined in sequence from the element with the lowest subscript to the element with the highest subscript (or vice versa).

Ordered Lists:

When the array elements are in ascending or descending order, a sequential search for a value that is not in the list can "give up" when the correct position is reached, but the value is not found there.

Files:

Default input and output files are always available. Although WATFIV-S supports other files, most WATFIV installations restrict their use, and special authorization and access numbers are usually required.

Unit Numbers:

Every file has a unit number, an integer from 1 to 99. The default input file is unit 5 and the default output file is unit 6.

The READ and WRITE Statements:

When reading and writing a file other than the default files, a long form of the READ statement and WRITE statement must be used in order to include the unit number.

The Problem: Credit Card Checking

When a customer presents a credit card in payment for goods or services, it is desirable to determine quickly whether it can be accepted or whether it previously has been reported lost or stolen or cancelled for any other reason. The programs in this section perform such an investigation. Companies that issue their own credit cards usually include such a card verification program in their combined charging, billing, and inventory control systems. Independent credit card companies offer a verification service, often by telephone, to the businesses that accept their credit cards.

Fortran Files

Between runs of a credit card checking program, the complete list of account numbers of cancelled cards is stored in computer-readable form on a magnetic disk. A READ statement used to obtain information from a file other than the default file is similar to a READ statement used to read data from the default input file except that it specifies which file to read from. Files are assigned to a **unit number** in control cards preceding the $JOB card and then are referenced by that unit number in READ or WRITE statements. For instance, if the file CRDFIL is associated with unit 11,

```
READ (11, *) NRCRDS
```

tells the computer to read a value from the file CRDFIL and to assign that value to the variable NRCRDS. The asterisk indicates that the default format is used. Since many different files may be used by the same program, any input or output statement that does not use the **default files** must specify the unit number of the intended file.

The default files also have unit numbers, preassigned by the WATFIV system. The default input file is unit 5 and the default output file is unit 6, traditional unit numbers that trace their ancestry to the first tape-based Fortran operating system.

Sequential Search Through an Unordered List

The first and simplest strategy for checking a given credit card is simply to search from beginning to end through the list of cancelled credit cards, card by card, either until the given account number is found in the list, or until the end of the list is reached without finding that account number. In the program CRDCH1 (card check, version 1), which implements this strategy, the **sequential search** is accomplished by a DO block with exit that scans the list until the given account number is found in the list or all of the numbers have been examined.

Style Note: It is good programming practice to make the searching part of the program a separate module. Other versions of the credit card program in this section will be obtained by modifying this module and leaving the other modules essentially unchanged.

The two ways of exiting from the search loop both pass control to the END statement that returns from the subroutine SEQSRC. However, they have a different effect on the dummy argument FOUND. When the credit card being checked is not in the list, the search loop is executed until the list is exhausted. This normal completion of the DO block allows control to fall through to the RETURN statement with the value of FOUND still false. When the card being checked is found in the list, the logical variable FOUND is set to true before exiting the DO block. The main program subsequently tests the variable FOUND to decide which of two output messages is appropriate.

```
C       PROGRAM CRDCH1
C       CHECKS WHETHER A CREDIT CARD
C       IS LOST, STOLEN, OR CANCELLED
C
C       THE FILE 'CRDFIL' CONTAINS A LIST
C       OF ALL CANCELLED CARDS.
C       IT IS ASSIGNED EITHER TO UNIT 11
C       IF NONDEFAULT FILES ARE AVAILABLE
C       OR UNIT 5 IF ONLY THE DEFAULT FILES MAY BE USED
C
        INTEGER MAXCRD, CDUNIT
        INTEGER NRCRDS, CARDNR, LSTCRD (10000)
        LOGICAL FOUND
C
        MAXCRD = 10000
        CDUNIT =5
C
        CALL REDCRD (LSTCRD, MAXCRD, NRCRDS, CDUNIT)
        READ, CARDNR
        PRINT, 'CARD NUMBER TO BE CHECKED:', CARDNR
        CALL SEQSRC (LSTCRD, NRCRDS, CARDNR, FOUND)
        IF (FOUND) THEN DO
           PRINT, 'CARD #', CARDNR, 'CANNOT BE ACCEPTED.'
        ELSE DO
           PRINT, 'CARD #', CARDNR, 'IS ACCEPTABLE.'
        END IF
        STOP
        END
C
C
        SUBROUTINE REDCRD (LSTCRD, MAXCRD, NRCRDS, CDUNIT)
        INTEGER MAXCRD, NRCRDS, LSTCRD (10000)
        INTEGER I, CDUNIT
C
        READ (CDUNIT, *) NRCRDS
        DO 18 I = 1, NRCRDS
           READ (CDUNIT, *) LSTCRD (I)
   18   CONTINUE
        RETURN
        END
C
C
        SUBROUTINE SEQSRC (LSTCRD, NRCRDS, CARDNR, FOUND)
C       SEQUENTIAL SEARCH
C
        INTEGER NRCRDS, LSTCRD (NRCRDS), CARDNR
        LOGICAL FOUND
        INTEGER I
C
```

```
      FOUND = .FALSE.
      DO 18 I = 1, NRCRDS
         IF (CARDNR .EQ. LSTCRD (I)) THEN DO
            FOUND = .TRUE.
            GO TO 19
         END IF
   18 CONTINUE
   19 RETURN
      END
```

Testing the Search Program

Since most WATFIV-S users are permitted to access only the default files, we have made the unit number for the file of lost or stolen credit cards a variable. If non-default files are available, and there are control cards in the run file associating the file CRDFIL with unit 11, the program can run as written. In the more likely event that only the default input file is available, the single change

```
CDUNIT = 5
```

in the main program redirects READ requests to the default input file. Of course, the list of account numbers for credit cards reported lost or stolen must now appear following the $ENTRY line in the default input file. If an editor is available, the instructor can create a public file, available to all, with the list of account numbers, and each student can copy the list from the public file to the WATFIV-S run file. This was the procedure we used in all sample executions in this section.

```
CARD NUMBER TO BE CHECKED:      3572065
CARD #      3572065 IS ACCEPTABLE.

CARD NUMBER TO BE CHECKED:      2718281
CARD #      2718281 CANNOT BE ACCEPTED.
```

The dilemma that had prevented the efficient programming of a sequential searching application is now solved by reading the list of lost or stolen cards into an array. Each card number in the list can be referenced individually using LSTCRD (1), LSTCRD (2), LSTCRD (3), and so on, yet the single expression LSTCRD (I) may refer to any one card, because the value of the index variable I may be the location in the list of any particular card.

Improving the Efficiency

The basic strategy of the program CRDCH1 is to check a credit card account number, supplied as input, against each account number, in turn, in the list of cancelled or lost cards, either until a match is found or until the list is exhausted. These alternatives are not equally likely. Most credit cards offered in payment for purchases or services represent the authorized use of active, valid accounts. Thus, by far the most usual execution of the program CRDCH1 terminates when the list is exhausted and the computer prints the message that the credit card presented is acceptable.

The number of comparisons a program must make before accepting a credit card is some measure of the efficiency of that program. For example, when searching for an acceptable credit card in a list of 10,000 cancelled credit cards, the program CRDCH1 always makes 10,000 comparisons. The actual elapsed computer time for the search section of the program depends on the time it takes the computer to make one comparison and to prepare to make the next comparison.

Sequential Search of an Ordered List

The lack of order in the list of cancelled cards is the reason so many comparisons are needed before a presented card is accepted. If the list of cancelled credit cards is maintained in order of increasing card number, then some improvement is possible. As soon as one cancelled card number examined in the search is too high, all subsequent ones will also be too high, so the search can be abandoned early. The program CRDCH2 presumes that the list is in increasing order. The only changes are in the subroutine SEQSR2 which replaces the subroutine SEQSRC in the program CRDCH1.

```
C       PROGRAM CRDCH2
C       CHECKS WHETHER A CREDIT CARD
C       IS LOST, STOLEN, OR CANCELLED
C
C       THE FILE 'CRDFIL' CONTAINS
C       A LIST OF ALL CANCELLED CARDS
C       IN ASCENDING ORDER
C       DEFAULT UNIT 5 IS USED FOR TESTING
C
        INTEGER MAXCRD, CDUNIT
        INTEGER NRCRDS, CARDNR, LSTCRD (10000)
        LOGICAL FOUND
C
        MAXCRD = 10000
        CDUNIT = 5
C
        CALL REDCRD (LSTCRD, MAXCRD, NRCRDS, CDUNIT)
        READ, CARDNR
        PRINT, 'CARD NUMBER TO BE CHECKED:', CARDNR
        CALL SEQSR2 (LSTCRD, NRCRDS, CARDNR, FOUND)
        IF (FOUND) THEN DO
           PRINT, 'CARD #', CARDNR, 'CANNOT BE ACCEPTED.'
        ELSE DO
           PRINT, 'CARD #', CARDNR, 'IS ACCEPTABLE.'
        END IF
        STOP
        END
C
C
        SUBROUTINE REDCRD (LSTCRD, MAXCRD, NRCRDS, CDUNIT)
        INTEGER MAXCRD, NRCRDS, LSTCRD (10000)
        INTEGER I, CDUNIT
C
        READ (CDUNIT, *) NRCRDS
        DO 18 I = 1, NRCRDS
           READ (CDUNIT, *) LSTCRD (I)
   18   CONTINUE
        RETURN
        END
C
C
        SUBROUTINE SEQSR2 (LSTCRD, NRCRDS, CARDNR, FOUND)
C       SEQUENTIAL SEARCH OF AN ORDERED LIST
C       SEARCH IS TERMINATED
C       IF A HIGHER ENTRY IS REACHED WITHOUT A MATCH
C
```

```
      INTEGER NRCRDS, LSTCRD (10000), CARDNR
      LOGICAL FOUND
      INTEGER I
C
      FOUND = .FALSE.
      DO 18 I = 1, NRCRDS
         IF (CARDNR .LE. LSTCRD (I)) THEN DO
            FOUND = (CARDNR .EQ. LSTCRD (I))
            GO TO 19
         END IF
   18 CONTINUE
   19 RETURN
      END
```

```
CARD NUMBER TO BE CHECKED:      4629076
CARD #      4629076 IS ACCEPTABLE.
```

For the same input data, the output of the program CRDCH2 would be identical to that produced by the program CRDCH1, but the execution times are not identical. Before accepting a presented account number, CRDCH1 always must search the entire list, but CRDCH2 stops as soon as it reaches a number in the list of cancelled account numbers that is larger than the presented number.

Roughly speaking, the average number of comparisons needed for an acceptance by CRDCH2 is about half the list size, plus one additional comparison to determine whether the last entry examined was exactly the account number of the credit card being checked. For a list of 10,000 cancelled cards, it would take an average of 5,001 comparisons, significantly better than the 10,000 for CRDCH1.

To a limited extent, this increased efficiency in the checking program is counterbalanced by some additional computer time needed to maintain the list of cancelled credit cards in increasing order. Nevertheless, almost any increase in the efficiency of the checking program results, in practice, in an increase in the efficiency of the entire operation.

Program Notes

The sequential search loop in the subroutine SEQSR2 is not quite as straightforward as it seems at first glance. When the presented card CARDNR is compared against an entry LSTCRD(I), three things can happen:

1. LSTCRD (I) is too low, in which case the search continues.
2. They match, in which case the presented card CARDNR has been found.
3. LSTCRD (I) is too high, in which case further search is futile.

The three possibilities are not equally likely. Case 1 can occur as many as 10,000 times in one search. Cases 2 and 3 can happen only once per search. It is important to test first for the most frequently occurring case. Otherwise, there will be two tests per iteration, slowing the search loop appreciably. This program tests for the first case, and then if it is false, it determines whether case 2 or case 3 applies.

6.3 Better Algorithms For Searching

Sequential search is a brute force technique. It works well for short lists but succeeds only by sheer persistence for large ones. Significant improvements in efficiency are possible if the strategy is modified so that only small lists are searched sequentially. A large list is subdivided into "pages" small enough to search sequentially. The correct page to search is located by examining the last entry on each page in sequence.

A somewhat different strategy, **divide and conquer**, is employed in a **binary search**. Half of the list can be eliminated at once by testing the middle element. Then half the remaining elements are eliminated by another test. Before long, there are hardly any candidates left and the search is completed quickly.

Section Preview

Multilevel Search:

If an ordered list is divided into pages, it takes less time to examine the last entry on each page and then to search the appropriate page for a given value than it takes to search the entire list sequentially.

If there are more levels, perhaps "volume", "chapter", "page", and "line", the search at each level is shorter and the total search time is shorter.

Binary Search:

Binary search uses a **divide and conquer** strategy to search an ordered list. At each step, the middle location still under consideration is tested, thereby eliminating half the remaining candidates for the location where the given value might be found. After very few steps, there is only one candidate left.

EQUIVALENCE statement:

The EQUIVALENCE statement is used to allow multiple names for the same variable and to overlay arrays to conserve memory.

General form:

EQUIVALENCE (*variable, variable*), ...

Example:

```
EQUIVALENCE (X, Y), (Z, A (17)), (A, B)
```

Multilevel Search

A better search strategy for a sequential search is to imitate the procedure of looking up a word in a dictionary. It makes no sense to search through every word in the dictionary, starting with aardvark in hopes of finding zebra. Most dictionaries have the first and last words defined on a page printed at the top of that page, for easy visibility. There is no point in searching through all the words on a page if a glance at the top of the page confirms that the correct page has not yet been reached. For this purpose, 10,000 entries in a list of cancelled credit cards might be divided arbitrarily into 100 pages of 100 entries each.

The basic strategy of the program CRDCH3 is a **two-level search**, first for the correct page, and second for the correct entry (if there is one) on that page.

Both the page search loop and the entry-by-entry search loop here are modelled on the search loop of CRDCH2, except that the page search loop does not have to check for exact agreement with the credit card number being presented.

```
C       PROGRAM CRDCH3
        INTEGER MAXCRD, CDUNIT
        INTEGER NRCRDS, CARDNR, LSTCRD (10000)
        LOGICAL FOUND
C
        CDUNIT = 5
        MAXCRD = 10000
        CALL REDCRD (LSTCRD, MAXCRD, NRCRDS, CDUNIT)
        READ, CARDNR
        PRINT, 'CARD NUMBER TO BE CHECKED:', CARDNR
        CALL SEQLV2 (LSTCRD, NRCRDS, CARDNR, FOUND)
        IF (FOUND) THEN DO
           PRINT, 'CARD #', CARDNR, 'CANNOT BE ACCEPTED.'
        ELSE DO
           PRINT, 'CARD #', CARDNR, 'IS ACCEPTABLE.'
        END IF
        STOP
        END
C
C
        SUBROUTINE REDCRD (LSTCRD, MAXCRD, NRCRDS, CDUNIT)
        INTEGER MAXCRD, NRCRDS, LSTCRD (MAXCRD)
        INTEGER I, CDUNIT
C
        READ (CDUNIT, *) NRCRDS
        DO 18 I = 1, NRCRDS
           READ (CDUNIT, *) LSTCRD (I)
   18   CONTINUE
        RETURN
        END
C
C
        SUBROUTINE SEQLV2 (LSTCRD, NRCRDS, CARDNR, FOUND)
C       TWO-LEVEL SEQUENTIAL SEARCH
C
C       THE LIST OF CANCELLED OR LOST CARDS MUST BE
C       IN INCREASING ORDER BY ACCOUNT NUMBER
C       FOR THIS SUBROUTINE TO WORK
C
        INTEGER NRCRDS, LSTCRD (NRCRDS), CARDNR
        LOGICAL FOUND, PAGFND
        INTEGER PAGSIZ, FIRST, LAST, I
C
        PAGSIZ = 100
C
C       SEARCH FOR THE CORRECT PAGE
C       FIRST IS THE FIRST ENTRY ON A PAGE
C       LAST IS THE LAST ENTRY ON A PAGE
C       EACH PAGE HAS PAGSIZ ENTRIES
        PAGFND = .FALSE.
        FIRST = 1
```

```
          IF (PAGSIZ .LE. NRCRDS) THEN DO
            DO 18 LAST = PAGSIZ, NRCRDS, PAGSIZ
              IF (CARDNR .LE. LSTCRD (LAST)) THEN DO
C                 CARDNR IS ON THIS PAGE
                  PAGFND = .TRUE.
                  GO TO 19
              ELSE DO
                  FIRST = FIRST + PAGSIZ
              END IF
   18       CONTINUE
          END IF
C
   19     IF (.NOT. PAGFND) THEN DO
C             CARDNR EXCEEDS LAST ENTRY ON LAST FULL PAGE
C             PREPARE TO SEARCH LAST (POSSIBLY EMPTY) PARTIAL PAGE
              LAST = NRCRDS
          END IF
C
C         SEARCH THE PAGE SEQUENTIALLY TO SEE IF
C         THE PRESENTED CARD IS THERE
          FOUND = .FALSE.
          IF (FIRST .LE. LAST) THEN DO
            DO 28 I = FIRST, LAST
              IF (CARDNR .LE. LSTCRD (I)) THEN DO
C                 TERMINATE SEARCH
                  FOUND = (CARDNR .EQ. LSTCRD (I))
                  GO TO 29
              END IF
   28       CONTINUE
          END IF
   29     RETURN
          END
```

Efficiency of a Multilevel Search

No sample execution output for the program CRDCH3 is given, because it would look identical to the output of CRDCH1 and to the output of CRDCH2. The speed of execution, however, is quite different. At the very worst, if the credit card presented is the last card in a list of 10,000 cancelled cards, the program CRDCH3 must scan through 100 pages and through 100 entries on the last page, and then make one final comparison for equality, a total of 201 comparisons. On the average, only half the pages must be checked, and only half the comparisons on the selected page are needed before a conclusion is reached. Thus the average number of comparisons of account numbers made by CRDCH3 is about 101, as compared to 5,001 for CRDCH2 and 10,000 for CRDCH1. The extra time spent writing the longer program CRDCH3 is quickly repaid in savings of computer time required for running the credit card checking program.

It is easy to see how a four-level search program could reduce the maximum number of comparisons to scan a list of 10,000 entries to 10 + 10 + 10 + 10 + 1 = 41, with the average number of comparisons roughly half of that. The 10,000 entries are divided arbitrarily into blocks of 1,000, then the correct block of 1,000 is divided into subblocks of 100, then the correct block of 100 is divided into subblocks of 10, and finally the correct block of 10 is searched sequentially to see if the presented card is there. There are no nev programming ideas in the writing of a program CRDCH4 to implement this four-level searching algorithm, so it is left as an exercise. A comparison of the efficiencies of CRDCH4 with the other programs of this section appears at the end of the section.

Binary Search

The number of comparisons required by the one-level, the two-level, and the four-level search procedures seems to indicate that, in spite of increasing the number of levels that must be checked, if the maximum number of comparisons on any one level is reduced, the total number of comparisons is reduced. Thus the ultimate in searching efficiency might be achieved by reducing the number of alternatives on each level to 2, even though the number of levels increases. This leads to an extremely efficient search procedure called a **binary search**. In fact, if the first alternative on any level is incorrect, then the second alternative must be correct. Thus only one test is needed on each level. With the use of such a binary search, it is possible to search a list of over 10,000 entries in only 15 comparisons, 14 comparisons to reduce the alternatives down to one entry, plus 1 more comparison to test that entry.

Surprisingly, the program CRDCH5 (listed later) to implement the binary search strategy has fewer statements than the program CRDCH3, which implements the much less efficient two-level search strategy. It is not necessary to write 14 successive loops for the binary search, because what is done at each level is sufficiently repetitive to form the only loop of the program. In order to clarify the details of a binary search, two examples are now provided.

Examples of Binary Search

Table 6.2 shows how a binary search is used to seek the number 2415495 in a list of 16 numbers. The numbers are given in increasing order in the first column. The presented number 2415495 is not in the list, but this fact plays no role in the search procedure until the very last step.

As a first step in binary searching, the list is divided in half. An asterisk follows the eighth number in column 1 because it is the last entry in the first half of the list. Since the given number 2415495 is less than (or equal to) the eighth entry 2980957, the second half of the list can be eliminated from further consideration. Column 2 shows only the first half of the original list, entries 1 through 8, retained as the segment still actively being searched.

The procedure is repeated. An asterisk follows the fourth entry in column 2 because it is the last entry in the first half of the segment of the list still actively being searched. Since the given number 2415495 is greater than the fourth number 1627547, this time it is the first half of the active segment that is eliminated and the second half (entries 5 through 8 of the original list) that is retained. This is shown in column 3 of Table 6.2.

In the next stage, the second remaining number 2202646, which was the sixth entry in the original list, is marked with an asterisk because it is the last entry of the first half of the segment still being searched. Since this number is exceeded by the given number 2415945, the second half of the segment in column 3 (entries 7 and 8) is retained as the active segment in column 4. The seventh entry of the original list, the number 2718281, is the last entry of the first half of the remaining list of two entries and thus is marked with an asterisk in column 4 to indicate its role as a comparison entry. Since the given number 2415495 is less than this, the other entry (the eighth original entry) is discarded, and column 5 shows that after four comparisons, only the seventh entry 2718281 remains.

Table 6.2 Binary search for the number 2415495 in a list of 16 numbers. An asterisk denotes the last entry of the first half of the segment still under active consideration.

Before any comparisons	After one comparison	After two comparisons	After three comparisons	After four comparisons	Given number
1096633	1096633				
1202604	1202604				
1484131	1484131				
1627547	1627547*				
2008553	2008553	2008553			
2202646	2202646	2202646*			
2718281	2718281	2718281	2718281*	2718281 ≠	2415495
2980957*	2980957	2980957	2980957		
3269017					
4034287					
4424133					
5459815					
5987414					
7389056					
8103083					
8886110					

Since only one entry remains, a test for equality is made between the given number 2415495 and the one remaining entry 2718281. They are not equal. Thus the given number is not in the list. Note that the previous comparisons of these two numbers was merely to determine whether the given number was less than or equal to the seventh entry.

Table 6.3 shows how the binary search works for the number 7389056, which is found in the list of 16 numbers.

As before, the first column lists the original numbers, with an asterisk following the last number of the first half of the list, the eighth entry. The number 7389056 is greater than the eighth entry, so the second half of the list (entries 9 to 16) is retained in column 2. A comparison of the given number 7389056 with the last entry of the first half of the segment remaining in column 2, the twelfth original entry 5459815, eliminates entries 9 through 12.

A comparison with the fourteenth entry, marked with an asterisk in column 3, eliminates the fifteenth and sixteenth entries. One more comparison of the given number 7389056 against the thirteenth entry, marked with an asterisk in column 4, eliminates that entry and leaves only the fourteenth entry 7389056. The final test for equality of the given number and the only remaining candidate in the list yields success, and it can be reported that the given number is the fourteenth entry in the list.

For the purpose of explanation it is most convenient to use a list size that is an exact power of 2 (2, 4, 8, 16, 32,...). This avoids fractions when the size of the list segment still under consideration is halved repeatedly. Since the smallest power of 2 greater than 10,000 is 2^{14} which is 16,384, it takes the same number of comparisons to perform a binary search on a list of 16,384 entries as on a list of 10,000 entries. The program CRDCH5 does a binary search on a list of 16,384 entries, but because the integer division operator (/), is used to locate the last element of the first half of the list segment still under active consideration,

Table 6.3 Binary search for the number 7389056 in a list of 16 numbers. An asterisk denotes the last entry of the first half of the segment still under active consideration.

Before any comparisons	After one comparison	After two comparisons	After three comparisons	After four comparisons		Given number
1096633						
1202604						
1484131						
1627547						
2008553						
2202646						
2718281						
2980957*						
3269017	3269017					
4034287	4034287					
4424133	4424133					
5459815	5459815*					
5987414	5987414	5987414	5987414*			
7389056	7389056	7389056*	7389056	7389056	=	7389056
8103083	8103083	8103083				
8886110	8886110	8886110				

no fractions are possible and this binary search subroutine can search a list of arbitrary length.

```
C       PROGRAM CRDCH5
        INTEGER MAXCRD, CDUNIT
        INTEGER NRCRDS, CARDNR, LSTCRD (16384)
        LOGICAL FOUND
C
        MAXCRD = 16384
        CDUNIT = 5
C
        CALL REDCRD (LSTCRD, MAXCRD, NRCRDS, CDUNIT)
        READ, CARDNR
        PRINT, 'CARD NUMBER TO BE CHECKED:', CARDNR
        CALL BINSRC (LSTCRD, NRCRDS, CARDNR, FOUND)
        IF (FOUND) THEN DO
           PRINT, 'CARD #', CARDNR, 'CANNOT BE ACCEPTED.'
        ELSE DO
           PRINT, 'CARD #', CARDNR, 'IS ACCEPTABLE.'
        END IF
        STOP
        END
C
C
        SUBROUTINE REDCRD (LSTCRD, MAXCRD, NRCRDS, CDUNIT)
        INTEGER MAXCRD, NRCRDS, LSTCRD (MAXCRD)
        INTEGER I, CDUNIT
C
        READ (CDUNIT, *) NRCRDS
```

```
      DO 18 I = 1, NRCRDS
         READ (CDUNIT, *) LSTCRD (I)
   18 CONTINUE
      RETURN
      END
C
C
      SUBROUTINE BINSRC (LSTCRD, NRCRDS, CARDNR, FOUND)
C     THE VARIABLES FIRST, LAST, AND HALF
C     REFER TO THE PART OF THE LIST STILL UNDER CONSIDERATION.
C     INITIALLY, THIS IS THE WHOLE LIST.
      INTEGER NRCRDS, LSTCRD (NRCRDS), CARDNR
      LOGICAL FOUND
      INTEGER I, FIRST, HALF, LAST, ONLY
C
      FIRST = 1
      LAST = NRCRDS
      DO 18 I = 1, NRCRDS
         IF (FIRST .EQ. LAST) THEN DO
            GO TO 19
         END IF
         HALF = (FIRST + LAST - 1) / 2
         IF (CARDNR .LE. LSTCRD (HALF)) THEN DO
C           DISCARD SECOND HALF
            LAST = HALF
         ELSE DO
C           DISCARD FIRST HALF
            FIRST = HALF + 1
         END IF
   18 CONTINUE
C
C     THE ONLY REMAINING LOCATION TO CHECK IS FIRST ( = LAST)
   19 ONLY = FIRST
      FOUND = (CARDNR .EQ. LSTCRD (ONLY))
      RETURN
      END
```

The subroutine BINSRC (binary search) is the only new module in the program CRDCH5. The upper limit NRCRDS on the DO block is deliberately too high. The real exit test is in the following line

```
      IF (FIRST .EQ. LAST) THEN DO
```

When the part of the list still under consideration has been reduced to a single element by repeated bisection, the first element left is the last and only element left and the DO block is exited to statement 19 to test it.

Efficiency of a Binary Search

As before, we can get a reasonable indication of the efficiency of a search method by seeing how many times the given account number is compared against account numbers in the list of lost or stolen cards in the most usual event that the card number is not in the list.

The number of comparisons required in the binary search can be counted easily. With one comparison, an original list of 16,384 is cut down to 8,192. A second comparison leaves only 4,096 candidates. A third leaves 2,048; a fourth 1,024; a fifth 512; a sixth 256; a seventh 128; an eighth 64; a ninth 32; a tenth 16; an eleventh 8; a twelfth 4; a thirteenth 2; and finally a fourteenth comparison leaves only 1 candidate. The fifteenth and final comparison determines whether that candidate is the credit card being searched for or not. Thus, whether the presented credit card is in the list or not, the number of comparisons against elements of the list is always 15.

When the number of entries is less than 16,384, the number of candidates at each stage never exceeds the number of candidates for an original list size of 16,384. Thus 15 comparisons suffices for binary searching all lists of length up to 16,384 (= 2^{14}), although sometimes even fewer are required.

Comparison of the Efficiency of the Search Procedures

Table 6.4 summarizes the number of comparisons required by each of the programs in this section to check a credit card against a list of 10,000 (or in the case of the binary search, up to 16,384) cancelled credit cards. For each program and search method, the minimum, maximum, and average number of comparisons is given for the most likely circumstance that the presented credit card is acceptable and is not to be found in the list.

Table 6.4 Comparison of Five Search Procedures Based on a 10,000-Entry List.

		Comparisons		
Search Method	Program Name	Minimum	Maximum	Average
Sequential search (unordered)	CRDCH1	10,000	10,000	10,000
Sequential search (ordered)	CRDCH2	2	10,001	5,001.5
Two-level sequential search	CRDCH3	3	201	102
Four-level sequential search	CRDCH4	5	41	23
Binary search	CRDCH5	15	15	15

The information in Table 6.4 shows the clear superiority of binary searching over all the other methods, even those whose programs are much more complicated. This superiority even increases as the list becomes longer, because it takes the binary search only one additional comparison to search a list with twice as many entries, 32,768, two additional comparisons to search 65,536 entries, and only three additional comparisons to extend the length of the list that can be searched to 131,072 entries. The other searching methods cannot begin to match this feat, as shown in Table 6.5.

Perhaps surprisingly, only the very slowest of the searching procedures is implemented by a program shorter than the binary search, and then not very much shorter. Binary search techniques are recommended, therefore, for searching all ordered lists, except possibly very short lists.

Searching Two Lists

Suppose that there are two large files, one listing stolen credit cards, and the other listing cancelled or never issued account numbers. The card checking strategy might be

```
PROGRAM TWOLST
Read account number to be checked
Read file of lost cards into array LSTCRD
Search for account number in LSTCRD
```

Table 6.5 Comparison of Five Search Procedures Based on a 100,000-Entry List, based on most efficient partitioning of the list.

		Comparisons		
Search Method	Program Name	Minimum	Maximum	Average
Sequential search (unordered)	CRDCH1	100,000	100,000	100,000
Sequential search (ordered)	CRDCH2	2	100,001	50,001.5
Two-level sequential search*	CRDCH3	3	634	318.5
Four-level sequential search**	CRDCH4	5	73	39
Binary search***	CRDCH5	18	18	18

*Based on 316 × 317 = 100,172 entries
**Based on 18 × 18 × 18 × 18 = 104,976 entries
***Based on 2^{17} = 131,072 entries

```
        IF found THEN DO
           PRINT, 'THE CARD IS LOST OR STOLEN'
        ELSE DO
           Read file of cancelled cards into array CANCRD
           Search for account number in CANCRD
           IF found THEN DO
              PRINT, 'THE ACCOUNT IS CANCELLED'
           ELSE DO
              PRINT, 'THE ACCOUNT IS ACCEPTABLE'
           END IF
        END IF
```

A new feature, the EQUIVALENCE statement, allows efficient use of memory in this program. The EQUIVALENCE statement causes two or more values to be stored in the same memory location. This is illustrated by the simple program that causes LSTCRD (1) and CANCRD (1) to be stored in the same memory location, It also causes LSTCRD (2) and CANCRD (2) to be stored in the same memory location, and so on.

```
        INTEGER LSTCRD (10000), CANCRD (10000)
        EQUIVALENCE (LSTCRD, CANCRD)
C
        LSTCARD (1) = 12345
        PRINT, LSTCRD (1), CANCRD (1)
C
        CANCRD (1234) = 5678
        PRINT, LSTCRD (1234), CANCRD (1234)
C
        STOP
        END
       12345          12345
        5678           5678
```

Without the EQUIVALENCE statement, space would be reserved in memory for both lists, despite the fact that they are not needed simultaneously. The EQUIVALENCE statement allows them to share the same memory locations. Sometimes this is the only way to fit a program into the computer.

It is also possible to use an EQUIVALENCE statement to assign a name to an array element. For example, we can save the actual NUMLST and NUMCAN in element 10001 of the arrays using the declarations

```
      INTEGER LSTCRD (10001), CANCRD (10001)
      EQUIVALENCE (LSTCRD, CANCRD),
     +        (LSTCRD (10001), NUMLST),
     +        (CANCRD (10001), NUMCAN)
C
      NUMLST = 100
      PRINT, NUMLST, LSTCRD (10001)
      NUMCAN = 50
      PRINT, NUMLST, LSTCRD (10001)
C
      STOP
      END
```

```
       100          100
        50           50
```

6.4 Sorting

The credit card checking programs in the previous section search unordered and ordered lists of cancelled credit cards to determine whether a particular number is in the list. This section presents another kind of searching application, searching an unordered list to find the smallest element. (If the list is ordered, then finding the smallest element is very easy.) The program developed to search for the smallest element in an unordered list is employed subsequently as the basis for several programs to **sort** the entire unordered list into increasing order.

A second theme of this section is that programs need to be tested thoroughly. The programs written in this chapter are not completely obvious to most beginners, partly because understanding the concept of a subscript requires some practice and partly because the programs involve complex ways of processing data. It becomes increasingly important, therefore, for a programmer to know how to test a program to be sure that it does what it is supposed to do.

A third theme is loops. As illustrated by the credit card checking programs in the previous section, loops are essential for sequential scanning. Searching for the smallest element in an unordered list also requires sequential scanning.

Section Preview

Smallest Element In a List:

A sequential search loop is adapted to finding the smallest element in a list and its location by keeping, as running variables, the smallest value found so far and the location in the list of that smallest value.

Sorting:

The elements of a list may be extracted in increasing order by repeatedly finding the smallest element, copying it to the sorted list, and "crossing it out" by replacing it with a very large value. The second attempt to find the smallest element in the list will find the second smallest element of the original list, because the smallest element was "crossed out". The process continues for the remaining elements. This method is not efficient, but it is easy to program.

Interchange Sort:

Swapping the smallest element found in each pass with the element in its intended position in the sorted list doubles the speed of sorting and halves the memory required.

Independent Testing of Subprograms:

The input, output, and find-smallest-element subprograms are sufficiently modular that they may be tested independently of the sorting subprogram. With the correctness of the subprograms independently verified in advance, there is little that could go wrong in the sorting program.

Arrays of Character Strings:

An array of character strings needs both subscript bounds and string length declarations. In a main program, these are usually parameters or constants. In a subroutine, the subscript bounds and the string length are often dummy arguments.

Program Example:

```
CHARACTER STRLST *20 (100)
```

Subroutine Example:

```
SUBROUTINE SUBNAM (STRLST, STRLEN, HISUB)
INTEGER STRLEN, HISUB
CHARACTER STRLST *(STRLEN) (HISUB)
```

Earned Run Averages for Baseball Pitchers

In baseball, a pitcher's earned run average (ERA) is roughly the average number of runs per game scored against him and his team while he is pitching, not counting "unearned" runs scored because of fielding errors, which do not have a direct bearing on the pitcher's ability as a pitcher. While a low earned run average for a particular pitcher does not guarantee that his team will win the games he pitches, it certainly makes that outcome more likely. For this reason, newspapers and sports periodicals frequently publish lists of names of pitchers in ascending order of earned run average, so that the best pitcher in this regard appears first.

The program SMLERA (smallest earned run average) tells the computer to read data on pitchers and their earned run averages and to print out the name and earned run average for the pitcher with the smallest earned run average. Input data for the program consist of one line for each pitcher in the league, containing the pitcher's name and his earned run average, and a trailer line containing a termination signal. Data for the first sample execution are based on a memorable American League season.

Lists of Character Strings

The main part of the program SMLERA resembles the program AVGSC3 in Section 6.1 in that both of them read all the data before the main processing is done. A new feature of this program is that the list PITCHR has values that are character strings, that is, the names of the pitchers.

Arrays of character strings require two kinds of size declarations. Like any other arrays, they require a declaration of subscript bounds. They also require a length declaration specifying the maximum number of characters in each entry in the list. For example, the declaration

```
      CHARACTER PITCHR *20 (MAXPIT)
```

declares subscript bounds 1 to MAXPIT and string lengths of NAMLEN.

In the subroutine RDERAS, the array PITCHR is a dummy argument. Its declared subscript bound MAXPIT and character string length NAMLEN are dummy arguments.

```
C     PROGRAM SMLERA
C     FINDS THE SMALLEST EARNED RUN AVERAGE (ERA)
C     OF ANY PITCHER IN THE LEAGUE
C
      INTEGER MAXPIT, NRPIT, NAMLEN, LOCSML
      REAL ERA (1000), SMLEST
      CHARACTER PITCHR *20 (1000)
C
      MAXPIT = 1000
      NAMLEN = 20
C
      CALL RDERAS (ERA, PITCHR, MAXPIT, NRPIT, NAMLEN)
      CALL FNDSML (ERA, NRPIT, SMLEST, LOCSML)
      PRINT, 'OUT OF', NRPIT, 'PITCHERS,'
      PRINT 15, 'THE BEST EARNED RUN AVERAGE IS', SMLEST
   15 FORMAT (T2, A30, F7.2)
      PRINT, 'PITCHED BY', PITCHR (LOCSML)
      STOP
      END
C
C
      SUBROUTINE RDERAS (ERA, PITCHR, MAXPIT, NRPIT, NAMLEN)
C     READ ALL PITCHER'S NAMES AND ERA'S
C
      INTEGER MAXPIT, NRPIT, NAMLEN, I
      REAL ERA (MAXPIT)
      CHARACTER PITCHR *20 (MAXPIT)
      CHARACTER SIGNAL *11
C
      SIGNAL = 'AARON GROSS'
C
      DO 18 I = 1, MAXPIT
         READ, PITCHR (I), ERA (I)
         PRINT, 'INPUT DATA  PITCHR:', PITCHR (I)
         PRINT 15, '            ERA:', ERA (I)
   15    FORMAT (T2, A19, F10.5)
         IF (PITCHR (I) .EQ. SIGNAL) THEN DO
            NRPIT = I - 1
            GO TO 19
         END IF
   18 CONTINUE
   19 RETURN
      END
C
C
      SUBROUTINE FNDSML (ERA, NRPIT, SMLEST, LOCSML)
C     FINDS THE SMALLEST ENTRY (SMLEST) IN THE ARRAY ERA
C     AND ITS SUBSCRIPT OR LOCATION (LOCSML) IN THE ARRAY
C
```

```
C       VARIABLES:
C          SMLSOF = SMALLEST ERA FOUND SO FAR
C          LOCSOF = LOCATION OR SUBSCRIPT OF SMLSOF IN ARRAY ERA
C
        INTEGER NRPIT, LOCSML, LOCSOF, I
        REAL ERA (NRPIT), SMLEST, SMLSOF
C
        SMLSOF = ERA (1)
        LOCSOF = 1
        DO 18 I = 2, NRPIT
           IF (ERA (I) .LT. SMLSOF) THEN DO
              SMLSOF = ERA (I)
              LOCSOF = I
           END IF
   18   CONTINUE
C
        SMLEST = SMLSOF
        LOCSML = LOCSOF
        RETURN
        END
```

The name AARON GROSS is used to terminate reading of the data. A termination signal of "***" is safer, but programmers need to have some fun. Actually, Aaron Gross converted from baseball to javelin at an early age and never pitched an inning of major league baseball, so his name cannot be confused with real data for this program. Baseball fans remember him best as a termination signal.

The basic strategy of the search is to examine each earned run average in turn and to remember it if it is the smallest encountered so far, or to forget it if it is not. The location (i.e., subscript) of the smallest earned run average so far is also remembered, so that the pitcher's name may be printed out at the end.

Handling Ties

Before running this program, we make one improvement. In case of ties, the program SMLERA locates and prints only the earliest of the equal entries. Since it makes little sense to ignore the other equally good pitchers, the following lines may be added to the main program SMLERA to print their names also.

```
        NXTLOC = LOCSML + 1
        IF (NXTLOC .LE. NRPIT) THEN DO
           DO 18 I = LOCSML + 1, NRPIT
              IF (ERA (I) .EQ. SMLEST) THEN DO
                 PRINT, 'AND', PITCHR (I)
              END IF
   18      CONTINUE
        END IF
```

This loop is another reason to find the location of the smallest earned run average in the list as well as its value. Incorporating these instructions to handle ties into the program SMLERA results in the program SMERA2. The sample execution of the program SMERA2 has been reduced to reasonable size by using an alphabetical listing of only the best 10 pitchers in one season. The full execution, using all 122 pitchers who pitched in 12 or more games, is quite similar but much longer.

```
C       PROGRAM SMERA2
C       FINDS THE SMALLEST EARNED RUN AVERAGE (ERA)
C       OF ANY PITCHER IN THE LEAGUE
C
        INTEGER MAXPIT, NRPIT, NAMLEN, LOCSML, NXTLOC
        REAL ERA (1000), SMLEST
        CHARACTER PITCHR *20 (1000)
C
        MAXPIT = 1000
        NAMLEN = 20
C
        CALL RDERAS (ERA, PITCHR, MAXPIT, NRPIT, NAMLEN)
        CALL FNDSML (ERA, NRPIT, SMLEST, LOCSML)
        PRINT, 'OUT OF', NRPIT, 'PITCHERS,'
        PRINT 15, 'THE BEST EARNED RUN AVERAGE IS', SMLEST
   15   FORMAT (T2, A30, F7.2)
        PRINT, 'PITCHED BY', PITCHR (LOCSML)
        NXTLOC = LOCSML + 1
        IF (NXTLOC .LE. NRPIT) THEN DO
           DO 18 I = NXTLOC, NRPIT
              IF (ERA (I) .EQ. SMLEST) THEN DO
                 PRINT, 'AND', PITCHR (I)
              END IF
   18      CONTINUE
        END IF
        STOP
        END
INPUT DATA   PITCHR: VIDA BLUE
                ERA:     3.01
INPUT DATA   PITCHR: BERT BLYLEVEN
                ERA:     3.00
INPUT DATA   PITCHR: STEVE BUSBY
                ERA:     3.08
INPUT DATA   PITCHR: DENNIS ECKERSLEY
                ERA:     2.60
INPUT DATA   PITCHR: ED FIGUEROA
                ERA:     2.90
INPUT DATA   PITCHR: CATFISH HUNTER
                ERA:     2.58
INPUT DATA   PITCHR: RUDY MAY
                ERA:     3.06
INPUT DATA   PITCHR: JIM PALMER
                ERA:     2.09
INPUT DATA   PITCHR: FRANK TANANA
                ERA:     2.63
INPUT DATA   PITCHR: RUSTY TORREZ
                ERA:     3.06
INPUT DATA   PITCHR: AARON GROSS
                ERA:     9.99
OUT OF             10 PITCHERS,
THE BEST EARNED RUN AVERAGE IS   2.09
PITCHED BY JIM PALMER
```

Program Testing

It is easy enough to check from the echoes of input data provided in the sample execution of SMERA2 that the correct smallest earned run average is found and printed. However, before adopting this program for regular use, additional checking should be done using different data to reduce or eliminate the likelihood that the program runs correctly only because of some special property of this first batch of data. Be especially suspicious of the testing data if the smallest earned run average turns out to be either the first one in the list or the last one in the list. Even an incorrect program might obtain the right answer in these very special circumstances.

Since the pitcher with the smallest earned run average in the sample execution is the eighth pitcher out of 10, the data used are suitable on this account. Of course, for a complete testing of the program, test data should also be used in which the smallest earned run average does come first or last, because programs also can fail when the data have special properties.

There is one eventuality allowed for in the program that is not tested by the data given, the possibility of ties. Since the actual historical data do not oblige us with a tie for the smallest earned run average, fictitious pitchers are manufactured to help test the tie feature.

```
INPUT DATA  PITCHR: VIDA BLUE
               ERA:    3.01
INPUT DATA  PITCHR: BERT BLYLEVEN
               ERA:    3.00
INPUT DATA  PITCHR: STEVE BUSBY
               ERA:    3.08
INPUT DATA  PITCHR: CARL CURVEBALL
               ERA:    2.09
INPUT DATA  PITCHR: DENNIS ECKERSLEY
               ERA:    2.60
INPUT DATA  PITCHR: ED FIGUEROA
               ERA:    2.90
INPUT DATA  PITCHR: FIREMAN FINK
               ERA:    2.09
INPUT DATA  PITCHR: CATFISH HUNTER
               ERA:    2.58
INPUT DATA  PITCHR: RUDY MAY
               ERA:    3.06
INPUT DATA  PITCHR: JIM PALMER
               ERA:    2.09
INPUT DATA  PITCHR: FRANK TANANA
               ERA:    2.63
INPUT DATA  PITCHR: RUSTY TORREZ
               ERA:    3.06
INPUT DATA  PITCHR: AARON GROSS
               ERA:    9.99
OUT OF          12 PITCHERS,
THE BEST EARNED RUN AVERAGE IS   2.09
PITCHED BY CARL CURVEBALL
AND FIREMAN FINK
AND JIM PALMER
```

After examining this somewhat fanciful execution, it is likely that the program SMERA2 could handle correctly the case of ties if that situation ever came up in real data.

A Uniform Main Program for Sorting

Sorting data is a very common and very important programming application. **Sorting** means putting a list in either increasing or decreasing order. In the credit card checking application in Section 6.3, for instance, all the efficient programs require that the list of lost or stolen credit cards already be in increasing order.

Recognizing the need for sorting in many different applications, the sorting programs presented in this chapter use general variable names, like LIST, that fit many different circumstances. All the sorting programs in this chapter are refinements of the program DOSORT.

```
PROGRAM DOSORT
Read all the data
Sort the data
Write the sorted list
END
```

Although the input, output, and sorting subroutines written in this section will use general, nonspecific names for their variables, the argument passing conventions introduced in Chapter 5 will permit these subroutines to be used without change in many applications.

Every sorting program in this chapter calls the same subroutine READL (read list) to read all the data. READL employs a loop whose execution is stopped when a termination signal is read. It places the data in an array LIST, and counts the number of data items LSTSIZ. An index variable is used to control where in the list the data are placed. When the signal data item is finally read, the value of this index variable gives the count of the items that were read. The subroutine READL closely resembles the subroutine READLI (read a list of integers) in Chapter 5.

```
      SUBROUTINE READL (LIST, MAXSIZ, SIGNAL, LSTSIZ)
C     READ INPUT DATA INTO THE LIST, LIST
C     STOPPING WHEN THE VALUE SIGNAL IS READ.
C     THE ACTUAL NUMBER OF DATA ITEMS READ IS LSTSIZ.
C
      INTEGER MAXSIZ, LIST (MAXSIZ), SIGNAL, LSTSIZ
      INTEGER DATUM, I
C
      LSTSIZ = 0
      DO 18 I = 1, MAXSIZ
         READ, DATUM
         PRINT, 'INPUT DATA  DATUM:', DATUM
         IF (DATUM .EQ. SIGNAL) THEN DO
            GO TO 19
         ELSE DO
            LIST (I) = DATUM
            LSTSIZ = I
         END IF
   18 CONTINUE
   19 RETURN
      END
```

The subroutine WRITEL (write list) is called to write the sorted list produced by the sorting programs to be considered. It employs a simple DO block and introduces no new features or methods.

```
      SUBROUTINE WRITEL (LIST, LSTSIZ)
      INTEGER LSTSIZ, LIST (LSTSIZ), I
C
```

```
      DO 18 I = 1, LSTSIZ
         PRINT, LIST (I)
   18 CONTINUE
      RETURN
      END
```

Testing the Input and Output Subroutines

It is possible to test the input subroutine READL and the output subroutine WRITEL without doing the sort in between. Since the sorting subroutine is slightly more complicated than these subroutines, it would be nice to know before checking the sorting subroutine that the input and output subroutines do not contribute any errors that might be attributed to the sorting subroutine. A test program TESTIO accomplishes this testing by printing the input list without sorting. To avoid possible confusion, it writes a disclaimer that the output list remains unsorted.

```
C     PROGRAM TESTIO
      INTEGER MAXSIZ, SIGNAL, LIST (1000), LSTSIZ
C
      MAXSIZ = 1000
      SIGNAL  = 9999
C
      CALL READL (LIST, MAXSIZ, SIGNAL, LSTSIZ)
      PRINT, ' '
      PRINT, 'I/O TEST ONLY -- NO SORTING ATTEMPTED'
      PRINT, ' '
      PRINT, 'THE LIST FOLLOWS:'
      PRINT, ' '
      CALL WRITEL (LIST, LSTSIZ)
      STOP
      END
```

```
INPUT DATA  DATUM:          256
INPUT DATA  DATUM:          -37
INPUT DATA  DATUM:            8
INPUT DATA  DATUM:           45
INPUT DATA  DATUM:         9999

I/O TEST ONLY -- NO SORTING ATTEMPTED

THE LIST FOLLOWS:

       256
       -37
         8
        45
```

Sorting by Finding the Smallest Element Remaining in a List

A subroutine to find the smallest element in a list can be used as a step in a subroutine to sort a list. All that is required is to cross out the smallest element from the list after it has been placed in the new, sorted list. Then, the subroutine finds the smallest remaining element, which was the second smallest original element. The second smallest is placed in the new list and "crossed out" in the original list. The next attempt to find the smallest remaining element will find the third smallest original element. Ultimately, the repetition of this process produces a sorted list consisting of all the original items in increasing order.

The sorting subroutine SORT1 repeatedly uses a subroutine FNDSML (find smallest) to locate the smallest remaining element in the list LIST. That smallest remaining element is then recorded in the sorted list SLIST. To trick the computer into thinking that the number has been crossed out, it is replaced by a number too large to be plausible data. This number never will be found by the next application of the subroutine FNDSML. The current subroutine FNDSML is the subroutine FNDSML in the earned run average example, with its variable names changed to conform to the greater generality of the current program.

```
      SUBROUTINE SORT1 (LIST, SLIST, LSTSIZ)
C     SORTS LIST AND PLACES RESULT IN SLIST.
C     LIST IS DESTROYED IN THE PROCESS.
C
      INTEGER LSTSIZ, LIST (LSTSIZ), SLIST (LSTSIZ)
      INTEGER SLOC, LOCSML, SMLEST, BIGNUM
C
      BIGNUM = 99999
C
      DO 18 SLOC = 1, LSTSIZ
         CALL FNDSML (LIST, LSTSIZ, SMLEST, LOCSML)
         SLIST (SLOC) = SMLEST
C        CROSS OUT THE SMALLEST ENTRY JUST FOUND
         LIST (LOCSML) = BIGNUM
   18 CONTINUE
      RETURN
      END

      SUBROUTINE FNDSML (LIST, LSTSIZ, SMLEST, LOCSML)
C     FINDS SMALLEST ELEMENT (SMLEST) IN LIST LIST
C     AND ITS LOCATION LOCSML.
C
      INTEGER LSTSIZ, LOCSML, LOCSOF, I
      INTEGER LIST (LSTSIZ), SMLEST, SMLSOF
C
      SMLSOF = LIST (1)
      LOCSOF = 1
      IF (LSTSIZ .GE. 2) THEN DO
         DO 18 I = 2, LSTSIZ
            IF (LIST (I) .LT. SMLSOF) THEN DO
               SMLSOF = LIST (I)
               LOCSOF = I
            END IF
   18    CONTINUE
      END IF
C
      SMLEST = SMLSOF
      LOCSML = LOCSOF
      RETURN
      END
```

If execution speed is important, a small amount of time could be saved by using the same variables SMLSOF and LOCSOF after the search as during the search. However, the sorting subroutine SORT1 is by no means the most efficient sorting subroutine possible, only one of the simplest. Thus, improved clarity of variable names is preferred in this case to increased execution speed.

Accordingly, the last two instructions of the subroutine FNDSML introduce two new variables, SMLEST and LOCSML, to reflect the fact that the search has been completed.

Testing Individual Subroutines

It can be verified by hand that the subroutine SORT1 sorts a list into increasing order, assuming that the subroutine FNDSML supplies correct values for the variables SMLEST and LOC. Verification that the subroutine FNDSML works properly might also be done by hand. Since FNDSML is a separate subroutine, it can be checked further using the small test program TSTFND (test FNDSML) that runs independently of the subroutine SORT1.

```
C       PROGRAM TSTFND
C       TESTS THE SUBROUTINE FNDSML (FIND SMALLEST)
C
        INTEGER LIST (5), SMLEST, LOCSML, LSTSIZ
C
        LSTSIZ = 5
C
        LIST (1) = 45
        LIST (2) = 27
        LIST (3) = 32
        LIST (4) = 24
        LIST (5) = 43
        CALL FNDSML (LIST, LSTSIZ, SMLEST, LOCSML)
        PRINT, 'THE SMALLEST IS', SMLEST
        PRINT, 'THE LOCATION IN THE LIST IS', LOCSML
        STOP
        END
```

```
THE SMALLEST IS            24
THE LOCATION IN THE LIST IS            4
```

More Program Testing

In the test program TSTFND, the values for the list are assigned by program steps to save the trouble of preparing input data. If more extensive testing is desired, the subroutine READL may be used to facilitate the reading of data to test FNDSML. The program MORTHO (more thorough test) illustrates this idea. Only one sample run is shown for this program, but it may be used as often as needed with different sets of test data, until the programmer is convinced that FNDSML works correctly for all possible data.

```
C       PROGRAM MORTHO
C       MORE THOROUGH TEST OF SUBROUTINE FNDSML
C
        INTEGER MAXSIZ, SIGNAL
        INTEGER LIST (100)
        INTEGER LSTSIZ, LOCSML, SMLEST
C
        MAXSIZ = 100
        SIGNAL = 9999
        CALL READL (LIST, MAXSIZ, SIGNAL, LSTSIZ)
        CALL FNDSML (LIST, LSTSIZ, SMLEST, LOCSML)
```

```
      PRINT, 'THE SMALLEST IS', SMLEST
      PRINT, 'THE LOCATION IN THE LIST IS', LOCSML
      STOP
      END
INPUT DATA  DATUM:            81
INPUT DATA  DATUM:            35
INPUT DATA  DATUM:             0
INPUT DATA  DATUM:            14
INPUT DATA  DATUM:            -3
INPUT DATA  DATUM:            45
INPUT DATA  DATUM:           -27
INPUT DATA  DATUM:            36
INPUT DATA  DATUM:            12
INPUT DATA  DATUM:          9999
THE SMALLEST IS             27
THE LOCATION IN THE LIST IS           7
```

The computer correctly recognizes that the number −27 is less than all positive numbers and less than the negative number −3. The echoes of input data that appear in the output are produced by the subroutine READL, which must be supplied along with the subroutine FNDSML to create a complete executable program.

Fitting All The Subroutines Together

The program DOSRT1 combines several subroutines that have been checked more or less independently of each other, with favorable results in each case. The program DOSRT1 itself must now be tested to see if its way of combining the subroutines actually provides a program for sorting data. The sample test run shown uses the same data used to test the subroutine FNDSML, in order to guarantee that at least the first call to FNDSML will work correctly, permitting a test of what happens after the first time.

```
C     PROGRAM DOSRT1
C     SORTS A LIST OF INTEGERS
C
      INTEGER MAXSIZ, SIGNAL
      INTEGER LIST (1000), SLIST (1000)
      INTEGER LSTSIZ
C
      MAXSIZ = 1000
      SIGNAL = 9999
      CALL READL (LIST, MAXSIZ, SIGNAL, LSTSIZ)
      CALL SORT1 (LIST, SLIST, LSTSIZ)
      PRINT, ' '
      PRINT, 'THE SORTED LIST FOLLOWS:'
      PRINT, ' '
      CALL WRITEL (SLIST, LSTSIZ)
      STOP
      END
INPUT DATA  DATUM:            81
INPUT DATA  DATUM:            35
INPUT DATA  DATUM:             0
INPUT DATA  DATUM:            14
INPUT DATA  DATUM:            -3
INPUT DATA  DATUM:            45
```

```
INPUT DATA  DATUM:          -27
INPUT DATA  DATUM:           36
INPUT DATA  DATUM:           12
INPUT DATA  DATUM:         9999

THE SORTED LIST FOLLOWS:

        -27
         -3
          0
         12
         14
         35
         36
         45
         81
```

Doubling the Sorting Speed While Saving Space As Well

The subroutine SORT1 is based on two key ideas. One is to use a search subroutine to find the locations of the smallest remaining item. The other is to form a sorted list by transferring items there one at a time, in ascending order, from an unsorted list. Replacing numbers in the unsorted list with very large dummy numbers is more of an incidental trick than a key idea. In fact, the "crossing out" trick is unnecessarily expensive in both time and space.

Toward the end of the execution of SORT1, when very few of the original numbers remain in the unsorted list, the search procedure spends most of its time examining and bypassing the dummy numbers, hardly productive labor. Moreover, the space occupied by the dummy numbers ultimately becomes as great as the space occupied by the whole original list.

Another sorting method, considered next, preserves both of the key ideas of SORT1. However, by using an interchange, it saves both time and space. Consider starting with the list supplied as input in the sample execution of the program TESTIO.

256 −37 8 45 (original list)

The first step in sorting by the interchange method is to locate the smallest by searching the original list in its entirety. It is the number −37 at location 2. The smallest item is then interchanged with the first item of the original list, as shown below. A vertical bar is drawn immediately after the sorted item in order to separate it from the remaining items. The sorted list is being formed to the left of the vertical bar.

−37 | 256 8 45

The second smallest item cannot be to the left of the vertical bar, because that is where the smallest item is. Thus the second smallest item of the original list is the smallest item to the right of the bar, and it can be found by searching the three locations to the right. This time the search locates the number 8 at location 3 of the list. This item, the second smallest item in the original list, is now interchanged with the item at location 2, yielding the following rearrangement of the list.

−37 8 | 256 45

This time the bar separates the two smallest items from the remaining items. To find the third smallest item of the original list, it is sufficient to search the items to the right of the bar, because the third smallest is the smallest of those two items.

The third smallest item of the original list is the number 45, at location 4 of the list. The interchange method of sorting now requires that it be exchanged with whatever number is at location 3 of the list as shown below.

−37 8 45 | 256

With each step, the sorted initial segment grows and the unsorted final segment shrinks. When the final segment disappears, the list is completely sorted. Indeed, when the unsorted final segment has length one, as it does here, the list is completely sorted because the last number must be the largest number of the original list.

Because the unsorted final segment is constantly shrinking, it takes the computer less and less time to find the smallest remaining item. By way of contrast, the search time for every item using the method of the subroutine SORT1 remains the same as the search time for the first item. Because of the reduced search time, this interchange method is about twice as fast as the "crossing out" method. The program DOSRT2 calls the subroutine SORT2 to apply this interchange method of sorting. Since the list is sorted in place, there is no need to reserve space for a second array to receive the sorted list.

```
C       PROGRAM DOSRT2
C       SORTS A LIST OF INTEGERS FASTER THAN DOSRT1
C
        INTEGER MAXSIZ, SIGNAL
        INTEGER LIST (1000)
        INTEGER LSTSIZ
C
        MAXSIZ = 1000
        SIGNAL = 9999
        CALL READL (LIST, MAXSIZ, SIGNAL, LSTSIZ)
        CALL SORT2 (LIST, LSTSIZ)
        PRINT, ' '
        PRINT, 'THE SORTED LIST FOLLOWS:'
        PRINT, ' '
        CALL WRITEL (LIST, LSTSIZ)
        STOP
        END
C
C
        SUBROUTINE SORT2 (LIST, LSTSIZ)
        INTEGER LSTSIZ, LIST (LSTSIZ)
        INTEGER NEXTEL, ALMOST, LOCSML, SMLEST
C       VARIABLE:  NEXTEL = SUBSCRIPT OF FIRST ELEMENT
C                  NOT YET IN SORTED SEGMENT OF LIST
C
        ALMOST = LSTSIZ - 1
        DO 18 NEXTEL = 1, ALMOST
           CALL FNDNXT (LIST, LSTSIZ, SMLEST, LOCSML, NRSRTD, NEXTEL)
C          INTERCHANGE SMALLEST FOUND
C          WITH FIRST ITEM AFTER SORTED SEGMENT
           LIST (LOCSML) = LIST (NEXTEL)
           LIST (NEXTEL) = SMLEST
     18 CONTINUE
        RETURN
        END
C
```

```
C
      SUBROUTINE FNDNXT (LIST, LSTSIZ, SMLEST, LOCSML, NEXTEL)
C     FIND THE SMALLEST ELEMENT IN THE UNSORTED SEGMENT OF LIST
      INTEGER LSTSIZ, LOCSML, LOCSOF, I, STARTL
      INTEGER LIST (LSTSIZ), SMLEST, SMLSOF, NEXTEL
C
      SMLSOF = LIST (NEXTEL)
      LOCSOF = NEXTEL
      IF (LSTSIZ .GE. NEXTEL + 1) THEN DO
         STARTL = NEXTEL + 1
         DO 18 I = STARTL, LSTSIZ
            IF (LIST (I) .LT. SMLSOF) THEN
               SMLSOF = LIST (I)
               LOCSOF = I
            END IF
   18    CONTINUE
      END IF
C
      SMLEST = SMLSOF
      LOCSML = LOCSOF
      RETURN
      END
INPUT DATA  DATUM:          81
INPUT DATA  DATUM:          35
INPUT DATA  DATUM:           0
INPUT DATA  DATUM:          14
INPUT DATA  DATUM:          -3
INPUT DATA  DATUM:          45
INPUT DATA  DATUM:         -27
INPUT DATA  DATUM:          36
INPUT DATA  DATUM:          12
INPUT DATA  DATUM:        9999

THE SORTED LIST FOLLOWS:

          -27
           -3
            0
           12
           14
           35
           36
           45
           81
```

Readings

Knuth, Donald E. *The Art Of Computer Programming, Vol. 3: Sorting and Searching*. Reading, Mass.: Addison-Wesley Publishing Co., 1973.

Martin, William A. "Sorting". *Computing Surveys* 3: 147-174.

Rich, Robert P. *Internal Sorting Methods Illustrated with PL/I Programs*. Englewood Cliffs, N.J: Prentice-Hall, 1972.

Wirth, Nicklaus. *Algorithms + Data Structures = Programs*. Englewood Cliffs, N.J.: Prentice-Hall, 1976.

6.5 Testing and Debugging: Common Array Errors

Arrays and subscripts bring with them a whole new class of programming techniques, and, of course, a whole new class of programming errors. In this section, we illustrate a few of the most common programming errors associated with arrays, and how you might find and remove them.

Section Preview

DATA Statement:

General form:

DATA *list of variables / list of values /*

Examples:

```
DATA A, B, C / 3, 4, 5 /
DATA (LIST (I), I = 1, 4) / 4 * 0 /
DATA A, B, (LIST (I), I = 1, 2) / 10, 20, 30, 40 /
```

Array and Subscript Errors:

Two common array and subscript errors are discussed with complete programming examples.

1. Confusing an array element LIST (I) with its subscript I.
2. Using a subscript outside the declared subscript bounds for an array.

Error 1: Confusing an Array Element With Its Subscript

Suppose we have a list NAME of ten names in alphabetic order, and a list RANK of the ranks in the graduating class of the 10 people in the list NAME. If this seems like a very small graduating class, it is because we don't want to type an excessive amount of data to make the illustrative program run.

The problem is to write a program that accepts as input a rank in the class, and prints as output the name of the person with that class rank. The basic algorithm employed in the program RANKLU (look up by rank) below is a sequential search for equality in the list RANK. Since the list of ranks is not in order (it is the names that are in order), only the simplest sequential search algorithm is applicable.

The DATA Statement

A new feature, the DATA statement is used to supply data for the arrays NAME and RANK. The general form

DATA *list of variables / list of values /*

follows its function. Rather than read the data for these arrays during execution, they are written into DATA statements in the Fortran source program. These arrays will have the desired values as soon as the program RANKLU is loaded.

Table 6.6 gives the names and class ranks to be used.

Each variable in the list of variables is assigned the corresponding value from the list of values. When an array name appears in the list of variables, it is understood to stand for the complete list of its elements in order. The same

Table 6.6 Class ranks for the graduating class of '06.

Name	Rank
Aaron Aardvark	2
Betty Banana	7
Charles Canary	3
Dolores Donut	1
Edgar Elephant	5
Frederick Farkle	10
Greta Giraffe	3
Harry Hippopotamus	9
Ichobod Igloo	6
Jason Jackrabbit	8

effect also could be achieved with an implied DO loop. For example, the two following DATA statements are equivalent.

```
      DATA RANK / 2, 7, 3, 1, 5, 10, 3, 9, 6, 8 /
      DATA (RANK (I), I = 1, 10)
     +     / 2, 7, 3, 1, 5, 10, 3, 9, 6, 8 /
```

We use the shorter DATA statement in the program RANKLU (rank lookup).

```
C     PROGRAM RANKLU
C     PRINTS THE NAME OF THE PERSON
C     WITH A GIVEN RANK IN THE CLASS
C
      CHARACTER NAME *20 (10)
      INTEGER RANK (10), I, INRANK
C
      DATA NAME / 'AARON AARDVARK', 'BETTY BANANA',
     +            'CHARLES CANARY', 'DOLORES DONUT',
     +            'EDGAR ELEPHANT', 'FREDERICK FARKLE',
     +            'GRETA GIRAFFE', 'HARRY HIPPOPOTAMUS',
     +            'ICHOBOD IGLOO', 'JASON JACKRABBIT' /
      DATA RANK / 2, 7, 3, 1, 5, 10, 3, 9, 6, 8 /
C
      READ, INRANK
      PRINT, 'RANK IN THE GRADUATING CLASS':, INRANK
C
C     SEARCH FOR THE GIVEN RANK
      DO 18 I = 1, 10
         IF (INRANK .EQ. I) THEN DO
            PRINT, 'THE PERSON RANKING', INRANK,
     +                'IN THE CLASS IS', NAME (I)
         END IF
   18 CONTINUE
      END
```

```
RANK IN THE GRADUATING CLASS:           5
THE PERSON RANKING           5 IN THE CLASS IS EDGAR ELEPHANT
```

The test run was successful! Edgar Elephant is fifth in the graduating class. Let us congratulate ourselves on how cleverly we wrote the program, and how carefully we chose the test data. We deliberately did not test for the extreme ranks, 1 and 10, because these might be special in some way that would allow the program to run successfully without being correct.

We have recognized that it is possible to have ties for a class rank and have provided for this possibility both in the test data and in the program. In the test data, both Charles Canary and Greta Giraffe have class rank 3, a tie, and no one has class rank 4. The program RANKLU provides for ties by not exiting the DO block when an exact match is found. Instead, the DO block continues execution to the full 10 iterations so that any other person with the same class rank will also be recognized and printed. Let us demonstrate this by a sample run searching for the class rank 3 as the input value.

```
RANK IN THE GRADUATING CLASS:           3
THE PERSON RANKING             3 IN THE CLASS IS CHARLES CANARY
```

This was almost a successful run. Charles Canary is third in the graduating class, but so is Greta Giraffe, and the program is supposed to handle ties. There must be something wrong with the way it handles ties because the program worked when there was no tie, and it found the first name with a given rank when there was a tie. Nevertheless, it does seem exceedingly unlikely that the DO block was exited before all 10 iterations were performed, because there is no statement in the DO block that can cause an exit.

We now have two standard strategies for debugging open to us. We could put a PRINT statement in the body of the DO block to determine whether all 10 iterations are performed, or we could try another test case designed to shed more light on our current theories about what is going wrong. (If you already know what the error is, read on anyway. The debugging techniques we are describing are also useful in more complex programs.) Why not try both? We will put the statement

```
      PRINT, 'ITERATION', I
```

in the DO block and try another case. Still avoiding the extreme cases, which might somehow be different, we try a random case, search for rank 7.

```
RANK IN THE GRADUATING CLASS:         7
ITERATION            1
ITERATION            2
ITERATION            3
ITERATION            4
ITERATION            5
ITERATION            6
ITERATION            7
THE PERSON RANKING           7 IN THE CLASS IS GRETA GIRAFFE
ITERATION            8
ITERATION            9
ITERATION           10
```

This is not a successful run of the program RANKLU. Greta Giraffe has rank 3 in the graduating class, not rank 7. However it does provide a great deal of useful information for debugging purposes. For one thing, it shows clearly that all 10 iterations are performed, even the three iterations after a match was found. This fact never should have been in doubt, but when you have a bug that you can't locate and explain, everything seems to be in doubt. Now, with the added information from the last run, we can rephrase the problem: why did the IF test succeed on the seventh iteration, causing the computer to print the name Greta Giraffe, when it should have succeeded on the second iteration, causing the computer to print the correct answer, Betty Banana? There isn't much room left for the bug to hide. We reexamine the IF test

```
IF (INRANK .EQ. I) THEN DO
```

and the answer is clear. The reason this IF test succeeded when the DO variable I was 7 is simply that the given rank in class INRANK is being compared to the subscript I instead of the rank in class RANK (I). This explains everything! It explains the last incorrect run. It explains the previous partially correct run. It even explains the coincidence that allowed the first test of this incorrect program to print the correct answer. In fact, we would have been better off if the first test run had failed also. We would have had less confidence in the correctness of the program, and probably would have found the bug sooner. The correct IF test is

```
IF (INRANK .EQ. RANK (I)) THEN DO
```

We have simply made the common mistake of confusing the array element RANK (I) with its subscript I.

Data for Paired Lists

Since both a list of names NAME and a paired list of ranks RANK were initialized with DATA statements in this problem, a more readable way to make the assignment of values to these lists would be to place each person's rank in class next to his/her name in the data list as follows. Some WATFIV systems do not allow this many continuation lines; in that case, two names and two ranks can be put on one line. The system used to test the programs in this book printed a warning message, but processed the program correctly.

```
      DATA (NAME (I), RANK (I), I = 1, 10)
+           / 'AARON AARDVARK', 2,
+             'BETTY BANANA', 7,
+             'CHARLES CANARY', 3,
+             'DOLORES DONUT', 1,
+             'EDGAR ELEPHANT', 5,
+             'FREDERICK FARKLE', 10,
+             'GRETA GIRAFFE', 3,
+             'HARRY HIPPOPOTAMUS', 9,
+             'ICHOBOD IGLOO', 6,
+             'JASON JACKRABBIT', 8 /
```

The values assigned by a DATA statement are assigned to their variables only once, before execution begins. Subsequently, the values of these variables may be changed by READ and assignment statements.

When there are repeated values in the value list of a DATA statement, it is permissible to put a multiplier before the repeated value. For example, the two statements

```
REAL FREQ (1000)
DATA FREQ / 1000 * 0.0 /
```

declare the variable FREQ to be an array of 1000 reals and initialize each of the 1000 entries in the array FREQ to 0.0.

Error 2: Subscript Out of Bounds

Our next example of an array bug consists of referencing an array element using a subscript that is not within the declared limits for the array. Some Fortran systems catch this error, but many do not, with unpredictable results. The application is also a search, this time for the first value in an array LIST that exceeds a value TEST read as input. Three sample executions are shown.

```
C      PROGRAM SEARCH
C      SEARCH FOR THE FIRST ELEMENT OF AN ARRAY
C      THAT EXCEEDS THE INPUT VALUE, TEST
C
       INTEGER LIST (10), TEST, I
       DATA LIST /136, 178, 207, 342, 471,
     +            511, 692, 701, 899, 914 /
C
       READ, TEST
       PRINT, 'SEARCH VALUE:', TEST
       DO 18 I = 1, 10
          IF (LIST (I) .GT. TEST) THEN DO
             GO TO 19
          END IF
   18  CONTINUE
   19  PRINT, 'THE FIRST NUMBER THAT EXCEEDS',
     +          TEST, 'IS', LIST (I)
       STOP
       END
```

```
SEARCH VALUE:          361
THE FIRST NUMBER THAT EXCEEDS            361 IS            471
SEARCH VALUE:           692
THE FIRST NUMBER THAT EXCEEDS          692 IS          701
```

```
SEARCH VALUE:               992
***ERROR***  SUBSCRIPT NUMBER 1 OF LIST    HAS THE VALUE          11
```

The WATFIV-S error message gives the maximum information. The kind of error messages produced in this and similar situations is what makes WATFIV-S one of the best "student" or "debugging" Fortran systems ever written. The question is, why does the first (and only) subscript, I, of the array LIST have the value 11 in the third sample execution? Hand simulating this execution, and referring to the DATA statement which conveniently gives the values for the array LIST in the program listing, we see that the input value for TEST is 992, and that value exceeds all of the values in the array LIST. Thus the IF test for early exit never succeeds and the DO block executes its full 10 iterations. When the DO block is completed, the DO variable I has as its value the first value in the sequence 1, 2, 3, ..., that exceeds 10. Thus I is 11 upon normal exit from the DO block. Since subscripts from 1 to 10 are declared for the array LIST, the attempt to use the subscript 11 in the final PRINT statement is indeed an error. If you are using a debugging compiler, you will be glad you got the error message. The results are unpredictable using Fortran compilers that do not check subscript bounds. On some systems, the value printed might be the value from the variable stored next to the array LIST in memory. The programmer has no knowledge of which variable this might be, and consequently might not be able to recognize that a wrong answer has been printed.

Programming Note: It is better to get an error message for a mistake than to have the program continue and calculate garbage.

If you compare this search loop with the search loops earlier in this chapter, you will notice that we always used a logical variable FOUND to indicate whether the search is successful. At the conclusion of the search, the variable FOUND is tested to determine whether normal or error output should be generated by the program. In the current example, assuming the search loop is modified to correctly set the variable FOUND, the following IF block would be appropriate.

```
19  IF (FOUND) THEN DO
       PRINT, 'FIRST NUMBER THAT EXCEEDS', TEST, 'IS', LIST (I)
    ELSE DO
       PRINT, TEST, 'EXCEEDS ALL THE VALUES IN THE LIST'
    END IF
```

6.6 What You Should Know

1. A list is a sequence of values, all representing data of the same kind.
2. In Fortran, the most usual way of storing a list is in an array.
3. A subscript indicates which element of the list is referenced.
4. The subscript of a subscripted variable may itself be a variable or an expression.
5. An index variable is a variable subscript.
6. WATFIV-S provides an execution-time error message if a subscript is out of bounds.
7. Except for dummy arguments, Fortran requires fixed constant limits for the range of subscripts in an array declaration in the main program or subprogram where the array is first declared. Another variable is used to keep track of the number of elements actually in the list.
8. In the declaration of an array that is a dummy argument, expressions using other dummy arguments may be used to indicate the range of subscripts.
9. Standard input and output files are available without being opened. Other files must be opened.
10. A sequential search algorithm examines each element of an array in increasing or decreasing order of subscript.
11. If the list is ordered, the sequential search can stop early either successfully on finding an exact match or unsuccessfully on passing the expected location of the test item without finding a match.
12. In a multilevel search, the list is scanned in large steps to determine quickly which smaller regions of the array should be searched in more detail.
13. A binary search quickly locates the position of a value in a list by halving the number of candidates with each step.
14. For large lists, multilevel search methods are much more efficient than simple sequential search methods and binary search methods are more efficient than multilevel search methods.
15. A list is sorted when its elements are in order.
16. A list may be sorted by successively finding the smallest remaining element.
17. Modules may sometimes be tested independently. Thereafter, the debugging effort can be confined to testing whether the modules fit together.
18. Successful test runs with atypical data are not sufficient evidence that a program will run with more usual data. On the other hand, programs also must be tested with such unusual data, because they must work in all cases.

6.7 Self-Test Questions

Section 6.1

1. How do you declare the variable PROFIT to be an array of 100 real values?
2. How do you declare a character string variable NAME to be an array of 50 items, each of length 30?
3. How do you handle lists of data that vary in length?
4. True/false:
   a. The smallest subscript in any array is always 1.
   b. Array subscripts must be integers.
   c. If the problem has a list of values, then an array must be used.
   d. An array is always written or read using a DO block.
   e. In an executable statement, the subscript written for an array element may be a variable.

Section 6.2

1. True/false:
   a. In using a sequential search, the main advantage of scanning ordered data rather than unordered data is that ordered data is easier for humans to read.
   b. If you need to find something in a list, you should always sort the list first.
   c. If you have a choice of searching an unordered list of objects or an ordered list containing the same objects, the search of the ordered list always will be faster.
2. What two purposes does the file CRDFIL serve in the credit card checking programs?

Section 6.3

1. True/false:
   a. A sequential search is an efficient way to search an ordered list.
   b. A sequential search is an efficient way to search an unordered list.
   c. In general, the more levels a multilevel search has, the more efficient it is.
   d. A binary search can be performed even if a list has gaps between adjacent values.
   e. A binary search program is much more complicated than a multilevel search program.
   f. Although binary search is more efficient than four-level search for lists of size 100,000, the four-level search catches up in efficiency for larger lists.
2. Suppose a computer had memory space for a little more than 100 entries from a list. How could a list of 10,000 entries be searched efficiently on such a computer?
3. The information in Table 6.5 about the comparative speed of the two-level search program of 100,000 items is based on 316 pages of 317 entries each. How many comparisons would be necessary (minimum, maximum, and average) if the two-level searching procedure were based on 1,000 pages of

100 entries each? Can you formulate a general principle about minimizing the number of comparisons in a two-level search?

Section 6.4

1. True/false:
   a. In executing subroutine SORT1, the computer examines every item in the unsorted list in order to determine which item is the smallest.
   b. If the input list to the "interchange sort" happens to be in sorted order, the execution time is less than for the usual case in which the input data are randomly ordered.
   c. The "interchange sort" works correctly even when there are duplicates in the input data.
2. What must be changed to make the sorting programs in this section sort into decreasing order, i.e., largest value first?
3. Hand simulate the execution of the subroutine SORT1, starting with a list whose values are 45, 32, 16, 32, 45. This is an important type of data to test, because the equality of two or more list items might upset the execution or the subroutine FNDSML.
4. Prove that to sort a list of nine items the subroutine SORT1 requires 72 comparisons. How many comparisons does SORT1 take for a list of length n?
5. Prove that to sort a list of nine items the subroutine SORT2 requires 36 comparisons. How many comparisons does SORT2 take for a list of length n? Contrast this answer to your answer for the previous question.

6.8 Programming Exercises

1. **Purpose:** To write a useful list manipulation subroutine.

   The problem: Inserting an item at location k of a list of length n means increasing the list length to $n + 1$, moving the values in locations $k + 1$, $k + 2$, ..., n to locations $k + 1$, $k + 2$, $k + 3$, ..., $n + 1$, respectively, and storing the value of the new item at location k.
   Write a subroutine

   ```
   SUBROUTINE INSERT (LIST, LOCATN, NEWITM, SIZE)
   ```

   that inserts NEWITM (new item) in the list LIST at location LOCATN in the list, moving subsequent items, if any, down one location. The fourth dummy argument SIZE will be the upper subscript bound declared for the array LIST.

   Hint: One of the nice things about subprogram modules is that once they are written and debugged, they can be considered as new operations added to the Fortran library. The subroutines READL and PRINTL in this chapter will be extremely useful in reading the data for the test program and in printing the list after executing the subroutine INSERT to see if it worked.

   Input data: A list of positive integers, one per line, followed by the signal value 0. After that comes the value of the new item to insert, followed by the location in which to insert it. For example,

```
123
234
345
456
```

```
0
333
3
```

Sample output:

```
ORIGINAL LIST

INPUT DATA  DATUM:  123
INPUT DATA  DATUM:  234
INPUT DATA  DATUM:  345
INPUT DATA  DATUM:  456
INPUT DATA  DATUM:    0

INPUT DATA  NEWITM:  333
INPUT DATA  LOCATN:    3

THE LIST AFTER INSERTION
123
234
333
345
456
```

2. **Purpose:** To calculate a useful statistic from a list using subroutines introduced in this chapter.

   The problem: The *median* of a list of numbers is the middle value, if the list has odd length, or the average of the two values closest to the middle, if the list has even length. The problem is to write a function subprogram

   ```
   MEDIAN (LIST, SIZE)
   ```

   to calculate the median of a list and to write a main program to test this function.

   The algorithm: First read a list using the subroutine READL. Then sort the list. The median will then be found in the middle position of the list, if the list length SIZE is odd, or it will be the average of the two middle elements of the list if the list length is even.

   Input data: A list of integers, all less than 100 in absolute value, followed by the signal value 9999. You should test your program on both of our test files.

```
 830
 260
-123
 589
 212
9999
```

Sample output:

```
INPUT DATA  DATUM:    830
INPUT DATA  DATUM:    260
INPUT DATA  DATUM:   -123
INPUT DATA  DATUM:    589
INPUT DATA  DATUM:    212
INPUT DATA  DATUM:   9999

THE SORTED LIST IS AS FOLLOWS:
```

```
  -123
   212
   260
   589
   830

THE MEDIAN IS 260.000
```

Input data:

```
35
12
18
23
9999
```

Sample output:

```
INPUT DATA  DATUM:    35
INPUT DATA  DATUM:    12
INPUT DATA  DATUM:    18
INPUT DATA  DATUM:    23
INPUT DATA  DATUM:  9999

THE SORTED LIST IS AS FOLLOWS:

  12
  18
  23
  35

THE MEDIAN IS  20.5000
```

3. **Purpose:** To calculate the median of a list without sorting the list as we did in Exercise 2.

   The problem: The problem is the same as Exercise 2, to write a program to find the median of a list and to test that program. Only the solution method is different.

   The algorithm: This time, we write a function subprogram HOWMNY (LIST, SIZE, ITEM) to count how many elements in the array LIST are less than ITEM. Then, for each element in the list, we use the function HOWMNY to count how many elements of the list are less than it. Assuming there are no duplicated values in the list, the median can be recognized in the following way: if the list length is odd, the median has (SIZE − 1) / 2 elements less than it. If the list length is even, then the median is the average of the elements with (SIZE / 2) − 1 and SIZE / 2 predecessors.

   Input data: The same two test files as Exercise 2.

   Sample output: The same output as in Exercise 2, except that the list is not sorted.

4. **Purpose:** To practice using DO loops and implied DO loops with arrays.

   The problem: To find the angle between two 3-dimensional vectors. (If vectors are not already familiar from physics or calculus, we suggest omitting this problem.)

   Background information: A 3-dimensional vector a is given by a triplet of real numbers (a_1, a_2, a_3). The dot product of two vectors a and b is given by the formula

$$a \cdot b = a_1 b_1 + a_2 b_2 + a_3 b_3$$

The magnitude of a vector is calculated by the formula

$$||a|| = \sqrt{a \cdot a}$$

The cosine of the angle θ between two vectors a and b is given by the following formula

$$\cos(\theta) = \frac{a \cdot b}{||a|| \; ||b||}$$

The Fortran built-in function ACOS may be used to find the angle with a given cosine. The answer is in radians.

Input data: There are two lines in the input file. Each line contains the three components of one of the vectors. For example,

```
3 -5 7
8 1 -2
```

Program requirement: The two vectors must be stored in arrays. Implied DO loops must be used for input and output, and DO blocks must be used for sums.

Sample output:

```
INPUT DATA  A:  3.00000 -5.00000  7.00000
INPUT DATA  B:  8.00000  1.00000 -2.00000
THE ANGLE BETWEEN THESE VECTORS IS ______ RADIANS
THE ANGLE BETWEEN THESE VECTORS IS ______ DEGREES
```

5. **Purpose:** To design a more complex subprogram using a search function as a building block. As a further wrinkle, the list being read and searched is a list of character strings instead of numbers.

   The problem: Five copies of a petition were circulated by members of a civic action group. By the time the petitions were to be presented to the Borough Council, they had 253, 311, 45, 217, and 529 signatures on the five copies. Unfortunately, some overzealous supporters of their cause had signed more than one copy of the petition, so that the number of distinct individuals signing the petition was lower than the apparent total of 1355. The problem is to write a program to read the complete list of 1355 names, and to produce a smaller list that contains no duplicates.

   Hints: Modify the subroutines READL and PRINTL to read and print lists of character strings. Write a subroutine UNIQUE (LIST, SIZE, ULIST, USIZE) that takes an array of character strings, LIST, and produces a new array, ULIST, which contains the same character strings without duplicates. One way to do this is to search through all names already in ULIST to see if a name is already there before adding it to ULIST. If a name is found in ULIST, then it is not added to ULIST a second time.

   Input data: The data should consist of a list of 1355 names, one per line, with the termination signal name, 'NO MORE NAMES' at the end. However, since all lists and subprograms to process these lists should be written to handle variable-length lists (up to a declared maximum size), it is sufficient to test the program on a list of approximately 25 names containing some duplicates, some triplicates, and perhaps one name occurring five times. Part of the fun of doing this exercise is making up an imaginative list of names.

   Sample output: It looks a lot like the input, but without duplicates. You must echo the input list containing the duplicates to show that your sample execution did not start with a list containing no duplicates.

6. **Purpose:** To speed up the program written in Exercise 5 by using a binary search algorithm instead of a sequential search.

   The problem: The problem is again to remove duplicates from a list. However, this time, the subroutine UNIQUE is modified to use a binary search to determine whether a name is already in the array ULIST. In order for the binary search to work, the names in ULIST must be maintained in alphabetic order. (As far as the program is concerned, it doesn't matter if this is alphabetic order by last name or by first name—the search simply needs the list in order as an array of character strings.) Thus, when a name that is not a duplicate is inserted in ULIST it must be inserted in order. As a result, more information must be extracted from the binary search subprogram than previously returned. Not only must it report success or failure of the search, (which is the desired case for adding a new name), it must report the location or subscript of the first name that is later than the new name in alphabetic order in case of failure. This information is readily available in the binary search. At the last stage of binary search, all names but one have been eliminated. Names before the final test name are definitely too low, and names after the final test name are definitely too high. All that remains to be determined is whether the new name precedes or follows the final test name.

   Input data: Use the same list of 25 names, followed by a signal, that you used for Exercise 5.

   Sample output: It is the same as Exercise 5, except that they are in alphabetic order. We suggest retesting the program of Exercise 6 on an input list without duplicates. It sorts the list! This method is called insertion sorting.

7. **Purpose:** To combine the list processing techniques of reading, printing and searching with accumulating an array of totals.

   The problem: A questionnaire was given to 2000 people and 1326 people gave usable responses to the most important question. Although the questionnaire did not require the respondents to choose from a prepared list of alternatives, many answers appeared more than once. Modify the program you wrote for Exercise 5 or Exercise 6 in the following ways. Declare two arrays, RESPON (response) and FREQ (frequency of occurrence of a response). When a duplicate response is detected, it is still not added a second time to the list of responses, but the frequency count for that response is incremented by one.

   Input data: You should use a bigger input file than we show below, but we don't want to make the book too long. These are responses to the question "Who was the greatest scientist of all time?"

```
ALBERT EINSTEIN
ALBERT EINSTEIN
ISAAC NEWTON
ALBERT EINSTEIN
DR. BUNSEN HONEYDEW
ISAAC NEWTON
THE INSTRUCTOR OF THIS COURSE
ALBERT EINSTEIN
NO MORE RESPONSES
```

Sample output:

```
INPUT DATA  RESPON:  ALBERT EINSTEIN
   .
   .
   .
INPUT DATA  RESPON:  NO MORE RESPONSES

RESPONSE                          FREQUENCY
ALBERT EINSTEIN                           4
ISAAC NEWTON                              2
DR. BUNSEN HONEYDEW                       1
THE INSTRUCTOR OF THIS COURSE             1
```

8. **Purpose:** To compare two algorithms.

   The problem: The problem is again to remove the duplicates as in Exercise 5. This time the method of removing duplicates involves first sorting the original list. In the sorted list, duplicates can be recognized very easily. They are the same as the entry that precedes them.

   Input data: A list of names containing duplicates, followed by the signal 'NO MORE NAMES'.

   Sample output: The sample output will contain echoes of input data, and then the same names without duplicates. The final list will be in alphabetic order.

   Observation: If your computer system prints the length of time an execution took, or if the executions are long enough to time by hand, compare the execution time of the solutions to Exercise 5 or 6 and Exercise 8. Hand timing may require a relatively small and slow computer, or a relatively large list.

9. **Purpose:** To give a new but easy list processing method.

   The problem: A list of names produced by another programmer is supposed to be in alphabetic order, but is suspected not to be. Write a program to check. Do not sort the list.

   Hint: If each pair of adjacent names is in order, then the whole list is in order.

   Input data: A list of names.

   Sample output: The same list of names, echoed as they were read, and the single word SORTED or UNSORTED, whichever is appropriate.

10. **Purpose:** To make the point that in computer programming there is little difference in searching or sorting lists of numbers or character strings.

    The problems: Do Exercises 5 – 9 using lists of numbers instead of lists of character strings. In most of the problem descriptions, just replace the person's name with the social security number to get an adequate numerical problem statement.

    Input data: Lists of numbers this time.

    Sample output: Similar to corresponding character string exercise.

7 CHARACTER DATA

Many programming applications are concerned with information appearing in the form of written text, rather than as numbers. Such text may represent names, places, responses to a survey, literary works, and so on. Most programming languages have special features for the manipulation of character data.

This chapter provides a systematic study of character data processing techniques, devoting particular attention to their applications in word processing and text analysis.

7.1 Processing Character Data

In a computer program, a piece of written text is called a **character string**. This emphasizes the fact that the computer treats a character string as a sequence of individual characters, and it does not understand the meaning of the text the characters represent. Character strings have been used since Chapter 2 to retain messages and identifying information that are printed out but not processed in any other way. This section reviews this simple use of character strings and presents computer programs in which the character strings themselves are the center of interest.

Section Preview

Character String Constant:

A character string constant is a sequence of characters in apostrophes

Example: 'ABC'

Character Variable Declaration:

General Form:

CHARACTER *variable name *integer*
CHARACTER **integer list of variable names*
CHARACTER *list of variable names*

Examples:

```
CHARACTER NAME *20
CHARACTER *20 FNAME, LNAME
CHARACTER LINE (80)
```

Trimmed Length:

The trimmed length of a string is its length after discarding terminal blanks. Unlike the declared length, the trimmed length of a character variable depends on the value of the variable.

Character String Declarations

A character string variable in a Fortran program is declared to be type character. In addition, each object of type character has a length, which is the maximum number of characters that the string may have. For example, the declaration

```
CHARACTER STR7 *7
```

declares the variable STR7 to be a character string of length 7. If the declared length is omitted, a default length of one character is used.

Character Constants

As a program might contain numeric constants, such as -4.23, 7, or 0.0031, it also might contain character string constants, such as 'LOVE', 'GOOD MORNING.', or 'BG7*5 AD'. In a program, a character constant is always enclosed in apostrophes, also referred to as single quotes. This makes it easy for the computer to tell the difference between the character constant 'YES' and the variable YES, or between the character constant '14' and the integer constant 14. Even a character constant that could not possibly be regarded as anything else is enclosed in apostrophes when it appears in a program.

When a character constant appears in a PRINT or WRITE statement, execution of that statement causes printing of the constant itself and not any meaning of it. This may be recalled, for instance from the program CLC1V2 (calculation 1, version 2) reprinted from Section 2.1. The character constant '84 + 13 =' is printed verbatim while the arithmetic expression 84 + 13 is evaluated before printing the result, 97.

```
C       PROGRAM CLC1V2
        PRINT, '84 + 13 =', 84 + 13
        STOP
        END
```

```
84 + 13 =                97
```

We repeat this example to reemphasize that enclosing a numeric expression in apostrophes identifies it as character data, so that it is not evaluated as a numeric expression.

Assigning Values to Character Variables

A variable that has been declared to be a character string may be assigned a value that is a character string. Selectively assigning written text to a character variable used in a PRINT statement provides an alternative to executing alternative PRINT statements containing different messages, as shown by the program TSTSGN (test sign).

```
C       PROGRAM TSTSGN
C       TESTS THE SIGN OF A NUMBER
        REAL NUMBER
        CHARACTER SIGN *8
C
        READ, NUMBER
C
        IF (NUMBER .GT. 0) THEN DO
           SIGN = 'POSITIVE'
        ELSE DO
        IF (NUMBER .EQ. 0) THEN DO
           SIGN = 'ZERO'
        ELSE DO
           SIGN = 'NEGATIVE'
        END IF
        END IF
        PRINT, NUMBER, 'IS', SIGN
        STOP
        END
           -2.3000000 IS NEGATIVE
```

Length of a Character String

The **length** of a character string is the number of characters in the string. The length of a Fortran character string is fixed and must be greater than zero. Each blank occurring in a string is counted in its length. During execution of a program, a character string variable always has its declared length. However, the length of a character string assigned to a character variable may be different from the length declared for that variable. For example, if the input number is zero in the program TSTSGN (test sign), the 4-character constant 'ZERO' is assigned to the 8-character variable SIGN. This assignment is legal. Four blanks are added to the end of the string 'ZERO' to make its length 8, the declared length of the variable SIGN. Thus the new value of the variable SIGN is 'ZERO   '.

On the other hand, if the character string to be assigned to variable is longer than the declared length of the variable, characters are truncated from the right end of the string prior to assignment. For example, if the string NAME has a declared length of 3, the assignment statement

```
        NAME = 'JONATHAN'
```

results in the string 'JON' being assigned to NAME.

Although these assignments are allowed, some WATFIV systems issue a warning message if the length of the right side exceeds the length of the left side.

Input of Character Strings

When character strings are supplied as input using a READ statement with the default format, the string must be enclosed in apostrophes, just like a character constant. When using an A format, however, surrounding apostrophes must be omitted: any apostrophes among the characters read are considered to be part of the character constant.

Comparison of Character Strings

In Fortran the comparison operators

.LT. .LE. .EQ. .NE. .GE. .GT.

may be used to compare two character strings. The ordering of strings is an extension of the ordinary lexicographic (i.e., dictionary) ordering of words. When two character strings of unequal length are compared, the shorter one is automatically extended with blanks for purposes of the comparison. Comparison of character strings is discussed in detail in Section 3.5.

Substrings

Many character processing applications require breaking down a string into individual characters or special sequences of characters. Examples are decomposing a word into letters or a sentence into words. The key idea in such a decomposition is a substring.

A **substring** of a character string is any consecutive sequence of characters in the string. for example, 'J', 'NE D', and 'DOE' are substrings of the character string 'JANE DOE', but 'JDOE' is not a substring. Every character string is regarded as a substring of itself. The following table indicates all the substrings of the character string 'THEN'.

Length 1: 'T' 'H' 'E' 'N'
Length 2: 'TH' 'HE' 'EN'
Length 3: 'THE' 'HEN'
Length 4: 'THEN'

Referencing Substrings

There is no convenient way to refer to substrings of a character string in WATFIV-S. To be able to reference individual characters of a character string, the string must be represented as an array of CHARACTER *1 variables. The *n*th character of the string is then the *n*th element of the array. The program SGLLTR (single letters) tells the computer to print, one at a time, the characters of a string supplied as input.

```
C       PROGRAM SGLLTR
C       PRINT INDIVIDUALLY THE LETTERS OF AN INPUT STRING
        INTEGER K
        CHARACTER STRING (10)
C
        READ 15, STRING
   15   FORMAT (10A1)
        PRINT, 'INPUT DATA  STRING:', STRING
C
        DO 18 K = 1, 10
           PRINT, STRING (K)
   18   CONTINUE
C
        PRINT, '====='
        STOP
        END
```

```
INPUT DATA  STRING:  S H A Z A M
S
H
A
Z
```

A
M

=====

When an array name appears without subscripts in a READ or PRINT list, Fortran treats it as though all the elements of the array were listed in order of increasing subscript. Thus the statements

```
READ 15, STRING
PRINT, 'INPUT DATA STRING:', STRING
```

are equivalent to the statements

```
READ 15, (STRING (K), K = 1, 10)
PRINT, 'INPUT DATA STRING:', (STRING (K), K = 1, 10)
```

Note that the format for reading an array of CHARACTER *1 values is 10A1 and not A10 which would be used to read a CHARACTER *10 variable.

There are four blank lines in the output of the program SGLLTR because there are are four blank letters following the characters "SHAZAM" in the value of the variable STRING. This is because STRING is declared to have length 10, but "SHAZAM" contains only 6 characters. If the input file is in card format, each record or line has 80 characters. Thus the letters "SHAZAM" are followed by 74 blanks, only 4 of which are read. Using a disk based system with interactive editing, the input line might not have 10 characters and an out-of-data error message will result.

Trimmed Length of a String

It is a nuisance that the length of a character variable is always the same regardless of its value. A definition of length that is suitable for many applications is the length of the substring that includes all characters up to and including the last nonblank character, but excluding terminal blanks. It is possible to write a function subprogram TRMLEN (trimmed length) that computes this value.

```
      FUNCTION TRMLEN (STRING, MAXLEN)
      INTEGER TRMLEN, MAXLEN, K, KK
      CHARACTER STRING (MAXLEN)
      LOGICAL NONBLK
C
      NONBLK = .FALSE.
      DO 18 KK = 1, MAXLEN
C        OR UNTIL NON BLANK FOUND
         K = MAXLEN + 1 - KK
         IF (STRING (K) .NE. ' ') THEN DO
            NONBLK = .TRUE.
            GO TO 19
         END IF
   18 CONTINUE
C
   19 IF (NONBLK) THEN DO
         TRMLEN = K
```

```
      ELSE DO
         TRMLEN = 0
      END IF
      RETURN
      END
```

Programming Note: The use of the length declaration MAXLEN for the dummy argument STRING enables this function program to find the trimmed length of a supplied character string argument of any declared length.

The program SBSTL2 (substrings of length two) prints all substrings of length two of any character string supplied as input. The upper bound TRMLEN (STRING, MAXLEN) − 1 on the DO variable K is the starting point of the last substring of length two that doesn't contain a trailing blank.

```
C     PROGRAM SBSTL2
      CHARACTER STRING (20)
      INTEGER K, TRMLEN, LAST
C
      READ 15, STRING
   15 FORMAT (20A1)
      PRINT, 'INPUT DATA  STRING:', STRING
      LAST = TRMLEN (STRING, 20) - 1
      DO 18 K = 1, LAST
         PRINT, (STRING (K + L - 1), L = 1, 2)
   18 CONTINUE
C
      PRINT, '====='
      STOP
      END
```

```
INPUT DATA  STRING:  H I G H   T H E I R
H I
I G
G H
H
  T
T H
H E
E I
I R
=====
```

By adapting the method of the program SBSTL2, we could write a program to print out all the substrings of any given length. By using a double loop, we could write a program that lists all substrings of all possible lengths. These tasks are exercises at the end of this chapter.

Reassigning the Value of a Substring

It is possible to reassign the value of a substring without affecting the rest of the string. For instance, if the value of the character array NAME is 'J', 'O', 'H', 'N', ' ', 'X', '.', ' ', 'P', 'U', 'B', 'L', 'I', 'C', the statements

```
      INITL = 'Q'
      NAME (6) = INITL
```

tell the computer to change the value of the array NAME from 'JOHN X. PUBLIC' to 'JOHN Q. PUBLIC'.

If more than one character is changed, a loop is required. For example if the array NAME holds the string 'JOHN XAVIER PUBLIC' one character per array element, and the array NEWMDL (new middle name) holds the string 'QUINCY', then the loop

```
      DO 18 LTR = 1, 6
         NEWLTR = LTR + 5
         NAME (NEWLTR) = NEWMDL (LTR)
   18 CONTINUE
```

directs the computer to change the value of the array NAME from 'JOHN XAVIER PUBLIC' to 'JOHN QUINCY PUBLIC'.

In reassigning the value of a substring as in the above two examples, the length of the new substring value was exactly equal to the length of the old substring value. The following example shows how to make room for a longer replacement substring. It is assumed that the declared length of NAME is at least 17 characters, that its first 16 elements represent the character string 'JOHN PAUL PUBLIC', and that the first five letters in the array NEWMDL are 'PETER'.

```
C     MOVE LAST NAME AND BLANK ONE POSITION TO THE RIGHT
      DO 18 L = 10, 16
         LTR = 26 - L
         NAME (LTR + 1) = NAME (LTR)
   18 CONTINUE
C     INSERT MIDDLE NAME
      DO 28 LTR = 1, 5
         NEWLTR = LTR + 5
         NAME (NEWLTR) = NEWMDL (LTR)
   28 CONTINUE
```

Note that it would not be correct to have the variable LTR count forward from 10 to 16 in the first DO loop. That loop would first move the blank in position 10 to position 11, which is what is desired. However, for the second iteration of the loop, the value of LTR would be 11 and the blank just placed in position 11 would be moved to position 12. Next, the blank in position 12 would be moved to position 13. The total effect of the loop would be to put blanks in positions 11 through 17.

Finding the Position of One String in Another

There are numerous reasons for wanting to know if one string is contained as a substring in another. We might want to know if a particular letter is in a word or if a certain word is in a sentence. The pseudocode function INDEX, available in FORTRAN 77 but not in WATFIV-S, tells even more than that; it tells where to find the first instance of one character string as a substring of another. For example

```
      INDEX ('MONKEY', 'ON') = 2
```

because the substring 'ON' begins at the second letter of the string 'MONKEY' and

```
      INDEX ('MONKEY', 'KEY') = 4
```

because the substring 'KEY' begins at the fourth letter of 'MONKEY'.

If the string supplied as the second argument occurs more than once as a substring of the string supplied as the first argument, the function value is the location of the beginning of the leftmost occurrence, so that

```
      INDEX ('BANANA', 'ANA') = 2
```

even though characters 4 to 6 of 'BANANA' also are 'ANA'. If the second argument is not a substring of the first argument, rather than calling it an error and halting, a signal function value of zero is used. For example,

```
      INDEX ('MONKEY', 'OFF') = 0
```

A program that calls the function INDEX can test for the signal value zero if desired.

The function INDEX is not a built-in function in WATFIV-S, but we can write a programmer-defined version of the function. The arguments of the WATFIV version of INDEX are TEXT, a CHARACTER *1 array of size LENTXT, and STRING, a CHARACTER *1 array of *trimmed length* LENSTR. If the supplied argument for STRING contains any blanks in the first LENSTR characters, these blanks must also appear in the corresponding positions in TEXT for the function INDEX to find the substring.

```
      FUNCTION INDEX (TEXT, LENTXT, STRING, LENSTR)
C     SEARCHES FOR STRING AS A SUBSTRING OF TEXT
C     IF FOUND, INDEX IS THE POSITION OF THE FIRST CHARACTER
C     OF THE LEFTMOST OCCURRENCE OF STRING IN TEXT
C     IF NOT FOUND, INDEX = 0
C
      INTEGER INDEX, LENTXT, LENSTR
      CHARACTER TEXT (LENTXT), STRING (LENSTR)
      INTEGER LFTEND, LASTLF, TXTLTR, STRLTR
      LOGICAL STRFND
C
      STRFND = .FALSE.
      LASTLF = LENTXT - LENSTR + 1
      DO 28 LFTEND = 1, LASTLF
C        TEST IF (TEXT (LFTEND : LFTEND + LENSTR - 1) .EQ. STRING)
         DO 18 STRLTR = 1, LENSTR
            TXTLTR = LFTEND + STRLTR - 1
            IF (TEXT (TXTLTR) .NE. STRING (STRLTR)) THEN DO
               GO TO 28
            END IF
   18    CONTINUE
         STRFND = .TRUE.
         GO TO 29
   28 CONTINUE
C
   29 IF (STRFND) THEN DO
         INDEX = LFTEND
      ELSE DO
         INDEX = 0
      END IF
      RETURN
      END
```

Blanking Out Punctuation

The subroutine BLKPCT (blank out punctuation) uses the function INDEX to replace with a blank every character in the text supplied as the argument that is not already a blank or letter. Keep in mind that a function value zero means the function subprogram INDEX has determined that the second supplied argument is not a substring of the first supplied argument. The subroutine BLKPCT regards any character other than a letter or a blank as a "punctuation mark" to be blanked out.

```
      SUBROUTINE BLKPCT (TEXT, LENTXT)
C     BLANK OUT PUNCTUATION
C     RETAIN ONLY LETTERS AND BLANKS
C     ARRAY NAME:  LTRORB = LETTER OR BLANK
C
      INTEGER LENTXT
      CHARACTER TEXT (LENTXT), LTRORB (27)
      INTEGER I, TRMLEN
C
      LTRORB (1) = 'A'
      ...
      LTRORB (26) = 'Z'
      LTRORB (27) = ' '
C
C     REPLACE ANY CHARACTER THAT IS NOT A BLANK OR LETTER
C     WITH A BLANK
      DO 18 I = 1, LENTXT
         IF (INDEX (LTRORB, 27, TEXT (I), 1) .EQ. 0) THEN DO
            TEXT (I) = ' '
         END IF
   18 CONTINUE
      RETURN
      END
```

The program TESTBP (test blank out punctuation) is intended to show how the subroutine BLKPCT works.

```
C     PROGRAM TESTBP
      CHARACTER TEXT (37)
      READ 15, TEXT
   15 FORMAT (37A1)
      PRINT, 'INPUT DATA  TEXT:', TEXT
C
      CALL BLKPCT (TEXT, 37)
      PRINT, TEXT
      STOP
      END
INPUT DATA  TEXT: S U P P R E S S 5 $ , E X T R A * 3 / S Y M B O L S
S U P P R E S S       E X T R A       S Y M B O L S
```

Excising a Character From a String

When a character of a string is blanked out, as by the subroutine BLKPCT, that character is replaced by a blank and the length of the character string remains unchanged. When a character is *excised* from a string, not only is the character removed, but also all of the characters to the right of the excised characters are moved one position to the left. Thus, when a character is excised from a string, the trimmed length (that is, not including trailing blanks) of the string is decreased by one. Of course, the declared total length of the string cannot change in Fortran. The subroutine EXCHAR (excise character) may be used to excise a character from a string.

```
      SUBROUTINE EXCHAR (C, TEXT, LENTXT)
C     EXCISES THE C-TH CHARACTER OF TEXT
C     ALL SUBSEQUENT CHARACTERS MOVE LEFT ONE POSITION
C
      INTEGER C, LENTXT, I, ALMOST
      CHARACTER TEXT (LENTXT)
C
      ALMOST = LENTXT - 1
      DO 18 I = C, ALMOST
         TEXT (I) = TEXT (I + 1)
   18 CONTINUE
C
      TEXT (LENTXT) = ' '
      RETURN
      END
```

The main reason for writing the subroutine EXCHAR is that its descriptive name makes it easier to read a program that uses it than the program one could obtain by inserting the code directly. This is apparent in the subroutine CMPBB (compress double blanks) that removes all double blanks from a string except those that occur at the right end. It calls the subroutine EXCHAR and is called by a program to list all the words in a string discussed in the next subsection.

```
      SUBROUTINE CMPBB (TEXT, LENTXT)
C     REMOVES DOUBLE BLANKS, EXCEPT AT RIGHT END
      INTEGER LENTXT
      CHARACTER TEXT (LENTXT)
      INTEGER TRMLEN, C, N, ALMOST
C
      C = 1
      ALMOST = TRMLEN (TEXT, LENTXT) - 2
      DO 18 N = 1, ALMOST
         IF (TEXT (C) .EQ. ' ' .AND. TEXT (C + 1) .EQ. ' ') THEN DO
            CALL EXCHAR (C, TEXT, LENTXT)
         ELSE DO
            C = C + 1
         END IF
   18 CONTINUE
      RETURN
      END
```

Listing All the Words

We now turn our attention to the problem of listing all the words in a text. For this purpose, the program WORDS regards a substring as a word if and only if it consists entirely of letters and both the character immediately before it (if any) and the character immediately after it (if any) are not letters. The computer does not consult a dictionary to see whether the word has been approved by a lexicographer.

```
C     PROGRAM WORDS
      CHARACTER TEXT (50), TEMP (50)
      INTEGER K, ENDWRD, TRMLEN, LTR, NEWBLK, ENDLTR
C
```

```
      READ 15, TEXT
   15 FORMAT (50A1)
      PRINT 25, 'INPUT DATA  TEXT:', TEXT
   25 FORMAT (T2, A17, T21, 50A1)
C
C     BLANKING OUT THE PUNCTUATION,
C     COMPRESSING THE MULTIPLE BLANKS,
C     AND ENSURING THAT THE FIRST CHARACTER IS A LETTER
C     ARE PREEDITING TASKS TO SIMPLIFY THE JOB
      CALL BLKPCT (TEXT, 50)
      CALL CMPBB (TEXT, 50)
      IF (TEXT (1) .EQ. ' ') THEN DO
         CALL EXCHAR (1, TEXT, 50)
      END IF
C
C     PRINT ALL THE WORDS
C     EACH WORD IS FOLLOWED BY EXACTLY ONE BLANK
      DO 38 K = 1, 50
C        OR UNTIL ALL WORDS ARE PRINTED
         IF (TRMLEN (TEXT, 50) .EQ. 0) THEN DO
            GO TO 39
         END IF
         ENDWRD = INDEX (TEXT, 50, ' ', 1) - 1
         PRINT, (TEXT (LTR), LTR = 1, ENDWRD)
C
C        DISCARD WORD JUST PRINTED
C        BY SETTING TEXT = TEXT (ENDWRD + 2 : 50)
         ENDLTR = 50 - ENDWRD - 1
         DO 18 LTR = 1, ENDLTR
            TEXT (LTR) = TEXT (LTR + ENDWRD + 1)
   18    CONTINUE
         NEWBLK = 50 - ENDWRD
         DO 28 LTR = NEWBLK, 50
            TEXT (LTR) = ' '
   28    CONTINUE
C
   38 CONTINUE
   39 RETURN
      END
```

```
INPUT DATA  TEXT:  THEN, DUE TO ILLNESS*, HE RESIGNED (FOR GOOD).
T H E N
D U E
T O
I L L N E S S
H E
R E S I G N E D
F O R
G O O D
```

If the string supplied as input to the program WORDS contains no letters, the pre-editing provides a string of all blanks to the DO 38 block that prints all the words. The DO block exits to statement 39 correctly on the first iteration without printing any words because the trimmed length is zero. In the usual case, however, a word starts at position 1 of TEXT and stops immediately before the first blank. The computer prints the word and discards it and the blank immediately following it, so that the next word to be printed begins at location 1 of the resulting character string.

7.2 Case Study: Word Processing and Text Editing

Since the invention of movable type, people have been concerned with the problem of producing a clean, error-free copy of a manuscript. In typed copy, a small number of typographic errors can be corrected cleanly by erasing, whiting out, or using some new miracle technologies for lifting the errant character from the page. The problems begin when a sentence, or sometimes even just a long word, must be inserted in the middle of a paragraph. When the insertion is long enough that the rest of the text must be moved down to make room for it, an entirely new copy of the page or document must be typed, introducing new typographic errors, and the process starts over again. Even with movable type, moving a partial line is a tricky process, involving redistributing the blank characters (spacers), and with linotype slugs (type), each line is one piece of metal, so the rest of the paragraph must be reset.

In recent years, an increasing share of document preparation is being done by computer-assisted word processing or text editing. Major newspapers and some books, including this one, are prepared using computer text-editing systems. Small, special-purpose computers supporting text-editing programs similar to the ones written in this section (with additional features, of course) are sold for office use as word processors or intelligent typewriters.

Some students, at installations with interactive terminals, have been using text editors from the very beginning to prepare programs and input files. This section will give such students a glimpse of one way that such a text editor might be written. For students with no previous experience with text editors or word processors, the sample executions will shed some light on how a word processor might be used.

Most WATFIV installations run in the batch mode. However, the text editing programs written in this section are, of necessity, interactive and cannot be run meaningfully in a batch environment. More detailed examples of character processing appear in this section, but there are no new syntactic features. If you have an interactive WATFIV system or a Waterloo Fortran interpreter for a microcomputer, you can run the programs in this section as written.

For demonstration purposes, we ran the program EDIT under batch WATFIV. The only changes were to add echoes of input data (in addition to the simulated input prompts) and to write an explicit programmer-defined end-of-file signal after the saved text file, which was copied from the standard output file to the appropriate place in the standard input file for the next run. Of course, a editor is not really worth much if it must be run in batch mode.

Some Editing Tasks

A text editing program can be broken into a supervisory main program that communicates with the user and individual subroutines, each of which performs one type of editing task. A text editing program should be able to maintain a copy of a document and perform the following editing operations:

1. Clear the system of all lines from the previous document.
2. Enter a new line of the document.
3. Delete a line of the document.
4. Replace an existing line of the document with a new line.

5. Print the most recent version of the document, or selected parts of it.
6. Locate and print all lines containing a given word, phrase, or other sequence of characters.
7. Replace all occurrences of a given word, phrase, or string of characters with another substitute word, phrase, or string of characters.
8. Renumber the lines of the document without changing the text itself.
9. Save the most recent version of the document for later use.
10. Recall the most recently saved version of the document.

A sophisticated text-editing system performs many additional operations as well, such as inserting extra blanks in order to align the right margin, centering lines to be used as titles or displayed formulas, setting tab stops for tables, lists, and paragraph indentation, and maintaining more than one document at a time. Suggestions are given in the exercises as to how some of these improvements might be implemented. The ten editing operations listed above are reasonably adequate for many purposes, and illustrate the basic principles of text editing and word processing.

A Program for a Simple Text Editor

As an introduction to the general structure of text-editing programs, a very simple text editing program EDIT is written first. It allows only the operations 1 to 5 and does operations 9 and 10 automatically. In a basic decision about how the text will be stored, we require every line of the document to have a unique line number, with the lines of the document being saved in order of increasing line number. This is the way it is done in many commercially available text editors. In the simple editor EDIT, lines of text are referenced by their line number, much as lines of a program are referenced in the language BASIC. In a better text editor, the program would keep track of the current line on which attention is focused, and new commands would specify actions relative to the current line.

Since each line of the document is a character string, the whole document might be represented as an array of character strings, one for each line. However, in order to modify individual characters in each line, the document is represented as a two-dimensional array of single characters. All of the characters in one row represent one line of text. The following declarations show the basic strategy for storing the document in the computer's memory.

```
      INTEGER LINENR (500)
      CHARACTER TEXT (500, 50)
```

The program EDIT is designed to recall automatically the most recent version of the text, created when the program was used last. Then, requests are processed until the request STOP is given. Finally, before terminating, the program EDIT always saves the most recently updated version of the document for later use. The values of variables and lists created in the computer's main memory during the execution of a program usually cannot be expected to remain unchanged in the main memory between runs of a program because space in the computer's main memory usually is too scarce and expensive to reserve for data which is at least temporarily not being used. A text file with a name of the user's choice is used to save the most recent version of the document on a less expensive auxiliary storage device such as magnetic disk or tape between runs. Many different documents can be maintained and edited by the program EDIT, as long as each document is assigned a different file name.

```
C     PROGRAM EDIT
C     A VERY SIMPLE EDITOR
C
```

```
      CHARACTER TEXT (500, 50)
      INTEGER LINENR (500)
      CHARACTER REQEST *7
      INTEGER NRLINS, REQNR
C
C     RETRIEVE PREVIOUS VERSION OF THE DOCUMENT FROM DISK
      CALL GETDOC (LINENR, TEXT, NRLINS)
C
C     PROCESS REQUESTS
      DO 18 REQNR = 1, 1000
         PRINT, 'REQUEST:'
         READ 15, REQEST
   15    FORMAT (A7)
         IF (REQEST .EQ. 'CLEAR') THEN DO
            CALL CLEAR (NRLINS)
         ELSE DO
         IF (REQEST .EQ. 'ENTER') THEN DO
            CALL ENTER (LINENR, TEXT, NRLINS)
         ELSE DO
         IF (REQEST .EQ. 'DELETE') THEN DO
            CALL DELETE (LINENR, TEXT, NRLINS)
         ELSE DO
         IF (REQEST .EQ. 'REPLACE') THEN DO
            CALL REPLAC (LINENR, TEXT, NRLINS)
         ELSE DO
         IF (REQEST .EQ. 'PRINT') THEN DO
            CALL PRINTD (LINENR, TEXT, NRLINS)
         ELSE DO
         IF (REQEST .EQ. 'STOP') THEN DO
            GO TO 19
         ELSE DO
            PRINT, 'ILLEGAL REQUEST'
         END IF
         END IF
         END IF
         END IF
         END IF
         END IF
   18 CONTINUE
C
C     SAVE CURRENT VERSION OF DOCUMENT ON DISK
   19 CALL SAVDOC (LINENR, TEXT, NRLINS)
      STOP
      END
```

In true top-down fashion, we have written an executable main program EDIT first. All we now need is to refine the subroutines it calls.

Double Checking Before Clearing

As long as each subroutine maintains the working copy of the document in the proper format, with the line numbers in increasing order and the count of the number of lines correctly computed, the design of the text editor can be completely modular. The main program EDIT has the responsibility for initiating the dialogue with the user and finding out which kind of request the user wants performed next. It then turns further processing of that request over to a specialized subroutine that continues the dialogue and finishes processing the request. Each specialized subroutine for processing a request can be written completely independently of the other subroutines of the text editor. This assumes, of course, that each one leaves the saved copy of the document in good order. With such modularity, it is very easy first to construct a very simple text editor that executes a limited number of operations, and later to add additional operations on the text by appending additional specialized subroutines.

In creating a new document with our simple editor, the first request issued must be CLEAR. Accordingly, we refine this section of the program first.

```
      SUBROUTINE CLEAR (NRLINS)
      INTEGER NRLINS
      CHARACTER ANSWER *1
C
      PRINT, 'ARE YOU SURE YOU WANT TO DESTROY',
     +         'THE ENTIRE DOCUMENT?'
      PRINT, 'IF SO, CONFIRM BY ANSWERING YES (Y):'
      READ 15, ANSWER
   15 FORMAT (A1)
      IF (ANSWER .EQ. 'Y') THEN DO
         NRLINS = 0
      ELSE DO
         PRINT, 'NO ACTION TAKEN.'
      END IF
      RETURN
      END
```

The reason for double checking a CLEAR request is that clearing the entire working text is a very serious step, and its accidental use could destroy thousands of lines of text and waste many hours of work entering the text. It is perfectly reasonable to be even more careful than EDIT and allow a CLEAR request to be processed only upon presentation of a closely guarded password or authorization code.

Entering a New Line

The refinement of the subroutine ENTER is equally easy, with all of the hard work pushed off into the subroutines LOCATE and INSERT. Pseudocode versions of these subroutines are given after the subroutine ENTER in a top-down fashion.

```
      SUBROUTINE ENTER (LINENR, TEXT, NRLINS)
C     ENTER A SINGLE NEW LINE OF TEXT
C
      INTEGER NRLINS, MAXLNS
      INTEGER LINENR (500)
      CHARACTER TEXT (500, 50), NEWTXT (50)
      INTEGER NWLNNR, LOC, LTR
      LOGICAL INDOC
      MAXLNS = 500
C
      IF (NRLINS .EQ. MAXLNS) THEN DO
         PRINT, 'REQUEST CANNOT BE PROCESSED;',
     +            'DOCUMENT IS FULL.'
```

```
      ELSE DO
         PRINT, 'NEW LINE NUMBER:'
         READ, NWLNNR
         CALL LOCATE (LINENR, NRLINS, NWLNNR, LOC, INDOC)
         IF (INDOC) THEN DO
            PRINT, 'REQUEST NOT PROCESSED;'
            PRINT, 'LINE NUMBER', NWLNNR,
     +             'IS IN DOCUMENT ALREADY.'
            PRINT, 'THIS LINE READS:'
            PRINT 25, (TEXT (LOC, LTR), LTR = 1, 50)
 25         FORMAT (T2, 50A1)
         ELSE DO
            PRINT, 'TEXT:'
            READ 15, NEWTXT
 15         FORMAT (50A1)
            CALL INSERT (LINENR, TEXT, NRLINS, NWLNNR, NEWTXT, LOC)
         END IF
      END IF
      RETURN
      END
      SUBROUTINE LOCATE (LINENR, NRLINS, NUMBER, LOC, INDOC)
      Locate the first line of text with a line number
            equal to or greater than NUMBER (search line number)
      Assign its subscript to LOC
      Set INDOC to indicate if there is already a line with this number
      END
      SUBROUTINE INSERT (LINENR, TEXT, NRLINS, NWLNNR, NEWTXT, LOC)
      Increase NRLINS (number of lines) by 1
      Make room for the new line by moving all lines
            following it down one location
      Insert new line number and new text into document
      END
```

The location of the first line of the existing text with a line number equal to or greater than the value of NWLNNR (new line number) can be determined by a procedure differing but little from the subroutine SEQSR2 in Section 6.2 that searches for an entry in a table. For simplicity, we build the subroutine LOCATE using a sequential search algorithm. It is left as an exercise to rewrite the subroutine LOCATE to use the more efficient binary search algorithm. Both algorithms require the list of line numbers to be maintained in increasing order. If the line number being searched for is greater than all entries of the search list, or otherwise does not appear, then the value of the logical variable INDOC (in document) is set to false as a signal.

```
      SUBROUTINE LOCATE (LINENR, NRLINS, NUMBER, LOC, INDOC)
C     LOCATES THE FIRST LINE NUMBER IN THE DOCUMENT
C     THAT EQUALS OR EXCEEDS THE DUMMY ARGUMENT NUMBER
C     RETURNS:
C        LOC = SUBSCRIPT OF LINE FOUND
C        INDOC = TRUE IF LINE NUMBER IS ALREADY IN DOCUMENT
C                FALSE IF NOT ALREADY USED
C
      INTEGER NRLINS, LINENR (500), NUMBER, LOC
      INTEGER LINE
      LOGICAL INDOC, FOUND
C
```

```
      FOUND = .FALSE.
      IF (NRLINS .GT. 0) THEN DO
         DO 18 LINE = 1, NRLINS
            IF (LINENR (LINE) .GE. NUMBER) THEN DO
               FOUND = .TRUE.
               GO TO 19
            END IF
18       CONTINUE
      END IF
C
   19 IF (FOUND) THEN DO
         LOC = LINE
         INDOC = (LINENR (LINE) .EQ. NUMBER)
      ELSE DO
         LOC = NRLINS + 1
         INDOC = .FALSE.
      END IF
      RETURN
      END
```

The subroutine INSERT is relatively easy to refine. The only potential trouble spot is remembering to move down both line numbers and text lines so that they continue to correspond after the subroutine is executed.

```
      SUBROUTINE INSERT (LINENR, TEXT, NRLINS, NWLNNR, NEWTXT, LOC)
C     INSERTS NEWTXT (NEW TEXT) WITH NEW LINE NUMBER NWLNNR
C     AT POSITION LOC IN THE ARRAYS TEXT AND LINENR.
C     EXISTING LINES OF TEXT ARE MOVED DOWN TO MAKE ROOM
C
      INTEGER NRLINS, LINENR (500), NWLNNR, LOC
      CHARACTER TEXT (500, 50), NEWTXT (50)
      INTEGER LINE, LTR, LOC1, L
C
      NRLINS = NRLINS + 1
C     MAKE ROOM FOR NEW LINE BY MOVING ALL LINES
C     FOLLOWING IT DOWN ONE LOCATION.
C     THIS MUST BE DONE FROM BOTTOM TO TOP
C     TO AVOID OVERWRITING.
      LOC1 = LOC + 1
      IF (LOC1 .LE. NRLINS) THEN DO
         DO 28 L = LOC1, NRLINS
            LINE = NRLINS + LOC + 1 - L
            LINENR (LINE) = LINENR (LINE - 1)
            DO 18 LTR = 1, 50
               TEXT (LINE, LTR) = TEXT (LINE - 1, LTR)
   18       CONTINUE
   28    CONTINUE
      END IF
C
C     INSERT NEW LINE
      LINENR (LOC) = NWLNNR
      DO 38 LTR = 1, 50
         TEXT (LOC, LTR) = NEWTXT (LTR)
   38 CONTINUE
      RETURN
      END
```

Using a Simple Text Editor

Before proceeding to similar refinements for the steps to delete a line, a sample execution is shown, using mainly the requests CLEAR and ENTER. Most of the session takes the form of a dialogue in which the computer asks a question, and the user types a response followed by a carriage return.

Of particular interest in this session are the computer's actions when the user mistakenly attempts to use the line number 60 a second time, and when the user fails to give the only acceptable confirming response, Y, after making the second request to clear the document. (Actually any response starting with Y has the same effect since A1 format is used to read the response.)

```
TYPE NAME OF FILE TO BE EDITED:
SPEECH
EDITING FILE:  SPEECH
REQUEST:
CLEAR
ARE YOU SURE YOU WANT TO DESTROY THE ENTIRE DOCUMENT?
IF SO, CONFIRM BY ANSWERING YES (Y):
Y
REQUEST:
ENTER
NEW LINE NUMBER:
          10
TEXT:
EIGHTY-SEVEN YEARS AGO, OUR
REQUEST:
ENTER
NEW LINE NUMBER:
          20
TEXT:
FOREFATHERS BROUGHT FORTH ON
REQUEST:
ENTER
NEW LINE NUMBER:
          30
TEXT:
THIS CONTINENT, A NEW NATION.
REQUEST:
ENTER
NEW LINE NUMBER:
          40
TEXT:
FOUNDED ON DEMOCRATIC PRINCIPLES,
REQUEST:
ENTER
NEW LINE NUMBER:
          50
TEXT:
CONCEIVED IN LIBERTY, AND DEDICATED
REQUEST:
ENTER
NEW LINE NUMBER:
          60
TEXT:
TO THE PRINCIPLE THAT ALL MEN ARE
```

```
REQUEST:
ENTER
NEW LINE NUMBER:
         60
REQUEST NOT PROCESSED;
LINE NUMBER          60  IS IN DOCUMENT ALREADY.
THIS LINE READS:
TO THE PRINCIPLE THAT ALL MEN ARE
REQUEST:
ENTER
NEW LINE NUMBER:
         70
TEXT:
EQUAL IN THE EYES OF THE LAW.
REQUEST:
CLEAR
ARE YOU SURE YOU WANT TO DESTROY THE ENTIRE DOCUMENT?
IF SO, CONFIRM BY ANSWERING YES (Y):
I GUESS NOT
NO ACTION TAKEN.
REQUEST:
PRINT
   10 EIGHTY-SEVEN YEARS AGO, OUR
   20 FOREFATHERS BROUGHT FORTH ON
   30 THIS CONTINENT, A NEW NATION.
   40 FOUNDED ON DEMOCRATIC PRINCIPLES,
   50 CONCEIVED IN LIBERTY, AND DEDICATED
   60 TO THE PRINCIPLE THAT ALL MEN ARE
   70 EQUAL IN THE EYES OF THE LAW.
REQUEST:
STOP
```

This sample execution gives some idea of what it is like to use this simple text editor. The most frequent request is usually ENTER, by a large margin. Thus, better text editors have an "enter multiple lines" request that allows the user to specify the first line number of an insertion or addition to the text, and then automatically supplies line numbers for all subsequent lines.

One of the best features of even a simple text editor is the ability to produce a clean, complete, error-free copy of the most recent version of the document at any time. The back of an old envelope cannot do as well. The coding to produce such a printout is straightforward.

```
      SUBROUTINE PRINTD (LINENR, TEXT, NRLINS)
      INTEGER NRLINS, LINENR (500)
      CHARACTER TEXT (500, 50)
      INTEGER LINE, LTR
C
      IF (NRLINS .EQ. 0) THEN DO
         PRINT, 'DOCUMENT IS EMPTY.'
```

```
      ELSE DO
         DO 18 LINE = 1, NRLINS
            PRINT 15, LINENR (LINE), (TEXT (LINE, LTR), LTR = 1, 50)
15          FORMAT (I5, 1X, 50A1)
18       CONTINUE
      END IF
      RETURN
      END
```

Deleting a Line

The coding required to delete a line is quite similar to that required to enter a line. The line with the given line number must be located, deleted, and all subsequent lines must be moved up one location in the arrays TEXT and LINENR. The subroutine LOCATE again is used to search for the line of text with line number equal to the line number to be deleted. The value of the logical variable INDOC (in document) distinguishes between an exact match and locating the next higher line number.

```
      SUBROUTINE DELETE (LINENR, TEXT, NRLINS)
C     DELETES A SPECIFIED LINE FROM THE TEXT
C
      INTEGER NRLINS, LINENR (500), LOC
      CHARACTER TEXT (500, 50)
      INTEGER LINE, OLDLIN, LTR
      LOGICAL INDOC
C
      PRINT, 'LINE NUMBER TO BE DELETED:'
      READ, OLDLIN
      CALL LOCATE (LINENR, NRLINS, OLDLIN, LOC, INDOC)
      IF (INDOC) THEN DO
         NRLINS = NRLINS - 1
         DO 28 LINE = LOC, NRLINS
            LINENR (LINE) = LINENR (LINE + 1)
            DO 18 LTR = 1, 50
               TEXT (LINE, LTR) = TEXT (LINE + 1, LTR)
18          CONTINUE
28       CONTINUE
      ELSE DO
         PRINT, 'THERE IS NO LINE NUMBER', OLDLIN
      END IF
      RETURN
      END
```

The following sample execution of EDIT shows the effect of the requests DELETE and PRINT on the version of the document that was saved at the conclusion of the last sample execution shown previously.

```
TYPE NAME OF FILE TO BE EDITED:
SPEECH
EDITING FILE:  SPEECH
REQUEST:
PRINT
   10 EIGHTY-SEVEN YEARS AGO, OUR
   20 FOREFATHERS BROUGHT FORTH ON
   30 THIS CONTINENT, A NEW NATION.
   40 FOUNDED ON DEMOCRATIC PRINCIPLES,
   50 CONCEIVED IN LIBERTY, AND DEDICATED
```

```
   60 TO THE PRINCIPLE THAT ALL MEN ARE
   70 EQUAL IN THE EYES OF THE LAW.
REQUEST:
DELETE
LINE NUMBER TO BE DELETED:
          40
REQUEST:
ENTER
NEW LINE NUMBER:
          70
REQUEST NOT PROCESSED;
LINE NUMBER          70  IS IN DOCUMENT ALREADY.
THIS LINE READS:
EQUAL IN THE EYES OF THE LAW.
REQUEST:
DELETE
LINE NUMBER TO BE DELETED:
          70
REQUEST:
ENTER
NEW LINE NUMBER:
          70
TEXT:
CREATED EQUAL.
REQUEST:
PRINT
   10 EIGHTY-SEVEN YEARS AGO, OUR
   20 FOREFATHERS BROUGHT FORTH ON
   30 THIS CONTINENT, A NEW NATION.
   50 CONCEIVED IN LIBERTY, AND DEDICATED
   60 TO THE PRINCIPLE THAT ALL MEN ARE
   70 CREATED EQUAL.
REQUEST:
STOP
```

Saving the Document Between Runs

In the sample execution, the previous version of the document does not have to be reentered. It is automatically saved at the end of each execution and recalled automatically at the start of the next execution of EDIT. Saving the document is accomplished by writing it into a file. Each line in the file will contain a pair of values, an integer-valued line number in the document and the complete text corresponding to that line number. The subroutine SAVDOC (save document) implements this operation. It differs little from the subroutine PRINTD (print document).

```
      SUBROUTINE SAVDOC (LINENR, TEXT, NRLINS)
C     SAVES BOTH LINE NUMBERS AND TEXT ON DISK
C     THE CORRECT FILE NAME WILL HAVE BEEN ASSOCIATED WITH UNIT 11
C     IN ANOTHER, PREVIOUSLY EXECUTED SUBROUTINE (GETDOC)
C     OR BY AN OPERATING SYSTEM COMMAND
C
      INTEGER NRLINS, LINENR (500)
      CHARACTER TEXT (500, 50)
      INTEGER LINE, LTR, DOCFIL
C
```

```
      DOCFIL = 11
C     SAVE COMPLETE DOCUMENT WITH LINE NUMBERS IN A FILE
      IF (NRLINS .GT. 0) THEN DO
         DO 18 LINE = 1, NRLINS
            WRITE (DOCFIL, 15) LINENR (LINE),
     +                    (TEXT (LINE, LTR), LTR = 1, 50)
   15       FORMAT (I5, 50A1)
   18    CONTINUE
      END IF
      RETURN
      END
```

Variable File Names

The subroutine GETDOC (get document) that restores the internal arrays LINENR and TEXT at the start of each execution to the exact values they contained at the conclusion of the previous execution is equally easy, merely reversing the steps of the subroutine SAVDOC.

```
      SUBROUTINE GETDOC (LINENR, TEXT, NRLINS)
C     READS A DOCUMENT FROM DISK INTO MAIN MEMORY
C
      INTEGER NRLINS, LINENR (500)
      CHARACTER TEXT (500, 50)
      CHARACTER FILNAM *6
      INTEGER LINE, LTR, DOCFIL
C
C     GET MOST RECENT VERSION OF A DOCUMENT
C     FROM A PERMANENT FILE
      PRINT, 'TYPE NAME OF FILE TO BE EDITED:'
      READ 15, FILNAM
   15 FORMAT (6A1)
      PRINT, 'EDITING FILE:', FILNAM
      DOCFIL = 11
      NRLINS = 0
      DO 18 LINE = 1, 500
         READ (DOCFIL, 15, END = 19)
     +         LINENR (LINE), (TEXT (LINE, LTR), LTR = 1, 50)
   15    FORMAT (I5, 50A1)
         NRLINS = NRLINS + 1
   18 CONTINUE
   19 RETURN
      END
```

The way in which a particular file name is associated with unit 11 may depend on which WATFIV system is being used. A common way to do this is to put information about files being used by a program in the command line that causes execution of the program. Check to see how your system deals with file names.

Replacing an Existing Line

In the sample execution, line 70 was replaced by first deleting it and then entering its replacement as a new line using the request ENTER. This method is wasteful of both the user's and the computer's time. The subroutine REPLAC simply locates the line to be replaced and substitutes a new line.

```
      SUBROUTINE REPLAC (LINENR, TEXT, NRLINS)
C     REPLACES AN EXISTING LINE OF THE DOCUMENT
C     WITH NEW TEXT AT THE SAME LINE NUMBER
C
      INTEGER NRLINS, LINENR (500)
      CHARACTER TEXT (500, 50)
      INTEGER OLDLIN, MAXLEN, LOC, LTR
      LOGICAL INDOC
      MAXLEN = 50
C
      PRINT, 'LINE NUMBER TO BE REPLACED:'
      READ, OLDLIN
      CALL LOCATE (LINENR, NRLINS, OLDLIN, LOC, INDOC)
      IF (INDOC) THEN DO
         PRINT, 'REPLACEMENT TEXT:'
         READ 15, (TEXT (LOC, LTR), LTR = 1, 50)
15       FORMAT (50A1)
      ELSE DO
         PRINT, 'THERE IS NO LINE NUMBER', OLDLIN
      END IF
      END
```

The next sample execution shows the use of the request REPLACE.

```
TYPE NAME OF FILE TO BE EDITED:
SPEECH
EDITING FILE:  SPEECH
REQUEST:
REPLACE
LINE NUMBER TO BE REPLACED:
       20
REPLACEMENT TEXT:
FATHERS BROUGHT FORTH ON
REQUEST:
PRINT
  10 EIGHTY-SEVEN YEARS AGO, OUR
  20 FATHERS BROUGHT FORTH ON
  30 THIS CONTINENT, A NEW NATION.
  50 CONCEIVED IN LIBERTY, AND DEDICATED
  60 TO THE PRINCIPLE THAT ALL MEN ARE
  70 CREATED EQUAL.
REQUEST:
STOP
```

It is clear from this execution that it is a convenience to be able to change a single word in a line instead of having to replace the entire line as is required so far by EDIT. This feature involves a deeper understanding of the processing of character strings to extract and replace substrings (i.e., parts) of a character string.

A Better Text Editor

Text editors grow by adding operations and convenience features. We could add the capability of printing a single line and locating and changing any sequence of words or characters *within a line*. Users of commercial text editors will realize that even these improvements will still not make EDIT an excellent text editor. Incorporating some of these improvements are left as one of the programming exercises at the end of the chapter.

7.3 Case Study: Text Analysis

There are numerous reasons for examining text in minute detail, word by word and letter by letter. One of the reasons is to determine the authorship of an historical or literary work. Such quantities as the average length of a word or the frequency of the usage of certain letters can be an important clue. Computers have been useful in studying text from this viewpoint.

Success has been reported distinguishing certain ancient Greek authors by analyzing the frequency with which common pronouns were used in the genitive form. Several measures, including distribution of word lengths and distribution of sentence lengths, have given confirming evidence that of the 14 epistles attributed to St. Paul, only four have a common author. An unfinished Jane Austen novel, completed in conscious imitation of her style by an anonymous admirer, easily is recognized as having two authors by the frequency of occurrence of certain pairs of words. In the forensic field, attempts have been made to determine authorship of confessions presented in evidence, but denied by the alleged confessor.

Section Preview

Text Analysis:

Statistics of various kinds are collected and computed based on an input text. Interpretation of these statistics, including average word length and letter frequencies, is not attempted. The programs make extensive use of substrings, the function INDEX, and DO loops, and illustrate top-down design and modular structure.

Palindromes:

A palindrome is a character string that reads the same forward as backward.

Average Word Length

In order to compute the average length of words in a given text, it is necessary to determine both the total number of letters in the text and the total number of words. The most direct way that comes to mind is used by the program WDLEN1 (average word length, version 1).

```
PROGRAM WDLEN1
Initialize word count and letter count to zero
Read text
Start scan at leftmost character of the text
Do while end of text is not yet reached
   Locate the beginning and end of a word
   If no more words then exit the loop
   Increase the letter count by the number of letters in the word
   Increase the word count by 1
Print 'Average word length = ', letter count / word count
END
```

After reading in the text, the computer starts to look for the first word at the extreme left. Blanks, commas, and other nonletters are passed over to find the beginning of a word. Then letters are counted until the first nonletter such as a blank or punctuation mark which signals the end of the word. These steps are repeated for each word in the text. Each time it locates a word, the computer increases the letter count by its length and the word count by one.

The refinement of WDLEN1 is straightforward.

```
C       PROGRAM WDLEN1
C       CALCULATE THE AVERAGE WORD LENGTH OF INPUT TEXT
C
        CHARACTER TEXT (50)
        INTEGER WORD, SCNLOC, WRDBEG, WRDEND, WRDLEN
        INTEGER WRDCNT, LTRCNT
        LOGICAL WRDFND
        CHARACTER ALFBET (26)
C
        ALFBET (1) = 'A'
        ALFBET (2) = 'B'
        ...
        ALFBET (26) = 'Z'
        LTRCNT = 0
        WRDCNT = 0
        READ 15, TEXT
    15  FORMAT (50A1)
        PRINT, 'INPUT DATA  TEXT:', TEXT
C
C       SCNLOC IS LOCATION IN TEXT CURRENTLY BEING SCANNED
        SCNLOC = 0
        DO 18 WORD = 1, 50
C          OR UNTIL NO MORE WORDS IN TEXT
C
C          LOCATE BEGINNING OF NEXT WORD
           CALL LOCBEG (TEXT, SCNLOC, WRDBEG, WRDFND, ALFBET)
           IF (.NOT. WRDFND) THEN DO
              GO TO 19
           END IF
C
C          LOCATE END OF WORD
           CALL LOCEND (TEXT, SCNLOC, WRDEND, ALFBET)
           WRDLEN = WRDEND - WRDBEG + 1
           LTRCNT = LTRCNT + WRDLEN
           WRDCNT = WRDCNT + 1
    18  CONTINUE
C
    19  PRINT, 'AVERAGE WORD LENGTH =', FLOAT (LTRCNT) / WRDCNT
        STOP
        END
C
C
        SUBROUTINE LOCBEG (TEXT, SCNLOC, WRDBEG, WRDFND, ALFBET)
C       LOCATE THE BEGINNING OF THE NEXT WORD
C       SEARCH STARTS AFTER POSITION SCNLOC
C       IF A WORD IS FOUND, SCNLOC AND WRDBEG RETURN
C       THE POSITION OF ITS FIRST LETTER
C
        CHARACTER TEXT (50), ALFBET (26)
        INTEGER SCNLOC, WRDBEG, LOC, SLOC1
        LOGICAL WRDFND
C
```

```
      WRDFND = .FALSE.
C     SCAN FOR NEXT ALPHABETIC CHARACTER
      SLOC1 = SCNLOC + 1
      DO 18 LOC = SLOC1, 50
         IF (INDEX (ALFBET, 26, TEXT (LOC), 1) .GT. 0) THEN DO
            WRDFND = .TRUE.
            GO TO 19
         END IF
   18 CONTINUE
C
   19 WRDBEG = LOC
      SCNLOC = LOC
      RETURN
      END
C
C
      SUBROUTINE LOCEND (TEXT, SCNLOC, WRDEND, ALFBET)
C     LOCATE THE END OF THE WORD THAT BEGINS AT SCNLOC
C
      CHARACTER TEXT (50), ALFBET (26)
      INTEGER SCNLOC, WRDEND, LOC
      LOGICAL ENDFND
C
      ENDFND = .FALSE.
C     SCAN FOR NEXT NONALPHABETIC CHARACTER
      SLOC1 = SCNLOC + 1
      DO 18 LOC = SLOC1, 50
         IF (INDEX (ALFBET, 26, TEXT (LOC), 1) .EQ. 0) THEN DO
            ENDFND = .TRUE.
            GO TO 19
         END IF
   18 CONTINUE
C
   19 IF (ENDFND) THEN DO
         WRDEND = LOC - 1
         SCNLOC = LOC
      ELSE DO
         WRDEND = 50
      END IF
      RETURN
      END
```

```
INPUT DATA  TEXT: N E V E R   M I N D   T H E   W H Y S   A N D   W H E R E F O R E S .
AVERAGE WORD LENGTH =             4.8333330

INPUT DATA  TEXT: I   C O M P U T E D   T H E   A V E R A G E   W O R D   L E N G T H .
AVERAGE WORD LENGTH =             4.8333330
```

The sample execution printouts of the program WDLEN1 might suggest that to use average word length as a test for authorship, one should have a fairly large sample of text. In any case, average word length is no absolute criterion for deciding authorship. Nor is it an absolute indicator of artistic merit.

Modification for a Large Quantity of Text

If the amount of text is very large, then the computer might not have enough memory to hold it all at one time. Also, in some Fortran systems, there is a maximum length for character strings. For these reasons, it may be desirable to modify the program WDLEN1 so that it reads the text one line at a time, rather than all at once. The program WDLEN2 incorporates such a modification. Much of the main program WDLEN1 is put into the subroutine ONELIN (process one line). Note that some of the declarations that were in the main program of WDLEN1 are now in the subroutine ONELIN (process one line). The subroutines LOCBEG and LOCEND are not shown; they are the same as for the program WDLEN1.

```
C        PROGRAM WDLEN2
C        CALCULATE THE AVERAGE WORD LENGTH
C        OF INPUT TEXT WITH MANY LINES
C        STOP ON END OF FILE
C
         CHARACTER TEXT (50)
         INTEGER WRDCNT, LTRCNT, LINE
C
         LTRCNT = 0
         WRDCNT = 0
C
         DO 18 LINE = 1, 1000
            READ (5, 15, END = 19) TEXT
   15       FORMAT (50A1)
            PRINT, 'INPUT DATA  TEXT:', TEXT
            CALL ONELIN (TEXT, WRDCNT, LTRCNT)
   18    CONTINUE
C
   19    PRINT, 'AVERAGE WORD LENGTH =', FLOAT (LTRCNT) / WRDCNT
         STOP
         END
C
C
         SUBROUTINE ONELIN (TEXT, WRDCNT, LTRCNT)
C        ACCUMULATE STATISTICS ON ONE LINE OF INPUT TEXT
C
         CHARACTER TEXT (50)
         INTEGER WRDCNT, LTRCNT
         CHARACTER ALFBET (26)
         INTEGER WORD, SCNLOC, WRDBEG, WRDEND, WRDLEN
         LOGICAL WRDFND
C
         ALFBET (1) = 'A'
         ALFBET (2) = 'B'
         ...
         ALFBET (26) = 'Z'
C        SCNLOC IS LOCATION IN TEXT CURRENTLY BEING SCANNED
         SCNLOC = 0
         DO 18 WORD = 1, 50
C           OR UNTIL NO MORE WORDS IN TEXT
C
C           LOCATE BEGINNING OF NEXT WORD
            CALL LOCBEG (TEXT, SCNLOC, WRDBEG, WRDFND, ALFBET)
```

```
          IF (.NOT. WRDFND) THEN DO
             GO TO 19
          END IF
C
C         LOCATE END OF WORD
          CALL LOCEND (TEXT, SCNLOC, WRDEND, ALFBET)
          WRDLEN = WRDEND - WRDBEG + 1
          LTRCNT = LTRCNT + WRDLEN
          WRDCNT = WRDCNT + 1
   18  CONTINUE
   19  RETURN
       END
INPUT DATA  TEXT: O N E   O F   T H E   M O R E   I M P O R T A N T   U S E S
INPUT DATA  TEXT: O F   T H E   C H A R A C T E R   M A N I P U L A T I O N
INPUT DATA  TEXT: C A P A B I L I T Y   O F   C O M P U T E R S   I S
INPUT DATA  TEXT: I N   T H E   A N A L Y S I S   O F   T E X T .
AVERAGE WORD LENGTH =          4.8947360
```

Frequency of Occurrence of Letters

There are two basic ways to count the number of occurrences of each letter of the alphabet in a given text. Both ways use 27 counters, one for each letter of the alphabet and one to count all the other characters.

One way to tabulate letter frequencies in a line of text is first to scan it for all occurrences of the letter "A", then to scan it for all occurrences of the letter "B", and so on through the alphabet. This requires 26 scans of the whole line. This method is embodied in the program LTRCT1 (letter count 1).

```
      PROGRAM LTRCT1
      Initialize
      DO 28 LINE = 1, MANY
         Read line of text
         If no more text, exit loop
         DO 18 LETTER = 'A', 'Z'
            Scan line of text, counting occurrences of that letter
            Calculate the number of nonletters and increment nonletter total
   18    CONTINUE
   28 CONTINUE
      Print the counts
      END
```

The second way to count letter frequencies in a line of text is to begin with the first symbol of the text, to decide which of the 27 counters to increment, to continue with the second letter of the line of text, to see which counter to increment this time, and so on through the text. This second way is implemented by the program LTRCT2.

```
      PROGRAM LTRCT2
      Initialize
      DO 28 LINE = 1, MANY
         Read a line of text
         If no more text, exit loop
```

```
         DO 18 for each character in the line of text
            If the character is a letter then
               increment the count for that letter
            else
               increment the nonletter count
            end if
   18    CONTINUE
   28 CONTINUE
      Print the counts
      END
```

By the method of the program LTRCT1, the text must be scanned completely once for each letter of the alphabet. By the method of the program LTRCT2, the text is scanned just once. Thus the second program executes considerably faster than the first one and so only the program LTRCT2 is refined.

Unfortunately, in Fortran, the subscripts of the array of counters cannot be 'A', 'B', etc. A subscript must be type integer. Therefore, subscripts 1 through 26 are used to count the number of occurrences of each letter of the alphabet and subscript 27 is used to count the characters that are not letters.

```
C     PROGRAM LTRCT2
C     COUNT FREQUENCY OF OCCURRENCE IN A TEXT
C     OF EACH LETTER OF THE ALPHABET
C     VARIABLES:
C        COUNT (1) - COUNT (26) = COUNTS OF A - Z
C        COUNT (27) = COUNT OF NONLETTERS
C
      CHARACTER TEXT (50), ALFBET (26)
      INTEGER LETTER, COUNT (27)
      INTEGER LINE
C
      ALFBET (1) = 'A'
      ALFBET (2) = 'B'
      ...
      ALFBET (1) = 'Z'
      DO 18 LETTER = 1, 27
         COUNT (LETTER) = 0
   18 CONTINUE
C
      DO 28 LINE = 1, 1000
         READ (5, 15, END = 29) TEXT
   15    FORMAT (50A1)
         PRINT, 'INPUT DATA  TEXT:', TEXT
C        COUNT THE LETTERS IN THE CURRENT LINE
         CALL CNTLTR (TEXT, ALFBET, COUNT)
   28 CONTINUE
C
C     PRINT THE FREQUENCY COUNTS
   29 CALL PRINTC (COUNT, ALFBET)
      STOP
      END
C
C
      SUBROUTINE CNTLTR (TEXT, ALFBET, COUNT)
C     COUNT LETTERS IN ONE LINE OF TEXT
C
```

```
      CHARACTER TEXT (50), ALFBET (26)
      INTEGER COUNT (27)
      INTEGER I, LETTER, TRMLEN, TLEN
C
      TLEN = TRMLEN (TEXT, 50)
      DO 18 I = 1, TLEN
         LETTER = INDEX (ALFBET, 26, TEXT (I), 1)
         IF (LETTER .EQ. 0) THEN DO
            LETTER = 27
         END IF
         COUNT (LETTER) = COUNT (LETTER) + 1
   18 CONTINUE
      RETURN
      END
C
C
      SUBROUTINE PRINTC (COUNT, ALFBET)
C     PRINT THE FREQUENCY COUNTS
C
      INTEGER COUNT (27), LETTER
      CHARACTER ALFBET (26)
C
      PRINT, ' '
      PRINT 15, 'LETTER', 'FREQUENCY'
   15 FORMAT (T2, 2A10)
      DO 18 LETTER = 1, 26
         PRINT 25, ALFBET (LETTER), COUNT (LETTER)
   18 CONTINUE
      PRINT 25, 'OTHER', COUNT (27)
   25 FORMAT (T2, A10, I10)
      RETURN
      END
INPUT DATA  TEXT: O N E   O F   T H E   I M P O R T A N T
INPUT DATA  TEXT: T E X T   A N A L Y S I S   T E C H N I Q U E S
INPUT DATA  TEXT: ( T O   D E T E R M I N E   A U T H O R S H I P )
INPUT DATA  TEXT: I S   T O   M A K E   A   F R E Q U E N C Y   C O U N T
INPUT DATA  TEXT: O F   L E T T E R S   I N   T H E   T E X T .

    LETTER FREQUENCY
         A         6
         B         0
         C         3
         D         1
         E        15
         F         3
         G         0
         H         5
         I         7
         J         0
         K         1
         L         2
         M         3
         N         8
         O         8
         P         2
```

```
         Q         2
         R         5
         S         6
         T        16
         U         4
         V         0
         W         0
         X         2
         Y         2
         Z         0
     OTHER        19
```

Palindromes

Another aspect of text analysis is searching for patterns. Perhaps the text repeats itself every so often, or perhaps the lengths of the words form an interesting sequence of numbers. One pattern for which we search here is called a "palindrome", meaning that the text reads the same from right to left as from left to right. The word "radar" is a palindrome, for example. Liberal palindromers customarily relax the rules so that punctuation, spacing, and capitalization are ignored. To liberal palindromers, the names "Eve", "Hannah", and "Otto" are all palindromes, as is the sentence

"Able was I ere I saw Elba."

something Napoleon might have said, except that he preferred speaking French.

The program PAL satisfies the most conservative palindromers. As the two sample runs show, it accepts the string

"NAT SAW I WAS TAN"

as a palindrome, but it rejects the string

"MADAM I'M ADAM"

One of the exercises involves writing a subroutine that excises from a string everything but the letters and another exercise deals with writing a program using this subroutine that applies a more liberal palindrome test.

```
C     PROGRAM PAL
C     TESTS FOR A PALINDROME
C
      CHARACTER TEXT (50), CORBLK *5
      INTEGER I, J, TRMLEN, JJ
      LOGICAL MATCH
C
      READ 15, TEXT
   15 FORMAT (50A1)
      PRINT, 'INPUT DATA  TEXT:', TEXT
C
      J = TRMLEN (TEXT, 50)
      JJ =J
      MATCH = .TRUE.
      DO 18 I = 1, JJ
         IF (TEXT (I) .NE. TEXT (J)) THEN DO
            MATCH = .FALSE.
            GO TO 19
```

```
            ELSE DO
               J = J - 1
            END IF
   18    CONTINUE
C
   19    IF (MATCH) THEN DO
            PRINT, 'PALINDROME'
         ELSE DO
            PRINT, 'NOT A PALINDROME'
            CALL CONVRT (TEXT (I), CORBLK)
            PRINT, 'CHARACTER', I, 'FROM THE LEFT IS', CORBLK
            CALL CONVRT (TEXT (J), CORBLK)
            PRINT, 'CHARACTER', I, 'FROM THE RIGHT IS', CORBLK
         END IF
         STOP
         END
C
C
         SUBROUTINE CONVRT (C, CORBLK)
C        TESTS IF C IS BLANK
C        RETURNS 'BLANK' IF IT IS,
C        RETURNS C OTHERWISE
         CHARACTER CORBLK *5, C *1
C
         IF (C .EQ. ' ') THEN DO
            CORBLK = 'BLANK'
         ELSE DO
            CORBLK = C
         END IF
         RETURN
         END
INPUT DATA  TEXT: N A T   S A W   I   W A S   T A N
PALINDROME

INPUT DATA  TEXT: M A D A M   I ' M   A D A M
NOT A PALINDROME
CHARACTER              5 FROM THE LEFT IS M
CHARACTER              5 FROM THE RIGHT IS BLANK
```

Readings

Morton, A.Q. *Literary Detection: How to Prove Authorship and Fraud in Literature and Documents*. New York: Charles Scribner's Sons, 1979. (Reviewed in *Scientific American*, Nov. 1979, p. 39.)

7.4 What You Should Know

1. A character string is a sequence of characters.
2. Character constants are enclosed in apostrophes.
3. Character string variables are declared of type CHARACTER.
4. Each character variable has a declared length, written after the variable name (and an asterisk) in the declaration.
5. Character string values may be assigned to a character variable by an assignment statement.

6. If the assigned value is too short for the variable receiving the value, blanks are added on the right; if the assigned value is too long, characters are dropped from the right.
7. Character input data to be read using the default format is enclosed in apostrophes.
8. Using default format, short input strings are padded with blanks on the right and long input strings are truncated on the right.
9. Character input data to be read using an A format descriptor is not enclosed in apostrophes. The length in the A format descriptor determines how many input characters are read.
10. Character values may be compared using the six operations .LT., .GT., .EQ., .LE., .GE., and .NE.
11. One character value is "less than" another if the first value precedes the second value in an extension of lexicographic (i.e., dictionary) order.
12. A substring of a character string is any sequence of consecutive characters from the character string.
13. If the individual characters of a string must be accessed, a character string is stored as an array of single characters.
14. A loop is used to move or change a substring of length more than one.
15. The programmer-defined function INDEX returns the starting position where one character string (specified by its first and second argument) is found as a substring of another character string (specified by its third and fourth argument). If the search string never appears as a substring, the function value is zero. If it appears more than once, the starting position of the leftmost occurrence is the function value.
16. The trimmed length of a character string is the length of the string if terminal blanks are ignored. A programmer-defined function TRMLEN is used to calculate trimmed lengths.
17. A document may be stored as an array of text lines.
18. A word processing or text-editing program allows the user to create, modify, save, and print a document using a computer.
19. Documents are saved in disk files in auxiliary memory for permanence.
20. Documents are recalled from disk files at the start of an editing session.
21. Computer programs can compute statistics about the characteristics of an input text to aid in its analysis for authorship, authenticity, etc.
22. A palindrome is a character string that reads the same from right to left as it does from left to right.

7.5 Self-Test Questions

Section 7.1

1. What is the length of each of the following character strings?

```
'5 FEET'
'ALPHABET'
'ABCDEFGHIJKLMNOPQRSTUVWXYZ'
'42'
```

2. List all the substrings of length 3 of the string 'ALPHABET'.

7.6 Programming Exercises

1. **Purpose:** To practice using substrings.

   The problem: Read a character string of maximum length 50, and print all substrings of length 3.

   Input data: If you can't think of anything better, use

```
'THESE ARE THE TIMES THAT TRY MEN'S SOULS'
```

Sample output:

```
THE
HES
ESE
.
.
.
ULS
```

2. **Purpose:** To become familiar with comparison of character strings.

   The problem: Sort a list of at most 200 character strings.

   Input data: Each character string is at most 50 characters long and occupies the leftmost positions of one line in the input file. Use the end-of-file test to terminate reading of input data.

   Sample output: First a line-by-line echo of the input data as it is read from the input file. Then a printout of the sorted list.

   Remarks: You may be surprised at what happens if you accidentally type a blank in the leftmost column of one of the lines in the input file. Then again, after you think about it, you might not be.

3. **Purpose:** To combine searching a list and character strings.

   The problem: A computer system maintains a list of valid passwords. Write a program that accepts an 8-character password and checks it against its list of valid passwords. The program should print OK if the password is in the list and TRY AGAIN if it is not. Give the user two additional tries, replying with successively nastier messages each time the user fails to give the correct password.

   Hint: Keep a list of responses as well as a list of passwords.

   Input data: An 8-character password.

   Sample output:

```
WELCOME TO THE SUPER SPECIAL SIMULATED SYSTEM
ENTER YOUR PASSWORD:
BUG FREE
TRY AGAIN
ENTER YOUR PASSWORD:
SILICON
ARE YOU SURE YOU ARE HAVE A PASSWORD
ENTER YOUR PASSWORD:
FORTRAN
OK
```

4. **Purpose:** To provide some practice in decomposing and combining character strings.

   The problem: Mark Twain wrote in "The Awful German Language" (in *A Tramp Abroad*) that he heard a California student in Heidelberg say, in one of his calmest moods, that he would rather decline two drinks than one German adjective. Write a program to help out this California student.

Input data: A German adjective, for example

```
GUT
```

Sample execution:

```
INPUT DATA  ADJ:  GUT

DER GUTES MANN       DIE GUTE FRAU       DAS GUTE KIND
DES GUTEN MANNES     DER GUTEN FRAU      DES GUTEN KINDES
DEM GUTEN MANN       DER GUTEN FRAU      DEM GUTEN KIND
DEN GUTEN MANN       DIE GUTE FRAU       DAS GUTE KIND
```

5. **Purpose:** To test extracting individual characters from a character string.

   The problem: Read a character string of maximum length 50 as input and print it in reverse order. Ignore trailing blanks.

   Program requirement: You must use a subroutine REVERS (STRING) to reverse the input string. You can't just read the string and run the subscript in the PRINT loop backward.

   Input data: A character string, for example,

```
UNTIL
```

Sample Output:

```
INPUT DATA  STRING:  UNTIL
LITNU
```

6. **Purpose:** To have some more fun with character strings.

   The problem: Nicely displayed headings add impact to a document. Write a program to take a character string as input and print it surrounded by a border of asterisks. Again, ignore trailing blanks in the input. Leave one blank before the first character and after the last character in the display.

   Input data: A character string representing the title of a document.

```
PAYROLL REPORT
```

Sample execution:

```
INPUT DATA  TITLE:  PAYROLL REPORT

******************
* PAYROLL REPORT *
******************
```

7. **Purpose:** To practice excising substrings.

   The problem: In a Fortran program, all blanks not within a character constant are ignored. Most Fortran compilers immediately remove these blanks to simplify the processing.

   a) Write a program to move all blanks that occur in an input string to the end of the string.

   b) Modify the program so that blanks within matched pairs of apostrophes are not removed.

   Input data:

```
DO 18 I = 1, 10
```

Sample execution:

```
INPUT DATA  SOURCE:  DO 18 I = 1, 10
DOI81=1,10
```

8. **Purpose:** To add features to the word processing program EDIT written in this chapter.

   The problem: A word processor grows in power and convenience by adding new features and capabilities, without altering the basic structure or making previously written features obsolete. Add to EDIT the capability of printing a single line, locating any sequence of characters within a line, and replacing a sequence of characters within a line with another sequence of characters. Use both the original and the modified versions of the text editor EDIT to convert the most recent version of the text shown in the sample executions of EDIT into an appropriate portion of the Gettysburg Address. Use the results as a basis of comparison of the ease of use of the two text editors.
9. **Purpose:** To get some practice analyzing a text.

   The problem: Calculate the ratio of letters in the first half of the alphabet to letters in the second half of the alphabet in an input text. If you have any idea about the significance of this statistic, tell us or publish it. We just give this problem for practice in programming.

   Input data: About 1000 words of typical text.

   Sample output: One real number, the ratio.
10. **Purpose:** Partly pure party pastime; partly programming proficiency.

    The problem: An alliteration is a sequence of words all starting with the same letter. Write a program ALLIT that counts how many consecutive words in an input text start with the letter P.

    Input data: Try this sentence

```
IN HIS POPULAR PAPERBACK, "PARTY PASTIMES PEOPLE PREFER,"
PROMINENT POLO PLAYER PAUL PERKINS PRESENTS PLEASING PALINDROMES.
```

Sample output:

```
14
```

MULTI-DIMENSIONAL ARRAYS

The array construct allows the name of a particular piece of information to be specified by a two-step process. First, the array name specifies a group of data items, and second, the subscript identifies a particular item within the group. The arrays in Chapter 6 were all one-dimensional arrays, also called **linear lists**, because position within the array or list is specified by one subscript.

Some data are naturally organized in such a way that it takes two independent indices to specify which item is meant. A **table** is an organization of data in which each entry is uniquely specified by its row number and its column number. In Fortran, such a structure is a **two-dimensional array**, a construct just like a one-dimensional array, except, of course, that two subscripts are used.

Digital images are pictures made by selectively coloring or shading a two-dimensional array of dots. Television images and newspaper or magazine pictures, called "halftones", are familiar examples. The individual dots are called **pixels**, short for "picture elements". The quality of the image depends on the size of the pixels. Large pixels create images that are obviously digital. Extremely small pixels, below the level of visual resolution at the usual viewing distances, create digital images indistinguishable from continuous images. The same principles of digital image processing apply to both coarse, low-resolution digital images and to fine, high-resolution computer graphics.

Sections 8.2 and 8.3 discuss how to write programs to produce **digital computer graphics** based on input data or equations, and to process digital images acquired by photographic means. Depending on the hardware available for printing or displaying the image and the number of pixels that can be processed in the available computer time, the resulting image may vary from a "cross stitch" design with pixels the size of printed letters to a high-resolution digital image with pixels the size of individual ink molecules.

8.1 Tables

An array variable with two subscripts is a **table**. The first subscript is often called the **row** number, and the second subscript the **column** number. After elementary examples involving a multiplication table and a telephone rate table, the next section concentrates on tables used in computer graphics, including visual image processing.

Section Preview

Table:

A table is an array with two subscripts.

General Form:

type name (constant, constant)

Examples:

```
REAL TABLE (5, 10)
CHARACTER FLAG *1 (21, 41)
```

Multiplication Table

One of the most familiar tables is the multiplication table. Each entry is the product of its row number and its column number. The program MULTT produces a copy of the multiplication table.

```
C       PROGRAM MULTT
        INTEGER MTABLE (10, 10), ROW, COL
C
        DO 28 ROW = 1, 10
           DO 18 COL = 1, 10
              MTABLE (ROW, COL) = ROW * COL
   18      CONTINUE
   28   CONTINUE
C
C       PRINT TABLE
        DO 38 ROW = 1, 10
           PRINT 35, (MTABLE (ROW, COL), COL = 1, 10)
   35      FORMAT (10I5)
   38   CONTINUE
        STOP
        END
```

```
    1    2    3    4    5    6    7    8    9   10
    2    4    6    8   10   12   14   16   18   20
    3    6    9   12   15   18   21   24   27   30
    4    8   12   16   20   24   28   32   36   40
    5   10   15   20   25   30   35   40   45   50
    6   12   18   24   30   36   42   48   54   60
    7   14   21   28   35   42   49   56   63   70
    8   16   24   32   40   48   56   64   72   80
    9   18   27   36   45   54   63   72   81   90
   10   20   30   40   50   60   70   80   90  100
```

As shown in the assignment and PRINT statement of the program MULTT, two subscripts are written within parentheses. The second subscript must be separated from the first by a comma. As illustrated, it is quite common in programs that deal with tables to have a DO block for the columns nested within a DO block for the rows. The section of the program MULTT that prints the table also contains two nested loops: an outer DO block for the row, and an inner implied DO loop for the column in the PRINT statement. The inner loop must be an implied DO loop because all ten values are to be printed on the same line.

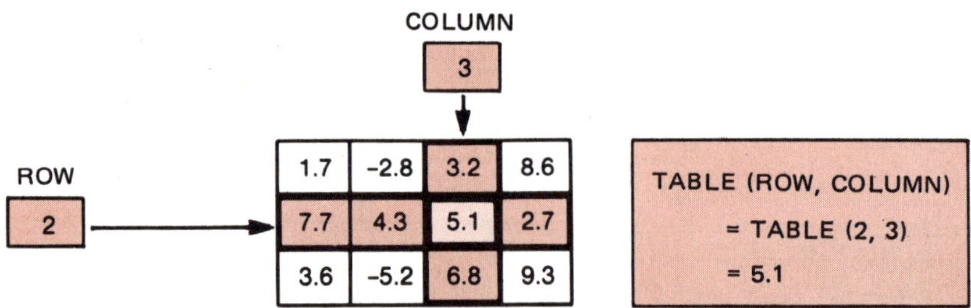

Figure 8.1 Referencing an entry in a table.

Case Study:

Calculating the billing charges for a long-distance telephone call is another elementary example of the use of a table. The rates depend upon the time of the day the call is placed. To encourage use of the telephone company's facilities and equipment during under-utilized hours, the rates in effect during peak daytime hours are usually reduced somewhat in the evening, and further reduced at night. Table 8.1 is a simplified version of such a telephone rate table, giving the charge for the initial 3 minutes of direct-dialed long-distance calls from Fun City to selected garden spots on the eastern seaboard. Weekend and holiday rates are omitted to simplify the program PHONE, which computes the long-distance telephone charges based on this table.

Table 8.1 Telephone Charges for the Initial 3 Minutes of Direct-Dialed Long-Distance Calls Placed from Fun City.

	Code for City	Day, Code 1	Evening, Code 2	Night, Code 3
Hoboken	1	.65	.45	.25
Paramus	2	.70	.50	.25
Peapack	3	.80	.55	.30
Piscataway	4	.70	.50	.25
Secaucus	5	.60	.40	.20
Tenafly	6	.60	.40	.20
Weehauken	7	.65	.45	.25

If a call lasts 3 minutes or less, then the customer pays the 3-minute basic rate. If the call runs over, there is an overtime charge proportional to the basic rate. The full charge before tax is the sum of the basic rate and the overtime charge. A tax of 10 percent is added, and the resulting amount is rounded to the nearest whole cent for printing.

```
C       PROGRAM PHONE
C       CALCULATES CHARGES FOR A LONG DISTANCE CALL
C
```

```
      INTEGER NRCITY, NRRATE, CTYCOD, RATCOD
      REAL BASTIM, TAXRAT
      REAL RATE (7, 3)
      REAL BASCHG, OVRTIM, BEFTAX, COST, DURATN
C     INITIALIZE NAMED CONSTANTS
      NRCITY = 7
      NRRATE = 3
      BASTIM = 3.0
      TAXRAT = 0.10
C
C     READ RATES
      DO 18 CTYCOD = 1, NRCITY
         READ, (RATE (CTYCOD, RATCOD), RATCOD = 1, NRRATE)
   18 CONTINUE
C
C     READ DATA PERTINENT TO CHARGES FOR THIS CALL
      READ, CTYCOD, RATCOD, DURATN
      PRINT, 'INPUT DATA  CTYCOD:', CTYCOD
      PRINT, '            RATCOD:', RATCOD
      PRINT 15, '            DURATN:', DURATN
   15 FORMAT (T2, A19, F6.2)
C
C     CALCULATE THE CHARGE
      BASCHG = RATE (CTYCOD, RATCOD)
      IF (DURATN .LE. BASTIM) THEN DO
         OVRTIM = 0
      ELSE DO
         OVRTIM = DURATN - BASTIM
      END IF
C
      BEFTAX = BASCHG + OVRTIM * (BASCHG / BASTIM)
      COST = BEFTAX * (1 + TAXRAT)
C
C     PRINT CHARGE TO CUSTOMER
      PRINT 25, 'CHARGE FOR THIS CALL:  $', COST
      FORMAT (T2, A24, F5.2)
      STOP
      END
```

```
INPUT DATA  CTYCOD:           3
            RATCOD:           2
            DURATN: 19.00
CHARGE FOR THIS CALL:  $ 3.83
```

8.2 Graphics

Viewed from a sufficient distance, a closely spaced array of dots looks like a continuous image. A computer produces digital images from instructions on the location and intensity of the dots. The same techniques are used, regardless of the resolution of the image.

Section Preview

A **digital image** is made up of an array of pixels, or picture elements.

In **printer graphics** each pixel is displayed as a printable character.

Superposition:

A method of building a digital image by using an array to hold values for each pixel of the digital image. The values in the array may be modified, thereby "superimposing" several patterns, before the digital image is printed or displayed.

Digital Images

A **digital image** consists of a two-dimensional array of pixels. The digital image is produced by displaying or printing different shades of black, white, gray, or different colors in some of the **pixels**.

In a newspaper photograph, each pixel is printed as a black dot whose size varies from pixel to pixel. Extremely dark regions have dots so large that they overlap and fill almost all the available space. Light regions have small dots with a great deal of white paper showing between them. A small magnifying glass will show the dots clearly. It is only when the digital image is viewed at a sufficient distance that the individual pixels are not the focus of attention and the effect of a continuous image is produced.

Television pictures are digital images produced using pixels of three different colors. If you look at a color television screen with a magnifying glass, you will see that its pixels come in groups of three, a red pixel, a green pixel, and a blue pixel. Each pixel is controlled individually to produce an intensity of its primary color from black (off) to the maximum intensity of that color the television screen is capable of producing.

Most computer display screens, including the ones usually used for displaying text, use digital images whose pixels are either on (bright) or off (dark). If you look at a display screen closely or with a magnifying glass, you will see how selected pixels are turned on and others turned off to form the letters and characters of the text. Many dot matrix printers use the same technique to form characters.

Although the size of the pixels and number of different possible colors or shades for an individual pixel certainly affect the resolution and quality of the digital image, the basic principles of digital image production are the same, no matter how many pixels are used. The standard language Fortran has no special features for controlling graphic output devices. However, in Fortran systems where graphic output is available, there are usually additional, nonstandard built-in subroutines to control the graphic output devices.

In **printer graphics**, printable characters are used to display the pixels. The resolution is not good. Ten characters per inch horizontally and six characters per inch vertically is typical. However, the programming principles are the same, and a full page of printer graphics, viewed from a sufficient distance, appears somewhat continuous. The major problem is that no printable character is truly black, filling with ink 100% of the space allocated to a character.

The programs in this section and Section 8.3 produce printer graphics. The higher resolution digital graphics shown in these two sections were produced using a microcomputer that supports Fortran and dot image graphics. The modifications to the programs were minor, consisting largely of increasing the size of the image arrays and using the nonstandard built-in subroutines for graphic output.

Tables of Characters

There is no reason why the values in a table must be numeric. The program ASTRSK prints a 9 × 20 rectangle of asterisks, a simple graphic. Since the length of each element of the array BLOCK is one, the output format prints the characters with no extra blanks inserted between them.

> *Programming Note:* The print list can be shorter than the format specifications. The extra format specifications are ignored.

```
C       PROGRAM ASTRSK
        INTEGER NRROWS, NRCOLS
        INTEGER ROW, COL
        CHARACTER BLOCK *1 (9, 20)
C
        NRROWS = 9
        NRCOLS = 20
C       FILL BLOCK WITH ASTERISKS
        DO 28 ROW = 1, NRROWS
           DO 18 COL = 1, NRCOLS
              BLOCK (ROW, COL) = '*'
   18      CONTINUE
   28   CONTINUE
C
C       PRINT BLOCK OF ASTERISKS
        DO 38 ROW = 1, NRROWS
           PRINT 35, (BLOCK (ROW, COL), COL = 1, NRCOLS)
   35      FORMAT (T4, 99A1)
   38   CONTINUE
        STOP
        END
```

```
   ********************
   ********************
   ********************
   ********************
   ********************
   ********************
   ********************
   ********************
   ********************
```

Superposition

The fundamental principle in printing more complicated graphics is to decompose them into simple shapes. In applying this principle, a programmer may make good use of **superposition**, superimposing new shapes over pre-existing parts of the graphic. The program GRAPHIC uses the superposition of shapes to produce a rectangular box with an X in it.

```
C       PROGRAM GRAPHIC
        INTEGER NRROWS, NRCOLS, NRROW2, NRCOL3
        CHARACTER STAR *1, BLANK *1
        INTEGER ROW, COL, STRTCL, STOPCL, STRTC5, STOPC5
        CHARACTER GRAPH *1 (17, 48)
C
```

```
      NRROWS = 17
      NRCOLS = 48
      STAR = '*'
      BLANK = ' '
C
C     START WITH A BLOCK OF STARS
      DO 28 ROW = 1, NRROWS
         DO 18 COL = 1, NRCOLS
            GRAPH (ROW, COL) = STAR
   18    CONTINUE
   28 CONTINUE
C
C     SUPERIMPOSE A BLOCK OF BLANKS IN THE MIDDLE
C     LEAVING A BORDER OF STARS
      NRROW2 = NRROWS - 2
      DO 48 ROW = 3, NRROW2
         NRCOL3 = NRCOLS - 3
         DO 38 COL = 4, NRCOL3
            GRAPH (ROW, COL) = BLANK
   38    CONTINUE
   48 CONTINUE
C
C     DIAGONAL BAR FROM UPPER LEFT TO LOWER RIGHT
      STRTCL = 4
      DO 68 ROW = 3, NRROW2
         STRTC5 = STRTCL + 5
         DO 58 COL = STRTCL, STRTC5
            GRAPH (ROW, COL) = STAR
   58    CONTINUE
         STRTCL = STRTCL + 3
   68 CONTINUE
C
C     DIAGONAL BAR FROM UPPER RIGHT TO LOWER LEFT
      STOPCL = NRCOLS - 3
      DO 88 ROW = 3, NRROW2
         STOPC5 = STOPCL - 5
         DO 78 COL = STOPC5, STOPCL
            GRAPH (ROW, COL) = STAR
   78    CONTINUE
         STOPCL = STOPCL - 3
   88 CONTINUE
C
C     PRINT THE GRAPHIC
      DO 98 ROW = 1, NRROWS
         PRINT 95, (GRAPH (ROW, COL), COL = 1, NRCOLS)
   95    FORMAT (T4, 99A1)
   98 CONTINUE
      STOP
      END
```

```
************************************************
************************************************
*********                              *********
***   ******                        ******   ***
***      ******                  ******      ***
***         ******            ******         ***
***            ******      ******            ***
***               *************              ***
***                  ******                  ***
***               *************              ***
***            ******      ******            ***
***         ******            ******         ***
***      ******                  ******      ***
***   ******                        ******   ***
*********                              *********
************************************************
************************************************
```

Plotting a Histogram

Another type of computer graphic easily produced on a printer is a histogram, a frequency distribution bar graph. Suppose, for example, that at a liberal arts college the registrar reports that there were 5281 As, 6003 Bs, 6717 Cs, 3118 Ds, 2644 Fs, and 241 grades of incomplete given out in the fall semester. The program GRADES plots a vertical bar graph in which the height of each bar is proportional to the number of letter grades of that type given out. This makes it easier to see the general characteristics of the grade distribution pattern.

```
C       PROGRAM GRADES
C       PLOT A HISTOGRAM
C
        INTEGER NRLTRS, NRROWS, NRCOLS, LINLEN, J, NINT
        INTEGER LETTER, ROW, COL, NRGRDS, BARHGT, TOPBAR, TOPBR1
        INTEGER BEGCOL, ENDCOL, FREQ (6)
        REAL PERCNT (6), X
        CHARACTER STAR *1, BLANK *1
        CHARACTER HSTGRM *1 (20, 36)
C
        NINT (X) = INT (X + 0.5)
C
        STAR = '*'
        BLANK = ' '
        NRLTRS = 6
        NRROWS = 20
        NRCOLS = 36
        LINLEN = 40
C
C       READ GRADE FREQUENCIES AND
C       CALCULATE TOTAL NUMBER OF GRADES
C       1, 2, ..., 6 REPRESENT GRADES A, B, C, D, F, INC
        NRGRDS = 0
        PRINT, 'INPUT DATA  FREQUENCIES:'
```

```
      DO 18 LETTER = 1, NRLTRS
         READ, FREQ (LETTER)
         PRINT, FREQ (LETTER)
         NRGRDS = NRGRDS + FREQ (LETTER)
   18 CONTINUE
C
C     COMPUTE PERCENTAGES AND CREATE HISTOGRAM
      DO 68 LETTER = 1, NRLTRS
         PERCNT (LETTER) = 100 * (FREQ (LETTER) / FLOAT (NRGRDS))
         BARHGT = NINT (PERCNT (LETTER) / 5)
C
C        ROW 1 IS AT TOP OF GRAPH
         TOPBAR = 21 - BARHGT
         BEGCOL = 6 * LETTER - 5
         ENDCOL = 6 * LETTER - 1
         DO 48 COL = BEGCOL, ENDCOL
C           BLANK OUT PART ABOVE BAR
            TOPBR1 = TOPBAR - 1
            IF (TOPBR1 .GE. 1) THEN DO
               DO 28 ROW = 1, TOPBR1
                  HSTGRM (ROW, COL) = BLANK
   28          CONTINUE
            END IF
C
C           FILL IN BAR WITH STARS
            IF (TOPBAR .LE. NRROWS) THEN DO
               DO 38 ROW = TOPBAR, NRROWS
                  HSTGRM (ROW, COL) = STAR
   38          CONTINUE
            END IF
C
   48    CONTINUE
C
C        PUT BLANKS BETWEEN BARS
         DO 58 ROW = 1, NRROWS
            HSTGRM (ROW, 6 * LETTER) = BLANK
   58    CONTINUE
C
   68 CONTINUE
C
      PRINT, ' '
      PRINT 15, ('_', J = 1, LINLEN)
   15 FORMAT (T5, 99A1)
      PRINT 25, 'LETTER GRADE DISTRIBUTION'
   25 FORMAT (T5, A25)
      PRINT, ' '
C
C     PRINT THE ROWS THAT ARE NOT ALL BLANK
      DO 88 ROW = 1, NRROWS
```

```
C          CHECK IF ROW IS ALL BLANK
           DO 78 COL = 1, NRCOLS
              IF (HSTGRM (ROW, COL) .NE. BLANK) THEN
                 PRINT 15, (HSTGRM (ROW, J), J = 1, NRCOLS)
                 GO TO 88
              END IF
   78      CONTINUE
   88   CONTINUE
C
        PRINT 15, ('_', J = 1, LINLEN)
        PRINT 35, 'A', 'B', 'C', 'D', 'F', 'INC'
   35   FORMAT (T2, 5A6, A7)
        PRINT, ' '
        PRINT 45, 'VERTICAL SCALE:  1 LINE = 5%'
   45   FORMAT (T5, A28)
        PRINT, ' '
        PRINT 55, 'PERCENTS:',
     +          (PERCNT (LETTER), LETTER = 1, NRLTRS)
   55   FORMAT (T5, A9, 6F6.2)
        STOP
        END
INPUT DATA  FREQUENCIES:
         5281
         6003
         6717
         3118
         2644
          241

 ________________________________________
 LETTER GRADE DISTRIBUTION

             *****
       ***** *****
 ***** ***** *****
 ***** ***** ***** *****
 ***** ***** ***** ***** *****
 ***** ***** ***** ***** *****
 ________________________________________
   A     B     C     D     F    INC

    VERTICAL SCALE:  1 LINE = 5%

    PERCENTS: 22.00 25.01 27.98 12.99 11.01  1.00
```

The first step in plotting this histogram is to obtain a total number of grades for the college during that semester. Next, each frequency is divided by the total number of grades to obtain the proportion of the total for each letter grade, and then multiplied by 100 to obtain the percentage. In the program grades, each bar is five columns wide, with one blank between the bars. Each 5 percent of the total distribution is plotted as a bar one line high. Rounding of the computed bar heights is necessary because, in the printed output, the height of each bar must be an integer. For a different distribution, a programmer might make different decisions about the size and scale of the histogram.

Based on the same data as in the sample execution of the program grades, the higher-resolution HSTGRM shown in Figure 8.2 was plotted using a microcomputer. To match the resolution of screen graphics on this computer, the array, HSTGRM, was increased in size to 160 rows by 280 columns.

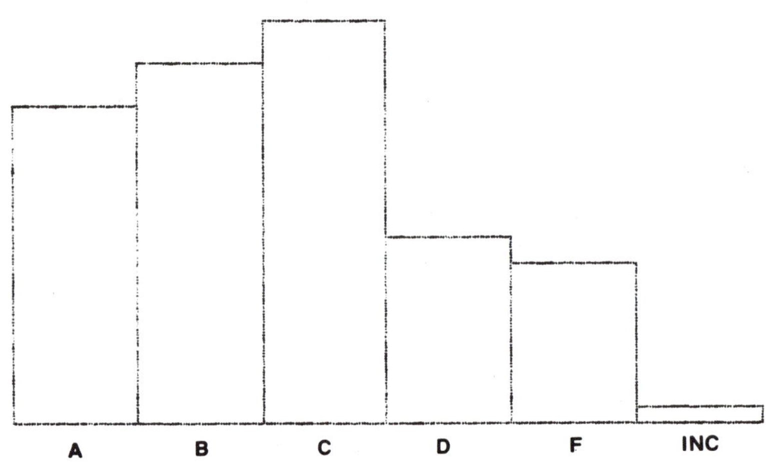

Figure 8.2 Higher-resolution histogram using the same data as in the program grades.

Plotting a Graph

Many computer installations have special graph-plotting equipment that can be directed by a computer. At installations that have an incremental plotter or a television-type display tube, a collection of graphics subroutines is usually available written in popular computer languages. This allows a programmer to write the calculation part of a program in a general-purpose computer language and call the appropriate graphics subroutine to display the answers. Besides general graphics subroutines, some installations have a library of specialized graphics subroutines designed for specific applications like architectural drawing, contour mapping, and so on (see Figure 8.3).

Rather than use specialized equipment, the program PRBOLA (parabola) uses the printer to plot a graph of the function $y = x^2$.

```
PROGRAM PRBOLA
Put blanks everywhere
Put minus signs on the x-axis
Put vertical lines on the y-axis
Put a plus sign at the origin
DO for each column in the graph
   Convert the column number to an X value
   Calculate Y = X ** 2
   Convert Y value to row number
   Put an asterisk in the correct row and column in the graph
Print the graph
```

Before the program PRBOLA can be refined, it is necessary to specify in more detail what is wanted. One important detail is the selection of a range for the variables X and Y. A decision is made to graph the region of the plane with both x and y coordinates between -1 and $+1$. Then a decision is made

Figure 8.3 Graphic display terminals produce complex images as combinations of lines, points, and curves. Using the same generating techniques as for printer graphics, much finer detail is possible on a television-type display screen. The light pen shown may be used for graphic input by transmitting its coordinates to a computer.

to use 20 columns for each unit distance in the x direction, and only 10 lines per unit distance in the y direction, because the spacing between lines is somewhat greater than that between successive characters on the same line. Thus the range of subscripts is from 1 to 41 for column numbers, and from 1 to 21 for row numbers. The "extra" row and column, $2 \times 20 + 1$ and $2 \times 10 + 1$, are used so that both end points of the interval from -1 to 1 may be plotted. The function NINT is written as a one-line statement function that rounds positive values to the nearest integer.

The program PRBOLA can now be refined as shown.

```
C       PROGRAM PRBOLA
C       DRAWS A PARABOLA
C
        INTEGER ROWMAX, COLMAX
        CHARACTER GRAPH *1 (21, 41)
C
        ROWMAX = 21
        COLMAX = 41
        CALL BLANKS (GRAPH, ROWMAX, COLMAX)
        CALL XAXIS (GRAPH, ROWMAX, COLMAX)
        CALL YAXIS (GRAPH, ROWMAX, COLMAX)
        CALL ORIGIN (GRAPH, ROWMAX, COLMAX)
        CALL CURVE (GRAPH, ROWMAX, COLMAX)
```

```
      CALL PRINTG (GRAPH, ROWMAX, COLMAX)
      STOP
      END
C
C
      SUBROUTINE BLANKS (GRAPH, ROWMAX, COLMAX)
      INTEGER ROWMAX, COLMAX
      CHARACTER GRAPH *1 (ROWMAX, COLMAX)
      INTEGER ROW, COL
C
C     PUT BLANKS EVERYWHERE IN GRAPH
      DO 28 ROW = 1, ROWMAX
         DO 18 COL = 1, COLMAX
            GRAPH (ROW, COL) = ' '
 18      CONTINUE
 28   CONTINUE
      RETURN
      END
C
C
      SUBROUTINE XAXIS (GRAPH, ROWMAX, COLMAX)
      INTEGER ROWMAX, COLMAX
      CHARACTER GRAPH *1 (ROWMAX, COLMAX)
      INTEGER COL, CENTER
C
C     PUT MINUS SIGNS ON X AXIS
      CENTER = (ROWMAX + 1) / 2
      DO 18 COL = 1, COLMAX
         GRAPH (CENTER, COL) = '-'
 18   CONTINUE
      RETURN
      END
C
C
      SUBROUTINE YAXIS (GRAPH, ROWMAX, COLMAX)
      INTEGER ROWMAX, COLMAX
      CHARACTER GRAPH *1 (ROWMAX, COLMAX)
      INTEGER ROW, CENTER
C
C     PUT BARS ON Y AXIS
      CENTER = (COLMAX + 1) / 2
      DO 18 ROW = 1, ROWMAX
         GRAPH (ROW, CENTER) = '|'
 18   CONTINUE
      RETURN
      END
C
C
      SUBROUTINE ORIGIN (GRAPH, ROWMAX, COLMAX)
      INTEGER ROWMAX, COLMAX
      CHARACTER GRAPH *1 (ROWMAX, COLMAX)
C
```

```
C       PUT PLUS AT ORIGIN
        GRAPH ((ROWMAX + 1) / 2, (COLMAX + 1) / 2) = '+'
        RETURN
        END
C
C
        SUBROUTINE CURVE (GRAPH, ROWMAX, COLMAX)
        INTEGER ROWMAX, COLMAX
        CHARACTER GRAPH *1 (ROWMAX, COLMAX)
        INTEGER ROW, COL
        REAL X, Y, Z
C
        NINT (Z) = INT (Z + 0.5)
C
C       PUT STARS ON CURVE
        DO 18 COL = 1, COLMAX
           X = 2.0 * (COL - 1) / (COLMAX - 1) - 1
           Y = X ** 2
           ROW = NINT (1 + (Y + 1) / 2 * (ROWMAX - 1))
C          LARGER Y VALUES HAVE SMALLER ROW NUMBERS
           ROW = ROWMAX + 1 - ROW
           IF (ROW .GE. 1 .AND. ROW .LE. ROWMAX) THEN DO
              GRAPH (ROW, COL) = '*'
           END IF
   18   CONTINUE
        RETURN
        END
C
C
        SUBROUTINE PRINTG (GRAPH, ROWMAX, COLMAX)
C       PRINT THE GRAPH
C
        INTEGER ROWMAX, COLMAX
        CHARACTER GRAPH *1 (ROWMAX, COLMAX)
        INTEGER ROW, COL
C
        PRINT, 'GRAPH OF THE FUNCTION Y = X ** 2'
        PRINT, '    -1 <= X <= 1, -1 <= Y <= 1'
        PRINT, ' '
        DO 18 ROW = 1, ROWMAX
           PRINT 15, (GRAPH (ROW, COL), COL = 1, COLMAX)
   15      FORMAT (T3, 99A1)
   18   CONTINUE
        RETURN
        END
```

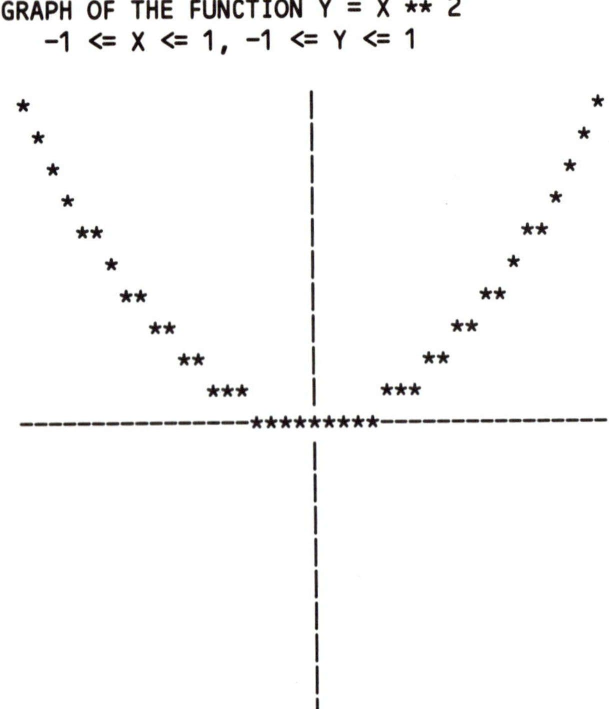

The smoothness of the graph is limited only by how closely points may be plotted. Using a microcomputer that displays 280 columns across and 192 rows vertically on a 12-inch video monitor, the authors have produced very good results (see Figure 8.4). The major changes in the program are to increase the number of columns from 41 to 280, the number of rows from 21 to 192, and to replace assignments to the array element GRAPH (ROW, COL) with calls to a built-in subroutine that displays a dot of a specified color on the screen in that row and column. The syntax and even the name of this subroutine vary from machine to machine, but all Fortran systems that support screen graphics have such a subroutine.

The graphs of other functions are easily obtained by minor modifications of the program PRBOLA. For example, the graph of the cubic equation $y = x^3$ over the same range of x and y values can be obtained merely by changing two lines, the line that computes the y value and the line that prints the description of the function on the output above the graph. Only the sample execution printout of the resulting program cubic is shown, because the program itself is so similar to the parabola. Modifications in the range of x and y values are discussed in the exercises.

8.3 Case Study: Digital Image Processing

Digital image processing consists of four major steps:

1. Acquiring the image
2. Digitizing the image
3. Enhancing the image
4. Plotting or displaying the enhanced image.

Acquisition and digitization of the image require special-purpose hardware. This section concentrates on programs for displaying and enhancing an image.

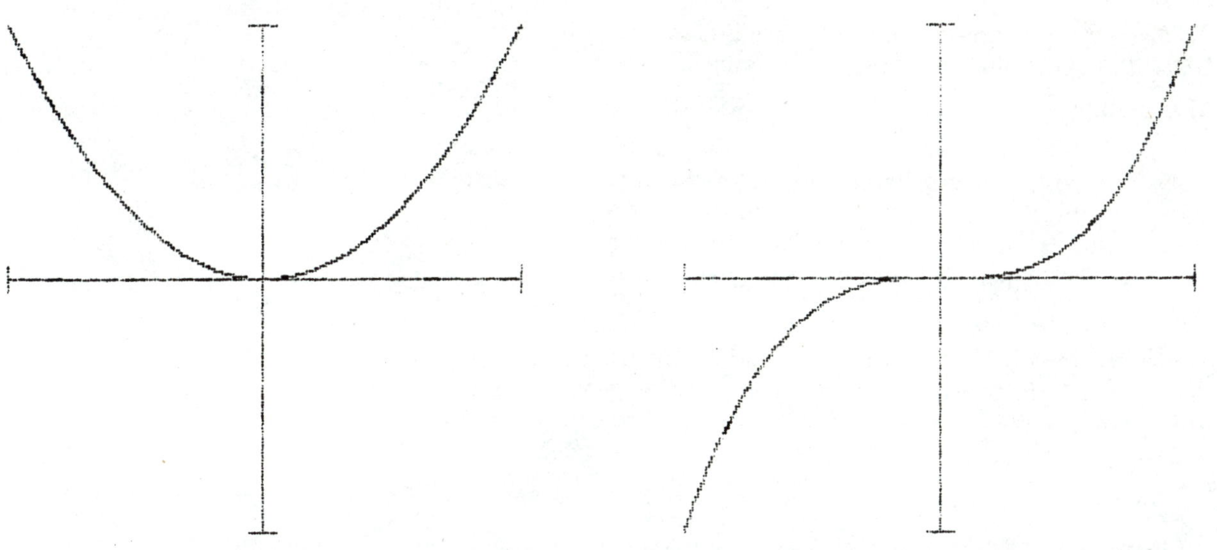

Figure 8.4 Graphs of the functions $y = x^2$ and $y = x^3$. These graphs were calculated on a grid of 191 × 191 pixels on a popular microcomputer and a dot matrix, higher-resolution printer.

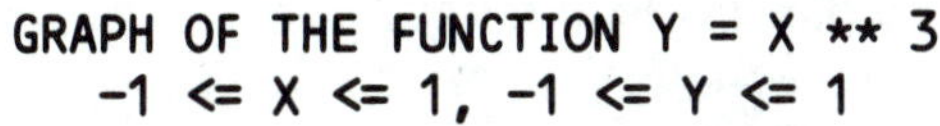

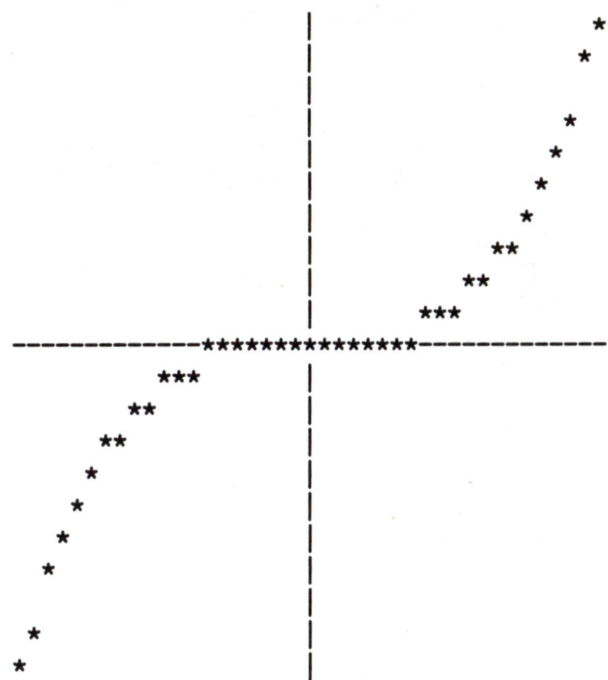

Section Preview

Visual Image Processing:

When photographic images are digitized, each pixel is assigned a number representing the intensity of light in the image at that location.

Gray Scale Output:

If display hardware permits, the brightness of each displayed pixel is proportional to its numerical intensity value.

Halftoning:

If only white and black are available in the display medium, gray tones are produced by filling part of the area allocated to a pixel with black and part with white in such a way the the fraction of the total pixel area that is white (or black) is proportional to the numerical intensity value.

Image Enhancement:

Between input of the digitized numerical intensity values and output of the final digitized image, the array of numerical intensities can be processed to enhance features of the image or to remove defects from the image.

Visual Image Processing

When equipped with special hardware for input and output, a computer can be programmed to process visual images such as computer portraits of the kind that can be found at shopping malls, science museums, and amusement parks. At the other end of the spectrum, it includes the synthesis, enhancement, and analysis of photographs transmitted back to Earth from space probes. The special hardware needed for input, a **video digitizer**, scans one frame of a television camera image and converts the light intensity at each image point in the picture to an integer that encodes the intensity. For the sake of further discussion, we assume that the digitizer encodes light intensity as an integer from 0 to 9, with 0 meaning the brightest possible image point and 9 the darkest possible image point.

Matching the input hardware, a computer used for image processing usually has a television-type **cathode ray tube (CRT)** for display and the associated circuits for converting a table of digitized light intensities into visual intensities on the screen. However, the image on a CRT is not permanent unless photographed. A second form of visual output, the printed page, is used during debugging of programs and whenever the lower cost and greater convenience of printed output outweigh the loss in image quality. The program IMAGE uses a digitizer for input but a printer for output. Of course, if no digitizer is available for program testing, the digitized image data can be simulated by hand and read from another input device.

```
      PROGRAM IMAGE
C     INITIAL VERSION
      Read a table of digitized light intensities
            from the video digitizer
      Convert each digitized light intensity
            to a printable character
            of appropriate print density
      Print the resulting image
```

The refined version of the program IMAGE is broken into four subroutines representing the phases of the process, the input, the echo of the input, the conversion of digits to characters, and the output. An echo of the input data is inserted to make it possible to check the execution of the program.

To complete the refinement of the subroutine CONVRT (convert image), 10 printable characters are chosen to represent the 10 possible digitized light intensities. Since no print character fills more than a small fraction of the space in which it is printed, it is not possible to obtain really dark image points in the printed output. The following 10 printable characters form a progression from very light to as dark as possible for a single character:

.	:	-	=	+	%	&	$	#	@
0	1	2	3	4	5	6	7	8	9

Refinement of the subroutine CONVRT is now straightforward.

```
C       PROGRAM IMAGE
C       READ AND PRINT A DIGITIZED IMAGE
C       VARIABLES:
C          DIMAGE = DIGITIZED IMAGE, A 2-DIMENSIONAL ARRAY
C                   OF LIGHT INTENSITIES FOR EACH PIXEL
C          PIMAGE = PRINTABLE IMAGE, A 2-DIMENSIONAL ARRAY
C                   OF PRINTABLE CHARACTERS OF VARYING DENSITY
C          CHARS  = A SEQUENCE OF PRINTABLE CHARACTERS
C                   OF GRADUATED DENSITY
C
        INTEGER NRROWS, NRCOLS, I
        INTEGER DIMAGE (12, 24)
        CHARACTER PIMAGE *1 (12, 24)
        CHARACTER CHARS *1 (10)
C
C       DATA FOR THE ARRAY OF PRINTABLE DENSITIES
        DATA CHARS / '.', ':', '-', '=', '+',
     +               '%', '&', '$', '#', '@', /
C
        NRROWS = 12
        NRCOLS = 24
C
        CALL READI (DIMAGE, NRROWS, NRCOLS)
        PRINT, 'DIGITIZED IMAGE POINTS:'
        CALL PRINTD (DIMAGE, NRROWS, NRCOLS)
        CALL CONVRT (DIMAGE, PIMAGE, NRROWS, NRCOLS, CHARS)
        CALL PRINTI (PIMAGE, NRROWS, NRCOLS)
        STOP
        END
C
C
        SUBROUTINE READI (DIMAGE, NRROWS, NRCOLS)
        INTEGER NRROWS, NRCOLS
        INTEGER DIMAGE (NRROWS, NRCOLS)
        INTEGER ROW, COL
C
C       READ DIGITIZED VERSION OF VIDEO IMAGE
        DO 18 ROW = 1, NRROWS
           READ, (DIMAGE (ROW, COL), COL = 1, NRCOLS)
   18   CONTINUE
        RETURN
        END
C
C
```

```
      SUBROUTINE PRINTD (DIMAGE, NRROWS, NRCOLS)
      INTEGER NRROWS, NRCOLS
      INTEGER DIMAGE (NRROWS, NRCOLS)
      INTEGER ROW, COL
C
C     ECHO DIGITIZED VERSION OF IMAGE
      DO 18 ROW = 1, NRROWS
         PRINT 15, (DIMAGE (ROW, COL), COL = 1, NRCOLS)
   15    FORMAT (T2, 99I3)
   18 CONTINUE
      RETURN
      END
C
C
      SUBROUTINE CONVRT (DIMAGE, PIMAGE, NRROWS, NRCOLS, CHARS)
      INTEGER NRROWS, NRCOLS
      INTEGER DIMAGE (NRROWS, NRCOLS)
      CHARACTER PIMAGE *1 (NRROWS, NRCOLS)
      INTEGER ROW, COL
C
C     CONVERT DIGITS TO PRINTABLE CHARACTERS
      DO 28 ROW = 1, NRROWS
         DO 18 COL = 1, NRCOLS
            PIMAGE (ROW, COL) = CHARS (DIMAGE (ROW, COL) + 1)
   18    CONTINUE
   28 CONTINUE
      RETURN
      END
C
C
      SUBROUTINE PRINTI (PIMAGE, NRROWS, NRCOLS)
      INTEGER NRROWS, NRCOLS
      CHARACTER PIMAGE *1 (NRROWS, NRCOLS)
      INTEGER ROW, COL
C
C     PRINT PRINTABLE IMAGE CONTAINING CHARACTERS
C     OF VARYING DENSITIES
      PRINT, ' '
      DO 18 ROW = 1, NRROWS
         PRINT 25, (PIMAGE (ROW, COL), COL = 1, NRCOLS)
   25    FORMAT (T3, 99A1)
   18 CONTINUE
      RETURN
      END
```

The next phase is testing the program. If a video digitizer is not available, simulated input data can be read from a more usual input device. The test data for the sample execution shown for IMAGE are based on a small section of a picture of Deimos, the smaller satellite of Mars, transmitted to Earth by the Viking I space probe orbiting Mars. The region chosen shows a small circular crater about 10 kilometers in diameter, with a raised rim. The original computer-generated photograph from which the input data are derived shows the entire disk of Deimos, using approximately three times as many scan lines in the vertical direction as the sample execution does for the same region. To be seen, the printed image of the program IMAGE must be far enough away that the individual print characters cannot be recognized as characters. At that distance, they appear as varying shades of white and gray. The main problems with the sample execution are the lack of a truly dark print character and the small number of points used to form the image. The crater is seen more distinctly when a larger region is shown in the same detail.

```
DIGITIZED IMAGE POINTS:
  4 4 4 4 4 4 4 4 3 3 3 2 2 1 1 1 1 1 1 0 0 0 0 0
  4 4 4 4 4 4 4 3 2 2 2 2 1 0 0 0 0 0 1 1 1 0 0 0
  4 4 4 4 4 4 3 2 8 8 8 8 9 9 9 9 9 0 0 0 1 1 0 0
  4 4 4 4 3 6 6 7 7 7 7 7 7 7 7 8 8 9 9 0 0 1 1 1
  4 4 4 3 5 6 6 6 5 6 6 6 6 6 6 7 7 8 9 9 1 1 3 3
  5 4 4 4 5 6 6 5 5 5 6 6 6 6 6 6 5 7 7 7 7 4 5 4
  5 5 5 5 4 4 6 6 5 6 6 6 6 6 6 5 5 5 6 6 7 5 6 6
  5 5 5 5 3 4 4 4 4 6 4 4 4 4 6 6 6 6 6 4 5 6 6 6
  5 5 5 5 2 1 1 1 2 2 3 4 4 4 4 4 4 4 4 5 6 6 6 7
  5 5 5 5 8 1 1 1 1 1 1 2 1 2 2 2 3 3 5 6 6 6 7 8
  5 5 5 5 7 6 8 8 1 1 1 1 1 1 2 2 5 6 6 6 6 7 8 8
  5 5 5 5 5 5 6 6 8 8 8 8 8 8 6 6 6 6 6 6 7 7 8 8
```

```
++++++++===--::::::.....
+++++++=----:.....:::...
++++++=-####@@@@@...::..
++++=&&$$$$$$$$##@@..:::
+++=%&&&%&&&&&&$$#@@::==
%+++%&&%%&&&&&&%$$$$+%+
%%%%++&&%&&&&&&%%&&$%&&
%%%%=++++&++++&&&&&+%&&&
%%%%-:::--=++++++++%&&&$
%%%%#::::::-:---==%&&&$#
%%%%$&##::::::--%&&&&$##
%%%%%&&######&&&&&&$$##
```

Halftone Images

A more satisfactory display of the digitized image is produced using a rectangle of displayed characters for each pixel. In Figure 8.5, each of the 12 × 24 pixels of the image printed by the program IMAGE is displayed as a rectangle of dots, 10 dots high and 5 dots across. If the numerical intensity value for a pixel is n, the fraction $n/9$ of the 50 possible dots is black in a random pattern. Thus, numerical intensity 0 prints as white and numerical intensity 9 prints as black. Intermediate intensities appear as gray from a distance great enough that the individual dots cannot be seen clearly.

This method of producing pixels that appear as varying shades of gray is **halftoning**. A satisfactory printer image halftone display can be produced by printing each pixel using a very dark print character, perhaps "*" or "@", in an appropriate fraction of a 5 × 5 rectangle. (*Note:* Each pixel then will be rectangular and not square because each printer character occupies a rectangle and not a square.)

Image Enhancement

The processing of the video image done by the program IMAGE consists of nothing more than a conversion from one form of representation to another. When a video camera and digitizer are available, this is all that is needed to print computer portraits. The subject sits before the video camera and a selected frame of the video image is digitized and printed. However, once the

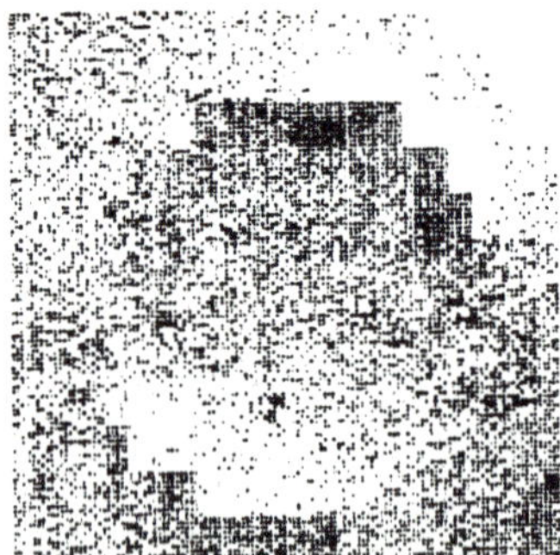

Figure 8.5 Digital image of a crater and the negative digital image of the same crater printed by a random halftone process.

image is digitized, the stage is set for computer enhancement of the image to reveal details more clearly, to reduce the amount of static or snow in the image, and to perform other modifications of the image difficult or impossible to obtain photographically. For example, digital TV sets now employ a microprocessor to enhance the image of commercially broadcast programs by smoothly interpolating extra scan lines to double the apparent resolution of the picture, and by comparing consecutive images to filter out random static. (See Exercise 7 at the end of this chapter.)

Heightened Contrast Image

Details can sometimes be seen more clearly if the image is converted into a high-contrast image. What this involves is altering the digitized light intensities so that only the extreme intensities encoded as 0 and 9 are represented. The program HICON (high contrast) to do this results from adding a fifth subroutine ENHANC, called between the echo of the input data and the conversion subroutines of the program IMAGE. In this subroutine, all light intensities from 0 to 4 are changed to a light intensity of 0, the brightest intensity, and all light intensities from 5 to 9 are changed to a light intensity of 9, the darkest intensity. Only the new main program HICON and the subroutine ENHANC are shown below. Other subroutines are unchanged.

```
C       PROGRAM HICON
C       PRINT A HIGH CONTRAST IMAGE
C       VARIABLES:
C          DIMAGE = DIGITIZED IMAGE, A 2-DIMENSIONAL ARRAY
C                   OF LIGHT INTENSITIES FOR EACH PIXEL
C          PIMAGE = PRINTABLE IMAGE, A 2-DIMENSIONAL ARRAY
C                   OF PRINTABLE CHARACTERS OF VARYING DENSITY
C          CHARS  = A SEQUENCE OF PRINTABLE CHARACTERS
C                   OF GRADUATED DENSITY
C          TRSHLD = THRESHHOLD, ALL DIGITIZED INTENSITIES <=
C                   TRSHLD ARE CONVERTED TO WHITE;
C                   ALL INTENSITIES > TRSHLD BECOME BLACK
C
        INTEGER NRROWS, NRCOLS, I, TRSHLD
        INTEGER DIMAGE (12, 24)
```

```
      CHARACTER PIMAGE *1 (12, 24)
      CHARACTER CHARS *1 (10)
C
C     DATA FOR THE ARRAY OF PRINTABLE DENSITIES
      DATA CHARS / '.', ':', '-', '=', '+',
     +             '%', '&', '$', '#', '@', /
C
      NRROWS = 12
      NRCOLS = 24
      TRSHLD = 4
C
      CALL READI (DIMAGE, NRROWS, NRCOLS)
      PRINT, 'DIGITIZED IMAGE POINTS:'
      CALL PRINTD (DIMAGE, NRROWS, NRCOLS)
      CALL ENHANC (DIMAGE, NRROWS, NRCOLS, TRSHOLD)
      PRINT, ' '
      PRINT, 'MODIFIED IMAGE POINTS:'
      CALL PRINTD (DIMAGE, NRROWS, NRCOLS)
      CALL CONVRT (DIMAGE, PIMAGE, NRROWS, NRCOLS, CHARS)
      CALL PRINTI (PIMAGE, NRROWS, NRCOLS)
      STOP
      END
C
C
      SUBROUTINE READI (DIMAGE, NRROWS, NRCOLS)
      INTEGER NRROWS, NRCOLS
      INTEGER DIMAGE (NRROWS, NRCOLS)
      INTEGER ROW, COL
C
C     READ DIGITIZED VERSION OF VIDEO IMAGE
      DO 18 ROW = 1, NRROWS
         READ, (DIMAGE (ROW, COL), COL = 1, NRCOLS)
   18 CONTINUE
      RETURN
      END
C
C
      SUBROUTINE PRINTD (DIMAGE, NRROWS, NRCOLS)
      INTEGER NRROWS, NRCOLS
      INTEGER DIMAGE (NRROWS, NRCOLS)
      INTEGER ROW, COL
C
C     ECHO DIGITIZED VERSION OF IMAGE
      DO 18 ROW = 1, NRROWS
         PRINT 15, (DIMAGE (ROW, COL), COL = 1, NRCOLS)
   15    FORMAT (T2, 99I3)
   18 CONTINUE
      RETURN
      END
C
C
      SUBROUTINE ENHANC (DIMAGE, NRROWS, NRCOLS, TRSHLD)
      INTEGER NRROWS, NRCOLS, TRSHLD
      INTEGER DIMAGE (NRROWS, NRCOLS)
      INTEGER ROW, COL
```

```
C       CHANGES ALL INTENSITIES 0..TRSHLD TO 0
C       AND ALL INTENSITIES TRSHLD+1..9 TO 9
        DO 28 ROW = 1, NRROWS
           DO 18 COL = 1, NRCOLS
              IF (DIMAGE (ROW, COL) .LE. TRSHLD) THEN DO
                 DIMAGE (ROW, COL) = 0
              ELSE DO
                 DIMAGE (ROW, COL) = 9
              END IF
   18      CONTINUE
   28   CONTINUE
        RETURN
        END
C
C
        SUBROUTINE CONVRT (DIMAGE, PIMAGE, NRROWS, NRCOLS, CHARS)
        INTEGER NRROWS, NRCOLS
        INTEGER DIMAGE (NRROWS, NRCOLS)
        CHARACTER PIMAGE *1 (NRROWS, NRCOLS)
        INTEGER ROW, COL
C
C       CONVERT DIGITS TO PRINTABLE CHARACTERS
        DO 28 ROW = 1, NRROWS
           DO 18 COL = 1, NRCOLS
              PIMAGE (ROW, COL) = CHARS (DIMAGE (ROW, COL) + 1)
   18      CONTINUE
   28   CONTINUE
        RETURN
        END
C
C
        SUBROUTINE PRINTI (PIMAGE, NRROWS, NRCOLS)
        INTEGER NRROWS, NRCOLS
        CHARACTER PIMAGE *1 (NRROWS, NRCOLS)
        INTEGER ROW, COL
C
C       PRINT PRINTABLE IMAGE CONTAINING CHARACTERS
C       OF VARYING DENSITIES
        PRINT, ' '
        DO 18 ROW = 1, NRROWS
           PRINT 25, (PIMAGE (ROW, COL), COL = 1, NRCOLS)
   25      FORMAT (T3, 99A1)
   18   CONTINUE
        RETURN
        END
```

```
DIGITIZED IMAGE POINTS:
  4 4 4 4 4 4 4 4 3 3 3 2 2 1 1 1 1 1 1 0 0 0 0 0
  4 4 4 4 4 4 4 3 2 2 2 2 1 0 0 0 0 0 1 1 1 0 0 0
  4 4 4 4 4 4 3 2 8 8 8 8 9 9 9 9 9 0 0 0 1 1 0 0
  4 4 4 4 3 6 6 7 7 7 7 7 7 7 7 8 8 9 9 0 0 1 1 1
  4 4 4 3 5 6 6 6 5 6 6 6 6 6 6 7 7 8 9 9 1 1 3 3
  5 4 4 4 5 6 6 5 5 5 6 6 6 6 6 6 5 7 7 7 7 4 5 4
  5 5 5 5 4 4 6 6 5 6 6 6 6 6 6 5 5 5 6 6 7 5 6 6
  5 5 5 5 3 4 4 4 4 6 4 4 4 4 6 6 6 6 6 4 5 6 6 6
  5 5 5 5 2 1 1 1 2 2 3 4 4 4 4 4 4 4 4 5 6 6 6 7
```

```
  5  5  5  5  8  1  1  1  1  1  1  2  1  2  2  2  3  3  5  6  6  6  7  8
  5  5  5  5  7  6  8  8  1  1  1  1  1  1  2  2  5  6  6  6  6  7  8  8
  5  5  5  5  5  5  6  6  8  8  8  8  8  8  6  6  6  6  6  6  7  7  8  8

MODIFIED IMAGE POINTS:
  0  0  0  0  0  0  0  0  0  0  0  0  0  0  0  0  0  0  0  0  0  0  0  0
  0  0  0  0  0  0  0  0  0  0  0  0  0  0  0  0  0  0  0  0  0  0  0  0
  0  0  0  0  0  0  0  0  9  9  9  9  9  9  9  9  9  0  0  0  0  0  0  0
  0  0  0  0  0  9  9  9  9  9  9  9  9  9  9  9  9  9  9  0  0  0  0  0
  0  0  0  0  9  9  9  9  9  9  9  9  9  9  9  9  9  9  9  9  0  0  0  0
  9  0  0  0  9  9  9  9  9  9  9  9  9  9  9  9  9  9  9  9  9  0  9  0
  9  9  9  9  0  0  9  9  9  9  9  9  9  9  9  9  9  9  9  9  9  9  9  9
  9  9  9  9  0  0  0  0  0  9  0  0  0  0  9  9  9  9  9  0  9  9  9  9
  9  9  9  9  0  0  0  0  0  0  0  0  0  0  0  0  0  0  0  9  9  9  9  9
  9  9  9  9  9  0  0  0  0  0  0  0  0  0  0  0  0  0  9  9  9  9  9  9
  9  9  9  9  9  9  9  9  0  0  0  0  0  0  0  9  9  9  9  9  9  9  9  9
  9  9  9  9  9  9  9  9  9  9  9  9  9  9  9  9  9  9  9  9  9  9  9  9

........................
........................
........@@@@@@@@@.......
.....@@@@@@@@@@@@@@.....
....@@@@@@@@@@@@@@@@....
@...@@@@@@@@@@@@@@@@@.@.
@@@@..@@@@@@@@@@@@@@@@@@
@@@@.....@....@@@@@.@@@@
@@@@...............@@@@@
@@@@@.............@@@@@@
@@@@@@@@.......@@@@@@@@@
@@@@@@@@@@@@@@@@@@@@@@@@
```

The data for the sample execution of HICON are the same data used in the sample execution of the program IMAGE. In the high-contrast printout, many details are lost, but the details that remain are seen more clearly. The threshhold between light and dark is critical in determining which details remain in the high-contrast printout. If, for example, instead of a threshhold intensity of 4, intensities of 5 or less are considered light, and intensities of 6 or greater are considered dark, the appearance of the high-contrast printout could change considerably. It is a simple matter to program a computer to produce a high-contrast printout based on any threshhold light intensity, particularly when the threshold is assigned to a variable. This and additional methods of image enhancement are discussed in the exercises.

COMMON Statement

Most of the subroutines in the program HICON use the arrays DIMAG, PIMAG, or both. If the number of shared arrays and values were much larger, the argument lists in subroutine calls would be uncomfortably long. The COMMON statement allows the program to share variables without using argument lists. For example, if each subroutine and the main program contained the statement

```
COMMON / DBLOCK / DIMAG, PIMAG, NRROWS, NRCOLS
```

after the relevant declarations, but before the first executable statement, the two arrays of the COMMON block named DBLOCK would be available to all these subprograms, along with the values of NRROWS and NRCOLS.

Variables in common may not be actual arguments of a subprogram call. They are already shared. For example, with the COMMON statement above, the call to the subroutines READI in PRINTD would become

```
CALL READI
CALL PRINTD
```

with no argument list.

Several named COMMON blocks (and one unnamed block) may be declared in a program. The variables of the COMMON block are available only to those subprograms that declare the block. Because the order in which variables are listed in a COMMON statement is critical to its interpretation, it is recommended that two programs sharing the same COMMON block use identical declarations and COMMON statements.

8.4 Three or More Subscripts

Arrays with more than two dimensions are allowed in Fortran. The maximum number of subscripts is seven. Multidimensional arrays are quite common in scientific programming, and they also arise from time to time in general applications.

The example in this section uses a three-dimensional array. Four or more dimensional arrays occur infrequently. Just as a rectangular table with entries in each unit square of the rectangular table serves as a model for a two-dimensional array, a three-dimensional rectangular solid with entries in each unit cube of the solid serves as a model of a three-dimensional array. (See Figure 8.6.)

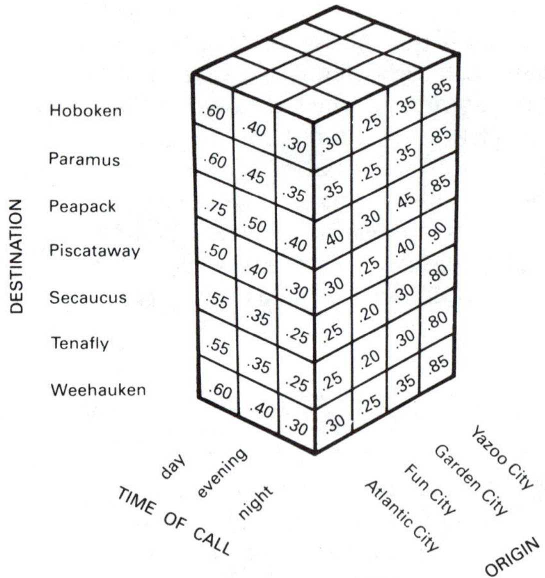

Figure 8.6 A three-dimensional table represented as a rectangular solid.

Section Preview

Multidimensional Arrays:

Arrays with from one to seven subscripts are permitted in Fortran.

A Three-Dimensional Telephone Rate Array

The telephone rate table in Section 8.1 has two subscripts. The row subscript of an entry in the table is a code for the destination city of the phone call, and the column subscript is a code for the time of day the call is placed. All telephone calls in the example in Section 8.1 originate from the same place, Fun City. In this section, we show how to use a three-dimensional array to generalize that example to take into account differing cities of origin of the telephone calls.

If four cities of origin, Atlantic City, Fun City, Garden City, and Yazoo City, are allowed for telephone calls, the four rate tables similar to Table 8.1 would be necessary to summarize all the applicable long distance telephone rates. Figure 8.6 shows how a $4 \times 7 \times 3$ array of rates can be used to amalgamate these four 7×3 rate tables. The front slab (completely visible) gives the telephone rate table for calls originating in Atlantic City. The next slab back (only partly visible) gives the telephone rate table for calls originating in Fun City. The night rates for such calls may be seen to agree with those in Table 8.1. The third and fourth slabs give the rate table for calls originating in Garden City and Yazoo City.

Based on the analysis of the complete rate schedule as a collection of rate tables for calls originating at different cities, we might declare the complete rate array as follows:

```
REAL RATE (4, 7, 3)
```

This declaration declares a $4 \times 7 \times 3$ array of real values. The subscripts always must be kept in the order in which they are declared. In any reference to the array RATE, for example,

```
RATE (ORGCOD, DESCOD, RATCOD)
```

the first subscript always must be a city-of-origin code from 1 to 4, the second subscript always must be a city-of-destination code from 1 to 7, and the third subscript always must be a time-of-day code from 1 to 3. This correspondence should be emphasized by replacing the constants 4, 7, and 3 by dummy arguments NRORG (number of cities of origin), NRDST (number of destination cities), and NRRAT (number of different rate scales).

```
REAL RATE (NRORG, NRDST, NRRAT)
```

Once the declaration of the rate array has been made properly, it is straightforward to modify the program PHONE in Section 8.1 to handle the case of varying city of origin as well as varying city of destination. We leave this as an exercise.

8.5 What You Should Know

1. An array name specifies a group of data items, and subscripts identify a particular item within the group.
2. One subscript is sufficient to locate an item in a linear list, or one-dimensional array.

3. Two subscripts, the row and column number, identify an item in a table, or two-dimensional array.
4. When processing a two-dimensional array, a DO block for the columns is often nested in a DO block for the rows.
5. Digital images are pictures made by selectively coloring or shading a two-dimensional array of dots. The dots are pixels.
6. The fundamental principle in printing more complicated shapes is to decompose them into simple shapes.
7. If the entire graphic is calculated in the computer's memory before being printed, new shapes can be superimposed over parts of pre-existing shapes. This is the method of superposition.
8. Neither negative nor zero subscripts are permitted in WATFIV.
9. The graph of a function has one plotted point in each column.
10. Until the number of points requires a change in computational strategy, the same techniques can produce high- or low-resolution digital images, depending on available computer time and output hardware.
11. Halftoning means producing shades of gray by alternating black and white areas in suitable proportion.
12. Examples of image enhancement include increasing contrast, making negatives and removing static and fixed imperfections of the image-acquisition apparatus.
13. Arrays with from one to seven subscripts are permitted in Fortran.

8.6 Self-Test Questions

Section 8.1

1. How do you declare a 20 × 20 table of characters to use for storing a crossword puzzle?
2. The input data to the following program consists of the numbers 9, 7, 2, and 5. Hand simulate the execution of this program and tell what the output will look like. Describe what this program will do.

```
C     PROGRAM EXAMPL
      INTEGER A (2, 2), B (2, 2)
      INTEGER I, J
C
      PRINT, 'INPUT DATA  A:'
      DO 18 I = 1, 2
         READ, (A (I, J), J = 1, 2)
         PRINT, (A (I, J), J = 1, 2)
   18 CONTINUE
C
      DO 38 I = 1, 2
         DO 28 J = 1, 2
            B (I, J) = A (I, J)
   28    CONTINUE
   38 CONTINUE
C
```

```
      PRINT, 'TABLE B:'
      DO 48 I = 1, 2
         PRINT, (B (I, J), J = 1, 2)
   48 CONTINUE
      STOP
      END
```

Section 8.2

1. How do you declare an array PICTUR to be used to print a digital image 35 pixels across by 20 pixels high?
2. What does the principle of superposition mean as applied to computer graphics?
3. If a computer has a graphic display device with pixels that can be either "on" or "off", how could the following array be used to store a digital image for such a graphic output device?

```
LOGICAL IMAGE (100, 100)
```

Section 8.3

1. How is a photographic image represented in a computer?
2. How are shades of gray produced in a digital image display?
3. What advantage does the process of digitizing and displaying an image have over merely reproducing the image by photographic or electronic means?

Section 8.4

1. True/false:
   a. The following two declarations for the triply subscripted array RATE used in Section 8.4 are equivalent.

   ```
   REAL RATE (4, 7, 3)

   REAL RATE (7, 3, 4)
   ```

   b. Arrays with four subscripts are permitted in Fortran.
   c. When you declare a multidimensional array in Fortran, the subscript with the largest maximum value must be the leftmost subscript for the array.
   d. As long as you refer to every subscript variable in this section by its correct name, like DSTCOD, ORGCOD, or RATCOD, the order in which the subscripts are written does not matter.

8.7 Programming Exercises

1. **Purpose:** To practice working with doubly subscripted arrays. To add a wrinkle, we suggest using an array of type LOGICAL, but an array of integers would also work.

   The problem: Ten student members of a committee would like to schedule a meeting at a time when none of them has a class. Classes meet starting at each hour from 9 A.M. to 5 P.M. on each of the days Monday to Friday. There are not Saturday or Sunday classes nor classes before 9 A.M. or starting at 6 P.M. or later. Each student will submit a list of times that are unavailable because of classes, and the computer will process these and print a list of all hours in the week seen when no one has classes.

Representing the data: We represent the days of the week Monday to Friday by the integers 1 to 5. For the time of day, we could either ignore the distinction between A.M. and P.M. and get nine distinct starting hours, or we could use the 24 hour time system and represent afternoon hours as numbers greater than twelve. We choose the latter and and encode starting times by numbers from 9 to 17. The times of the week free for meetings may be represented as the entries in an array

```
LOGICAL FREE (5, 17)
```

This array is initialized to .TRUE. and every time a student indicates a class meeting, the corresponding entry in FREE is set to .FALSE.

Input data: Pairs of integers consisting of day code and starting time of each of the classes of members of the committee. For example, a MWF class meeting at 10 A.M. is represented as

```
1 10
3 10
5 10
```

Sample output: The output is a list of all hours still available after all the student class hours read from input are deleted. For some specific sets of input data, the output might look like this:

```
INPUT DATA  DAY:     1
            TIME:   10
INPUT DATA  DAY:     3
            TIME:   10
INPUT DATA  DAY:     5
            TIME:   10
INPUT DATA  DAY:     2
            TIME:   14
INPUT DATA  DAY:     4
            TIME:   14

...
FREE TIME SLOTS REMAINING ARE
DAY 1  TIME  14
DAY 2  TIME   9
DAY 2  TIME  16
DAY 4  TIME  16
DAY 5  TIME   9
```

2. **Purpose:** To get some practice using superposition to create computer graphics.

   The problem: Draw a facsimile of the U.S. flag.

   Problem analysis: The size of the flag should depend on the physical characteristics of the output device you are using. Because there are 13 stripes, the height should be a multiple of 13 lines. On a standard printer output page, 65 lines is a good choice. To save space in the book, we will use 13 lines. A good width would be twice the height. Thus we use four times as many columns as rows because a printed character is only half as wide as it is high. Even an asterisk, which is round, is positioned within the same rectangular space as more obviously rectangular characters. The fact that the field of blue with stars makes the upper stripes shorter than the lower stripes should not complicate the program. You simply draw the 7 darker stripes across the entire rectangle, then superimpose the blue field with stars over it.

Input data: None.

Sample output: See for yourself.

Comment: This result really looks good on a microcomputer with color graphics. One student made the computer play the Star Spangled Banner after it drew the flag.

3. **Purpose:** To explore extensions and pitfalls in the graph plotting program PRBOLA. The concept of windowing is introduced.

   The problem: The program PRBOLA (parabola) in Section 8.2 plots the graph of a parabola $y = x^2$ for values of x and y between -1 and 1.

   a) Modify the program PRBOLA to plot the graph of the equation

   $$y = 2x^3 - x \quad \text{for } -1 \le x \le 1 \text{ and } -1 \le y \le 1$$

   The modification is easy because the function has the same actual range of values as that of PRBOLA.

   b) Modify the program PRBOLA to plot the graph of the equation

   $$y = x^2 \quad \text{for } -2 \le x \le 2 \text{ and } -2 \le y \le 2$$

   Some of the function values, for example, the y value when x is 2, are not within the plottable range of y values. If you don't take this into account, the row number calculated for this point will be outside the declared range of subscripts for row numbers, and the program will be terminated by an error message. What you must do is to pre-screen each point before it is plotted, which is called windowing. Those that lie within the window of the plottable region are stored in the array GRAPH, and those that are outside this window are not stored.

   Input data: None.

   Sample output: You will see it when you run the program.

4. **Purpose:** To illustrate plotting of points in two dimensions from a file of coordinate pairs.

   The problem: The program PRBOLA plotted sets of points that satisfy an equation.

   a) Read pairs of coordinates from the input file and plot them to the same size graph and range of x and y values as in the program PRBOLA.

   b) Enlarge the size of the graph by doubling or tripling the parameters ROWMAX and COLMAX, depending on the size of your display device.

   Input data: The x and y values of points to plot.

```
-1 1
-.95 .9025
-.9  .81
-.85 .7225
  .    .
  .    .
  .    .
 .9  .81
 .95 .9025
1 1
```

   Sample output: The output using the sample input should look like that of PRBOLA because the points in sample input file all lie on the parabola $y = x^2$.

5. **Purpose:** Draw a two-dimensional plot in three-dimensional space.

   The problem: Points in three-dimensional space given by coordinate triples (x, y, z) are no harder to plot than points in the plane given by coordinate pairs. Use the same array GRAPH as in the program PRBOLA and plot the points (X, Y, Z) using the formulas

```
ROW = NINT (4 * X - 10 * Z + 11)
COL = NINT (-10 * X + 20 * Y + 21)
```

Sample input: The corners of the unit cube:

```
-.5 -.5 -.5
-.5 -.5 +.5
-.5 +.5 -.5
-.5 +.5 +.5
+.5 -.5 -.5
+.5 -.5 +.5
+.5 +.5 -.5
+.5 +.5 +.5
```

Sample output: Not shown.

Comment: Connect the plotted points to see the cube.

6. **Purpose:** To get additional practice with two-dimensional arrays.

   The problem: Write a program to help keep track of the solution of a 20 × 20 crossword puzzle. First, clear the 20 × 20 table of characters to all blanks. Then accept input describing a word to be entered in the puzzle. Input has the following form:

   a) Row number (for the first letter of the word)

   b) Column number (for the first letter of the word)

   c) The single character A meaning across or the single character D meaning "down"

   d) The word to be entered

   Print or display the current state of the puzzle solution after each entry. Print a warning if a letter in the word to be entered does not agree with the letter already in that position in the array.

7. **Purpose:** To explore avenues of image enhancement.

   The problem: The program IMAGE in this chapter is a no-frills digital-image program. The program HICON makes an initial attempt at image enhancement.

   a) Modify the program HICON to convert any digitized intensity from 0 to 5 into an intensity of 0, and any intensity from 6 to 9 into an intensity of 9. Run the modification using the same input data used in this section.

   b) Write a program to make a negative print of a video image. This means that all light intensity relationships are reversed. The brightest points in the video image are to be printed darkest, and the darkest points in the original image are to be printed lightest.

   c) Simulate the effect of random interference or static in the transmission of the video picture to the computer by generating for each image point a random integer from 1 to 100. If the random integer is 96 or greater, then generate another random integer, this time from 0 to 9, and replace the actual digitized light intensity with this second random integer. Test your program two ways: using a completely uniform gray image with a digitized intensity of 4 at all points, and using the static generator to put static into the picture of the crater on Deimos.

   d) Write a program that accepts as input three consecutive images of the same object, each of which has random interference noise, or static in it. Use an array with three subscripts. Process the three images to reduce static by averaging the three values for the light intensity at each point in the image. Be sure to round the average to the nearest integer before conversion and printing. Use the random noise generator written for Part c to test the program.

e) Write a program that accepts three successive images of the same object and tries to reduce the random static in the images by computing a digitized light intensity at each point as follows. If two or more of the digitized intensities agree, accept that value regardless of what the other one is. If one value is more than twice as far from the other two as they are from each other, then reject that value and average the other two. If all three are relatively close, take their average, rounding to the nearest integer to obtain a valid digitized intensity. Test this program using the random static generator.

8. **Purpose:** To print a digital image using different data.

   The problem: a) Execute the program IMAGE in Section 8.3 using a different table of digitized light intensities as input data:

   Input data:

```
3 3 3 3 3 3 3 3 9 9 9 9 9 3 3 3 3 3 3 3 3 3 3 3
3 3 3 3 3 3 3 9 9 9 9 9 9 9 3 3 3 3 3 3 3 3 3 3
3 3 3 3 3 3 3 9 9 9 9 9 9 9 3 3 3 3 3 3 3 3 3 3
3 3 9 9 9 9 3 3 9 9 9 9 9 0 0 3 3 3 3 3 3 3 3 3
3 9 9 9 9 9 9 9 9 9 9 9 0 0 0 0 0 3 3 3 3 3 3 3
9 9 9 9 9 9 9 9 0 0 0 9 0 0 0 9 0 9 3 3 3 3 3 3
3 9 9 9 9 9 0 0 0 0 0 0 0 0 0 9 0 9 3 3 3 3 3 3
3 3 3 3 3 3 0 0 0 0 0 0 0 0 0 9 0 9 0 0 9 9 3 3
3 3 3 3 3 3 3 0 0 0 9 0 0 0 0 0 0 0 0 9 9 3 3 3
3 3 3 3 3 3 3 3 3 0 6 9 0 0 0 0 0 0 0 0 3 3 3 3
3 3 3 3 3 3 3 9 9 9 6 6 9 0 9 0 0 0 0 3 3 3 3 3
3 3 3 3 3 3 3 9 3 9 9 9 9 9 9 9 9 9 3 3 3 3 3 3
```

   Sample output: Not shown. Try to recognize who it is.

   b) Modify the program IMAGE so that each pixel is printed as a fraction of a 5 × 5 rectangle of asterisks. Print none of these 25 asterisks if the image intensity at that pixel is 0. Print all of these 25 asterisks if the intensity is 9 and print NINT (N * 25.0 / 9) of these asterisks if the intensity is N. You may use either random patterns of asterisks or regular patterns of asterisks within each pixel.

9. **The problem:** Write a program that reads input values for a 4 × 7 × 3 array of rates for long distance telephone calls. It then reads coded input for city of origin, city of destination, time-of-day rate code, and duration for a telephone call between cities used in the example in this section. The program should calculate and print the charge for the call.

   Input data: The sample represents a call from city 2 to city 5 at the evening rate (code 2) for seven minutes

```
65 45 25 80 60 30 50 35 25 75 55 30
70 50 25 70 50 40 70 50 35 70 50 25
80 55 30 60 40 20 80 65 40 60 40 20
70 50 25 70 50 35 55 35 20 55 40 20
60 40 20 80 60 30 65 45 25 50 30 30
60 40 20 80 60 30 75 55 30 50 35 20
65 45 25 75 55 30 75 55 30 45 30 15
2 5 2 7
```

Sample output:

```
THE CALL COSTS $1.54.
```

10. For each day of the month, a shot putter keeps a list of the distance he achieved in each of his shot puts that day. Write a program that reads each of these lists of distances into a row of a table and computes the average distance for the month for first puts, the average distance for second puts, and so on. Modify the program so that it also prints out the number of the put in which the shot putter has the greatest average distance.

9 ADDITIONAL CASE STUDIES

This chapter contains no new features of the Fortran programming language. Instead, some significant problems and techniques are examined in detail using case studies. They are applicable to computing science, regardless of the programming language used. The three topics considered are roundoff error, deterministic computer simulation, and nondeterministic computer simulation.

9.1 Roundoff

The subject of roundoff, or as it is less charitably called—roundoff error, occupies a curious position in an introduction to computer programming. It is one of those annoying practical details that prevent a perfectly reasonable looking program from doing exactly what it seems to say it should. Yet roundoff is not a characteristic of any one computer language or any one computer. It is a characteristic of the computational process itself.

To illustrate what roundoff is, and how likely it is to occur in actual computations, we give two simple examples. Using any computer or hand calculator, try the calculation

```
(1 / 3) * 3
```

Chances are the computed answer is something like 0.9999999 instead of 1. The difference is roundoff error. If the previous calculation comes out exactly to 1, as it does on some hand calculators and computer systems, try calculating

```
((1 / 3) * 3) - 1
```

Even fewer computers or hand calculators obtain exactly 0 as the answer for this calculation.

In our view, roundoff is a special problem, but one that is so important and so pervasive that, like debugging, it simply cannot be ignored if one wants to write real programs. Since roundoff refuses to confine itself to advanced mathematical and scientific applications, even the beginning programmer must be able to recognize when roundoff error has occurred and know how to apply first aid so that perfectly reasonable programs can be made to execute in a perfectly reasonable fashion.

In one major respect, this section differs from the rest of the book. The rest of the book emphasizes the similarity between ordinary usage and computer usage. This section emphasizes the differences between ordinary arithmetic and computer arithmetic.

Storing Numbers

For every variable a program uses, the computer must reserve a certain portion of its memory to store its values. It does not matter whether the computer memory consists of tiny magnetic doughnut-shaped cores, or transistor circuits, or magnetic film, tape, drum, or disk; the principle is the same: a fixed number of units of the computer's physical hardware is reserved to store the values. For simplicity, our examples are based on a computer that stores the seven digits that make the largest contributions to the value of the number. This corresponds approximately to the behavior of many contemporary computers.

Nonrepresentable Numbers

Some numbers, like 123, can be represented exactly in seven (or fewer) digits. Others, like $1/3$, cannot be so represented, although the seven-digit decimal value 0.3333333 is a very good approximation to the number $1/3$. The difference between the two is only $1/30000000$, so small as to be of no consequence whatsoever for most purposes. Moreover, the seven-digit value 0.3333333 is clearly the closest seven-digit value to the intended number $1/3$.

How A Small Roundoff Error Can Cause Big Trouble

In Section 2.3, we discussed how to use formatting to improve the appearance of output. In that case, roundoff created aesthetic problems, but didn't harm the computations in any way. We now examine some cases in which roundoff produces wrong answers. In spite of the fact that a roundoff error might be very small, it can create a serious problem, as in the program PRICES.

```
C     PROGRAM PRICES
      REAL PRICE, COST, YARDS
      INTEGER COUNT
C
      READ, PRICE
      PRINT 15, 'INPUT DATA  PRICE:', PRICE
   15 FORMAT (T2, A18, F7.2)
      PRINT 25, 'YARDS', 'COST'
   25 FORMAT (T2, A15, A10)
C
      YARDS = .3333333
      WHILE (YARDS .NE. 1) DO
         COST = YARDS * PRICE
         PRINT 35, YARDS, COST
   35    FORMAT (T2, F15.7, F10.2)
         YARDS = YARDS + .3333333
      END WHILE
      STOP
      END
```

```
INPUT DATA  PRICE:   2.75
          YARDS      COST
      0.3333333      0.92
      0.6666666      1.83
      0.9999999      2.75
      1.3333330      3.67
      1.6666660      4.58
      1.9999990      5.50
          .           .
          .           .
          .           .
```

The intended values for the variable YARDS are 1/3, 2/3, and 1. However, in actual computer execution, the values for YARDS might be slightly different. When a computer that retains seven-decimal digits is used, the first value is 0.3333333, the closest possible seven-digit approximation to the intended value 1/3. This value is only 1/30000000 too low. However, the next calculated value is 0.3333333 + 0.3333333 = 0.6666666, which is not the closest possible seven-digit approximation to the intended value 2/3. The value 0.6666667 is closer, although the difference between either approximation and the intended value 2/3 is still extremely small. The next computed value for YARDS might be a little further off the mark. Increasing the computed value 0.6666666 by the step size of 0.3333333 gives a new value for YARDS of 0.9999999, which differs by 0.0000001 from the intended value 1.

The difference between the computed and the intended values was very small, but it was large enough to cause the WHILE test to fail. In this example the largest roundoff error encountered so far was 1/10000000. In most cases, it takes a rather large number of arithmetic operations to produce a significant roundoff error.

In executing a loop, however, a more subtle problem arises: how does the computer know when to stop? The stopping value for YARDS in the program PRICES is 1, which is 1.000000 to 7 decimal places. The computed values for YARDS are 0.3333333, 0.6666667, 0.9999999, 1.3333333, ..., none of which is exactly equal to 1.000000. Yet the programmer clearly does not intend the loop to continue to the next calculated value for YARDS of 1.333333, which is nearly 1 1/3.

This is precisely the kind of annoying detail that most programmers would prefer not to have to cope with, because it does not correspond to any comparable difficulty in the original problem. In the absence of roundoff error, the loop in the program PRICES would work properly and print the correct number of lines of output. However, in this case, as there is some slight roundoff, the value of the variable YARDS is never exactly equal to 1. Thus the WHILE condition YARDS .NE. 1 is always true, and the loop never terminates. The failure of this loop to terminate is an instance of violating an important principle of prudent programming: *Avoid writing a test for equality of two quantities* if there is the slightest chance that one or both of the quantities, or even any of the preliminary calculations leading up to these quantities, can result in roundoff error. In practice, the only truly safe numbers are relatively small integers exactly representable on all machines, and even these have been known to fail equality tests on occasion.

How To Avoid Tests For Equality

One substitute for a test for equality is a test for approximate equality. Instead of testing whether two quantities X and Y are equal, one might test whether they are close to each other; that is, whether the difference between them is a small number. Since it may not be known which is larger, it is the absolute value of the difference that must be tested, as in the statement

```
IF (ABS (X - Y) .LT. 0.001) THEN DO
```

In the program PRICES, a simpler test suffices. Rather than comparing the absolute values of the difference between YARDS and 1 to 0.001, the simpler test

```
WHILE (YARDS .LE. 0.999) DO
```

can be made, since YARDS is increasing and will be greater than 1 − 0.001 = 0.999 for the first time during the program execution, when its value should be exactly equal to 1.

Writing Loops Resistant to Roundoff Error

A WHILE loop that refines a DO block terminates when the value of the loop variable is greater than the termination value. For example, the loop

```
      DO 18 Y = 1./6., 1./2., 1./6.
         PRINT, Y
   18 CONTINUE
```

continues until Y is greater than ½.

In selecting the significant digits to retain in a number, some computers round to the number of significant digits retained, and some computers **truncate,** that is, they merely drop the extra digits, however large. Thus the number of iterations in an execution of the loop above is not the same on all computers. If the number ⅙ is rounded to 0.1666667, the third value for Y is 0.1666667 + 0.1666667 + 0.1666667 = 0.5000001, which is greater than the termination value ½, so it is not printed. But if the number ⅙ is truncated to 0.1666666, the third value for Y is 0.1666666 + 0.1666666 + 0.1666666 = 0.4999998, which is less than the termination value ½, so this third value is printed.

If a programming language has loops that work in this manner, as Fortran does, they can be fixed by giving a termination value *between* two expected values of the loop variable. The loop given above could be rewritten as follows to avoid the roundoff problem.

```
Y = 1./6.
WHILE (Y .LE. 0.501) DO
   PRINT, Y
   Y = Y + 1./6.
END WHILE
```

In general, a pseudocode loop headed by a statement of the form

```
DO 18 X = START, FINISH, STEP
```

can be rewritten as follows to minimize roundoff problems.

```
X = START
WHILE (X .LE. FINISH + STEP / 2) DO
   Loop body
   X = X + STEP
END WHILE
```

Avoiding Roundoff Error in an Incremented Variable

If a loop is executed a large number of times, the value of an incremented variable may drift by more than half the step size, affecting the number of times the loop is executed. Even if the loop is executed the proper number of times, the variable may not assume values close enough to the ones needed for computations in the loop. The last general method given here to reduce roundoff error eliminates the cumulative roundoff that comes from adding an approximation to the step size during each iteration of a loop. The program ACCPRC (accurate prices) also uses the technique of calculating in advance the number of times the loop is to be executed, thereby minimizing the possibility that the loop executes the wrong number of times because of roundoff error.

```
C     PROGRAM ACCPRC
      REAL PRICE, COST, YARDS
      REAL FEWEST, MOST, STEP, X
      INTEGER NRCOST, COUNT, NINT
C
      NINT (X) = (X + 0.5)
C
      READ, PRICE
      PRINT 15, 'INPUT DATA  PRICE:', PRICE
   15 FORMAT (T2, A15, F7.2)
      PRINT 25, 'YARDS', 'COST'
   25 FORMAT (T2, A15, A10)
C
      FEWEST = 1./3.
      MOST = 1.0
      STEP = 1./3.
      NRCOST = NINT ( 1 + (MOST - FEWEST) / STEP)
C
      DO 18 COUNT = 1, NRCOST
         YARDS = FEWEST + (COUNT - 1) * STEP
         COST = YARDS * PRICE
         PRINT 35, YARDS, COST
   35    FORMAT (T2, F15.7, F10.2)
   18 CONTINUE
      STOP
      END
```

```
 INPUT DATA  PRICE:   2.75000
          YARDS      COST
      0.3333333      0.92
      0.6666667      1.83
      1.0000000      2.75
```

Table 9.1 compares three different sets of values for the variable YARDS. The intended values increase by exactly 1/3 per iteration, reaching 3000 exactly on the 6001st iteration. The increment values in the next column arise from successively adding the best computer representation of 1.0 / 3.0 to the value of YARDS. The right columns shows values computed by modifying the program ACCPRC so that FEWEST = 1000.0, MOST = 3000.0, and STEP remains 1.0 / 3.0.

The successive increment values will continue to drift farther and farther off the mark. The drift rate on your computer will depend on the number of significant digits retained. On most computers, by the 6001st iteration, roundoff

Table 9.1 A comparison of two methods for resisting roundoff error in a DO variable.

	Values of the DO variable YARDS		
Iteration	Intended value	Successive increment value	ACCPRC value
1	1000	1000	1000
2	1000 1/3	1000.333	1000.333
3	1000 2/3	1000.666	1000.666
4	1001	1000.999	1000.999
5	1001 1/3	1001.333	1001.333
6	1001 2/3	1001.666	1001.666
7	1002	1001.999	1001.999
8	1002 1/3	1002.332	1002.333
.	.	.	.
.	.	.	.
.	.	.	.
5997	2998 2/3	2998.178	2998.666
5998	2999	2998.511	2998.999
5999	2999 1/3	2998.845	2999.333
6000	2999 2/3	2999.178	2999.666
6001	3000	2999.511	2999.999

will be reaching the fourth digit from the right. In the seven-digit arithmetic shown in Table 9.1 the roundoff has reached the tenths place, and is larger than the step size. In ten-digit arithmetic, the roundoff would be in the thousandths place and still be relatively harmless. On the other hand, the values computed by the method of ACCPRC are usually the best computer representation of the intended value, regardless of the arithmetic precision used. This is why the method used in ACCPRC is highly recommended when there are difficulties with roundoff error.

Using Integers to Avoid Roundoff Error

If the intended values of a DO variable are all fractions with the same denominator, it is possible to avoid roundoff error by using the numerator of these fractions as the values of an integer DO variable in a related loop as shown in the program YARDS3. The DO variable THREEX (three times YARDS) has no roundoff error, and the printed value for the number of yards has only the rounding error of the most recent division by 3, and no error if THREEX is an integer multiple of 3.

```
C       PROGRAM YARDS3
        INTEGER THREEX
        DO 18 THREEX = 3000, 9000
           PRINT, FLOAT (THREEX) / 3.0
   18   CONTINUE
        STOP
        END
```

Double Precision

No discussion of roundoff error is complete without mention of double precision or extended precision arithmetic. Many computers provide hardware circuitry for performing the basic arithmetic operations on numbers with approximately double the ordinary number of significant figures for that machine. Fortran allows the programmer to request double precision arithmetic for the calculations of certain values by declaring which variables are to be of type double precision. An example is

```
DOUBLE PRECISION A, B, K47, Z93A (42)
```

On a machine that keeps the 7 most significant decimal digits in ordinary calculations, double precision arithmetic operations might keep the 14 most significant decimal digits. Since roundoff error first appears in the least significant digits, the use of double precision arithmetic forces the roundoff error to start 7 decimal places farther to the right. Thus the number of significant digits unaffected by roundoff error is likely to be 7 more when performing a calculation in double precision than when performing the same calculation using ordinary single precision arithmetic on a 7-digit computer. As a result, the digits and decimal places desired in the answers are more likely to be free from roundoff error when double precision arithmetic is used, although in some severe cases, roundoff error can propagate into the 7 more significant digits of a double precision answer.

Double precision arithmetic does not eliminate roundoff error. It only pushes it several digits to the right. Thus the problems of a small error causing incorrect termination of a WHILE block controlled by an incremented variable, or failure of a test for equality between two variables, are still present. The user of double precision must be aware that the calculations are still subject to some roundoff error, although a much smaller amount, and program accordingly. Moreover, hardware double precision arithmetic operations take longer to perform than ordinary, single precision arithmetic operations. When used on a computer where the double precision arithmetic must be simulated by software, that is, programming supplied with the computer language implementation, the double precision arithmetic operations can take several times as long as the single precision operations on the same machine. There is no doubt that double precision arithmetic is a powerful tool for the reduction of roundoff error, but it is by no means a panacea. The double precision data type was discussed in Section 4.5.

Binary Computers: A Postscript

A great many contemporary computers, probably the majority of them, do their internal arithmetic using a number system based on the number 2 instead of the ordinary base 10 decimal number system. In such a number system, called a **binary number system,** the place values of the integer places from right to left are 1, 2, 4, 8, 16, 32, ..., the powers of 2 instead of the usual decimal place values of 1, 10, 100, 1000, ..., the powers of 10. The places to the right of the binary point are worth successively 1/2, 1/4, 1/8, 1/16, 1/32, ..., as compared to the place values of 1/10, 1/100, 1/1000, ..., for the places to the right of the decimal point in the ordinary number system.

Binary number representations tend to be long and monotonous and are not at all felicitous for human usage. For example, the decimal number 650 is represented in binary as 1010001010, and the decimal number 100 is represented in binary as 1100100. For this reason, when computer languages are implemented on a binary computer or on a computer using number systems based on 8 ("octal") or 16 ("hexadecimal"), which are closely related to the binary number system, the user is still allowed to communicate with the computer using ordinary decimal numbers. The conversion of all input numbers from decimal notation into binary, and the reconversion from binary to ordinary decimal notation of all numbers to be printed or written as output in any other fashion for human use, are done automatically by the computer system. In fact, the user might not even know that the computer is binary.

The reason for mentioning binary computers at this point is the curious fact that, although 1/10 can be represented exactly in one significant decimal digit as 0.1, it cannot be represented exactly in binary, no matter how many significant digits are used. Just as the true decimal representation for 1/3 is 0.3333333333..., never ending, the true binary representation for 1/10 is 0.0001100110011001100..., without termination. In both cases, retaining the fixed number of significant places a particular computer's hardware is designed to handle results in a small but significant roundoff error. Thus 1/10 is represented exactly on every decimal machine but is never represented exactly on any binary machine. A tell-tale sign is that the expressions 10 * (1/10) and 1/10 + 1/10 + 1/10 + 1/10 + 1/10 + 1/10 + 1/10 + 1/10 + 1/10 + 1/10 are computed as exactly 1 on a decimal machine and usually as 0.9999999 on a binary machine.

Besides the fact that there are many common decimal fractions exactly representable in ordinary decimal notation but not exactly representable in binary computers, the problems caused by roundoff error and their solutions are pretty much the same for binary computers as for decimal computers. Small integers are exactly representable in binary notation, as they are in decimal notation, provided they are small enough to fit in the number of binary digits provided by the computer's circuits. Of course, since binary number representations tend to be longer than decimal number representations, the number of binary digits (sometimes called "bits") provided on a given binary computer is usually sufficiently large that the size of the numbers that can be represented is roughly comparable to those representable on decimal machines.

In summary, it is generally conceded that users want to communicate with computers using ordinary decimal numbers, even if the computer happens to be a binary machine. In most computer languages, including Fortran, the user does so, and perhaps the only surprises encountered are related to the fact that numbers like 1/10 cannot be represented exactly in a binary computer.

9.2 Simulation of Water Pollution

Deterministic simulation provides a natural way to solve many problems and is often easier to understand than any other method. Simple population growth is one of the least complicated forms of simulation, as demonstrated in Section 4.8 for the state of New Jersey. A deterministic simulation program that solves a problem about water pollution provides a second illustration of the technique.

In order to understand a phenomenon and to avoid performing experiments that are either too time-consuming, too expensive, or too dangerous to be done using the real situation and material, a scientist constructs a **model** of the situation and performs the experiments on the model. Sometimes the model is a physical model exhibiting the same phenomena on a much smaller and more tractable scale. More often these days, with computers available to do the huge amounts of computation involved, the model is a mathematical one.

All model building necessarily involves a compromise between a desire to retain as many characteristics of the original as possible and a desire to simplify the model so it can be solved or examined more conveniently. In mathematical model building, the values of the important physically meaningful quantities are included in the model along with mathematical rules describing how these values change. These rules model the physical laws that determine the behavior of the original physical system.

In a **deterministic simulation** of a situation, the mathematical rules describing how the values of the important quantities change are used to predict future values of these quantities. The word *deterministic* means that there is no element of chance in the rules for predicting future values. The random number generating function discussed in the next section can be used to construct **nondeterministic** or **probabilistic** simulations, which are discussed in Section 9.3.

Garbage In, Garbage Out

Neatly printed computer output has the ring of authority and truth. Especially in the area of simulation, the user needs to be reminded of the standard computer science warning: Garbage in, garbage out. If the mathematical model does not capture the important features of the original or if the starting data is in error, the predictions generated by the simulation program are worthless, even though they may be printed to seven decimal places. However, if the model is correct in essential detail and the data used are accurate, the results of the simulation are likely to be accurate predictions of what will happen in the real situation.

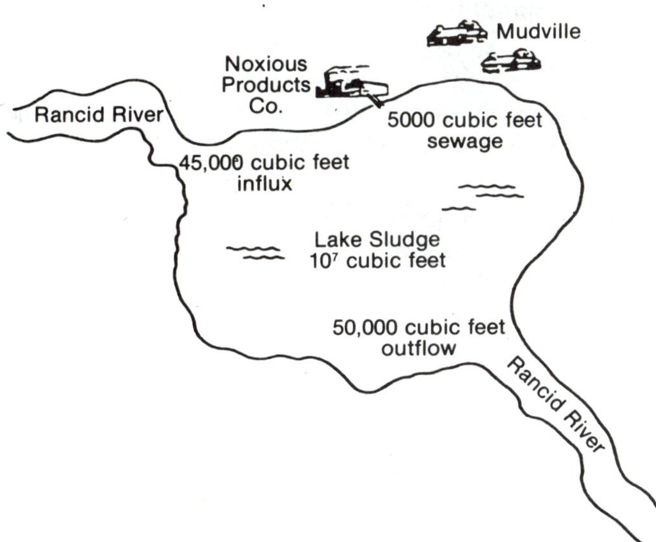

Figure 9.1 The environs of Mudville.

A Water Quality Problem

The residents of Mudville, located on the shore of Lake Sludge, notice that the quality of the water in their beautiful lake has deteriorated in recent years, and they make a special study of the situation producing some critical facts, illustrated in Figure 9.1.

First, they observe that the volume of Lake Sludge is 10 million cubic feet, and that the lake is 0.5 percent polluted. That is, the quantity of polluting materials is

$$0.005 \times 10{,}000{,}000 = 50{,}000 \text{ cubic feet}$$

Second, the influx from the Rancid River, which is 0.2 percent polluted, is 45,000 cubic feet per day. Third, the town of Mudville puts into the lake daily 5000 cubic feet of sewage, of which 10 percent is concentrated polluting materials.

A Simulation of the Water Flow

A deterministic simulation which can calculate when the pollution level in the lake reaches 1 percent needs to record only one item of information, the amount of pollutants in Lake Sludge. That is the value of the variable LAKGNK (lake gunk) in the program POLLUT. The initial value of LAKGNK is the current quantity of pollutants in the lake, which is $0.005 \times 1{,}000{,}000$ cubic feet. Each day, counted by the variable day, the value of LAKGNK is increased by the quantity of pollutants coming from sewage and the influx of the Rancid River. The value of LAKGNK is then decreased by the amount of pollutants that flow out of the lake. This calculation is repeated until the proportion of pollutants in the lake, LAKGNK / LAKVOL (lake volume), is more than 1 percent.

In the program POLLUT, some simplifying assumptions have been made.

1. There is no loss of water by evaporation, so the amount of liquid flowing out of Lake Sludge is equal to the amount flowing in.
2. The pollutants in the lake are completely mixed, so that the proportion of pollutants leaving Lake Sludge via the river is the same as the proportion for the whole lake.

The first simplification can be removed easily and is left for an exercise at the end of this chapter.

```
C       PROGRAM POLLUT
C       SIMULATES WATER FLOW AND POLLUTION CONTENT
C       FOR LAKE SLUDGE
C
C       CONSTANTS:
C          LAKVOL = LAKE VOLUME
C          RVRINF = RIVER INFLUX
C          SWGINF = SEWAGE INFLUX
C          RVRPOL = RIVER POLLUTION (FRACTION)
C          SWGPOL = SEWAGE POLLUTION (FRACTION)
C          INIPOL = INITIAL POLLUTION OF LAKE (FRACTION)
C          MAXPOL = MAXIMUM POLLUTION OF LAKE (FRACTION)
C          MAXDYS = MAXIMUM NUMBER OF DAYS TO RUN SIMULATION
C
        REAL LAKVOL, RVRINF, SWGINF, RVRPOL
        REAL SWGPOL, INIPOL, MAXPOL
        INTEGER MAXDYS
C
```

```
C       VARIABLES:
C          LAKGNK = LAKE GUNK, QUANTITY OF POLLUTANTS IN LAKE
C          RVRGNK = RIVER GUNK, QUANTITY OF POLLUTANTS IN RIVER
C          SWGGNK = SEWAGE GUNK, QUANTITY OF POLLUTANTS IN SEWAGE
C          RVROUT = RIVER OUTFLOW
C          DAY    = COUNTS DAYS IN SIMULATION
C          TOOPOL = LOGICAL VALUE RECORDING WHETHER LAKE IS TOO POLLUTED
C
        REAL LAKGNK, RVRGNK, SWGGNK, RVROUT
        INTEGER DAY
        LOGICAL TOOPOL
C
        LAKVOL = 1.0E7
        RVRINF = 45000.0
        SWGINF = 5000.0
        RVRPOL = 0.002
        SWGPOL = 0.1
        INIPOL = 0.005
        MAXPOL = 0.01
        MAXDYS = 10000
C
        RVRGNK = RVRPOL * RVRINF
        SWGGNK = SWGPOL * SWGINF
        RVROUT = SWGINF + RVRINF
        LAKGNK = INIPOL * LAKVOL
        TOOPOL = .FALSE.
C
        DO 18 DAY = 1, MAXDYS
           LAKGNK = LAKGNK + RVRGNK + SWGGNK
           LAKGNK = LAKGNK - (LAKGNK / LAKVOL) * RVROUT
           IF (LAKGNK / LAKVOL .GT. MAXPOL) THEN DO
              TOOPOL = .TRUE.
              GO TO 19
           END IF
   18   CONTINUE
C
   19   IF (TOOPOL) THEN DO
           PRINT, 'MUDVILLE IS DOOMED IN', DAY, 'DAYS.'
        ELSE DO
           PRINT, 'THERE IS NO DANGER TO MUDVILLE FOR AT LEAST',
     +                 MAXDYS, 'DAYS.'
        END IF
        STOP
        END
MUDVILLE IS DOOMED IN          271 DAYS.
```

Testing Corrective Actions

If the Noxious Products plant were closed and sewage treatment facilities built, the town could reduce the pollutant level of the sewage going into the lake to 0.1 percent. If the septic tanks along the Rancid River were replaced by a sewer system, the pollutant level of the river would drop to 0.03 percent. If these actions could be implemented immediately, how long would it be before the pollution level of the lake dropped to 0.1 percent?

The program CLENUP is similar to the program POLLUT. The pollutant levels of the water sources have been changed, and the simulation is stopped when LAKGNK < 0.001 × LAKVOL. Simply by changing the numbers in the program CLENUP, it is possible to predict the effect on the lake of any other changes in the pollutant levels of the river or of the town's sewage.

```
C       PROGRAM CLENUP
C       SIMULATES WATER FLOW AND POLLUTION CONTENT
C       FOR LAKE SLUDGE, BUT WITH LOWER POLLUTION LEVELS
C
C       CONSTANTS:
C          LAKVOL = LAKE VOLUME
C          RVRINF = RIVER INFLUX
C          SWGINF = SEWAGE INFLUX
C          RVRPOL = RIVER POLLUTION (FRACTION)
C          SWGPOL = SEWAGE POLLUTION (FRACTION)
C          INIPOL = INITIAL POLLUTION OF LAKE (FRACTION)
C          MINPOL = MINIMUM POLLUTION OF LAKE (FRACTION)
C          MAXDYS = MAXIMUM NUMBER OF DAYS TO RUN SIMULATION
C
        REAL LAKVOL, RVRINF, SWGINF, RVRPOL
        REAL SWGPOL, INIPOL, MINPOL
        INTEGER MAXDYS
C
C       VARIABLES:
C          LAKGNK = LAKE GUNK, QUANTITY OF POLLUTANTS IN LAKE
C          RVRGNK = RIVER GUNK, QUANTITY OF POLLUTANTS IN RIVER
C          SWGGNK = SEWAGE GUNK, QUANTITY OF POLLUTANTS IN SEWAGE
C          RVROUT = RIVER OUTFLOW
C          DAY    = COUNTS DAYS IN SIMULATION
C          CLEAN  = LOGICAL VALUE RECORDING WHETHER LAKE IS CLEANED UP
C
        REAL LAKGNK, RVRGNK, SWGGNK, RVROUT
        INTEGER DAY
        LOGICAL CLEAN
C
        LAKVOL = 1.0E7
        RVRINF = 45000.0
        SWGINF = 5000.0
        RVRPOL = 0.0003
        SWGPOL = 0.001
        INIPOL = 0.005
        MINPOL = 0.001
        MAXDYS = 10000
        RVRGNK = RVRPOL * RVRINF
        SWGGNK = SWGPOL * SWGINF
        RVROUT = SWGINF + RVRINF
        LAKGNK = INIPOL * LAKVOL
        CLEAN = .FALSE.
C
        DO 18 DAY = 1, MAXDYS
           LAKGNK = LAKGNK + RVRGNK + SWGGNK
           LAKGNK = LAKGNK - (LAKGNK / LAKVOL) * RVROUT
```

```
         IF (LAKGNK / LAKVOL .LT. MINPOL) THEN DO
            CLEAN = .TRUE.
            GO TO 19
         END IF
   18  CONTINUE
C
   19 IF (CLEAN) THEN DO
         PRINT 15, 'POLLUTION LEVEL DOWN TO', MINPOL * 100,
     +            '% AFTER', DAY, ' DAYS.'
   15    FORMAT (A24, F10.6, A7, I4, A6)
      ELSE DO
         PRINT 25, 'POLLUTANT LEVEL STILL NOT BELOW', MINPOL *100,
     +            '% AFTER', MAXDYS, ' DAYS.'
   25    FORMAT (A31, F10.6, A7, I4, A6)
      END IF
      STOP
      END
POLLUTION LEVEL DOWN TO  0.1000000% AFTER 398 DAYS.
```

The simulation technique illustrated in the program cleanup is being used to solve some very complex problems. In *American Scientist,* Walter Orr Roberts discussed a simulation program to model the weather system of the entire world.*

> Not only will the model, when built and tested, permit experiments to refine weather and climate forecasting research, but also we anticipate, as suggested above, that such a model will permit experiments in global weather modification—safely in the model, and not in nature. We should be able, for example, to level the Rockies or rotate the earth backwards and see what the impact is on weather. Or more usefully and realistically, we hope to be able to simulate, for a few thousand dollars, cleaning up world air pollution, so that we may be able to evaluate the meteorological consequences of such a clean-up—giving us a handle to the value of so doing in the real world. This would be a very powerful decision-making aid.

9.3 Probabilistic Simulation of Gambling Games

In Section 9.2, we solved a water pollution problem with a deterministic simulation. Another kind of simulation is called **probabilistic**, or **nondeterministic**. The programmer-defined function RNDINT, introduced below permits a programmer to generate a random integer from 1 to 6. By interpreting the result as the outcome of the roll of a single die, it is possible to simulate dice games. The uncertainty of the result is the reason the simulation is called nondeterministic. A nondeterministic simulation is used to calculate the proportion of rolls in a fair dice game that come up either 7 or 11. Later in the section we examine two betting strategies for the game of roulette.

Even if it is impossible to predict with certainty the outcome of any particular occurrence of a random event, it may be possible to ascertain some facts about what will happen if the event is repeated many times. A typical nondeterministic simulation program simulates a random event many times, recording information about the entire sequence of events. A nondeterministic simulation is often called a Monte Carlo simulation, after the casino famed for its games of chance.

---

* Walter Orr Roberts, "Man on a Changing Earth", *American Scientist,* Vol. 59, No. 1, pp. 16-19.

Generating Random Numbers

To simulate the throwing of one die, the computer needs to generate a number from 1 to 6. Some Fortran systems have a built-in function that can be used to generate random problems, but even on Fortran systems that do not have such a function built in, the function subprogram given in this section may be used as a programmer-defined function.

For any two integers R and S, the value of the expression

```
RNDINT (R, S)
```

is one of the integers from R to S, although exactly which one it will be cannot be predicted in advance. For instance, the value of the expression

```
RNDINT (0, 9)
```

could be any one of the integers 0, 1, 2, ..., 9. The likelihood that any one of these possibilities will be the computed value is the same as the likelihood that any other one will be. The user does not know in advance which of these 10 possible values will occur when the computer evaluates the expression

```
RNDINT (0, 9)
```

The user only knows that each possible value has a 1/10 chance of occurring. Moreover, each time the expression is evaluated, a completely new and independent choice is made for the random integer from the complete set of possibilities.

The problem simulating the throw of one die may be solved by executing the statement

```
DIE = RNDINT (1, 6)
```

Properties of Random Integers

In two consecutive evaluations of a random integer generating function, the second random integer is neither necessarily the same as nor necessarily different from the first. In fact, for the throw of the die, about 1/6 of the time they are the same, and about 5/6 of the time they are different. This property is illustrated by the program RNDDIG (random digits) that chooses a random integer from zero to nine, 50 consecutive times.

```
C       PROGRAM RNDDIG
C       GENERATES 50 DIGITS USING RNDINT (0, 9)
C
        INTEGER I, J, RNDINT
C
        DO 18 I = 1, 10
           PRINT, (RNDINT (0, 9), J = 1, 5)
   18   CONTINUE
        STOP
        END
C
C
        FUNCTION RNDINT (R, S)
C       GENERATES AN INTEGER IN THE RANGE R TO S
C
        INTEGER RNDINT, R, S
        INTEGER MAX, MULT, ADD, SEED
C
        DATA MAX, MULT, ADD, SEED / 1000, 21, 437, 1 /
C
```

```
SEED = MOD (MULT * SEED + ADD, MAX)
RNDINT = R + SEED * (S - R + 1) / MAX
RETURN
END
```

```
    4           0           5           8           6
    8           1           3           3           8
    7           7           6           3           5
    1           8           4           8           7
    9           3           7           8           4
    3           4           5           2           6
    2           0           8           2           2
    6           1           5           7           4
    5           7           8           7           1
    9           8           6           2           3
```

Evaluation of the same expression RNDINT (0, 9) in the PRINT statement of the program RNDDIG results in all 50 of the above random digits. Not every one of the 10 digits occurs exactly the same number of times in the above table, but surprising as it may seem at first sight, this is to be expected. Suppose, to make an analogy, that an experiment consisted of tossing a coin 8 times. The probability of obtaining exactly 4 heads and 4 tails is not a virtual certainty, but actually is less than 1/3. This may be verified either analytically by those who know how to compute combinatorial probabilities, or empirically by performing the experiment of tossing 8 coins a large number of times. To further illustrate why an exactly equal number of heads and tails in the coin tossing experiment, or exactly 5 repetitions of each digit in the random number table, is not the most reasonable or the most probable occurrence, imagine what a scrupulously fair coin would do in an experiment consisting of 5 coin tosses. Would it have to show up heads 2½ times?

There are two important rules for using the function RNDINT. Both of its arguments, the two numbers in the parentheses, should be integers, and the second integer should be at least as large as the first.

Pseudorandom Numbers (Optional Reading)

Computers don't really generate random numbers. What they generate has all of the important properties of a truly random collection of numbers, but it cannot actually be random because it is calculated by an algorithm.

Suppose, for example, that RNDINT (1, 73) is computed 7,300 times. The numbers produced would appear to be random, for our simple purposes, if each of the integers 1 to 73 is generated approximately 100 times, that is, approximately 1/73 of the time, and if there is no discernible pattern in the numbers generated. Of course, each will not occur exactly 100 times, but perhaps one number will occur 84 times, another will occur 107 times, and so on.

The Function Subprogram RNDINT

The function RNDINT generates random numbers by keeping a number called the **seed**. Each time a new random number is to be produced, the seed is multiplied by MULT and ADD is added to the result. Then all but the last three digits of the seed are discarded by taking the remainder (modulus) when the seed is divided by 1000. The number is an integer from 0 to 999. Next the interval 0 to 999 is divided into S − R + 1 parts, one for each possible value of RNDINT, yielding an integer from 0 to S − R. Then the value of R is added to this number to get an integer from R to S. The value of SEED is initialized to 1 in the DATA statement.

It is no easy matter to decide whether the function RNDINT does a good job of behaving like a true random generator, but it is entirely adequate for the present purpose of getting different values for the throw of dice.

The parameters 1000, 21, and 437 were chosen so that the quantity

```
SEED * MULT + ADD
```

would not cause overflow (i.e., exceed the maximum allowable size for integers) on any Fortran system. If your system supports larger integers, you might try parameters of 10,000, 201, and 3,437 or 32,768, 891, and 0. Some of the best random number generators use the method of RNDINT for suitably chosen parameters.

Simulating the Throw of a Die

We now consider the problem of calculating the proportion of times that the roll of two fair dice results in a 7 or an 11. One way to solve this problem by a simulation is to take a pair of dice and roll them a large number of times while recording the number of favorable outcomes. One might even use the results of a real dice game in progress, provided one is sure the dice are fair. An easier and faster way, however, is to have a computer probabilistically simulate the rolls of the dice, as described in this section.

Since a die has six faces with one to six dots on a face, a computer can simulate the throw of one die by evaluating the function RNDINT (1, 6). The value of the function represents the number of dots on the face of the die when it is rolled.

The program SVN11 estimates the percentage of rolls of two dice that yield a 7 or 11. The variable WINS records the number of *successes,* that is, the number of times the dice come up 7 or 11. The DO block that simulates each trial roll of the dice is executed 1000 times. The trial is successful if the value of the variable DICE, representing the total number of dots showing on the two dice, is 7 or 11, in which case the value of WINS is increased by 1. The final percentage is (WINS / 1000) * 100 = WINS / 10.

```
C        PROGRAM SVN11
C        SIMULATES THROWING TWO DICE
C        TO DETERMINE THE PERCENTAGE OF TIMES
C        A PAIR OF DICE COME UP 7 OR 11
C
         INTEGER ROLLS, DICE, I, WINS, RNDINT
C
         ROLLS = 1000
         WINS = 0
         DO 18 I = 1, ROLLS
            DICE = RNDINT (1, 6) + RNDINT (1, 6)
            IF ((DICE .EQ. 7) .OR. (DICE .EQ. 11)) THEN DO
               WINS = WINS + 1
            END IF
      18 CONTINUE
C
         PRINT 15,
     +         'THE PERCENTAGE OF ROLLS THAT ARE 7 OR 11 IS',
     +         100.0 * WINS / ROLLS
      15 FORMAT '(T2, A43, F6.2)',
         STOP
         END
```

```
THE PERCENTAGE OF ROLLS THAT ARE 7 OR 11 IS 22.40
```

It would be incorrect for the program SVN11 to use the statement

```
DICE = 2 * RNDINT (1, 6)
```

because this statement generates only one roll and doubles it, so that the result always would be even. The statement used in the program SVN11 generates two random numbers that might be the same, but more often are not.

The program SVN11 simulates the event of rolling two dice 1000 times. The problem of deciding how may times to simulate the event in order to obtain a good approximation to the true value is a difficult one. Ten times obviously is not enough, and a trillion simulations would require too much time on any computer.

One way to approach this problem is to run the program 3 or 4 times with some fairly small number of simulations of the event, but using different starting values for the seed. If the answers are all fairly close to each other, that is an indication that the number of simulations was sufficient. If the answers are quite different, then the number of simulations could be increased by a factor of 10 if there is sufficient computer time available to execute the program. One should not expect in rerunning the program SVN11 to duplicate the answer 22.40 percent shown in the sample execution. The authors ran the dice program four more times (changing the initial value of seed each time) with the following results:

21.80 percent	21.60 percent
22.10 percent	22.80 percent

The true answer is $6/36 + 2/36 = 8/36 = 22.22$ percent.

Roulette

Roulette is a popular game in gambling casinos. Many interesting questions about the game can be answered by simple simulation programs, which will be Monte Carlo simulations because of the uncertainty of the result of spinning the roulette wheel.

When the roulette wheel is spun, a metal ball is allowed to drop onto it and to come to rest in one of 38 different positions numbered 1 to 36, 0, and 00. Half of the positions 1 to 36 are colored red and the other half black, as noted in Figure 9.1. Positions 0 and 00 are colored green. Before the wheel is spun, bets may be placed on red, black, even, odd, any individual number, or several different combinations of numbers. Figure 9.2 shows what the betting table looks like, how bets are made, and the amount paid to the winners. A winner who bets on a combination that pays 6 to 1 is paid \$6 for each \$1 bet and the amount bet is also returned.

A Comparison of Two Betting Strategies; Computer-Assisted Decisions

Suppose a gambler enters a Las Vegas casino with \$1000. She decides to play roulette, betting each time on the red. She is considering two different betting strategies.

1. Bet \$1 each time.
2. Bet \$1 on the first spin and on any spin following a win. On any spin following a loss, bet \$1 more than the total losses since the last win, or whatever is left of the \$1000, whichever is smaller.

If each bet takes a minute, how much money should the gambler expect to have after an hour using one of these strategies?

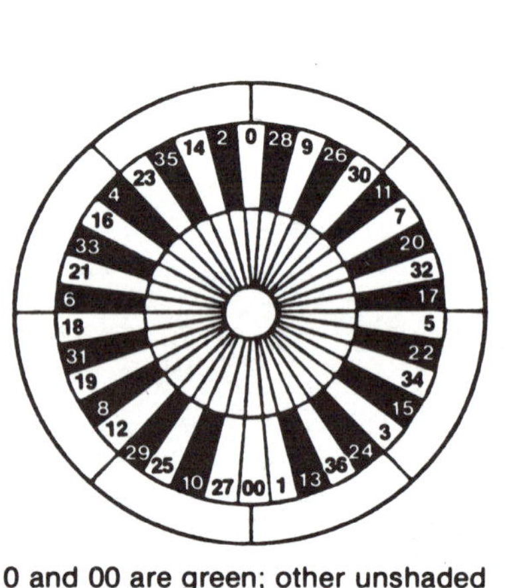

0 and 00 are green; other unshaded numbers are red

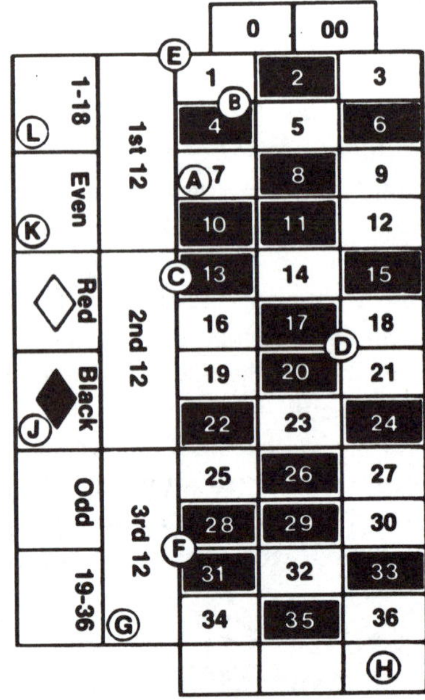

A Single numbers .... pays 35 to 1
B Two numbers....(split) .... pays 17 to 1
C Three numbers .... pays 11 to 1
D Four numbers .... pays 8 to 1
E Five numbers................. pays 6 to 1
F Six numbers .... pays 5 to 1
G Dozen .... pays 2 to 1
H Column .... pays 2 to 1
J Color .... pays even
K Odd or even .... pays even
L High or low.................. pays even

Figure 9.2 A roulette wheel and its payoffs.

A Session Using the Fixed-Bet Strategy

The program ROUFIX (roulette with fixed bet) simulates a 1-hour gambling session in which the gambler bets $1 each minute on the red. The information the program must record consists only of the amount of money in the gambler's possession and the number of bets that have been made.

```
PROGRAM ROUFIX
Start with $1000
DO 60 bets
   Place bet
   Spin roulette wheel
   IF position is red then
      Pay off
   END IF
CONTINUE
Print the amount of money left
END
```

In the more detailed version, the value of RNDINT (1, 38) simulates the spin of the roulette wheel; the values 37 and 38 represent 0 and 00, respectively. This random value is assigned to the variable WHEEL and checked to see if it is one of the 18 red positions to determine if the gambler wins.

As seen in Figure 9.2, the red numbers on the roulette wheel do not follow a simple pattern, such as all even numbers or all odd numbers, so no simple formula suffices to decide if the value of WHEEL represents a red number or not.

The variable MONEY represents the amount of money in the gambler's possession and is initialized at $1000. The loop that simulates one bet is executed 60 times. The value of MONEY is decreased by one when the bet is placed, and if the gambler wins, the variable MONEY is increased by the $1 won plus the $1 bet.

```
C      PROGRAM ROUFIX
C      SIMULATES A BETTING SESSION
C      AT THE ROULETTE TABLE
C      WITH A FIXED BETTING STRATEGY
C
       INTEGER NRBETS, MONEY, BETNR, WHEEL, RNDINT
C
       NRBETS = 60
C      START WITH ONE THOUSAND DOLLARS
       MONEY = 1000
C      SIMULATE BETS
       DO 18 BETNR = 1, NRBETS
C         PLACE BET
          MONEY = MONEY - 1
C         SPIN WHEEL
          WHEEL = RNDINT (1, 38)
C         CHECK IF RESULT IS RED
          IF (WHEEL .EQ. 1 .OR. WHEEL .EQ. 3 .OR.
     +        WHEEL .EQ. 5 .OR. WHEEL .EQ. 7 .OR.
     +        WHEEL .EQ. 9 .OR. WHEEL .EQ. 12 .OR.
     +        WHEEL .EQ. 14 .OR. WHEEL .EQ. 16 .OR.
     +        WHEEL .EQ. 18 .OR. WHEEL .EQ. 19 .OR.
     +        WHEEL .EQ. 21 .OR. WHEEL .EQ. 23 .OR.
     +        WHEEL .EQ. 25 .OR. WHEEL .EQ. 27 .OR.
     +        WHEEL .EQ. 30 .OR. WHEEL .EQ. 32 .OR.
     +        WHEEL .EQ. 34 .OR. WHEEL .EQ. 36) THEN DO
C            PAY OFF
             MONEY = MONEY + 2
          END IF
   18  CONTINUE
C
       PRINT, 'THE AMOUNT OF MONEY LEFT IS $', MONEY
       STOP
       END
THE AMOUNT OF MONEY LEFT IS $           996
```

The 1-hour gambling session is simulated only once by the program ROUFIX. The program would have to be run many times in order to obtain a good estimate of what the average win or loss would be. Of course, a loss should be expected, since a bet on the red pays even money, but there are 20 losing positions and only 18 winning ones on the roulette wheel. Don't forget to change the initial value of SEED for each simulation: it is set by the DATA statement in the function RNDINT.

Sessions Using the Strategy to Recoup Losses

Sessions using the second gambling strategy are simulated by the program ROUVAR (roulette with variable bet). The variable LOSS records the amount lost on the previous bets since the last win. For the first bet, and after any bet that is won, LOSS = 0. In the betting strategy simulated by the program, the amount of the bet is LOSS + 1 unless the gambler doesn't have that much money left. In that case, all that is left is bet. Thus the amount bet should be LOSS + 1 or MONEY, whichever is smaller.

The program ROUVAR simulates any number of 60-minute betting sessions. The number of sessions (NRSESS) is a parameter. The variable SESSON counts the sessions simulated. After each session, the amount of money remaining in the gambler's possession is added to TOTAL, so that the average amount left can be printed after all the sessions have been simulated. The value of the variable TOTAL is set to zero initially. As might be expected, the sample execution printout shows that a gambler employing this strategy either wins a few dollars or loses a lot almost every time.

By sacrificing the details of the roulette wheel positions, this program is able to achieve a highly efficient test for a red position without any loss of accuracy in its calculations. Since all positions on a roulette wheel are equally likely, it really does not matter for computational purposes which 18 of them are red. No matter which ones are red, over a long period, the proportion of spins yielding red is about 18/38, and the proportion of spins resulting in black or green is about 20/38. In the program ROUVAR, a value of RNDINT (1, 38) less than or equal to 18 is taken as a spin of red.

```
C     PROGRAM ROUVAR
C     SIMULATES A BETTING SESSION
C     AT THE ROULETTE TABLE
C     WITH A VARIABLE BETTING STRATEGY
C
      INTEGER NRBETS, NRSESS
      INTEGER MONEY, SESSON, TOTAL
C
      NRBETS = 60
      NRSESS = 25
C
C     INITIALIZE TOTAL OF AMOUNTS LEFT AFTER EACH SESSION
      TOTAL = 0
      PRINT 15, 'SESSION', 'AMOUNT LEFT'
   15 FORMAT (2A20)
      DO 18 SESSON = 1, NRSESS
C        START WITH ONE THOUSAND DOLLARS
         MONEY = 1000
         CALL BETS (MONEY, NRBETS)
         PRINT 25, SESSON, MONEY
   25    FORMAT (2I20)
C        ADD AMOUNT LEFT TO TOTAL
         TOTAL = TOTAL + MONEY
   18 CONTINUE
C
      PRINT, ' '
      PRINT 35,
     +      'THE AVERAGE AMOUNT OF MONEY LEFT IS $',
     +       REAL (TOTAL) / NRSESS
   35 FORMAT (T2, A38, F7.2)
      STOP
      END
C
C
      SUBROUTINE BETS (MONEY, NRBETS)
C     SIMULATES ONE BETTING SESSION
C
```

```
      INTEGER MONEY, NRBETS
      INTEGER WHEEL, LOSS, BET, BETNR, RNDINT
      LOGICAL BROKE
C
      BROKE = .FALSE.
C     LOSS IS AMOUNT SINCE LAST WIN
      LOSS = 0
C     SIMULATE BETS
      DO 18 BETNR = 1, NRBETS
C        BET IS PREVIOUS LOSS + 1
C        BUT NO MORE THAN GAMBLER HAS LEFT
         IF (LOSS .LT. MONEY) THEN DO
            BET = LOSS + 1
         ELSE DO
            BET = MONEY
         END IF
C        PLACE BET
         MONEY = MONEY - BET
C        SPIN WHEEL
         WHEEL = RNDINT (1, 38)
C        CHECK IF RESULT IS RED
         IF (WHEEL .LE. 18) THEN DO
C           PAY OFF
            MONEY = MONEY + 2 * BET
            LOSS = 0
         ELSE DO
            BROKE = (MONEY .EQ. 0)
            LOSS = LOSS + BET
         END IF
   18 CONTINUE
      RETURN
      END
```

SESSION	AMOUNT LEFT
1	1030
2	1024
3	1028
4	992
5	1028
6	999
7	1023
8	1028
9	1025
10	1029
11	1030
12	1025
13	1033
14	1027
15	1032
16	1026
17	1029
18	1031
19	1023
20	1031
21	1019
22	1023

```
                23                    1028
                24                    1022
                25                    1029

THE AVERAGE AMOUNT OF MONEY LEFT IS $1024.56
```

9.4 Self-Test Questions

Section 9.1

1. Perform the calculation (1 / 7) * 7 by hand, rounding the intermediate answer and the final answer to seven significant digits. (This involves calculating eight digits and then rounding to seven.) Is the answer equal to 1?
2. Perform the calculation (2 / 7) * 7 by hand, rounding the intermediate answer and the final answer to seven significant digits. Would a seven-decimal-digit computer call this answer equal to 2 in an IF test?
3. What significant difference is there between the calculations for Question 1 and for Question 2 that causes one to compute the exact answer and the other to show roundoff error?
4. Perform the calculation (1 / 7) * 7 by carrying 14 digits throughout the calculation and rounding the final answer to seven significant digits. How does this computation differ from that for Question 1?
5. A well-known fact of ordinary arithmetic, called the Associative Law, says that, for any three numbers a, b, and c,

   $$a + (b + c) = (a + b) + c$$

   Test whether this law holds in computer arithmetic using the values $a = 5.326451$, $b = 6.954603$, and $c = 1.719843$. Be sure to round each intermediate result so that it retains no more than seven significant digits.
6. In ordinary arithmetic, the expression

   $$(a + b) - a$$

   is exactly equal to b. Keeping seven significant digits in all intermediate and final results, what is the size of the roundoff error that occurs when $a = 12345$ and $b = 0.1234567$ in the expression above? Why is the roundoff error so large compared to the size of b?
7. In the calculation and comparisons for Question 6, try different values for a and b. In particular, find values for a and b such that the number of significant digits remaining from b is only one; find values such that all seven significant digits of b remain; and find values for a and b such that only four significant digits of b remain in the final answer.
8. Does addition or subtraction have the greater potential for roundoff error disasters?
9. The Associative Law of Multiplication says that in ordinary arithmetic

   $$x \times (y \times z) = (x \times y) \times z$$

   for any numbers x, y, and z. Find three computer-represented numbers such that this equality fails on a seven-digit machine. Hint: Try making the first significant digit of $x \times y$ small and the first significant digit of $y \times z$ large. (The same calculation may be tried on a three-digit machine to save arithmetic done by hand.) Does multiplication have the same potential for roundoff disaster as addition or subtraction?

Section 9.2

1. What are the principal advantages of simulation by computer?
2. What is the meaning of the phrase "garbage in, garbage out"?

Section 9.3

1. For each of the following three expressions, determine all possible values.
```
2 * RNDINT (0, 5)
RNDINT (0, 10)
RNDINT (0, 5) + RNDINT (0, 5)
```
2. Which two of the three expressions in Question 1 are the most nearly alike? How does the other expression differ from these two?
3. Is one run of a nondeterministic simulation program enough to establish an answer? How many simulations are enough?
4. What is the difference between a deterministic simulation and a nondeterministic simulation?
5. Why are nondeterministic simulations called Monte Carlo simulations?

9.5 Programming Exercises

1. **Purpose:** To investigate a subtle case of roundoff error.

   The problem: Calculate the sums

   0 + 1/3 + 2/3 + 1 + · · · + 19 2/3 + 20

   and

   20 + 19 2/3 + 19 1/3 + 19 + · · · + 1/3 + 0

   using a computer. Be sure to print the computer approximations to each of the numbers added to form the sum. How do the answers compare to the exact answer 610? Theoretically, these sums are formed by the same numbers added in reverse order. In the computer output, are the same numbers actually added in both sums? Explain any differences. Compute the same sums using the technique introduced in the program ACCPRC in Section 9.1 to minimize the roundoff error in the calculation. Are the same numbers now used in both sums? Are the sums equal to each other or to the exact answer 610?

   Input data: None.

   Sample output: It will vary depending on the computer.

2. **Purpose:** To investigate an obvious example of roundoff.

   The problem: In the absence of roundoff error, as the number n grows larger, the value of the expression

   $(1 + 1/n)^n$

   gets closer and closer to the important mathematical constant e = 2.718281828459045.... Using either a desk calculator or a computer, calculate the value of this expression for values of n in the following sequences until the answer is obviously wrong.

   1. 2, 4, 8, 16, 32, 64, 128, 256, 512, 1024, 2048, 4096, 8192, ...,
   2. 3, 6, 12, 24, 48, 96, 192, 384, 768, 1536, 3072, 6144, 12288, ...,
   3. 10, 100, 1000, 10000, 100000, ...,

This formula, which is closely related to compound interest formulas, is especially sensitive to roundoff error for large values of n, so the answers may differ considerably depending on the machine used.

Input: None.

Sample output: Varies depending on the computer.

3. **Purpose:** To program an example of a deterministic simulation.

   The problem: The population of the United States in 1970 was 203.2 million. By 1980 it had increased 11.5 percent to 226.5 million. If it increases by 11.5 percent each decade, what will the population of the United States be in 2000? In 2050?

   Input: None.

   Output:

```
IN THE YEAR 2000, THE POPULATION OF THE U. S. WILL BE 286.1 MILLION
IN THE YEAR 2050, THE POPULATION OF THE U. S. WILL BE 485.3 MILLION
```

4. **The purpose:** To program a more detailed deterministic simulation.

   The problem: The town of Bettysburg had 10,324 residents in the year 2073. Every year there is a new baby born for each 173 residents and one death for every 211 residents. Every year exactly 47 new residents move to town, and 76 move away. Write a deterministic simulation that will determine the population in the year 2084.

5. **Purpose:** To test alternatives in the Lake Sludge model.

   The problem: Suppose the pollutant level of the Rancid River is reduced to 0.03 percent, but the residents of Mudville are not willing to close the Noxious Products plant because most of them would lose their jobs. Therefore the pollutant level in the town's sewage will be 1 percent, even after installation of a treatment facility.

   a) What will happen to the pollution level of the lake? Put a PRINT statement in the simulation program that will display the pollution level of the lake only every 30 days.

   b) Modify the Lake Sludge program POLLUT to reflect the assumption that 500 cubic feet of pure, unpolluted water evaporate each day and the flow of water out of the lake into the Rancid River is 49,500 cubic feet.

6. **Purpose:** To simulate Mendel's Law.

   Background: The individuals of certain species of birds may be any one of three genetic types: BB, Bb, or bb. Individuals of types BB and Bb have brown eyes, and those of type bb have blue eyes. Each year during mating season, mating between the members of each pair of genetic types produces a number of offspring, which is equal to 10 percent of the number of individuals in the smaller of the two groups. To illustrate, if there are 31 million BB adults and 22 million bb adults, they will produce 0.1×22 million $= 2.2$ million offspring. The genotype of each offspring is determined by selecting at random one of the genes (B or b) from each parent. Each of the four not necessarily distinct genotypes comprises one-fourth of the offspring generation. Each year, after the offspring are produced, 15 percent of the brown-eyed adults and 5 percent of the blue-eyed adults die. The new offspring become reproducing adults in 1 year.

   The problem: If the current population distribution is given by the following table

Type	Population (Millions)
BB	16.3
Bb	41.2
bb	75.6

write a program to determine the population of each type in 30 years.

7. **Purpose:** To explore a practical application of simulation.

   The problem: A husband and wife plan to save money from their paychecks to make a down payment on a home. They intend to make monthly deposits of $800 in a savings account on which the bank pays monthly interest at the rate of 7/12 of 1 percent. (The bank advertises a nominal annual rate of 7 percent, but it actually pays somewhat more, because the interest is compounded monthly.) How many months will they need to accumulate $30,000?

8. **Purpose:** To program examples of nondeterministic simulation.

   The problem: Select one of the following problems and write the program to solve it.

   a) Write a program that determines by simulation the percentage of times the sum of two rolled dice will be 2, 3, or 12.
   b) Two dice are rolled until a 4 or 7 comes up. Write a simulation program to determine the percentage of times a 4 will be rolled before a 7 is rolled.
   c) Write a simulation program to determine the percentage of times exactly 5 coins will be heads and 5 will be tails, if 10 fair coins are tossed simultaneously.
   d) Use the function RNDINT to create a program which deals a five-card poker hand. Remember that the same card cannot occur twice in a hand.

9. **Purpose:** To program a more realistic nondeterministic simulation.

   The problem: A certain skier likes to have the snow 5 feet deep. He skis at a slope in New Hampshire where the snow begins falling as early as August 24. From August 24 to July 4 the percentage of days with snow is 25 percent. On a snowy day, there is always a deposit of exactly 2 feet. On other days, 4 inches of snow melt away.

   a) What percentage of skiing seasons will have a 5-foot accumulation by September 12?

   b) What percentage of days between August 24 and July 4 will there be 5 feet of snow on the ground?

10. **Purpose:** To determine by simulation the odds in three games of chance.

    The problem: Write a program to solve one of the following problems.

    a) If two cards are drawn from a standard deck of playing cards, what percentage of the time will the cards be an ace and a face card (10, jack, queen, or king)? When simulating the draw of the second card, remember that there are only 51 cards left in the deck, and that the same card cannot be drawn twice.
    b) Suppose a gambler bets $1 on the following game. Two dice are rolled. If the result is odd, the bettor loses. If the result is even, a card is drawn from a standard deck. If the card is 1 (an ace), 3, 5, 7, or 9, the bettor wins the value of the card, otherwise he loses. What, on the average, will the bettor win (or lose) in this game?

c) Write a simulation program to determine which of the following is better to bet on: (a) three or more heads when four fair coins are tossed, or (b) a sum of 9 or more on the roll of two fair dice.

11. **Purpose:** To use simulation to investigate alternate strategies.

    Background: A man on a vacation in Las Vegas strikes up a conversation at a bar with a regular casino patron, Ms. Lisa Bet. The man says he would really like to return home and be able to tell his friends he won money from the gambling casino, but he knows that all of the games favor the house, so he is reluctant to play. Ms. Bet makes the following proposal: "Let me advise you while you are gambling. You must be willing to risk losing up to $100. I am so confident that you will win some money from the casino that I will pay you $200 if you do not win. If you do win money, you must pay me $100 for my advice." The man agrees, figuring that, if he wins, it will be worth $100 (less what he wins) to say that he "beat the house" and, if he loses the $100, he will get $200 from Lisa and be $100 richer. Ms. Bet takes the man to the roulette table and tells him to bet $1 each time on the red. If his wins ever exceed his losses, he is to stop. He also must stop if he loses $100.

    The problem: Write a program to find the expected winnings for (a) the man, (b) Ms. Bet, and (c) the casino? (These three numbers, treating losses as negative, must sum to 0.)

12. **Purpose:** To program a nondeterministic ecological simulation:

    Background: Each January 1 in Smogsville the air pollution index is 100. Smoggy days and clear days occur "randomly", the probability of each being ½. On a smoggy day, the index goes up 10 points. On a clear day the index decreases by 10 percent of its value.

    The problem: Simulate 10 years of 365 days each to estimate the probability that the pollution index will be greater than 105 on any given day. In this simulation, the air pollution index magically returns to 100 each January 1, regardless of what its value was the previous day.

Appendix A
BUILT-IN FUNCTIONS

This appendix describes some of the Fortran built-in functions.

Type Conversion

The WATFIV built-in functions INT and IDINT produce a type integer value that is the integer part of the argument, which must be type real or double precision, respecively.

```
INT (4.73) = 4
IDINT (3.14159D1) = 31
INT (17.0) = 17
IDINT (-177D-1) = -17
INT (2./3.) = INT (.6666667) = 0
```

The functions FLOAT and DFLOAT convert an argument of type integer to type real or double precision, respectively. For example,

```
FLOAT (4) = 4.0
DFLOAT (-5) = -5.0D0
```

The functions SNGL and DBLE convert from double precision to real and vice versa.

The functions CMPLX and DCMPLX produce a complex value from two arguments of type real and double precision, respectively.

The functions REAL and AIMAG produce the real and imaginary parts of a complex value.

Absolute Value

The built-in function ABS is used to obtain absolute values of a real value in Fortran. To take the absolute value of an integer, double precision, or complex value, use the function IABS, DABS, or CABS, respectively. The result will be the same type as that of the argument, except that the absolute value of a complex argument is type real. For example,

```
ABS (6.75) = 6.75
ABS (0) = 0
DABS (-13.8D-2) = 13.8D-2
```

```
CABS ((5.0, -12))
   = SQRT (5.0 ** 2 + (-12.0) **2)
   = 13.0
```

Minimum and Maximum

The built-in functions MAX0, AMAX1, and DMAX1 have values which are respectively the maximum or two or more real, integer, or double precision values. The functions MIN0, AMIN1, and DMIN1 are similar, except that they produce the minimum of their arguments. For example,

```
AMIN1 (-99.9, -5.7) = -99.9
DMAX1 (-99.3D0, 3.6D0, 5.23D0) = 5.23D0
MIN0 (MAX0 (5, -7), 0) = MIN0 (5, 0) = 0
```

Square Root

The built-in Fortran functions SQRT, DSQRT, and CSQRT assign the best possible approximate square root to a number. The argument may be real, double precision, or complex, respectively. The argument for SQRT and DSQRT must not be negative. For example,

```
SQRT (2.0) = 1.414214
```

Remaindering

For integer arguments, the function MOD (N, D) computes the remainder when N is divided by D. The arguments for the remainder functions AMOD and DMOD may be integer or double precision, respectively. For each of these functions, the following formula gives the value of MOD.

```
MOD (N, D) = N - D * (N / D)
```

Complex Conjugate

The function CONJG forms the complex conjugate of its argument. For example,

```
CONJG ((3.2, -4.7)) = (3.2, 4.7)
```

Scientific Functions

Trigonometric, hyperbolic, logarithmic, and exponenetial functions are avaialable as Fortran built-in functions. The result is always the same type as the argument. Each of these functions has a double precision version whose name begins with the letter D. In addition, some have a complex version, whose name begins with the letter C.

Summary

Tables A.1 and A.2 summarize the WATFIV-S built-in functions.

Table A.1 Type Conversion Functions in WATFIV-S.

INT	IDINT	real and double precision to integer
FLOAT	DFLOAT	integer to real and double precision
SNGL	DBLE	double precision to real and vice versa
CMPLX	DCMPLX	two reals to complex (single and double precision)
REAL	AIMAG	real and imaginary parts of complex value

Table A.2 Other Intrinsic (Built-In) Functions in WATFIV-S.

Function	Argument				
	Integer	Real	Double Precision	Complex	Double Precision Complex
Remainder	MOD	AMOD	DMOD		
Maximum	MAX0	AMAX1	DMAX1		
Minimum	MIN0	AMIN1	DMIN1		
Absolute value	IABS	ABS	DABS	CABS	CDABS
Square root		SQRT	DSQRT	CSQRT	CSSQRT
Sine		SIN	DSIN	CSIN	CDSIN
Cosine		COS	DCOS	CCOS	CDCOS
Tangent		TAN	DTAN		
$e sup x$		EXP	DEXP	CEXP	CDEXP
Natural logarithm		ALOG	DLOG		
Common logarithm		ALOG10	DLOG10		
Arcsine		ARSIN	DARSIN		
Arctangent		ATAN	DATAN		
Arctan (y/x)		ATAN2	DATAN2		
Hyperbolic sine		SINH	DSINH		
Hyperbolic cosine		COSH	DCOSH		
Hyperbolic tangent		TANH	DTANH		
Normal error		ERF	DERF		
Error complemented		ERFC	DERFC		
Complex conjugate				CONJG	DCONJG

Appendix

FORMATTING

This appendix describes the major features of input and output formatting in Fortran.

The F and E format descriptors

The F and E format descriptors are used to print real double precision and complex quantities. The E stands for "exponential form" and the F stands for "floating point", a dark ages term for "real". The F and E format descriptors have the form

F*c*.*d* and E*c*.*d*

where *c* and *d* must be positive integer constants.

The format descriptors F*c*.*d* and E*c*.*d* indicate that a real quantity is to be printed using *c* columns and is to be rounded to *d* digits to the right of the decimal point. If there are more columns than needed, the number will be right justified in the *c* columns. If the number will not fit into *c* columns, *c* asterisks are printed. Table B.1 shows how the variable X = −26.78 would be printed using several different formats. The "b" in the table represents a blank.

Table B.1 Printing X = −26.78 Using F Format Descriptors

F6.0	bb−27
F6.1	b−26.8
F6.2	−26.78
F6.3	******
F7.3	−26.780
F8.3	b−26.780

When the F format descriptor is used for input, the result depends on whether the input contains a decimal point. If no decimal point is present, the rightmost *d* columns form the decimal part of the value. Blanks are treated as zeros. If a decimal point (and/or power of 10) is present, its position overrides the *d* specification.

When using the E format descriptor, it is important to remember to leave columns for the signed exponent as well as the sign of the number itself. A good rule is make *c* at least seven larger than *d*. Table B.2 shows how X = −26.78 would be printed using several different E format descriptors.

Table B.2 Printing X = −26.78 Using E Format Descriptors.

E12.1	bbbb−0.3E+02	or	bbbbb−.3E+02
E12.3	bb−0.268E+02	or	bbb−.268E+02
E12.4	b−0.2678E+02	or	bb−.2678E+02
E11.4	−0.2678E+02	or	b−.2678E+02
E7.4	*******		

Double precision numbers may be read and written using a D format descriptor, which works just like the E descriptor for real values. Complex numbers are treated as a pair of real numbers for input and output. For example, the specifications (F10.5, F10.5) or (2F10.5) are suitable for reading or printing a single complex value.

The I Format Descriptor

Integer quantities are printed using an I format descriptor, which has the form I*c*. The integer is printed right justified in *c* columns. Asterisks are printed if the number, including its sign if negative, will not fit into *c* columns.

When I format is used for input, *c* columns are read and interpreted as an integer. Only digits, plus and minus signs, and blanks may appear in the input. Blanks are treated as zeros. Thus the input line

```
12
```

is read as 1 in I1 format, 12 in I2 format, 120 in I3 format, and 1200 in I4 format.

The A Format Descriptor

The A (for "alphanumeric") format descriptor is used to read and print character values. Its form is A*c*.

In the following example

```
      REAL X
      INTEGER N
      PRINT 5, X, ' AND ', N
    5 PRINT '(F5.1, A5, I4)', X, ' AND ', N
```

the value of X = 6.3 is printed using the F5.1 format descriptor, so five columns are used and one digit after the decimal point is printed. The character string ' AND ' has length 5 and is printed using the A5 format descriptor, so it appears in five columns of the output line. Since N = −26 and it is printed using the I4 format descriptor, one blank precedes the minus sign and follows the single blank at the end of the string ' AND '.

If the A format descriptor is used for input, it is not necessary to put apostrophes around the character string to be read from the input file. The one-line input file

```
ROGER KAPUTNIK
```

can be used with the program WHO2.

```
C       PROGRAM WHO2
        CHARACTER WHATS *20

        PRINT, 'DO I REMEMBER WHATSHISNAME?'
        READ 15, WHATS
    15  FORMAT (A20)
        PRINT, 'OF COURSE, I REMEMBER', WHATS
        STOP
        END
DO I REMEMBER WHATSHISNAME?
OF COURSE, I REMEMBER  ROGER KAPUTNIK
```

Printer Carriage Control

When output lines are printed on some devices, primarily ordinary printers, the first character in the line is *not* printed. Instead, it controls the line skipping (carriage control) on the printer. Carriage control characters in Fortran are

1	skip to the first line of the next page
blank	single space
0 (zero)	double space
+	no space, print over the previous line

Most other characters, in general, have no effect (cause single spacing), but are not printed. Some printers also recognize other characters as causing special types of vertical spacing, such as positioning a certain number of lines down from the top of the page.

Some terminal devices attempt to duplicate the effect that would be realized on a printer, but some simply print all the characters, including the first one. Experimentation will determine how any particular device behaves. A simple rule to follow is to always put a blank in column one. The output appearing in this book was produced on a device that recognizes characters in column one for carriage control.

The T, X and / Format Descriptors

Each F, E, I, or A format descriptor is used to read or print one value from the input/output list. The T, X and / format descriptors affect the format of the data but do not correspond to any item in the input/output list. The T format descriptor must be of the form T*c* where *c* is a positive integer. When the T*c* format descriptor is encountered, the next item to be read or printed will begin in column *c* of the current line, even if column *c* is to the left of previously specified fields. The slash (/) format descriptor causes the current line to be terminated and the next item to be read from or printed on the next line. On devices with carriage control, the first character of the new line controls line spacing, just as it does for the first line. A comma before or after a slash may be omitted in a format specification. The X format descriptor has the form *n*X. It causes *n* columns to be skipped in input or output.

Repeated Fortran Descriptors

Any sequence of format descriptors may be repeated by enclosing them in parentheses and prefixing them with a multiplier. If the repeated sequence consists of a single I, A, F, E, or X descriptor, the parentheses may be omitted. Repeated sequences may be nested. The following format specifications are suitable for printing respectively an array of length 10, a 10 × 10 table, and a 10 × 10 × 10 array (T2, 10I4), (10 (/, T2, 10I4)), (10 (/, 10(/, T2, 10I4))).

Long and Short Fortran Specifications

If a format contains more format specifications than the corresponding input or output list, the extra specifications are ignored. If there are too few specifications, a new line is started and the specifications repeated from the rightmost left parenthesis.

Obsolete Format Specifications

A character constant (enclosed in apostrophes) is a valid format specification that does not correspond to any item in the output list. It is printed in the formatted output. With the introduction of the A format specification, the character constant format specification is unnecessary, but it is still used sometimes to avoid the necessity of counting characters. Still older Fortran programs used the awkward H format descriptor.

Appendix

FORTRAN STATEMENTS

Assignment Statement

variable = *expression*

IF Block

IF (*logical expression*) THEN DO
   statement
   ...
   statement
ELSE DO
   statement
   ...
   statement
END IF

Note: The ELSE clause is optional.

DO Block

DO *label variable* = *expression, expression, expression*
   statement
   ...
   statement
label CONTINUE

Notes:

1. If the third expression is omitted, an increment of 1 is assumed.
2. The labelled statement ending a DO block need not be a CONTINUE statement, but some statement types are forbidden and most DO blocks now end with a CONTINUE statement.

WHILE Block

WHILE (*logical expression*) DO
statement
...
statement
END WHILE

Implied DO Loop

(*list of expressions, variable = expression, expression, expression*)

Note: The implied DO loop is not a statement. It is a *list of expressions* suitable for use in WRITE and PRINT statements or a *list of variables* suitable for use in READ and DATA statements.

CALL Statement

CALL *subroutine name* (*actual argument,...,actual argument*)

Note: If there are no arguments in a subroutine call, the parentheses are omitted.

GO TO Statement

GO TO label

RETURN Statement

RETURN

STOP Statement

STOP

SUBROUTINE Statement

SUBROUTINE (*dummy argument,...,dummy argument*)

FUNCTION Statement

FUNCTION (*dummy argument,...,dummy argument*)

END Statement

END

READ Statement

READ *format, list of variables*
READ (*unit, format, other options*) *list of variables*

Notes:

1. A *format* may be either a) nothing for default format or b) the label of a FORMAT statement.
2. The phrases UNIT = and FMT = may be omitted if they are the first two options.

PRINT Statement

PRINT *format, list of expressions*

Note: See READ statement.

WRITE Statement

WRITE (*unit, format, other options*) list of expressions

Note: See READ statement.

FORMAT Statement

label FORMAT (*list of format specifications*)

REWIND Statement

REWIND (*unit*)

Type Declarations

INTEGER *list of variables*
REAL *list of variables*
DOUBLE PRECISION *list of variables*
COMPLEX *list of variables*
LOGICAL *list of variables*
CHARACTER *variable * length, variable * length, ...*
CHARACTER * *length list of variables*
IMPLICIT *type* (*letter - letter*), (*letter - letter*), ...

Note: An array declaration has one of the forms:

array name (*highest subscript*)
*character array name *length* (*highest subscript*)

DATA Statement

DATA *list of variables / list of values /*

COMMON Statement

COMMON */name of block/ list of variables and arrays*
COMMON *list of variables and arrays*

EQUIVALENCE Statement

EQUIVALENCE (*variable, variable...*), (*variable, variable....*)....

Notes:

1. *Variable* above includes array element and array name.
2. If an array name is used, it refers to the element of that array with the lowest subscript.

Obsolete Statements Still Supported

IF (*logical expression*) statement
IF (*arithmetic expression) label, label, label*

Other Statements

This list contains all Fortran statements a programmer is likely to need or encounter. However, Fortran contains other statements not described in this book. Some are obsolete or obsolescent. Others are rarely used. See the Fortran standard or your WATFIV manual for details.

THE GLOSSARY

absolute value The size of a number, disregarding its sign. For positive numbers and zero, the absolute value is the number itself. For negative numbers, the sign is changed. The built-in functions ABS, CABS, and DABS find absolute values.

actual argument The value, variable, or expression supplied to replace a dummy argument in a procedure or function call.

address The number by which a specific cell in the computer's memory is located.

algorithm An unambiguous set of instructions or steps that produce an answer or halt after a finite number of steps.

alternative computational procedures Sequences of program steps, only one of which is to be executed each time. The decision is made on the basis of a computed test.

argument A supplied or dummy variable used to communicate values between a calling program and a subroutine or function. Arguments appear in parentheses after the subroutine or function name.

arithmetic comparison An expression formed by comparing two arithmetic expressions using one of the comparison operator .LT. .GT. .EQ. .LE. .GE. .NE.

arithmetic expression An algebraic expression composed of numeric variables, constants, and functions, arithmetic operators, and parentheses.

array A subscripted variable. An array with one subscript is a sequence of values of the same type. An array with two subscripts is a table of values of the same type.

ASCII American Standard Code for Information Interchange. A 128-character code for representing characters in computer-readable form.

assignment operator The symbol = used to separate the variable on the left in an assignment from the expression whose value is to be assigned to it.

assignment statement A Fortran statement which directs the computer to evaluate an expression and assign the result as the new value of a variable.

automatic operation The ability of a computer to operate as much as possible without human direction or assistance.

auxiliary memory The slower access, higher capacity parts of a computer's memory such as magnetic disk and tape. Data written to auxiliary memory is saved more or less permanently between runs.

batch execution A mode of program execution in which all the input data is stored in files before the execution begins. In large computer systems, batching also means the system automatically collecting a number of jobs in the same computer language to run together.

binary computer A computer that does its internal arithmetic using a binary number system.

binary number system A number system using powers of 2 to determine place values.

binary search A search strategy that eliminates half of the remaining candidates for the location of a value by testing against the middle value of those remaining. Repeated halving quickly reduces the search to one possible candidate.

bit A binary digit, 0 or 1.

blank COMMON An unnamed block of common variables.

body of a loop The repeated part of a loop.

buffer A holding area where input/output data are stored temporarily, pending transfer. Input data are generally read into an input buffer and then transferred to other variables. Output data are often collected in an output buffer until enough data is accumulated to write.

bug A mistake in a program.

built-in functions Functions supplied with the Fortran system.

call To direct the computer to execute a subroutine or function.

CALL statement A statement invoking the execution of a subroutine.

case construct A decision procedure available in other languages resembling an IF block in which all the cases are distinguished on the basis of the value of a single expression.

cathode ray tube, CRT A television-type display screen.

character An intrinsic type whose values may be any one or more computer-representable characters.

character constant A sequence of characters enclosed in apostrophes.

character string A sequence of computer-representable characters.

character string variable A variable of type character.

collating sequence The ordinal sequence of all the computer-representable characters. The two most widely used collating sequences are based on the 128-character ASCII character set and the 256-character EBCDIC character set.

column The second subscript in a doubly subscripted variable (table).

comment A remark inserted in the program listing by placing a C in column 1. Comments have no effect on program execution, but they can improve the readability of a program.

COMMON block A named or unnamed block of variables made available to other subprograms.

COMMON statement A statement defining blocks of variables that will be available to other subprograms declaring the same common block.

COMMON variables A variable that is available to all subprograms because it it listed in a COMMON statement.

compiler A program that translates a higher-level language like Fortran into a computer's machine language for execution.

compound condition A logical condition formed by connecting simpler logical conditions with the logical operators .AND., .OR., and .NOT.

computer A general purpose machine for processing data automatically under control of a stored program.

computer program A set of directions telling a computer which sequence of operations to perform.

computer programming Writing computer programs.

computer terminal A device for communicating with a computer. It usually has a keyboard for typing, circuits for transmitting typed information to a computer as input, a screen or typing element for display, and circuits for receiving output from a computer and displaying the output.

computer-assisted instruction A flexible learning experience, presented to the student by means of a computer.

constant A named or unnamed value that cannot change during the execution of a program.

CONTINUE statement A statement that performs no operations at all. Its primary use is to provide a line on which to place a label to mark the end of a DO block or a destination of an early exit from a DO block.

creating a file Erasing the previous contents of the file, if any, and writing a file in the correct form with no data in it.

data transfer Moving data from one place to another in a computer.

debugging Locating and removing errors from a program.

debugging trace A trace of program execution for the purpose of locating bugs in a program.

decision A place in a computer program where the computer selects one of several alternative steps in its program to execute next.

declaration A nonexecutable statement (or statements) that specifies information needed later in the program such as the value of a constant or the type of a variable.

default A value, type, or declaration that is supplied automatically by the system without the programmer having to specify it.

deterministic simulation A simulation in which the algorithms for predicting future values of the simulated quantities involve no elements of chance.

digital computer graphics Digital images produced by computer.

digital image A picture made by selectively coloring or shading a two-dimensional array of dots called pixels.

direct access A file access method in which any record may be accessed next, regardless of which records were accessed previously.

DO block A sequence of Fortran statements starting with the DO statement and ending with the statement having the label referenced in the DO statement. This last statement usually is a CONTINUE statement. The body of a DO block is intended to be repeated a number of times specified in the DO statement.

DO loop A DO block.

DO statement The first statement in a DO block. The DO statement specifies the number of iterations of the DO block.

DO variable The variable whose values are determined by the DO statement.

documentation Material that explains, describes, annotates, clarifies, or elucidates the nature of the problem, the plan for its solution, the organization of the modules in the solution, the details of the solution, or which describes how to use the program, when to use the program, etc.; any supporting material that accompanies a program.

double precision A data type whose values resemble reals except that approximately twice as many significant digits are retained in the representation.

dummy argument An argument listed in the heading of a subroutine or function.

EBCDIC Extended Binary Coded Decimal Interchange Code. A 256-character code for representing characters in computer-readable form.

echo of input data After input data are read, the values are usually echoed to the screen or printer to verify what values were read and whether they were read correctly.

ELSE clause The part of an IF block that is executed if all the tested conditions are false. The ELSE clause is optional.

ELSE statement A statement in an IF block preceding a list of statements to be performed if all tests are false.

END BLOCK statement The last statement in a remote block.

END IF statement The last statement in an IF block.

END option in a READ statement An option in a READ statement giving the label of the statement to which control should be transferred if an end-of-file condition is encountered while reading.

END WHILE statement The last statement in a WHILE block.

endless loop A loop that never terminates. See infinite loop.

EXECUTE statement The equivalent of a CALL statement for a remote block. When an EXECUTE statement is executed, control passes to the remote block. Control is returned to the main program when the remote block is completed.

exit test A test in a loop to determine whether the loop should be exited before the full number of iterations.

exponential notation A form of scientific notation useful in writing very large or very small numbers. The value is multiplied by a power of ten (written after the character E). For example, 2.3E6 is 2.3×10^6, which is 2,300,000.

external documentation Documentation not in the program listing.

file A sequence of values or records, usually stored on an auxiliary memory device such as magnetic disk.

flag A logical value that will be tested later in the program execution.

flag setting A programming technique in which a logical value is set at one place in a program and tested at another (sometimes far removed) place in the program.

FORMAT statement A Fortran statement used to specify the form of input and output data.

formatted file A file of characters, similar in structure to the input and output files.

function subprogram A construct similar to a subroutine whose primary purpose is to return a single value as the function value.

function value assignment A statement like an assignment statement that assigns the value to be returned by the function.

garbage in, garbage out A computer science aphorism meaning that if the input data or algorithm are unreliable, the output also will be unreliable, even if it is neatly printed to seven decimal places.

GO TO statement A statement GO TO that directs the computer to change its execution sequence so that a specific labelled statement is executed next. The GO TO statement was much abused in the early days of computer programming and acquired a reputation as a statement to avoid if you want to write clear programs. Once a clear, structured programming style is established, situations such as early exit from a DO block can be found where a GO TO statement improves the clarity of a program.

gray scale A choice of display intensities to correspond to each digitized pixel intensity.

halftoning A technique for producing the effect of intermediate gray shades by combining suitable patterns of black and white image elements. Halftoning can also produce pastel shades by combining suitable patterns of dots of highly saturated primary colors.

hand simulation A debugging technique in which you put yourself in the role of the computer and perform by hand the steps which the computer is directed to perform by its program.

hard copy Printed output.

histogram A bar graph showing the frequency of occurrence of each of the categories.

IF block A sequence of Fortran statements starting with an IF statement and ending with an END IF statement.

IF statement The first statement in an IF block. If the condition in the IF statement is true, all statements between the IF statement and the next ELSE or END IF statements are executed.

IF test The condition or logical expression in an IF statement.

image enhancement Once an image is digitized, it can be processed by computer to improve, enhance, or modify the image before it is displayed.

increment The amount a variable is increased in each iteration of a loop.

incrementation Increasing the value of a variable.

index A subscript.

index file A file that is searched to find record numbers in a file accessed directly.

index variable A variable that appears as a subscript in an array reference.

INDEX A programmer-defined function to find the location of one character string as a substring of another character string.

infinite loop A loop that never terminates. See endless loop.

indirect addressing A flexible way to access memory cells in which the value in one memory cell determines which memory cell will be read from or stored into.

initialization Assigning starting values to variables at the beginning of a program, loop, or subprogram execution.

input All operations supplying a computer with information.

input buffer An area in memory into which input data is read in preparation to moving it to its intended destination.

input prompt A message sent to the user before an interactive input operation telling what kind of input is expected.

integer A type whose values are whole numbers not exceeding a system-defined maximum in absolute value.

integer constant A number written without a decimal point.

interactive When the computer responds relatively quickly to user requests.

interactive dialogue A conversational mode of communication between a user and a computer during interactive execution of a program.

interactive editing Preparing or changing a program or data file using an interactive program.

interactive execution Execution of a program while the user is at a computer terminal. The user may receive output on the terminal screen or printer, and may enter input data for the program execution during the execution.

internal documentation Documentation that appears in the program listing for the benefit of programmers who will later read the program to modify it, verify its correctness, or fix a bug.

interpreter A program that simultaneously translates and executes a higher level language.

iteration Repetition of a loop.

keyword A word or abbreviation that has a precise intrinsic meaning in the syntax of a programming language.

label An unsigned integer that precedes and identifies a statement. Labels are typed in columns 1 – 5 of a Fortran statement.

lexicographic order The order of words in a dictionary, alphabetic order.

linear list A one-dimensional array.

link To combine separately compiled modules for execution.

list A one-dimensional array, an array with one subscript.

local variable Except for subprogram arguments and variables declared in COMMON, all variables are local variables, inaccessible to other subprograms including the main program. Local variables help prevent side effects of a subroutine or function.

logical An intrinsic data type that has only two possible values: .TRUE. and .FALSE.

logical expression An expression whose value is either .TRUE. or .FALSE.

logical operator One of the logical connectives .AND. .OR. and .NOT. used to construct compound logical expressions.

logical variable A variable of type logical. The only values a logical variable may have are .TRUE. and .FALSE.

loop A sequence of program steps that may be executed more than once during a single execution of the program.

machine language A representation of the set of basic operations a computer is capable of performing.

magnetic disk A medium for storing data in computer-readable form on rotating disks coated with magnetizable iron oxide. Disks range in size from small, flexible floppy disks to large fixed disk packs storing billions of bytes of data.

magnetic tape A medium for sequentially storing relatively large quantities of data in computer-readable form. Although maximum read/write speeds are high, information in random parts of the reel are hard to access quickly.

main memory The main collection of high-speed, high-cost memory cells in a computer. Data in main memory is not usually saved between runs.

manual A set of directions for using a program or computer system.

mathematical model A scaled-down representation of a real situation using numerical values and equations or algorithms that specify how the values change.

memory The capacity of a computer to retain information and to recall that information later.

memory cell An individual unit of the computer's main memory.

MOD The remainder built-in function.

modular subprocess A part of the total algorithm that is reasonably self-contained, easily described, and which is a meaningful conceptual unit to the designer and reader of the program.

module A coherent set of instructions that serve a specific and well-defined purpose in the solution of a problem.

multi-level search A search strategy in which the elements of an ordered list are organized into several hierarchical levels of groupings. First, the correct highest-level grouping is located, then the correct next-level grouping, and so forth, until finally, the lowest level is searched to find the item.

nested IF blocks When an IF block is entirely contained within one of the conditionally executed clauses of another IF block.

nesting When one program structure is wholly contained within another structure. DO blocks and IF statements are often nested.

NINT Programmer-defined function whose value is the integer nearest to a real value.

number A real, integer, double precision, or complex constant.

operating system A program that controls the flow of information through the computer and schedules the use of the computer's hardware components. Usually the operating system is the first program run when the computer is turned on, and it then schedules all subsequent requests for computer use.

output All operations in which a computer transmits information to another device.

output buffer An area in the computer's memory into which data is transferred in preparation to writing it as output.

pixel An individual picture element or dot in a digital image.

positional notation The usual notation for numbers in which the position of a digit relative to the decimal point determines its value.

PRINT statement A statement that writes values to the default output device, usually a printer, terminal typing element or screen.

printer graphics Digital images produced using printable characters of differing densities to display the pixels.

program A set of directions telling a computer which sequence of operations to perform.

program listing A printed or displayed copy of a program.

program memory In some programmable calculators, program steps are stored in different memory cells than data. In most computers, memory is used interchangeably for program steps or data.

programmable A device is programmable if sequences of its basic operations can be selected in advance for automatic execution.

pseudocode A hybrid language used in top-down program design consisting of some constructs from the target language Fortran and some instructions written in terms closer to the language of the problem statement.

pseudorandom numbers A sequence of numbers that are extremely unpredictable except by simulating the algorithm that generates them. Good pseudorandom number sequences share many properties with random numbers including the correct distribution, mean and standard deviation of values, and negligible correlations between successive values.

punchcard A rectangle of cardboard in which information can be stored in computer-readable form by punching holes in appropriate positions. Invented in its present form by Herman Hollerith to tabulate census data, it was once the primary means of preparing input data for computers.

READ statement A statement that directs the computer to accept input and assign the values it reads to variables in the program.

reading Programmers usually speak of a computer reading all input, regardless of the source of the input.

real An intrinsic type whose values include numbers with and without fractional or decimal part.

real constant A number written with a decimal point, and possibly with a power of ten written after the character E.

recall To retrieve information from a computer's memory. Recall is more often used to describe this operation on a hand calculator.

record One of the components of a file.

reference argument, by-reference argument A dummy argument whose actual argument is a variable or array element. No memory space is reserved for an argument called by reference; the memory space reserved for the corresponding actual argument is used for the values.

refine To replace a step in a problem solution with the same step described in greater detail.

refinement of a program A new version of the program in which one or more steps have been described in greater detail.

remote block A construct like a subroutine, but which shares all variables with the calling program. A remote block is called with an EXECUTE statement.

REMOTE BLOCK statement The first statement in a remote block. The REMOTE BLOCK statement names the block so it can be referenced.

REWIND statement A statement that positions a file at its beginning.

roundoff, roundoff error Differences, usually small, between an exact answer and a computed answer. Roundoff occurs in type real quantities when the fixed number of significant digits is not sufficient to retain the exact answer.

row The first subscript in a doubly subscripted variable (table).

running a program Making the computer execute the steps of a program.

scheduling algorithm The rules by which an operating system decides when a request for program execution or a request for an editing operation or a request for any other computer use will be carried out.

scope of a declaration The set of lines in a program listing to which a particular declaration applies. In Fortran, the scope of each declaration is the subprogram in which the declaration appears.

seed The initial value that determines the starting point of the pseudorandom number generator.

self-documenting A variable name or program or subprogram is self-documenting if its meaning is clear without additional explanation.

sequential access A file access method in which the records are read in sequence.

sequential search A search strategy in which the elements of a list are tested, one at a time, in sequence, to locate a given item.

side effect A peripheral effect of one subroutine or function on another, unrelated to the well-defined task of the offending subprogram.

signed number A number, possibly preceded by a plus sign or minus sign.

sorting Arranging a list of data in order.

square root A number whose square is the given number. The built-in function SQRT finds the computer-representable number closest to the square root of its argument.

statement function A Fortran statement that defines a function without using a function subprogram.

stepwise or successive refinement The process of adding detail to the steps in a problem solution. If a refined step is still not described in executable Fortran statements, it is refined again. Successive stages of refinement continue until each step is executable.

store To save information in a computer's memory.

structured programming A style of programming that includes writing programs with clear and readable structure, top-down program design, using procedures to clarify the organization of the program, and using standard loop constructs and sections of code with one entrance and one exit.

subprogram call A statement invoking the execution of a subroutine or function. The subprogram call also establishes argument correspondences that allow information to be passed between calling program and called subprogram.

subprogram A subroutine or function subprogram. A part of a program that is executed only when a statement in another part of the program calls for its execution.

subroutine A subprogram invoked by a CALL statement.

subscript A value in parentheses in an array reference that specifies which element of the array is intended.

subscripted variable An array.

superposition A technique for forming a complex digital image by superimposing simple shapes.

supplied argument The value, variable, or expression written in a subroutine or function call to replace the corresponding dummy argument. An actual argument.

syntax The precise grammar of a computer language.

system of programs A collection of programs that share information written to or read from one or more common files.

system of subprograms A collection of subprograms that are part of the same execution. The subprograms in a system of subprograms may share data both through argument passing, COMMON blocks, and files.

table An array with two subscripts, a two-dimensional array.

termination signal An input data value that is recognized by the program as indicating that no more data (of the current kind) will follow.

THEN clause The statements of an IF block following an IF test that are executed if the test succeeds.

time sharing When many users share a central computer, a time sharing operating system schedules requests in such a way as to make each user feel that there are no other users on the system.

top-down program design A method of analyzing problems in which the solution is attempted first at the highest possible conceptual level, in terms closest to the problem statement. Then, details are added to each step of the proposed solution until the result is an executable program.

tracing Monitoring the progress of a program execution by means of frequent printouts showing which step is being executed. Tracing also may include printing the values of key variables at each step.

truncation the operation of removing the fractional part of a real number to get the integer part. The built-in function INT finds the integer part of a real quantity. Truncation also occurs when a real or double precision value is assigned to an integer variable.

two-level search A searching strategy that involves looking first for the correct page and then searching the correct page for the given entry.

type A description of the kind of values a variable will have.

type declarations Statements in a Fortran program which declare the types of variables, functions, the length of character strings, and the subscript bounds for arrays.

unit An integer used in Fortran programs to refer to an input or output file. Units are associated with file names with control statements. System defined default units are used by READ, WRITE, and PRINT statements that do not specify a unit.

updating a file Reading the contents of a file, making changes, and saving the new version of the file.

value argument A dummy argument whose actual argument is an expression more complex than a variable name, array element, or array name. A value argument receives an initial value from the calling program, but cannot return a value to the calling program. Changes in a value argument do not affect the corresponding actual argument.

variable name A name used in Fortran to refer to one or more memory locations. The name usually describes what the values represent.

video digitizer A device for digitizing frames of television pictures.

visual image processing When an optical image is digitized by assigning to each pixel a number representing the intensity of light in the image at that point, the image may be processed by computer and then displayed.

writing Programmers usually speak of writing all output, regardless of whether the output is transmitted to printer, screen, plotter, or magnetic disk.

WRITE statement A Fortran statement that writes values to an output device.

WHILE block A sequence of WATFIV statements starting with a WHILE statement and ending with an END WHILE statement. The body of a WHILE block is intended to be repeated as long as the WHILE condition is true at the start of each iteration.

WHILE condition The logical expression in a WHILE statement that determines whether the body of the WHILE block will be executed. If the

WHILE condition is true, the body of the WHILE block is executed; if false, the WHILE block is exited.

WHILE loop A WHILE block.

WHILE statement The first statment of a WHILE block. The WHILE statment contains the condition that must be satisfied in order for the next iteration of the WHILE loop body to begin.

ANSWERS TO SELF-TEST QUESTIONS

Chapter 1

Section 1.1

1. Automatic, accepts input, sends output, saves data, programmable (but has a very limited repertoire of basic operations), and decides when to turn on the radio. It does not perform arithmetic, move data, access memory flexibly, or store its program in the same cells as data.
2. Same as 1. Digital doesn't matter.
3. A simple 4-operation hand calculator can perform arithmetic, accept input and display output.
4. A programmable hand calculator usually has all 10 attributes of a computer, although some may lack flexible memory access (indirect addressing). A programmable hand calculator is usually a computer, although its input, output, and memory are often severely limited.
5. Babbage's Analytical Engine was missing flexible memory access and stored program. The program was stored on computer readable cards, but not in the same memory cells that could hold data.
6. All! A computer is a computer.
7. A player piano definitely is automatic and sends output to the listener's ears. It is a matter of opinion whether the piano roll that determines the music it plays is input or a program.
8. A record player is automatic, accepts records as input, produces sound as output. It can be programmed by means of a record or produce any reasonable sounds, but it probably cannot be programmed to do every reasonable sequence of movements of the tone arm.
9. An automatic speed control mechanism is automatic, accepts input about speed, sends output control impulses to the engine, and has so few meaningful sequences of operations that it probably passes the programmability test by default.

10. A Jacquard loom is automatic, programmable, and sends the output (the woven cloth) to the user. It probably accepts no input except its program.

Section 1.2

1. a) False, first you should make a high-level breakdown into major subproblems. b) True. c) False, many problems have no best solution.
2. It isn't necessary for the programmer to refine a program down to the level of machine language because a Fortran compiler can do this automatically for the programmer.
3. a) True. b) False, remember that in the vacation example, you had to refine the details of where you were going and what you were doing before you could refine the details of making reservations or packing your luggage.
4. a) True, computer programs are supposed to be perfect. Testing part of a program means making sure that no part of it has any flaws at all. b) False, comments are used to explain whatever in your program is not self-explanatory. Throwing them into a program that is already self-explanatory without them tends to clutter the program and make it harder to read. The program should be designed to be clear without many comments. (But don't be afraid to use comments when they are needed.) c) While this certainly is a side effect of modularizing, the main reason for modularizing is the central role modularizing plays in the systematic top-down approach to writing computer programs.

Chapter 2

Section 2.1

1-2. Program name is too long; BEGIN is not a Fortran statement; missing format specification; no STOP statement; no period after END.

3-4. Missing comma in PRINT statement; nothing is permitted after END.

5. Yes.
6. The correct answer will depend on your system.
7. a) True. b) False. It is *. c) False. It is **.
8. 1004
9. 14; PRINT * ((343 / 7) / 7) * 2
10. 12
11. IT IS EASY TO DO CALCULATIONS ON A COMPUTER.
12. 1024
13. 1 AND 1 MAKES 2; Some of the blanks surrounding the numbers may be missing in your output.
14.

4.82613E	−2.41E−3	3.8499E4
2.717E−1	−5.5E1	7.000001E0

15.

950.3	41679000000	.00002881
−442.1	−.00581	7.000001

Section 2.2

1. a) True, since they appear only in comment lines. b) True. c) False, there are default types for undeclared variables.
2. Valid names: NAME, PHONEY, REAL, IOU, IOU2, PACKET, LAURIE. Invalid names: ADDRESS (too long), PHONE# (illegal character), 4GOT-TEN (illegal character and too long).
3. assignment of value not allowed in type declaration; OK; missing comma.
4. The Fortran type is CHARACTER; colon not correct and type name comes first.
5. Correct; wrong assignment operator; interchange left and right sides of assignment; variable name too long. Correct.
7.

```
INPUT DATA  A:             27.9290000
INPUT DATA  B:             14.6499900
          13.2799900
```

6.

```
INPUT DATA  X:             3
            Y:             5
            Z:             7
         105
```

7.

```
         110.0000000 INCHES =              9.1666660 FEET
```

8. 7ELEVEN (Shouldn't start with digit); SVN 11 (valid); SVN-11 (minus prohibited); SEVEN11 (too long).
9. PH and PHD are valid; PH.D. contains invalid characters and DOCTOR OF PHILOSOPHY is too long.
10.

```
          3 WENT UP THE HILL.
```

11. Probably.
12. 46.6000

Section 2.3

1. b2.500bbbb6.3E+00
2. 9999.999 and −999.999
3. |bb0.33333|

Section 2.4

1. INT (X * 10 + 0.5) / 10.0 works for positive values of X.
2. When X / Y is an integer, or X is an integral multiple of Y.
3. If N < = X < N + .5 for some positive integer N or if N − .5 < = X < N for some negative integer N or N = 0.
4. 5.3; 4; −123.456; 1.1
5. Neither is always true in computer arithmetic because of roundoff.
6. MOD (N, 100)
7. MOD (N, 2)
8. MOD (N, 2) .EQ. 0

Section 2.5

1. a) False. b) False, but they must be prepared in some computer readable form before execution. c) True. d) False. e) False, a one-user microcomputer usually has interactive editing. f) True.
2. a) True. b) False. c) True, and very important. d) True. e) True. f) We insist for our students.
3. For batch execution, the input file is prepared in advance; interactive input is typed during execution. If the program is rerun, the batch input file may be reused. The interactive input must be retyped.
4. So the user will know what kind of information to enter.
5. The user might type the right information at the wrong time or the wrong information at the right time.
6. Usually not. On most interactive systems, all interactive input automatically appears in the default output device.
7. There is no one waiting during execution to prompt.
8. It provides a record of which data were used during an execution, and helps verify that it has been read correctly.

Section 2.6

1. They would be converted to type real, producing the same value for F.
2. Exchange and modify the READ and PRINT statements.

Chapter 3

Section 3.1

1-2. a) Incorrect. Missing END IF statement. b) Incorrect. In Fortran, the comparison operator is .EQ.: IF (X .EQ. Y) THEN. c) Since 5 is always 5, the single statement X = 6 would suffice. d) Correct. e) Incorrect. If this is intended to be a LOGICAL IF statement, the keyword THEN DO must be omitted. f) Correct. g) Incorrect. Use .EQ. for equality comparison and delete BEGIN. Also change END to END IF.

Section 3.2

1. a) Change END to END IF; add an END IF statement. b) Probably not a syntax error, but certainly a useless bit of code.
2.

```
      IF (LETTER .EQ. 'A'
     +    .OR. LETTER .EQ. 'E'
     +    .OR. LETTER .EQ. 'I'
     +    .OR. LETTER .EQ. 'O'
     +    .OR LETTER .EQ. 'U') THEN DO
         PRINT *, 'VOWEL'
      ELSE DO
         PRINT *, 'CONSONANT'
      END IF
```

Section 3.3

1. No output; 75 IS HIGH; 95 IS VERY HIGH
2. No output; 75 IS HIGH; 95 IS HIGH, 95 IS HIGH
3. 45 IS HIGH; No output; 95 IS VERY HIGH
4. 45 IS HIGH; 75 IS HIGH; 95 IS VERY HIGH

Section 3.4

1. a) Both are correct, but 'SIGNAL' will be assigned the value 'STO'. b) Both are correct. PUNCT is assigned a single apostrophe. c) Correct. The values are 'ONE ' and 'TWO '.
2. Both are wrong. The data type is CHARACTER. Moreover FIRSTNAME is too long.
3. a) Correct. b) Incorrect. The assignment operator is "=". c) Incorrect. Remove the apostrophes from 'YES'.
4. a) Valid and true. b) Valid, but false. c) Invalid. You can't compare a character string and an integer. d) Valid. Truth depends upon which collating sequence is used. e) Valid. False in ASCII. True in EBCDIC. f) Valid and true.
5. '123' .LT. 'ABC' in ASCII and 'ABC' .LT. '123' in EBCDIC.

Chapter 4

Section 4.1

1-2. a) Correct. b) Correct, but executes once. c) Correct. d) Incorrect. The DO statement should be correct as follows: DO 48 YEAR = 1960, 1984 e) Correct. f) Correct. g) Incorrect. An END IF cannot be the last statement of the DO block. Add another CONTINUE statement at the end and move to label 78 to that statement. h) Correct. Fortran does not require the label in a DO statement to end with the digit 8. The authors so label all their DO blocks so that they can tell at a glance which labels terminate DO blocks.

3.

```
N     PROD
-      2
2      2
3      6
4     24
```

4.

```
        1
        3
        5
        7
        9
       11
       13
       15
       17
       19
```

Section 4.2

1-2. a) No problems. RESULT = 10. b) No problems. RESULT = 1. c) RESULT is uninitialized. If RESULT is initialized to zero, the final value of RESULT = 11. d) RESULT is uninitialized. Any value but zero is a probable initialization, but a better one is READ, RESULT. The loop then reads until a signal of zero is read. The final value of RESULT = 0. e) RESULT is uninitialized. If it is initialized to zero, the final value of RESULT = 250000. However, the THEN clause GO TO 58 is not an exit from the DO block. Probably, GO TO 59 was intended. In that case, the final value of RESULT would be 121.

Section 4.3

1. The value of SUM is increased by 1.
2. a) 10 b) 55 c) 455 d) 15
3.

```
N        PROD
-        2
2        3
3        6
4        10
```

4. a) Requires initialization: SUM = 0. Final value of SUM = 45. b) Missing CONTINUE at end of DO block. Final value of SUM = 21 c) Needs initialization of N this time. Suggest READ, N. The final value of SUM will be the sum on the N values read for SCORE. d) The READ statement is incorrect. No initialization statement is necessary, but no sum is accumulated.

Section 4.4

1.

```
N =              1   SUM =           1
N =              2   SUM =           2
N =              3   SUM =           3
N =              4   SUM =           4
N =              5   SUM =           5
FINAL SUM =          5
```

The value of SUM is increasing by 1 each iteration instead of by N. Change the statement SUM = SUM + 1 to the statement SUM = SUM + N.

2. a) Well documented, good variable names, clear structure, a comment describing what the program does seems to be the only one that is necessary. More comments might get in the way. b) Structure is clear, but variable names are too short to tell what they represent. No comments. Only the identifying message on the final PRINT statement gives a hint of what this program does. It might be even harder to tell what this program does if we hadn't just read the better version above. c) Variable names are longer, but less helpful. Loop structure is still clear, but the overall purpose of the program is mysterious. The final PRINT statement of the program now makes a delightful literary statement, but very poor documentation.

Chapter 5

Section 5.1

1. CALL *subroutine name* (*actual argument, ..., actual argument*)
2. The Fortran standards have no requirement. Subroutines and main program can even be compiled separately. However, top-down programming style suggests putting the highest level analysis of the problem, the main program, first and successively more detailed refinements, the lower level subroutines below the subprogram that calls them.
3. None.
4. a) False. Variable names are local to a subprogram and do not conflict with identical variable names in another subprogram. b) True. c) True.

Section 5.2

1. Because the information about what the output should look like was available and specific. Refining the output routine first in this problem shed light on what calculations must be performed in order to produce this output.
2. A modular subprocess is a part of the program that is reasonably self-contained, its purpose is easily described, and it is a meaningful conceptual unit at a higher level of planning the solution of the problem.
3. False. The first real progress was when we wrote the pseudocode version of the main program.

Section 5.3

1. A value placed in the input file that cannot be a valid data value. It is intended to be recognized by the program as signalling the end of data.
2. If the return key hasn't been pressed, the mistake usually can be corrected before it is transmitted, the only thing the user can do is to finish with the incorrect report for that student as quickly as possible,

Section 5.4

1. The main program and subroutines for highest level tasks first, followed by subroutines for successively lower level tasks.
2. Internal documentation, external documentation, and a manual.
3. You can never test a program too many times. In practical terms, testing every essentially different alternative in the program is a desirable minimum. For complex programs, a belief based on reading the Fortran code that it will correctly handle all future cases as well becomes equally important.
4. The program crashes if the user handles this case wrong. The only way not to crash is not to mention this student to the computer. If you start by giving a name but no courses, there will be a division by zero error when GPA is calculated because the denominator REAL (CREDTS) is zero. Another way to save the run is to enter at least one fictitious course with nonzero credits for that student, and then throw away the output. This is riskier than never mentioning the student. Better still is to patch the program so that this case doesn't crash it.

Section 5.5

1. a) False. That was only the preliminary rule to be used before argument passing conventions were taught. b) True. c) True. d) False. Subprograms are independent.
2. To avoid side effects. Local variables is the default for subprograms.
3. If the actual argument is a variable name, an array element, or an array name, the dummy argument is called by reference. It is an expression different from these three kinds, the call is by value.
4. After swapping, I = 2, A (1) = 1, A (2) = 3. The change in the value of I to 2 during the execution of SWAPI does not affect the reference of the dummy variable B to A (I) = A (1) whose address reference was fixed before the subroutine execution began.

Section 5.6

1. A function returns a function value, while a subroutine can only return values through its arguments. Thus a function can be used in expressions while a subroutine is called by a separate CALL statement.
2. a) True. b) True. c) False. The last one assigned is the function value.
3. There is no function value assigned for these three actual arguments. Probably, an ELSE clause should be added assigning to the function a signal value to inform the calling program that an invalid triple of actual arguments were supplied.
4. This expression rounds X to N significant decimal digits. Thus for N = 3, the answers are 27.6, 4830000, and −.000190. For N = 1, the answers are 30, 5000000, and −.0002.

Chapter 6

Section 6.1

1. REAL PROFIT (100)
2. CHARACTER NAME *30 (50) or other variants.
3. You keep their actual length in a variable.
4. a) True. b) True. c) False, only if they are all needed simultaneously in memory. d) False. If the question said "usually", it is probably true. e) True.

Section 6.2

1. a) False. The main advantage is that the search can be given up as futile before the entire list is searched. b) False. Sorting is much more time consuming than even sequential searching. c) False. You might be lucky and find the item you are looking for at the start of the unordered list. Also, if the list contains the most frequently searched for entries at the beginning regardless of where they belong in numerical or alphabetic order, the search on such a list can be faster than searching an ordered list.
2. The file CRDFIL holds the account numbers of lost and stolen cards permanently between runs. It also provides a linkage with the programs that maintain and update this list.

Section 6.3

1. a) False, but it may be adequate for a small list. b) It is practically the only reasonable way to search it. c) True. d) True. e) False. f) False. The binary search just keeps improving its advantage.
2. Assume the list is sorted. Read the list one "page" of 100 entries at a time, look at the last entry on a page, and decide whether to search that page or to go on to the next one.
3. 551 comparisons average, 2 comparisons minimum, 1101 comparisons maximum, give or take a comparison. The closer the number of pages and the number of entries on a page are together, the more efficient the search. Thus both would be approximately the square root of the number of entries for a two-level search.

Section 6.4

1. a) True. b) False. The method takes no advantage of the fact that the list is in order. c) True.
2. Change .LT. to .GT. to make the search for the smallest element a search for the largest element.
3.

Original list	Sorted list
45 32 16 32 45	
45 32 99999 32 45	16
45 99999 99999 32 45	16 32
45 99999 99999 99999 45	16 32 32
99999 99999 99999 99999 45	16 32 32 45
99999 99999 99999 99999 99999	16 32 32 45 45

4. There are 9 passes, one to get each element of the sorted list. Each pass takes 8 comparisons to find the smallest remaining element. For general list length n, the formula is $n\ (n - 1)$.
5. The first scan to find the smallest takes 8 comparisons. With one fewer element remaining, the second pass takes 7 comparisons, and the next pass 6 comparisons, etc. The total number of comparisons is $8 + 7 + 6 + 5 + 4 + 3 + 2 + 1 = 36$. For a list of length n, the formula is $n\ (n - 1)\ /\ 2$. This is half the number of comparisons of SORT.

Chapter 7

Section 7.1

1. 6, 8, 26, 2.
2. 'ALP', 'LPH', 'PHA', 'HAB', 'ABE', 'BET'

Chapter 8

Section 8.1

1. CHARACTER CROSWD *1 (20, 20)
2.

```
INPUT DATA  A:
  9  7
  2  5
TABLE B
  9  7
  2  5
```

This program reads the 2 × 2 array A row by row, then it assigns to each element of the 2 × 2 array B the corresponding value from A, and finally, it prints the values in B row by row.

Section 8.2

1. CHARACTER PICTUR *1 (20, 35)
2. A complex graphic can be formed by overlaying simple shapes on top of each other.
3. A value of .TRUE. in any row and column of the array IMAGE can be interpreted as meaning turn that pixel on, and a value of .FALSE. can mean turn that pixel off.

Section 8.3

1. As a 2-dimensional array of digitized densities. For color photographs, each pixel has three component intensities, one for each primary color red, green, and blue. Thus, while a black and white photograph might become a 12 × 24 array of integers, a color photograph might become a 12 × 24 × 3 array of integers.
2. Two ways. If the display device has pixels in varying shades of gray such as different printer characters or TV tube dots of controllable intensity, these are used. If only maximum black and maximum white are available, a block of dots is used and a suitable fraction of these dots are turned fully one to achieve the desired shade of gray. This second process is halftoning.
3. Once the image is digitized, it can be enhanced before being displayed. Contrast can be increased, imperfections can be removed, features can be emphasized, and the whole image can be enlarged and improved.

Section 8.4

1. a) False. b) True. c) False. d) False. Fortran knows which subscript is which by its position within the list of subscripts. Unfortunately, it does not check to see if the name of the variable makes sense in a given position. In fact, Fortran never checks to see if any variable name makes sense in the context it is used in a Fortran program. It is the programmer who benefits from the use of self-descriptive variable names because they make many erroneous assignments read like nonsense.

Chapter 9

Section 9.1

1. When a calculational step is carried out below, it is first shown with eight significant digits and then rounded to seven digits. (1 / 7) * 7 = .14285714 * 7.000000 = .1428571 * 7.000000 = .99999970 = .9999997.
2. (2 / 7) * = .28571428 * 7.000000 = .2857143 * 7.000000 = 2.0000001 = 2.000000. The expression (1 / 7) * 7 would be unequal to 1 = 1.000000 in an IF test on a computer that rounds to seven significant decimal digits in type real.
3. The difference is that the answer to the first calculation is less than one, so all the nonzero digits are retained, even the last one that shows roundoff. In the second calculation, the answer spills over into the units position and the seven significant digits include only six decimal places.
4. Answers vary, depending on the machine you use.
5. (1 / 7) * 7 = .14857142857143 * 7.0000000000000 = .14285714285714 * 7.0000000000000 = .999999999999980 = .99999999999998 = 1.000000 = 1.000000. Although there was still roundoff in the 15 digit rounded to 14 digit answer, rounding the result to 7 digits gives the exact expected answer.
6. 5.326451 + (6.954603 + 1.719843) = 5.326451 + 8.674446 = 14.000897 = 14.000897 = 14.00090; (5.326451 + 6.954603) + 1.719843 = 12.281054 + 1.719843 = 12.28105 + 1.719843 = 14.000893 = 14.00089
7. (12345 + .1234567 − 12345 = (12345.00 + .1234567) − 12345.00 = 12345.123 − 12345.00 = 12345.12 − 12345.00 = .12 = .1200000. Very few significant digits of b are retained in the sum $a + b$.
8. If the value of a has n integer places, then $7 - n$ decimal places are retained in the sum $a + b$. Thus only $7 - n$ significant digits of b remain in the calculated value of $(a + b) - a$.
9. Subtraction of nearly equal quantities is a major cause of very large roundoff errors. The question as posed isn't quite meaningful since addition of numbers with nearly equal absolute value but opposite sign is the same as subtraction of their absolute values. In that sense, any subtraction problem is an addition problem and vice versa.
10. 3.123456 × (4.123456 × 2.123456) = 3.123456 × 8.7559773 = 3.123456 × 8.755977 = 27.348908 = 27.3489; (3.123456 × 4.123456) × 2.123456 = 12.879433 × 2.123456 = 12.87943 × 2.123456 = 27.348902 = 27.34890. Multiplication can only create roundoff in the last significant digit. Subtraction creates roundoff in all significant digits if the quantities subtracted are nearly normal.

Section 9.2

1. Simulation by computer is inexpensive, nondestructive, and rapid. Large numbers of alternatives can be tried, even dangerous ones, without risk and in a reasonable amount of time.
2. If either the information used as a starting point of the simulation or the model itself is invalid or inaccurate, the answers also will be invalid or inaccurate.

Section 9.3

1. 2 * RNDINT (0, 5) can be 0, 2, 4, 6, 8, or 10; RNDINT (0, 10) can be 0, 1, 2, 3, 4, 5, 6, 7, 8, 9, 10; RNDINT (0, 5) + RNDINT (0, 5) can be 0, 1, 2, 3, 4, 5, 6, 7, 8, 9, or 10. The last two can take on the same values. However, a value of 5 is more likely, and a value of 0 or 10 is less likely in the last expression than it is in the second. The first two expressions are similar in the sense that all possible values are equally likely. In the third expression, 5 is the most likely value, and the likelihood drops off in either direction to the extremes. For example, a value of 0 occurs approximately 1/25 of the time in the third expression and 1/10 of the time in the second expression.
2. a) One run of a nondeterministic simulation program may in fact give a good value, but there is usually no way of knowing whether the value is accurate or whether it is an accident. b) After several runs have been made, you can begin getting an idea of the variability that can be expected in the answers of the simulation. If the variability is low, that is, if the answers are all reasonably close, then there is reason to believe that future simulation runs will also give answers close to the ones already calculated. If the variability remains high after many runs, it may be the case that the actual situation is also unstable, and there may not be any one answer to the problem.
3. A nondeterministic simulation attempts to capture the notion of a random event by generating pseudorandom numbers to determine the outcome of the simulation.
4. Monte Carlo is famous for its gambling casinos.

INDEX